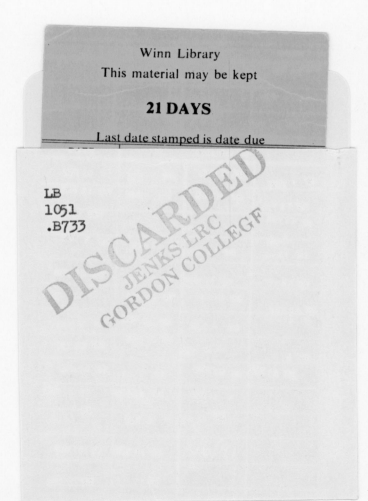

THE DIAGNOSIS AND TREATMENT
OF LEARNING DIFFICULTIES

TEXTBOOKS IN EDUCATION
William H. Burton, *Consulting Editor*

An Approach to Guidance, by Edna Dorothy Baxter.

Growth and Development of the Preadolescent, by Arthur Witt Blair and William H. Burton.

The Diagnosis and Treatment of Learning Difficulties, by Leo J. Brueckner and Guy L. Bond.

Student Teaching in the Elementary School, 2nd ed., by James R. Burr, Lowry W. Harding, and Leland B. Jacobs.

Guidebook for Elementary Student Teachers, by Isabel Miller, George E. Dickson, and Loren R. Tomlinson.

The Guidance of Learning Activities, 2nd ed., by William H. Burton.

Supervision, 3rd ed., by William H. Burton and Leo J. Brueckner.

Education for Effective Thinking, by William H. Burton, Roland B. Kimball, and Richard L. Wing.

Education and Morals, by John L. Childs.

Public Education in America, by George R. Cressman and Harold W. Benda.

The Third Curriculum, by Robert W. Frederick.

Educational Psychology, by Karl C. Garrison and J. Stanley Gray. Also accompanying *Workbook,* by Karl C. Garrison, Ira E. Aaron, and Joseph C. Bledsoe.

Introduction to Educational Research, by Carter V. Good.

Methods of Research, by Carter V. Good and Douglas E. Scates.

Human Relations in School Administration, by Daniel E. Griffiths.

Guidance in Democratic Living, by Arthur Hollingshead.

The Guidance Function in Education, by Percival W. Hutson.

Early Elementary Education, by Myrtle M. Imhoff.

The Child and His Curriculum, 3rd ed., by J. Murray Lee and Dorris May Lee.

The Child and His Development, by J. Murray Lee and Dorris May Lee.

The Preadolescent, by Mary Jane Loomis.

Changing the Curriculum, by Alice Miel.

Teaching Adolescents in Secondary Schools, by Harry N. Rivlin.

The American Secondary School, by L. O. Taylor, Don R. McMahill, and Bob L. Taylor.

Education and the Democratic Faith, by Ephraim Vern Sayers and Ward Madden.

Statistical Methods in Educational and Psychological Research, by James E. Wert, Charles O. Neidt, and J. Stanley Ahmann.

The
DIAGNOSIS AND TREATMENT
of
LEARNING DIFFICULTIES

by
Leo J. Brueckner
and
Guy L. Bond

Appleton-Century-Crofts
EDUCATIONAL DIVISION
Meredith Corporation

NEW YORK

LB
1051
.B733

Preface

THIS BOOK deals with procedures that teachers can use to appraise the outcomes of the educational program, the techniques that teachers may use to diagnose the nature and causes of learning difficulties, and the methods by which developmental and corrective measures of various kinds can be adjusted to meet the needs of the individual learner.

The discussion is primarily directed to the classroom teacher and to students enrolled in college courses. However, the specialist in the diagnosis of educational problems will find a wealth of information about available diagnostic techniques that may be applied in the study of disability cases, particularly in the basic skills of reading, arithmetic, and the other language arts.

Emphasis is placed on the techniques of diagnosis and treatment which experience has shown can be effectively applied by the average classroom teacher. However, the authors believe that all teachers should be familiar with the more scientific aspects of diagnosis so that they may be aware of the technical procedures that now are utilized in educational and psychological clinics. These diagnostic materials are sure to be adapted gradually by wide-awake teachers for use in daily classroom instruction, thereby greatly increasing the effectiveness of their work.

The authors believe that when the instructional program is effectively adjusted to the needs, ability, and development of the children there will be few of them who will not be able to learn the basic skills that are socially useful. The authors therefore include in the various chapters that deal with the teaching of the basic skills statements of the major objectives to be considered by the teacher and the principles of teaching that underlie effective instruction. The brief introduction is then followed by a systematic discussion of the diagnosis and treatment of difficulties in mastering the basic tools of learning. Emphasis is placed in the point of view that teachers who are conscious of the types of difficulties children encounter in their school work can do much to avert their development by "preventive" teaching.

Special consideration is given to methods of correcting difficulties and disabilities that are identified by diagnosis. The factors most commonly associated with learning difficulties are systematically analyzed and the types

v

of adjustments that experimentation has found most helpful are summarized. The great value of self-diagnosis by the learner as a basis of motivating corrective work is emphasized throughout.

The authors have drawn heavily on current research and their own clinical experience in selecting the remedial treatments that they recommend. The importance of adapting methods of instruction to the needs of each individual is emphasized, and many methods of doing so are illustrated in the various chapters.

To make the discussion as concrete as possible, frequent short descriptions of case studies are included which illustrate diagnostic procedures. These should be supplemented by the actual consideration of reports of cases studied by students and teachers in local schools. If an educational clinic is accessible, its files can be drawn on for illustrative material.

At the end of each chapter there is given a short list of "suggested activities" which will indicate the types of work that the authors have used in their own courses on diagnosis. There is also a short selected bibliography at the end of each chapter which supplements the books and articles referred to in the body of the chapter itself. The number of magazine articles listed has been kept to a minimum. Advanced students should be expected to extend the list by studies of special problems which should include current reports of investigations.

It is important that instructors develop a file of the diagnostic tests that are discussed in this book so that students can familiarize themselves with them. Demonstrations of their application should be included in the work of the course. The lists given in Chapters 2 and 4 should be regarded as a minimum.

Special acknowledgment for the critical reading of most of the chapters should be given to Theodore Clymer and Maynard Reynolds, associates of the authors in the faculty of the University of Minnesota.

L. J. B.
G. L. B.

Contents

Contents

Contents

THE DIAGNOSIS AND TREATMENT
OF LEARNING DIFFICULTIES

1 INTRODUCTION: THE NATURE OF EDUCATIONAL DIAGNOSIS

EDUCATIONAL DIAGNOSIS deals with three major problems which are the underlying themes of this book:

1. The appraisal of pupil progress toward desirable educational objectives.
2. The identification of factors in the teaching-learning situation that may be interfering with the optimum growth of individual learners.
3. The adjustment of aspects of the teaching-learning situation to the needs and characteristics of the learner so that his continued growth will be assured.

METHODS OF APPRAISING EDUCATIONAL OUTCOMES

Determining the extent to which desirable educational objectives are being achieved involves procedures that inform teachers about changes in the behavior of learners. These appraisal procedures vary from standardized tests of achievements in the various curriculum areas to informal observation of the learner's reactions in the classroom and elsewhere.

The survey movement early in the present century stimulated the development of standard tests of pupil achievement in the basic skills. Invariably, the results of these reveal a very large range of individual differences in achievement in all areas of the curriculum and at all levels of the school. In almost every class there are children who are seriously deficient in their control of some of the basic tools of learning, such as reading, oral and written communication, or arithmetic. They present difficult problems for teachers. In order to deal more effectively with problems growing out of the variations in the ability and achievements of pupils, many changes have been made in the organization of our schools and in the management of the instructional program itself.

In recent years much research has been done to devise methods by which teachers can appraise important but less tangible outcomes of education, for example, methods of study, interests, attitudes, and appreciations. To evaluate these learnings, teachers have found the use of interviews, anecdotal

1

records, systematic application of check-lists, and similar evaluative procedures of great value.

The achievements of the learner can be appraised by comparing his performance with established test standards, or where these are not available, by subjective appraisals based on the judgments of the teacher and other competent observers. In this way both the strengths and weaknesses of the individual pupil can be identified. In this book the diagnosis and treatment of learning difficulties is the topic of major concern.

IDENTIFYING FACTORS THAT INTERFERE WITH OPTIMUM GROWTH

Once weaknesses and deficiencies have been identified, the modern teacher who is familiar with effective diagnostic procedures takes steps to determine the nature of the difficulties, the degree of their seriousness, and the factors underlying them. This is especially necessary when a pupil's performance in some field is considerably below what can normally be expected of children of his learning potential and level of maturity. Considerable progress has been made in recent years in the development of standardized diagnostic techniques in reading, arithmetic, oral and written expression, spelling, and handwriting. Some are highly technical and their administration should be left to specialists. However, teachers who have informed themselves through reading and study about these methods of diagnosis, described in this book, can make informal adaptations of them in analyzing the work of their pupils from day to day. These methods of diagnosis are sure to be a great improvement over the crude procedures that good teachers formerly used to cope with learning difficulties.

Standard diagnostic procedures are the result of systematic studies of pupil learning difficulties and the evolution of objective methods of identifying them and estimating or measuring their severity. Their application helps the teacher both to understand the nature of an apparent deficiency and to analyze the factors that underlie it. In this book the authors not only describe these standard diagnostic methods but also illustrate numerous informal, practical procedures useful in studying the characteristics and behavior of learners whose work in any curriculum area is considerably below normal expectancy. Special attention is given to methods which the teacher can use to identify the kinds of behavior and responses of pupils that are symptomatic of specific types of deficiencies and of factors underlying them.

The factors that contribute to child growth and development may be identified in such elements of the total teaching-learning situation as the curriculum, the instructional procedures used, the materials of instruction, the socio-physical environment both in and out of school, and the mental, physical, emotional, social, and moral characteristics of the learner himself. Under optimum conditions, with educational programs adapted to their needs, abilities, and interests, most pupils will progress satisfactorily. However, in many schools such favorable conditions often do not prevail at the present time, for reasons that are quite apparent. For example, the curriculum may not be well organized or adapted to the learner's interest and levels of development; instructional procedures may be unskillful and may inadequately provide for adapting goals to the wide range of individual differences in the abilities of the various pupils; instructional materials may be inadequate and poorly constructed; social relations in the school and in the home may be unwholesome and unstimulating; obviously factors inherent in the pupil himself—for example, physiological handicaps such as poor vision and hearing deficiencies, low level of mental ability, and specific weaknesses in basic skills—may be sources of his difficulty.

In most cases of severe learning disability the difficulty cannot be traced to any single cause. Very often a complex of causes will be found. For instance, a reading disability may be due to a combination of such elements as an undetected visual defect in the learner, ineffective teaching at lower grade levels, the use of books that are beyond the pupil's level of reading ability, and indifference in the home to his reading difficulties. The teacher faces the problem of adjusting the instructional program to meet the needs of the individual pupil. The situation becomes increasingly complicated when problems of mental health and emotional adjustment enter into the picture. In many instances lack of success in school work is the cause of emotional maladjustment, a point often overlooked by psychologists and social workers; in others the tensions and strains of home life and actual mental illness may be primary causes of the learning problem. It is known that many cases of emotional maladjustment clear up when learning deficiencies are corrected.

ADJUSTING THE INSTRUCTIONAL PROGRAM TO THE NEEDS OF THE LEARNER

Whenever a pupil has a serious learning difficulty, the teacher should make every effort to determine the exact nature of the problem and the factors most probably contributing to it. Diagnosis is a logical process based on an analysis of all available pertinent information about the case at hand in the light of knowledge gained through experience and study. When the teacher feels that because of inexperience or lack of time the problem is too complex for classroom analysis, the case should be referred to specialists, if available, in educational or psychological clinics and other community agencies. Treatment can be rational only when diagnosis reveals the nature of the deficiency and leads to the identification of conditions that contribute to it.

Sometimes the underlying causal factors can be quite easily eliminated or corrected—for instance, by providing spectacles that correct visual handicaps. Sometimes specific learning difficulties, such as weakness in sub-traction of whole numbers, which may be the source of incorrect work in long division, respond quickly to carefully guided remedial instruction by the teacher. The correction of a serious disability in spelling may require a much longer period of remedial treatment, since many different elements may be involved: a low level of reading ability, possible physiological handicaps of hearing or vision, poor quality of handwriting, ineffective study habits, lack of appreciation of the social value of correct spelling, or emo-tional maladjustment. The important thing in remedial teaching is that the teacher takes steps to secure the interested co-operation of the learner and plan with him the action that will most likely bring about an improvement. In many instances the home and various community agencies may have to be called upon to assist in the corrective program.

THE ORGANIZATION OF THE CONTENTS OF THIS BOOK

A quick overview of the contents of this book will give the reader a conception of its specific contribution to problems of diagnosis and treat-ment of learning difficulties in the basic curriculum areas.

Chapter 2 contains a general discussion of the available appraisal pro-cedures that the teacher can use to determine pupil progress toward desir-able educational objectives. Here are described not only standardized tests and measurement procedures but also informal evaluative techniques which can be used in the appraisal of outcomes that do not readily lend themselves to paper-and-pencil methods.

There then follows in Chapter 3 a discussion of the factors that underlie unfavorable growth and development, particularly in the mastery of the knowledges, skills, abilities, and methods of work and study in the basic curriculum areas. Problems of diagnosis and treatment of learning difficul-ties in these fields are the primary concern of this book.

In Chapter 4 there is a discussion of techniques of diagnosis. Three levels of diagnosis are described: (1) general diagnosis by the use of comprehen-sive survey procedures; (2) analytical diagnosis which entails a variety of procedures for identifying specific areas of strength and weakness in the achievements of children in some particular field of learning; and (3) case-study procedures that can be utilized in the systematic study of the perform-ance and characteristics of individual learners with more or less severe disabilities to determine their nature and the underlying causes.

As necessary background for the study of specific methods of treatment of learning difficulties in all curriculum areas, Chapter 5 presents the basic principles underlying remedial and preventive teaching for the general guidance of teachers and clinical workers.

There then follows a series of chapters which describe the methods of diagnosing and treating learning difficulties in reading, arithmetic, oral and written expression, spelling, and handwriting. Each chapter begins with a brief statement of desirable objectives. Next there follows an analysis of the basic principles that underlie an effective instructional program in that area. Then both standardized and informal diagnostic procedures are systematically described and illustrated. The chief causes of learning difficulties are also discussed. Finally, specific remedial measures of known validity are described which can be applied in the correction of the most common learning difficulties.

The last chapter briefly discusses how to organize the schools for diagnostic work. The chapter also considers the types of special services a well-organized school system should provide to meet the needs of handicapped children, including educational and psychological clinics for the diagnosis and treatment of learning difficulties in serious disability cases. The authors believe that it is highly desirable for the regular teacher to integrate the diagnosis and treatment of learning difficulties in the daily work of the class, except in cases of severe disability where unusual adjustments or specialized kinds of treatment may be necessary.

2 APPRAISAL OF EDUCATIONAL OUTCOMES

IN THIS CHAPTER five important aspects of the appraisal of educational outcomes are discussed:

1. How to appraise the effectiveness of the educational program.
2. Methods of appraising the educational product.
3. The analysis of appraisal data.
4. Individual and trait differences.
5. Interpreting relationships among test scores.

HOW TO APPRAISE THE EFFECTIVENESS OF THE EDUCATIONAL PROGRAM

The Essential Elements of an Educational Program

The fundamentals of an effective educational program that is most likely to assure the well-rounded development of the learner can be stated briefly.

1. There should be a clear conception of the desired goals to be achieved at all stages of the educational program.

2. The school should provide a curriculum of rich, varied experiences adapted to the needs, abilities, and interests of the children.

3. The instructional program should be conducted by a staff of competent, well-adjusted individuals in accordance with modern principles of education and mental hygiene.

4. The school facilities should be adequate and attractive, and the classrooms should be constructed and equipped as learning laboratories for groups of not more than thirty children.

5. Instructional materials and learning aids widely varied in nature and appeal and of varying levels of difficulty should be available, so that the teacher can provide as effectively as possible for the wide range of individual differences of pupils in ability, interests, and level of development.

6. There should be a well-conceived guidance program which will aid the teacher in evaluating the characteristics of the educational product and the rate of growth of the individual at all stages of development and will help the teacher to assist pupils who are maladjusted in varying degrees

6

educationally, physically, socially, and emotionally to adapt themselves to normal school and community life.

The Basis of the Appraisal of the Educational Program

The most satisfactory way to determine the effectiveness of an educational program is to appraise the characteristics of the learners as revealed by their progress in school and by changes in their behavior in social situations both in and out of school. Increasingly, schools are formulating specific educational objectives in terms of desirable types of behavior. The progress made by learners toward the achievement of these objectives is a valuable means for measuring the effectiveness of the total educational program of the community.

For purposes of appraisal, educational outcomes can be grouped under three major headings:

1. Basic learnings directly related to areas of the curriculum, such as functional knowledge, skills, abilities, understandings and insights, and methods of thought, work, and study.

2. Outcomes of a broad developmental nature, such as the individual's mental, physical, social, moral, and emotional health; his interests, purposes, attitudes, and tendencies to act; his appreciations and satisfactions; his creativity in the arts and language expression; and his physical development.

3. Outcomes societal in nature, such as leadership, ability to deal with and solve problems of school and community life, skill in democratic co-operation, social sensitivity, and social creativity.

Recognition of the broad scope of educational outcomes has great significance for those who evaluate the results of instruction, for those who plan the curriculum, and for teachers whose problem it is to facilitate the development of all desirable aspects of the learner's personality. The traditional school primarily emphasized outcomes in the first of these three categories, namely, mastery of the basic skills and subject-matter content, while the developmental and societal aspects of educational outcomes were given little, if any, direct attention. The modern school fully recognizes the importance of an educational program that provides for all three of the outcomes outlined above.

In this volume we shall deal primarily with evaluation and diagnosis in the fundamental skills and learnings in the various curriculum fields, principally reading, arithmetic, and the language arts. However, the authors wish to make it clear that they recognize fully the importance of the other outcomes. It is a fact, as will be shown, that effective learning of skills and curriculum content is closely related to the developmental nature of the child. Obviously, learning is most effectively motivated by providing experiences in which children utilize what is learned in schools in social situations where outcomes of a societal nature are also important.

METHODS OF APPRAISING THE EDUCATIONAL PRODUCT

The Meaning of Measurement and Evaluation

Current educational literature describes many improved methods of appraising the educational product. However, for many valuable, generally accepted objectives of the educational program there are no satisfactory techniques of evaluation now available. In recent years specialists in psychology and sociology have carefully sought methods of appraising pupil characteristics and behavior relevant to the developmental and societal outcomes discussed above. Considerable progress has been made along these lines, but much remains to be done.

Methods of appraisal may be classified in two general types: (1) those involving *measurement,* that is, the application of precision units and objective norms expressed in numerical terms, such as educational age, grade score, and standard norms; and (2) those involving *evaluation,* that is, the gathering and study of qualitative information for which standard norms expressed in objective terms are neither available nor perhaps even appropriate.

The term *measurement* applies to the use of precise objective methods which yield data about those aspects of the individual that lend themselves to quantitative analysis, such as achievements in curriculum areas, level of intelligence or scholastic aptitude, and physical characteristics such as height and weight. In these instances the data can be compared directly with objective standards.

Evaluation, on the other hand, refers to the gathering of facts by more subjective procedures, for example, anecdotal records, interviews, interest inventories, and observation of activities. These data are valuable for making judgments about the quality of an individual's behavior, his reactions, the effectiveness of his methods of work, and his thought processes. In recent years considerable progress has been made in the development of objective standards by which to appraise qualitative data gathered by informal evaluative methods.

An Analysis of Methods of Appraisal

In the analysis given below, a wide variety of appraisal methods are grouped under two major headings: (1) those methods that involve tests and standardized measures, yielding objective scores which can be expressed in quantitative terms; and (2) those methods that make possible evaluation by less formal, subjective approaches.

A. OBJECTIVE TESTS AND STANDARDIZED MEASURES
    1. Standardized tests and measures.
        a. Achievement tests.

       b. Mental and intelligence tests.
       c. Tests of motor skills and abilities.
       d. Aptitude and readiness tests.
       e. Physiological measures and medical examinations.
       f. Personality and adjustment tests.
       g. Interest inventories and attitude scales.
  2. Unstandardized short-answer objective tests.
       a. Simple recall or free response tests.
       b. Completion tests.
       c. Alternate response tests.
       d. Multiple choice tests.
       e. Matching tests.
  3. Improved essay types of tests consisting of questions so formulated that they can be scored on a fairly objective basis.
  4. Scales for analyzing and rating a performance or a product.
  5. Tests involving evaluation of responses using projective methods.

B. EVALUATION OF BEHAVIOR BY LESS FORMAL PROCEDURES

  1. Problem-situation tests.
       a. Direct experience.
          (1) Experiment to be performed.
          (2) Actual life situation to be met.
       b. Indirect approach.
          (1) Improved essay-type examinations.
          (2) Expressing judgments about described situations.
          (3) "What would you do?"
  2. Behavior records concerning in- and out-of-school activities.
       a. Controlled situations.
          (1) Use of check-lists, rating scales, score cards, codes for evaluating personality traits, behavior, attitudes, opinions, interests, and so on.
          (2) Self-rating devices, "Guess-Who?"
          (3) Time studies of attention, activities.
          (4) Photographs and motion pictures.
          (5) Stenographic reports.
          (6) Dictaphone and tape recordings.
       b. Uncontrolled situations.
          (1) Log or diary; autobiographical reports.
          (2) Anecdotal records; behavior journals.
          (3) Records of libraries, police, welfare agencies, and so on.
          (4) Still or motion pictures.
          (5) Tape recordings.
  3. Inventories and questionnaires of work habits, interests, activities, associates, and the like.
  4. Interviews, conferences, personal reports.
       a. With the individual learner himself.
       b. With others, such as parents or associates.
  5. Analysis and evaluation of a creative act or product, such as a poem, music, constructions, and so forth.
  6. Sociometric procedures for studying group relationships.
  7. Evaluation of reactions using projective and expressive techniques.
       a. Psychodrama and play technics.

    b. Free-association tests.
    c. Interpretation of reactions to selected pictures and drawings.
    d. Interpretation of free oral and written expression.
    e. Interpretation of artistic and constructive products.

Differences Between Standardized Tests and Informal Evaluative Procedures

The principal characteristics of a standard test are the following:

1. The contents of the test are selected and arranged systematically according to accepted specifications.

2. The conditions under which the test is to be given, the directions to be followed in giving it, and the time allowances are all standardized to insure uniformity in its administration.

3. The specified method of scoring the test is definite and objective, so that the personal judgment of the rater is eliminated as far as possible in marking the test paper.

4. Standards or norms based on the performances of large numbers of typical pupils are provided, making it possible to evaluate and interpret the scores of an individual pupil.

It should be borne in mind that norms are based on average results for average pupils taught by average teachers with average materials, and hence that they are at best measures of mediocrity. These standards are usually surpassed where there is high-grade instruction.

The application of informal evaluative procedures requires the observer to select suitable techniques from among those available. When informal evaluation is used there are no standardized procedures or norms, and the interpretation of the data secured must be based upon estimates of values and subjective personal judgments.

The Essentials of a Testing Program

The staff of a school system should plan a long-range testing program to provide a basis for intelligent judgments about the progress of pupils from year to year in important curriculum areas, so as to determine strengths and weaknesses in the instructional program of the schools. Insofar as the individual teacher is concerned, the testing program should provide information which will enable him to plan learning experiences adapted to the needs, abilities, and interests of each pupil.

In many elementary schools a basic testing program similar in scope to the one given below is undertaken, preferably early in the school year, so that the test results will be of immediate value to the classroom teacher. Similar tests also should be used systematically in secondary schools.

SUGGESTED MINIMUM TESTING PROGRAMS

ELEMENTARY SCHOOLS, GR. K-6

1. Health and physical examinations: yearly and as the need arises.
2. Intelligence tests: group tests, three times in grades K-6; individual tests as the need arises.
3. Basic skills:
   a. Readiness tests in reading within the first month of the first grade; in arithmetic, within first two months.
   b. Reading achievement test at the beginning of grades 2 to 6.
   c. Battery of comprehensive achievement tests in spelling, language, and arithmetic: yearly in grades 3 to 6.
   d. Study skills: one or two times, grades 4 to 6.
4. Personality tests: at least once, grades 5 or 6.

SECONDARY SCHOOLS, GR. 7-12

1. Health and physical examinations: yearly and as need arises.
2. Intelligence tests: group tests, grade 9; individual tests as need arises.
3. Basic skills:
   a. Reading achievement test at beginning of each grade.
   b. Battery of comprehensive achievement tests in basic curriculum areas, grades 7 and 8.
   c. Study skills: once in grades 7 to 9, once in grades 10 to 12.
4. Personality and adjustment tests: twice in grades 8 to 12.

In addition to this basic testing program, the staff of a school or the individual teacher will almost always find it necessary to administer other tests from time to time to secure information needed in dealing with some particular individual or problem. Informal evaluative procedures such as those listed on page 9 also must be used continuously by the teacher as an integral part of the appraisal program in any well-managed school. The children should also learn to evaluate their own work and their behavior in social situations both in and out of school. Evaluation should be a continuing process throughout the learning experience. From the point of view of its effects on learning, there can be no doubt that an intelligent evaluation of performance and achievement by the learner himself is likely to be of far greater significance than an appraisal made by any other agency.

A selected list of suitable intelligence, achievement, and personality tests is given below:

A. INTELLIGENCE TESTS
   1. Group tests.
      a. California Test of Mental Maturity (California Test Bureau).
      b. Detroit Test of Learning Aptitude (Public School Publishing Co.).
      c. Kuhlman-Anderson Intelligence Tests.
      d. Kuhlman-Finch Intelligence Test (Educational Test Bureau).
      e. Otis Quick Survey Test of Mental Ability (World Book).
      f. SRA Primary Mental Abilities (Science Research Associates).
      g. Terman-McNemar Group Test of Mental Ability (World Book).

    2. Individual tests.
       a. Arthur Point Scale of Performance Tests (Commonwealth Fund).
       b. Kuhlman Test of Mental Development (Educational Test Bureau).
       c. Terman-Merrill Revision of the Stanford-Binet Test (World Book).
       d. Wechsler-Intelligence Scales for Children—Verbal and Non-Verbal (Psychological Corporation).

B. ACHIEVEMENT TEST BATTERIES
    1. California Achievement Tests (California Test Bureau).
    2. Co-ordinated Scales of Attainment (Educational Test Bureau).
    3. Iowa Every Pupil Tests of Basic Skills (Science Research Associates and Houghton Mifflin).
    4. Metropolitan Achievement Test (World Book).
    5. Modern School Achievement Test (Teachers College, Columbia Univ.).
    6. Stanford Achievement Test (World Book).

C. PERSONALITY AND ADJUSTMENT TESTS AND RATING PROCEDURES
    1. Bell Adjustment Inventory (Stanford Univ. Press).
    2. California Test of Personality (California Test Bureau).
    3. Detroit Adjustment Inventory (Public School Publishing Co.).
    4. Haggerty-Olson-Wickman Behavior Rating Scales (World Book).
    5. SRA Youth Inventory (Science Research Associates).

Most teacher-education centers and school systems have on file numerous standard tests which the student should become familiar with. Manuals for all tests should be consulted for the grade levels tested and the nature of the contents of each test.

THE ADDRESSES OF TEST PUBLISHERS

The addresses (1955) of the most prominent publishers of standard tests are:

Bureau of Educational Research, Univ. of Iowa, Iowa City, Ia.
Bureau of Publications, Teachers College, Columbia Univ., New York 27, New York.
California Test Bureau, 5916 Hollywood Boulevard, Los Angeles 28, Calif.
Educational Test Bureau, 720 Washington Ave. S.E., Minneapolis 14, Minn.
Educational Testing Service, Princeton, N. J.
Houghton Mifflin Co., 2 Park St., Boston 7, Mass.
Public School Publishing Co., 509 North East St., Bloomington, Ill.
Science Research Associates, 57 West Grand Ave., Chicago 10, Ill.
World Book Co., 313 Park Hill Ave., Yonkers 5, N. Y.

Sources of Information About Appraisal Methods

Space limitations make it impossible to illustrate in this book all of the above methods of appraisal.[1] However, many of them will be described

---

[1] A comprehensive discussion of appraisal procedures is given in W. H. Burton and L. J. Brueckner, *Supervision: A Social Process,* 3rd ed. (New York, Appleton-Century-Crofts, 1955), Ch. 9.

from time to time in the discussions of diagnosis in the chapters that follow. Those who may wish to familiarize themselves with the various appraisal methods should consult these references:

MENTAL AND PSYCHOLOGICAL TESTS

F. S. Freeman, *Theory and Practice of Psychological Testing* (New York, Holt, 1950).

A. M. Jordan, *Measurement in Education* (New York, McGraw-Hill, 1953).

ACHIEVEMENT TESTS AND GENERAL EVALUATIVE PROCEDURES

H. A. Greene, A. N. Jorgenson, and J. R. Gerberich, *Measurement and Evaluation in the Elementary School* (New York, Longmans, 1953).

E. F. Lindquist, *Educational Measurement* (Washington, American Council on Education, 1951).

H. H. Remmers and N. L. Gage, *Educational Measurement and Evaluation* (New York, Harper, 1943).

E. R. Smith and R. W. Tyler, *Appraising and Recording Student Progress* (New York, Harper, 1942).

R. M. Thomas, *Judging Student Progress* (New York, Longmans, 1954).

A. E. Traxler and associates, *Introduction to Testing and to Use of Test Results in Public Schools* (New York, Harper, 1953).

SOCIOMETRIC AND PROJECTIVE PROCEDURES

H. H. Anderson and Gladys Anderson, *An Introduction to Projective Techniques* (New York, Prentice-Hall, 1951).

Ruth Cunningham and associates, *Understanding Group Behavior of Boys and Girls* (New York, Bureau of Publications, Teachers College, Columbia Univ., 1951).

Hilda Taba and associates, *Diagnosing Human Relations* (Washington, American Council on Education, 1951).

EVALUATION OF MANY AVAILABLE TESTS

Oscar Buros, ed., *Fourth Mental Measurements Yearbook* (Highland Park, N. J., Gryphon Press, 1953).

Criteria to Be Considered in Selecting Appraisal Methods

The following criteria should be considered in selecting measurement and testing methods:

1. *The value of the characteristic or aspect of growth tested.* Does the test claim to measure an aspect or characteristic of pupil growth in which you are interested? Are the educational outcomes tested of undoubted value and significance?

2. *Validity.* Does the test actually measure what it purports to measure?

3. *Reliability.* Does the test measure accurately? Will the children tend to get the same scores if measured again?

4. *Ease of administration and scoring.* Are the directions for administering the test clear and easy to follow? Is the test fairly easy to score? Are the tabulation forms clear?

5. *Provision and usability of standardized norms.* Does the test yield scores that are well defined and adequately standardized? Are the scores readily understandable?

Test manuals almost always supply data to which each of the above criteria can be applied. For a technical discussion of the meaning and significance of each of the above criteria, the reader should consult such books on appraisal methods as those listed on page 13. An up-to-date and highly technical discussion of criteria for selecting psychological tests is contained in the report of a special committee of the American Psychological Association.[2]

When the teacher wishes to apply any of the less formal, unstandardized evaluative procedures listed on pages 9 and 10, he should carefully select those that are likely to yield valid reliable information about the aspect or characteristic of behavior that is being tested. The fact that norms will be lacking should suggest the need of caution in interpreting the findings.

Steps in the Informal Evaluation of Educational Outcomes

Whenever the teacher feels the necessity to appraise some educational outcome for which suitable standardized evaluative instruments or procedures are not available, a usable informal method of appraisal must be devised on the spot. The following sequence of steps suggests the method to be followed:

1. Specify clearly what outcome is to be evaluated.
2. Define the outcome in terms of observable behavior or characteristics of the learner.
3. Prepare test items or test situations by which the behavior or characteristics can most readily be evaluated.
4. Secure some kind of record of the behavior exhibited in the test or test situation.
5. Analyze the information secured and judge the significance of the findings.

Illustration of a Method of Informal Evaluation

These five steps can be illustrated by applying them to the evaluation of a pupil's ability to spell correctly the words he uses in free written work:

1. The teacher recognizes that an important measure of spelling ability is the correctness of spelling in all written work, not merely performance on words studied in the regular spelling lesson.

2. The teacher decides to secure a measure of correctness of spelling in ordinary written work by finding the percentage of words misspelled in a free writing activity, when the children are not particularly aware that spelling is being appraised.

---

[2] Technical Recommendations for Psychological Tests and Diagnostic Procedures: Preliminary Proposal. *The American Psychologist*, Vol. 7 (August, 1950), pp. 461-475.

3. The teacher arranges to secure an eager response to the suggestion that the children write a story for the school newspaper about an interesting or exciting experience they have had. There is a general discussion of what the contents of the story might be before actual writing is begun.

4. The pupils then write their stories. They are encouraged to write between 100 and 200 words. No assistance is given on the spelling of words about which pupils may be in doubt.

5. When the written work is completed, each pupil is told to count the number of words he has written and then to write the number under his name at the top of the paper. The teacher collects the papers, marks the words incorrectly spelled on each paper, counts them, and finally finds what percentage the number of words misspelled is of the total number of words written. The teacher also may decide to examine critically the poorest papers to determine the kinds of errors made.

Interpretation of Results of Informal Evaluations

This informal but rather systematic procedure gives the teacher valuable information about one aspect of the spelling ability of the pupils. It must be repeated several times in similar situations to secure reliable results. Although it is not possible to interpret the results by comparing them directly with standards based on the written work of typical pupils of their grade level on a similar test exercise, the procedure is sure to identify the pupils who are low in spelling ability.

The teacher cannot always directly compare spelling ability within the class on the basis of this procedure. For instance, a child may have a flare for creative writing and may choose to use colorful or unusual words that are in his speaking or hearing vocabulary but far beyond those taught in ordinary spelling instruction. Such a child, however, may spell correctly almost all of the words commonly used by other children of his grade level, as can be determined by an overview of his daily written work.

Similar informal procedures can be applied in evaluating outcomes in such fields as reading, arithmetic, and oral and written language. The choice of test or other evaluative procedure should depend on its effectiveness and appropriateness for the particular problem. The outcomes appraised should be of undoubted significance. Test situations should provide either the opportunity for the learner to demonstrate directly the behavior that is being appraised, or the opportunity to react in a way that is known to be a satisfactory index of the behavior.

The evaluative procedure selected should be practical and feasible from the standpoint of effort, time, and equipment required. The test should be comprehensive enough to insure reliable and valid information. Scoring should be objective and if possible expressed in quantitative terms. When evaluation is for diagnostic purposes, it should be carried to a satisfactory level of specificity.

Interpretation of any evaluative data should be done with caution in the absence of agreed-upon standards and dependable norms, and in the light of the general characteristics and capacity of the individual himself and his possible achievements. Teachers should always interpret the achievements of children on standard tests in terms of the abilities and opportunities of the individuals which constitute the group. It is quite obvious that a sixth-grade group of children from an underprivileged area cannot be expected to achieve as high a level as a group of sixth-grade children living in a favored suburban community. In general, however, knowledge of test results aids the teacher greatly in observing children in the more informal types of evaluation used in the classroom.

THE ANALYSIS OF APPRAISAL DATA

Methods of Analyzing the Results of Survey Tests

The following analysis suggests procedures for analyzing and interpreting the results of general survey tests of educational outcomes at various levels in the school system:

1. SUPERINTENDENT AND CENTRAL STAFF
   a. Analysis of city-wide results grade by grade in comparison with expected performance.
   b. Comparison with results of previous years.
   c. Consideration of the consolidated distributions of class results.
   d. Overview of results for various schools.
   e. Consideration of possible causes of these variations in results among the different schools.
   f. Planning next steps for improving the educational program.

2. STAFFS OF INDIVIDUAL SCHOOLS IN CO-OPERATION WITH CONSULTANTS
   a. Comparison of results for the school as a whole with city-wide scores and with standard scores at various grade levels.
   b. General trends of progress from grade to grade as compared with results for previous years.
   c. The deviation of each grade and class from expected levels of attainment in relation to the mental ability of the children, their social background, and health.
   d. Consistency of levels of attainment in the various areas tested.
   e. The range of test results for each area within individual classes.
   f. The overlapping of test scores at consecutive grade levels.
   g. Identifying strengths and weaknesses of the school's program on the basis of the test results.
   h. Considering possible next steps.

3. INDIVIDUAL TEACHERS IN CO-OPERATION WITH PRINCIPAL OR CONSULTANT
   a. Overview of the results for the class as a whole, sharing the information with the pupils.
   b. Analysis of the progress made by individual pupils based on comparison with previous tests, preferably summarized in graphic profile form.

c. Critical comparison of educational levels achieved in relation to the mental ability of individuals.
d. Consideration of factors that might throw light on variations in achievement of individuals and deviations from levels of expectancy.
e. Consideration of discrepancies between test results for individual pupils and teacher's estimates.
f. Analysis of the test items on survey tests that have possible diagnostic value.
g. Planning a program of remedial instruction.
h. Planning the ways in which to use the data most effectively in the public relations program.

Characteristics of Behavior to Be Considered in Evaluation

In evaluating the outcomes of learning, the teacher should consider at least six characteristics of performance: (1) rate of response, (2) accuracy, (3) quality, (4) altitude or level of development, (5) area of experience or range of ability, and (6) methods of thinking and performance.

1. *Rate of Response.* The pupil's rate of work is a valuable index of skill and control of a particular function. Rate of motor response increases with age until maturity is reached. Other things being equal, the pupil who can read, write, or compute rapidly has greater skill than the pupil whose rate of response is slow. A slow rate of response is often symptomatic of a learning difficulty.

Numerous efforts have been made to set up tentative norms for rates of reading, writing, and computing at various grade levels, but they are of doubtful validity because standard methods and materials for applying these norms are lacking. Such norms are of some value in evaluating the scores for a class, but because of individual differences in rates of mental growth and motor development they should be applied with caution to the performance of individual pupils.

Furthermore, many factors affect the rate at which an individual performs, including not only his level of maturity and physical development but also his interest in the task at hand and his mental attitude toward it. For instance, rate of reading is affected both by the purpose of the reader and by the difficulty of the reading matter. Hence it is not possible to state a norm for rate of reading in general. When in an arithmetic test pupils are asked to "write the answers to these questions as rapidly as you can," their scores will differ considerably from those made on a test when unlimited time is allowed. Two pupils whose scores are identical on a timed test in addition may actually differ considerably in ability to add, a fact that is not evident because of differences in their rates of writing answers after the answers have been recalled. The fast writer may be slow in addition as such, whereas the slow writer may be able to find the sums rather quickly but be slow in recording them.

There are several ways in which the teacher can measure the pupil's typical rate of work. For instance, the pupil's rate of reading can be measured informally by finding (1) the number of minutes it takes him to read a selection of average difficulty, or (2) how many words in the selection he can read in a given time, such as two or three minutes. Similarly, in arithmetic it is possible to measure the time it takes a pupil to give or write sums, or to find the number of sums he can write in a given time. In handwriting it is possible to measure rate of writing by similar procedures.

To measure a pupil's normal rate of work, it is necessary to use materials that are fairly uniform in difficulty so that his flow of work will not be slowed up unduly at times by difficult parts of the test. Very few of the available standard tests of basic skills provide measures of rates of work because of the difficulty of standardizing the procedures. It is clear not only that children differ in their rates of work but also that they can at will vary their speeds, within limits. Speed of work should always be considered and allowed for in interpreting test scores.

2. *Accuracy.* The term *accuracy* is synonymous with "freedom from error." Many responses in reading, spelling, written and oral expression, and arithmetic can readily be classified as correct or incorrect. In general, the greater the proportion of correct responses, the higher is the level of ability or performance. For most standard tests, norms are based on the number of correct responses made within generous time limits.

Rate and accuracy occur in various combinations, as shown by the diagram below.

		ACCURACY	
	High	Average	Low
RATE — High	I	II	III
	High in both rate and accuracy	High in rate— average in accuracy	High in rate— low in accuracy
RATE — Average	IV	V	VI
	Average in rate— high in accuracy	Average in both rate and accuracy	Average in rate— low in accuracy
RATE — Low	VII	VIII	IX
	Low in rate— high in accuracy	Low in rate— average in accuracy	Low in both rate and accuracy

Pupils whose scores on a test fall in groups I, IV, and VII are doing highly accurate work. Scores in groups I, II, and IV indicate excellent performance. Those pupils whose scores fall in group VII probably can improve their rate of work considerably. Pupils in group V present no special problems, although some may not be performing as well as can be expected of children of their learning aptitude. The work of pupils in group IX is exceedingly poor, an indication either of low mental ability or of serious learning difficulty requiring systematic analysis. It may be true that they are performing up to their maximum potentialities. The teacher should make a special study of the work of pupils in groups III, VI, and VIII, in order to discover the possible causes of their poor performances so as to have a basis on which to plan corrective measures.

It should be recognized that in tests an individual may choose to work at different rates. He may work at rates of speed that for him are rapid, and then his work is likely to be inaccurate or his performance may be inferior in quality. Likewise, under other circumstances he may choose to work slowly and carefully, and hence accurately. Therefore his performance may be of a higher than usual level or quality. It is important that this point be borne in mind when formulating test directions and selecting the form of motivation to be used. In general, an increase in effort increases both speed and accuracy of response. It also is true that under undue strain the performance of some learners breaks down. Test situations should be so arranged that as nearly as possible a typical normal performance will result.

3. *Quality.* The general merit or quality of performance in handwriting, drawing, and written composition can most appropriately be determined by comparing specimens with a series of standard examples of varying degrees of merit. The appraisal is based on the judgment of the rater, usually expressed numerically.

4. *Altitude or Level of Development.* The altitude of ability is measured by the height or level of difficulty of the tasks which the individual can perform successfully. There is a wide range in the difficulty of the tasks pupils undertake in school, the information they are to learn, and the concepts they are to master. In the primary grades the pupil is expected to learn only relatively easy elements. As he progresses through school, he comes into contact with more complex and difficult learnings. The higher on the scale of difficulty the learner can achieve, the more superior his general development is considered to be. Thus the more difficult the materials the pupil can read, the words he can spell, and the computations he can perform, the higher are the altitude of his ability and his level of development in these fields. Most standard achievement tests measure *altitude.*

5. *Area of Experience or Range of Ability.* Thorndike has suggested that it is necessary in appraising the individual's achievements to consider the breadth of his learning at each general level of difficulty. He has shown that the results of tests containing a number of items for each level of difficulty reveal that some persons have a much wider range of ability at all levels than others have, as indicated by the percentage of items answered correctly at each level.

The concept of area must also be borne in mind in appraising such general outcomes as ability in reading, ability in arithmetic, and ability in written language. As will be shown in Chapter 6, reading is not a single general ability but consists of a number of component skills and abilities, all of which must be developed under guidance if the field of reading itself is to be fully explored. Inferences about specific reading abilities should not be drawn from the results of a general reading test; their status should be determined by measurements of each specific ability itself. What is true of the scope of reading ability is likewise true of outcomes in all other areas of the curriculum.

The concept of area also includes such outcomes of learning and instruction as purposes, interests, attitudes, appreciations, and insights, all of which should be considered in evaluating educational outcomes. This should be done in addition to the appraisal of conventional knowledge, skills, and abilities.

6. *Methods of Work*. In evaluating any performance an important factor is the merit of the methods of work and the efficiency of the thought processes that the learner employs. A pupil's achievement often is lower than it should be because of inefficiency in his work habits and study skills.

Faulty methods of work cannot be measured directly by paper-and-pencil tests, although their existence can be suspected when the performance of a pupil is slow and clearly inferior to what ordinarily can be expected of a pupil of his level of ability. Faulty methods of work can be discovered by observing the behavior of a pupil while, for example, he is taking a test or preparing some assignment. A pupil may be able to write all answers to addition examples correctly, but observation may show that he uses a variety of methods of counting to find the sums. Similarly, it may be evident to an observer that a pupil uses ineffective, unsystematic methods when studying his spelling assignment.

The Structure of Achievement Tests

Standard achievement tests can be classified according to their structure as follows:

1. *Rate* tests, intended to measure rate of response; often also a measure of accuracy.
2. *Scaled* tests, consisting of a series of items arranged according to level of difficulty, essentially a measure of *altitude* of ability in reading, spelling, arithmetic, and written language.
3. *Quality* scales, consisting of specimens of standard quality, as in handwriting and composition.
4. *Area* tests, consisting of tests of a broad sampling of elements in some field, often suitable for diagnostic purposes.
5. *Performance* tests, used to evaluate some motor or manual skill.

INDIVIDUAL AND TRAIT DIFFERENCES

The Range of Individual Differences

Standardized tests provide basic data that must be considered in evaluating prevailing school organization and instructional practices. Perhaps the single most important fact that has been revealed by educational measurement, as far as instruction is concerned, is the wide range of individual differences in achievement and intelligence among the members of any typical class in our schools.

There apparently is an increase in variability in both achievement and intelligence grade by grade and age by age. Cook [3] has shown that in the typical school the range in the achievement of pupils (2nd to 96th percentile) in reading comprehension, vocabulary, mechanics of English composition, literary knowledge, science, geography, and history is between three and four years at the second-grade level, between five and six years at the fourth-grade level, and between seven and eight years at the sixth-grade level. In arithmetic reasoning and computation the range is somewhat less, being between six and seven years at the sixth-grade level.

DISTRIBUTION OF TOTAL SCORES ON THE PARTS OF THE
IOWA EVERY PUPIL TESTS OF BASIC SKILLS BY
A 5.1 CLASS (SEPTEMBER)

A. *Reading*		B. *Study Skills*		C. *Language*		D. *Arithmetic*	
8.0		8.3					
7.4	4	6.7	3	7.6		6.3	
6.0	3	5.7	4	6.1	2	6.0	1
5.2	5	5.0	2	5.2	3	5.0	7
4.5	1	4.5	9	4.4	3	4.5	5
4.0	5	4.0	3	4.0	4	4.0	9
3.6	4	3.3	7	3.3	15	3.7	5
3.1	3	2.7		2.9	1	3.4	1
2.5	4	2.1	1	2.5	1	3.1	1
N	29		29		29		29
Median	4.4		4.7		4.0		4.4
Norm	5.1		5.1		5.1		5.1
Difference	— .7		— .4		—1.1		— .7
Range	2.6-7.7		2.2-7.4		2.5-6.4		3.1-6.2

An illustration of the range of scores among the pupils of a single class is shown in the table above, which presents the distributions of individual scores of 29 pupils, grade 5.1, on the four parts of the Iowa Every Pupil Test of Basic Skills. The children were all about 10 years of age. The class

[3] W. W. Cook in E. L. Lindquist, ed., *Educational Measurement* (Washington, American Council on Education, 1951), pp. 10-12.

medians ranged from grade 4.0 in language skills to grade 4.7 in study skills. All of them were below the test norms as shown. There was a wide range in individual scores: approximately five grades in reading and study skills, four grades in language skills, and three grades in arithmetic. When faced with such a range of ability, the teacher has the problem of adjusting instruction to the needs of the individual pupils. Even wider ranges are often found in some classes.

Cook also has shown that in the typical school the first-grade teacher will find that 2 per cent of the pupils have mental ages of less than four years and 2 per cent have mental ages of more than eight years; the sixth-grade teacher will find 2 per cent with mental ages of less than eight years and 2 per cent with mental ages of more than sixteen years; the high-school teacher will find a range of from six to eight years in the mental ages of pupils at each grade level. Cook reports that these conditions prevail whether the school enforces strict policies of promotion and failure or promotes entirely on the basis of chronological age.

Application of less objective evaluative procedures, such as those listed on pages 9 and 10, reveals that almost as wide variations as are found in achievement and intelligence are typical of other less readily evaluated educational outcomes, such as health, interests, attitudes, appreciations, methods of work, creativeness, sociability, honesty, and problem-solving ability.

The purpose of measurement and evaluation is to enable the teacher to plan an educational program that is adapted insofar as possible to the age, needs, ability, and interests of each pupil.

Trait Differences in the Individual

The problem of adjusting instruction to the needs of individuals is complicated by unevenness in the development of the various abilities of an individual learner. Research has shown that the variability in the development of the various traits of an individual is practically as great as is the variability among a group of individuals in any single trait. Brown [4] has demonstrated that "dull boys and bright boys show an equal amount of unevenness in all abilities." He maintains that "the same type of class organization and treatment" is required for both groups.

The table on page 23 presents data that show the unevenness of the test scores of four grade 5.1 pupils in the same class on the various subtests of the Iowa Every Pupil Tests of Basic Skills and also the total scores for each major area. The total scores of Pupil I, IQ 120, varied from grade 7.6 in reading to grade 5.7 in arithmetic. All were considerably above the norms of the grade 5.1. On the other hand, the total scores of Pupil IV, IQ 90, were

---

[4] A. W. Brown, *Unevenness of the Abilities of Dull and Bright Children,* Contributions to Education No. 220 (New York, Bureau of Publications, Teachers College, Columbia Univ., 1926), p. 109.

all below the norms, ranging from grade 3.1 to grade 3.7. Note the range in the total test scores for Pupils II and III.

On the subtests there was a much wider range in scores for the individual pupils. For instance, the scores for Pupil II, IQ 154, ranged from grade 4.1 in number operations to grade 9.3 in language usage. The scores of Pupil II on use of reference and punctuation were almost as low as for arithmetic operations. The range of subtest scores for Pupil I was almost as great as for Pupil II. In both cases there is evidence of weak spots that require special attention by the teacher. These deficiencies probably can be remedied quite easily.

GRADE LEVELS OF FOUR GRADE 5.1 PUPILS ON THE SUBTESTS
OF IOWA EVERY PUPIL TESTS OF BASIC SKILLS

Test	*Pupil I*	*Pupil II*	*Pupil III*	*Pupil IV*
A. Reading	7.6	7.6	4.4	3.1
Comprehension	7.4	7.1	4.7	3.1
Vocabulary	7.8	7.8	4.0	3.1
B. Work Study Skills	6.7	6.1	4.1	3.7
Map reading	5.2	6.6	4.0	4.0
Use of references	5.4	4.3	2.8	2.2
Use of index	7.6	7.9	4.6	3.4
Use of dictionary	8.0	8.0	3.9	5.4
Alphabetization	9.0	5.6	5.0	3.4
C. Language Skills	6.5	5.8	3.5	3.1
Punctuation	4.8	4.3	2.4	3.6
Capitalization	4.6	5.0	3.3	2.6
Usage	9.3	9.3	5.6	2.7
Spelling	7.9	7.3	3.6	3.3
Sentence sense	7.5	4.7	4.1	2.3
D. Arithmetic	5.7	5.2	5.4	3.6
Fund. knowledge	7.0	6.3	5.6	4.4
Operations	5.0	4.1	5.0	3.6
Problems	6.1	6.1	6.1	2.6
Range in scores				
Totals	5.7-7.6	5.2-7.6	3.5-5.4	3.1-3.7
Specifics	4.6-9.3	4.1-9.3	2.4-6.1	2.2-4.4
Norms	5.1	5.1	5.1	5.1
IQ Ratings	120	154	106	92

The range of subtest scores for Pupil III, IQ 106, is greatest of the four cases reported in the table. All of the subtest scores of Pupil IV are considerably below the grade 5.1 norm and the range of scores is the smallest of the four cases. The scores for Pupil III indicate that he has a serious general deficiency in language skills and specific deficiencies in reading vocabulary and work study skills, whereas in arithmetic skills his scores are normal. On the whole, the scores for Pupil IV are low but fairly consistent, indicating a general low level of performance commensurate with his relatively low mental rating. His greatest weaknesses are in reading and language skills. Marked improvement can hardly be expected from Pupil IV because of his lack of mental ability. It is quite probable that his skills will continue to develop under good teaching, but at a slower rate than can be expected of Pupils I and II. The level of achievement that Pupil IV can reach must be considerably below the levels of Pupils I and II.

Profiles of test scores of almost every conceivable kind are found when an analysis is made of test results for several hundred children. This fact demonstrates clearly the necessity of administering early in the school year suitable tests which will enable the teacher to identify strengths and weaknesses in the achievement of individual pupils, so that steps can be taken to improve their basic skills. Similar variability is sure to be found when other aspects of achievement and personality are appraised by less formal methods.

Ways of Providing for Individual Differences

The schools have tried many ways of organizing classes to accommodate the wide range and variety of individual differences known to exist among the pupils. In large schools pupils have sometimes been grouped according to mental ability, so as to make the classes more homogeneous. However, research has shown that because of trait variability among individuals, homogeneous grouping actually cannot be achieved in this fashion. Even with the most painstaking grouping, large differences in pupil achievement in the various curriculum areas are found which must be provided for within the classes. The social desirability of ability grouping has been questioned, and in most schools the plan has been discarded. The present trend is to group children by age, taking into consideration their social maturity and social development.[5] Whatever the form of grouping used, it is essential that there be proper adaptations of experiences, methods of teaching, and materials of instruction.

Within any class the grouping for instructional purposes should be highly flexible. Sometimes the teacher will wish to work with the class as a unit in developing some skill that is needed by all or in carrying on some activity; at other times the teacher will wish to form several broad groupings according to levels of achievement to help in arranging activities of different levels of complexity and difficulty. Sometimes a group having a common interest may be formed to work together on some problem, but the pupils in the group may work on special tasks and with materials of different levels of difficulty; sometimes the teacher may give special assignments to the more able pupils; sometimes a group will be formed on the basis of level of ability in some field to help them increase power in that field; sometimes pupils will be grouped for extra help on some skill in which they are weak; sometimes

[5] W. W. Cook, *Grouping and Promotion in the Elementary School* (Minneapolis, Univ. of Minnesota Press, 1941).

the teacher will take time to make a special study of the work of some pupil whose performance indicates serious learning difficulties that should be diagnosed and remedied.

When groups of these and other kinds are made, it is possible to adjust the work of the class to individual differences in the needs, rates of growth, ability, and interests of the various pupils. When what is to be learned is complex and the goals are unlimited, so that the abilities of the most able pupils are taxed, the variability of the group actually will be increased under good instruction. When what is to be learned is relatively simple, and limited goals are set which a large proportion of the class can achieve, variability will be reduced under good instruction. Whatever the form of grouping, special attention must be given by the teacher to pupils whose work indicates they have learning difficulties that should be analyzed and eliminated.

INTERPRETING RELATIONSHIPS AMONG TEST SCORES

Methods of Relating Test Scores to Each Other

Various problems arise in interpreting relationships among test scores. Let us consider the following sets of data about two fifth-grade pupils:

	Pupil A	*Pupil B*
Chronological age	10.0	10.0
Mental age	14.0	8.5
Reading age	12.6	6.7
Arithmetic age	11.9	9.3
Spelling age	12.8	8.5

1. *Intelligence Quotients.* The ratio between a pupil's mental age and chronological age is called his *intelligence quotient.* Thus, Pupil *A*'s intelligence quotient is $14.0 \div 10.0 = 1.40$, or 140. This quotient indicates very superior intelligence. Pupil *B*'s intelligence quotient is 85, which is considerably below normal.

In recent years there has been much discussion of the usefulness and dependability of intelligence tests. It is generally recognized that scores on tests of mental ability may be influenced by such extrinsic factors as the emotional status of the individual tested, extremely unusual environmental conditions, and a relatively low level of reading ability, especially on verbal group tests.[6]

It is also recognized that the IQ varies within limits, as is true of scores on achievement tests. It is likely that the individual's mental growth curve

[6] Theodore Clymer, "The Influence of Reading Ability on the Validity of Group Intelligence Tests," unpublished Ph.D. thesis, Univ. of Minnesota, 1952.

G. L. Bond and L. F. Fay, "A Comparison of the Performance of Good and Poor Readers on the Individual Items of the Stanford-Binet Scale, Forms L and M," *Journal of Educational Research,* Vol. 43 (February, 1950), pp. 475-479.

is not uniformly consistent; he may be growing more rapidly at one time than at another. Furthermore, the tests are not completely reliable and hence there may be errors of measurement. Therefore one should not depend completely on the results of a single test given at some prior time. The most recent measurement is likely to be the most indicative of the pupil's present status, unless it is out of line with other evidence.

The results of group tests of intelligence are in general much less valid and reliable than such individual measurements as the Wechsler or Stanford-Binet tests, and therefore they should be given less weight in estimating mental capacity. In cases of doubt about the ratings of individuals on group tests, the results should be checked by individual tests.

No child should be assumed to be a slow learner because of low mental ability until all other causes of functional slowness such as physical handicaps, ill health, meager experiential background, social and emotional maladjustment, and unwholesome environmental conditions have been taken into account.

2. *Educational Quotient.* The ratio between reading age and chronological age for Pupil *A* is 126. This is called his *educational quotient* for reading. Pupil *B*'s educational quotient for reading is 67. Pupil *A*'s educational quotient for arithmetic is 119 and for spelling 128. Pupil *B*'s educational quotient for arithmetic is 93 and for spelling 85. Pupil *A*'s educational quotients are all above 100 whereas those of Pupil *B* are all below 100. Educational quotients have the same limitations as intelligence quotients, discussed above.

3. *Achievement Quotients.* Pupil *A*'s reading, arithmetic, and spelling ages are all considerably below his mental age. The ratio between mental age and educational age in each area is called the *achievement quotient.* Pupil *A*'s achievement quotients are 90 for reading, 85 for arithmetic, and 92 for spelling. They are all below 100, and considerably below his IQ. Pupil *B*'s achievement quotients are 79 for reading, 109 for arithmetic, and 100 for spelling. Except for reading, Pupil *B*'s achievement quotients are thus 100 or above. It is evident that his lack of proficiency in reading requires special attention by the teacher.

4. *Level of Expectancy.* Many teachers are uncertain about how to interpret the above data. Pupil *A* is performing at a level considerably below his mental age level, as is indicated by his AQ's which are all below 100. It is said by some that he is performing below his *expectancy level.* On the other hand, Pupil *B,* except for reading, is performing at or above his expectancy level. In general, it has been found that pupils who have high IQ's perform *below* their expectancy level whereas pupils with low IQ's perform *above* their expectancy level. There are those who maintain that Pupil *A*'s performance would be higher under more effective teaching, while Pupil *B*'s performance in arithmetic and spelling indicates that instruction in these fields has been effective and that he is achieving as well as can be expected.

However, his low AQ in reading clearly indicates a disability. An AQ below 80 is usually regarded as an indication of disability requiring systematic diagnosis and treatment.

The important point to bear in mind in interpreting test scores is that standards of achievement should not be the same for all pupils in a particular grade or age group, because of differences in their capacity to learn, in their experiential background, in their social, emotional, and physical maturity, and in their basic interests and purposes.

Setting up norms for various configurations of these and other factors that influence learning presents many interesting possibilities. In clinical and remedial work, individual norms are often used; the pupil's past performance is taken as the norm by which to measure his subsequent progress, so that his rate of growth can be considered in appraising his performance.

The teacher's aim should be to guide the pupil "from where he is to where he ought to be," as judged by the achievements of similar children and by his own potentialities and background of experience.

The authors strongly recommend that individual progress-growth goals that are meaningful to the learner be set up for each pupil who has a serious learning difficulty and that his growth be measured by the progress he makes in achieving these goals.

Types of Cases That Emerge

A variety of types of cases emerge when the results of appraisal are scrutinized.

1. There are many pupils at all levels of mental ability whose performance on tests of the basic skills is quite in line with their learning potential. For them the regular instruction program should be continued and strengthened.

2. A number of pupils will be found in almost every class who are performing at levels somewhat below their level of expectancy, but whose work does not indicate the presence of any serious learning deficiency. In these cases there often are found weaknesses in specific skills and abilities in some field, such as reading or arithmetic, that should be studied carefully by the teacher. The prognosis is good and the deficiency usually responds readily to carefully guided instruction. These pupils may be regarded as instances of *simple retardation*.

3. We shall use the category *specific disability case* to label cases in which there is something fundamentally wrong with the performance of a learner in some specific learning area. There always is present an interfering habit or an ineffective approach in this type of disability. For example, the child may be overanalytical or underanalytical in reading, or be confused by zeros in arithmetic operations. If the faulty habit or ineffective approach has become so well established over a period of time that correction will

require individualized instruction, it may be necessary to place the child in a special remedial group for a time until the condition is alleviated.

4. The category *complex disability case* includes the more subtle, complicated cases of disability. Such children often are normal in intelligence but are always severely retarded in some learning area, such as reading, although they may be bright, capable youngsters in other areas. These children have developed blockings, tensions, and faulty attitudes that make them ineffective learners. With the passing of time these tensions become more severe, and the children demonstrate fear and worry and often a lack of desire to learn. This group of cases should be given careful individual attention under expert guidance.

It should be pointed out that those *categories* should be regarded as descriptive designations and that there actually is no clear line of demarcation between them.

SUGGESTED ACTIVITIES

1. Tell about the planning and organization of the testing program used where you may be teaching or in some school with which you are familiar. Evaluate the program. How are the findings used? Should teachers have a voice in the selection of tests?

2. Tell about methods of informal evaluation in the same way. Which ones are regarded as most valuable? What is being done by the schools to improve the use of evaluation procedures? Use as the basis of discussion the list on pages 9 and 10.

3. Why should evaluation be a continuing process? How can pupils participate in evaluation? Account for the wide range of individual differences found in test scores in almost all classes and its significance for instruction.

4. Discuss difficulties you have had in interpreting test scores and in reporting or discussing test scores with parents and others.

5. Examine critically the test scores of the four pupils given on page 23. Define a disability case in reading; in arithmetic; in spelling.

6. Select a series of tests you would regard as basic in studying pupil growth and development. The outlines on pages 11 and 12 may be helpful. Apply the criteria given on pages 13 and 14.

7. Examine selected textbooks in some curriculum area for evidence of provisions for evaluation of achievements and diagnosis of learning difficulty. Arithmetic textbooks and reading workbooks sometimes contain the essentials of a well-rounded testing program.

8. What is the value of anecdotal records?

9. Apply a simple sociometric procedure in a classroom and chart the results.

10. A group of students may select some important educational outcome, list procedures for evaluation, and prepare brief descriptions of the necessary appraisal techniques.

11. How valid are criticisms of the educational product that appear in various publications? What are the limitations of these criticisms?

12. Describe cases which you believe fit each of the four categories described at the close of the chapter.

SELECTED BIBLIOGRAPHY

The list of books on page 13 contains the titles of the most valuable books available on tests and measurements and other methods of appraisal.

It is strongly recommended that copies of the tests listed on pages 11 and 12 together with the accompanying manuals be made available for examination by students and teachers. The authors have followed the practice of preparing portfolios of selected tests for purchase by individuals in their classes or by schools for their files.

3

FACTORS RELATED TO
LEARNING DIFFICULTIES

THE PROBLEM OF ISOLATING CAUSES OF
LEARNING DIFFICULTIES

A DISCUSSION of the factors which contribute to learning difficulties is important inasmuch as these must be taken into account when formulating a corrective program. It is relatively hard to isolate them but it is even more difficult to establish a causal relationship. Nonetheless, as a result of a large body of research, it has become clear that certain characteristics within the individual and factors in his environment influence his ability to master such difficult learnings as reading, arithmetic, spelling, and language usage.

The contributing factors to a specific learning difficulty are hard to isolate for several reasons. First, a child who is seemingly capable in other respects gets into difficulty in a specific field as a result of a whole series of inter-related causes. There is usually no single cause or condition that creates the learning difficulty. A child, for example, may have a moderate degree of hearing loss. This would not preclude his learning to read. But if this child is in a classroom on a noisy street and his teacher has a soft voice and uses a method that involves a large amount of oral instruction, serious difficulty may be encountered in learning to read. Learning difficulties are, for the most part, the result of the combined effects of many unfortunate circumstances.

Second, it is frequently hard to tell with exactness which is the cause and which is the effect of a learning difficulty. The typical child with a serious learning problem is quite likely to feel insecure in the classroom, and as a result, exhibits withdrawing tendencies. Whether the child withdraws because he has trouble with his school work or is in trouble with his school work because he tends to withdraw is a problem difficult to solve.

Third, the underlying causes of learning disabilities are frequently subtle and difficult to appraise. Quite often teachers are uncertain about assessing the difficulty when there is a complex disturbance within the child. For example, a teacher unaided cannot assess the degree to which the child may have a glandular imbalance. The teacher cannot readily determine the influence of certain types of emotional disturbance. The teacher should, however, know that such conditions are sometimes related to learning difficulties and know that there are specialists to whom he can go for technical assistance.

APPROACHES TO OVERCOMING KNOWN LIMITATIONS OF A CHILD

In spite of the difficulty inherent in assigning causality, it is important to discuss the factors that contribute to learning difficulty. Those who would help a child overcome a specific learning problem will need to take these factors into account in formulating their remedial plans. The teacher will find that, in general, there are three approaches to overcoming a known limitation or set of limitations of an individual child. In the first place, the teacher may find it possible to improve the limiting element so that the child can become a more effective learner. For example, if the child suffers from a visual defect that can be corrected, the correction should be made so that the child can learn more efficiently and comfortably. It must be remembered, however, that the mere correction of a known limitation does not correct the learning confusion which the limitation caused. Usually the teacher will have to institute a program of re-education to correct the confusions that have resulted from the child's handicap.

Another approach the teacher may use is to alter the method of instruction so that the child is not forced to apply the ability in which he is limited. The child who cannot hear, for example, can be taught to spell by emphasis on the visual characteristics of words. The teacher can encourage the child to make a careful visual analysis of the words being studied and thus avoid emphasizing the auditory method of sounding out the words. Or, if a child has a speech difficulty, the teacher need not delay instruction in reading until the speech difficulty has been corrected, but can modify the program of reading instruction to enable the child to grow in reading as the speech difficulty is being corrected.

A third possible adjustment to a known limitation is that of adjusting the expected outcomes. A child who is a slow learner cannot be expected to develop skill in arithmetic as fast as an average or more capable learner. The child who is limited in energy because of a health problem cannot be expected to develop as rapidly educationally. The spastic child cannot be expected to develop as high a standard in handwriting as a child who is not so affected. The slow-learning child should not be expected to learn to read with the same degree of critical insight as the normal or gifted child.

In the discussion of the factors related to learning difficulties which follows, their detection and significance, and possible adjustments to them, will be considered. The general categories are:

1. Intellectual and neurological factors.
2. Physical and sensory factors.

3. Personal and social adjustment as related to educational development, interests, and motivation.
4. Environmental and instructional factors, including learning omissions and overemphases.

INTELLECTUAL AND NEUROLOGICAL FACTORS

Relation of Intellectual and Neurological Conditions to Learning Difficulties

There can be no question that intellectual and neurological conditions bear a substantial relationship to the degree of competence a child is able to achieve in such learnings as reading, arithmetic, and language usage. In spelling and handwriting this relationship is not as close. In a group of very poor readers, a substantial number will be found to have low intelligence; likewise, in a group of children who are poor in arithmetic, a fairly large proportion will be found to be low in intelligence. These children, however, should not be classified as suffering from a specific learning difficulty. They are children who are growing, perhaps, as well as can be expected.[1] The children who are classified as having real learning difficulties are those children who are not living up to their level of expectancy. There are children with relatively high measured intelligence who find it difficult to progress in such fields as reading, arithmetic, or language usage. The truly disabled reader, for example, is usually found to be above average in intelligence.

So it is necessary, when appraising the influence of intellectual and neurological conditions, to consider in addition to general intelligence such specific mental limitations as faulty memory, perseveration, and ability to sense field and ground. The possibility also exists that neurological damage may be present and causing difficulty in learning to read or to spell. The role of brain dominance as a possible cause of certain types of difficulty must be carefully considered.

General Intelligence

In considering general intelligence as a cause of educational difficulty, we are confronted with a rather complicated relationship. In general, children of high intelligence will be successful in such learnings as reading, arithmetic, and language usage. The correlation between intelligence and achievement that has been demonstrated by research depends to a considerable degree upon the types of tests used. If group paper-and-pencil verbal tests are used to measure intelligence, the relationship between intelligence and reading, for example, seems very high because children who cannot read well are unable to demonstrate their true intellectual capability.

The case of Betty will serve to illustrate this point. Betty was supposed

[1] Helen Robinson, *Why Pupils Fail in Reading* (Chicago, Univ. of Chicago Press, 1946).

to have a diminishing intelligence quotient. At kindergarten age, Betty was measured with a Stanford-Binet Intelligence Test and was found to have an IQ of 108. At the fourth-grade level, she was measured with the Otis Self-Administering Test of Intelligence, a verbal group intelligence test, and her indicated IQ was 82. At the high-school level, she was measured with the Terman-McNamara Test of General Intelligence, an extremely verbal group intelligence test, and the result was an IQ of 54. Measurement showed also that Betty at high-school level was unable to read comfortably material of average third-grade difficulty. When measured by an individual Wechsler Intelligence Test, which requires no reading on the part of the person being examined, Betty had a nonverbal IQ of 109 and a verbal IQ of 100.

Betty was a specific reading disability case. She represents the type of learning difficulty which necessitates further search for causal factors. Betty had been grossly mismeasured by intelligence tests suitable for children of normal reading growth. They are invalid for disabled readers.

A study of group intelligence tests by Clymer [2] showed that

there can be no doubt that many of the current testing programs are under-estimating the capabilities of the poor reader. Reading achievement is definitely entering into the measurement of intelligence.

If teachers are to use present intelligence tests properly, they must realize that a low score on a group intelligence test which involves reading is not a true test if the child is a poor reader.

Even the scores on individual tests of intelligence, such as the Stanford-Binet, are influenced to some degree by poor reading ability. Bond and Fay [3] found that

children in the fourth, fifth, and sixth grades whose reading ages were less than their mental ages tended to be penalized by those items of the Revised Stanford-Binet Scale which are verbal in nature or which depend upon ability to understand a read passage. The effect of this penalty probably tends to increase as the difference between mental age and reading age of the poor reader increases.

Careful checks of measures must be made before classifying a poor reader as a person of low intelligence.

In considering the relationship between intelligence and learning difficulties, the teacher must recognize that there are two types of problems. One is the slow-learning child who, although living up to his level of expectancy, will be poor in certain learning fields. The teacher must adjust the methods of instruction to the learner's mental limitation and also alter the expected outcomes to correspond with his intellectual capability. The second type of problem is the more troublesome, namely, that of such cases as Betty, who

[2] Theodore W. Clymer, *The Influence of Reading Ability on the Validity of Group Intelligence Tests*. Unpublished Ph.D. thesis, Univ. of Minnesota, 1952.

[3] Guy L. Bond and Leo F. Fay, "A Comparison of the Performance of Good and Poor Readers on Individual Items of the Stanford-Binet, Forms L and M," *Journal of Educational Research*, Vol. 43 (February, 1950), pp. 475-479.

are capable children with a serious specific learning difficulty. The relationships between intelligence, as measured by individual mental aptitude tests such as the Stanford-Binet or the Wechsler, and educational accomplishments are not high. Hence many children of high intellectual capability can be in serious difficulty in complex learnings such as reading, arithmetic, spelling, and language usage. The solution of their problems depends upon a thorough diagnosis in which other causal factors are identified, so that the teacher can make the necessary adjustments. It is with this second type of child, who is having difficulty in learning the tool subjects, that the remainder of this chapter will deal.

The most useful tests for appraising the general intelligence of a child with an educational disability are individual tests such as the Stanford-Binet or the Wechsler Bellevue Intelligence Scales for Children. Group tests are often invalid for this type of child and should not be relied upon. In some school systems the teachers cannot obtain adequate measures of general intelligence. They can, however, make a rough estimate of the child's general intelligence by noting such indications as the following:

1. The extensiveness of his vocabulary.
2. His achievement in other academic learnings.
3. His ability to apply school learning to solve problems.
4. The knowledges he has been able to gain from radio and television.
5. The contributions to discussions he makes from his first-hand experiences.

In making such estimates from observed intellectual behavior, the teacher must recognize the possibility of misjudging intelligence because of the following pupil characteristics:

1. The aggressive or talkative child is likely to be overestimated.
2. The popular, social child is likely to be overestimated.
3. The unattractive, shy, or rejected child is likely to be underestimated.
4. The overage child is likely to be overestimated.

In summary, then, before concluding that a child is in difficulty because of inadequate general intelligence, the teacher must be sure that the measurement used gave the child an adequate chance to demonstrate his true capability and did not reflect his learning difficulty. Secondly, the decision must be made as to whether the child is a slow learner, for whom appropriate adjustments should be made, or truly a specific disability case, that is, one who in some important learning area is not living up to what can be expected of a pupil of his general capacity.

Specific Mental Limitations

Although it is recognized that a child of high general intelligence may have a learning difficulty, it is sometimes thought that this may be the result of a specific mental limitation. A child, for example, may be thought of as having high general intellectual capability but a poor memory. As the teacher deals with children in serious trouble in reading, arithmetic, or spelling, he may well be convinced that a particular child's trouble is due to a defect in his memory. The child may, for example, know how to spell a word on one day and seem to have forgotten the word on the next day. Or a child who is in serious difficulty in reading may have recognized a word, such as *learned,* on one day but when he is confronted with the same word the following day, he does not recognize it or seems to have forgotten it. Nonetheless, when we take a group of good readers and a group of poor readers of equal general intelligence and compare their memories, we can detect no difference. It is not memory in general, then, that is at fault; they did not perceive the word in the same way on one day as they did on the next. Perhaps the words looked different to the child. For example, the child may have known the word *learned* on one day when he separated the word into *learn-ed* and recognized it readily. On the next day he may have separated the word into *l-ear-ned* and could not blend the elements into the word *learned.* It was not that the child's memory was poor, but that his visual perception of the word changed so greatly he simply didn't recognize it. He saw something different on the two days. The evidence shows that such a faculty as faulty memory either does not exist or, if it does exist, it is not related to specific learning difficulties.

Another specific mental limitation might be perseveration, the tendency for a given response to persist. When the youngster, for example, breaks a word into parts that do not help him to recognize the word, as illustrated above with the word *learned,* he is unable to reject that view of the word and re-inspect it to find one that works. A study by Clymer [4] tends to indicate that perseveration may be a specific characteristic which influences reading growth, since a part of the reading process is one of reacting to a stimulus, rejecting it, reacting to the next, and so forth. An overlap or a lag of either stimulus might have implications for speed and comprehension, and even for word recognition.

A specific mental limitation that gives some evidence of being related to inefficient reading by a person with high general intellectual capability is the inability to distinguish "figure and ground." Reading is, in part, a process of rapid perception of field and ground. There is some evidence that the ability to see parts within a whole is related to word recognition. Adequacy in word recognition leans heavily upon the ability to see syllables, large elements such as root words, and the like within complex words. But, aside from this slight relationship which does warrant further study, it can be said that specific mental limitations do not seem to be highly related to specific learning difficulties; and until further evidence is available, it would be unwise for the teacher to devote time and effort to the identification of possible specific mental limitations.

[4] Theodore W. Clymer, *Interrelationships of Certain Mental Abilities and Reading of Fourth Grade Pupils.* Unpublished Master's dissertation, Univ. of Minnesota, 1951.

Neurological Damage

That neurological damage may constitute a basic cause of learning difficulties cannot be denied. There is evidence that sometimes as a result of brain injury, people lose their ability to read or to spell or to function in other ways linguistically. There is also evidence that many of these brain damage cases can be re-educated, although at times it is a long and arduous task. It is reasonable to suppose that birth injury or accident prior to learning to read, spell, or calculate may have some influence on the child's capability within these areas. It is quite possible, in certain rare cases, that such neurological conditions do interfere with educational progress and that the learning capacity of a youngster who is seemingly bright in many respects is limited because of neurological damage. However, the evidence seems to show that such cases are rare. Nonetheless, if a child shows evidences of lack of co-ordination, minor speech defects, or other indications of neurological difficulties, a thorough examination should be undertaken by a competent neurologist. It should be re-emphasized that only rarely is there a neurological explanation for specific learning difficulties.

Brain Dominance

It is often assumed that certain orientational confusions such as reading *was* for *saw,* or *not* for *ton* are attributable to mixed brain dominance. The transposition of letters in spelling, mirror writing, and the transposition of numbers in arithmetic are regarded as indications of such orientational confusions. The major evidence tends to support the point of view that these are learning difficulties—that is, the child has failed to learn the systematic, orderly progression of print and number—rather than the result of dominance confusion. Nonetheless, the teacher should be alert to the possibility that such a causal relationship may exist in rare cases and that any enforced change of handedness might set up confusions difficult for the child to overcome. It is likely that greater care will be necessary in establishing left-to-right sequence across the printed page and in spelling for the child who is left-handed; characteristically he tends to work from right-to-left prior to reading instruction, since in working thus he can more readily see what he is doing. These habits operate when brought to printed material, whether it be words or numbers, and may cause the child an unusual amount of confusion.

Summary

Summarizing the intellectual and neurological conditions that might cause learning difficulties, it is well for the teacher to recognize that because of low general intelligence a child will develop skills at a slower rate and that he cannot be expected to reach the ultimate level of achievement of children of higher general intelligence. But there are many children of high capability who get into learning difficulties. They present very important instructional problems in our educational system. The teacher should know that the search for special mental limitations has not proved very fruitful as a means of isolating causes of learning difficulties.

Neurological damage and dominance confusion may be important contributing conditions in certain cases, but they are relatively infrequent. When they do exist, they are extremely crucial.

When a child has an apparent neurological defect or intellectual lack, the important thing for the teacher to do is to adjust the instruction to the limitation. Whether physiological or functional, the teacher simply and directly teaches the child by methods that (1) do not stress what the child lacks, and/or (2) help the child overcome his weakness. The teacher's job is one of organizing the instruction to overcome the shortcoming. The origin of the trouble, which is left up to the neurologist, does not influence the teacher's method of adjusting to it.

PHYSICAL AND SENSORY FACTORS

Relationship to Learning Difficulties

Poor general physical condition, malnutrition, frequent illnesses, and certain glandular conditions are related, at least to some degree, to learning difficulties. Learning the fundamental subjects in school is both difficult and exacting. Any condition within the child that lessens his energy, distracts him, or makes him in any way uncomfortable may have deleterious effects upon his learning. The establishment of almost automatic responses to number combinations, for example, requires that the learner energetically attack the task of learning them. Wandering attention, restlessness, or fatigue are not conducive to effective learning. Poor motor control, visual limitations, and auditory deficiencies also contribute to learning difficulties. The physical and sensory characteristics of the child predispose him to specific difficulties in the basic learnings of reading, arithmetic, language usage, spelling, and handwriting. These conditions within the child, which make it more likely for him to get into learning difficulties, are also important in formulating remedial programs and warrant further attention.

General Physical Condition

The teacher who would help a child to overcome a specific learning difficulty needs to be alert to the possibility of poor general physical condition of the child. Poor general physical condition is related in a variety of ways to learning difficulties. The child who is absent from school misses some of the important instruction. The child who has frequent illnesses may lack the stamina necessary to be an effective student. He may be somewhat listless and show frequent signs of fatigue, and evidence boredom.

The teacher must recognize, however, that a well child who has difficulty in learning frequently shows these same symptoms. When a child finds that he is unable to learn his spelling effectively, he frequently forms the unfortunate pattern of dawdling over his spelling words, and his behavior shows symptoms of boredom or fatigue. The teacher should then look for evidence of lack of physical stamina in activities not related to the specific learning difficulty. If, for example, he tires quickly on the playground or is bored and restless when the teacher reads interesting stories to the children, then attention should be given to his general physical condition.

It may be that rather than having poor health the child is lacking in physical stamina because he is tired. Many children lose valuable rest time because of unwise use of television at home. It has been found, for example, that third-grade children have reported as their favorite programs those which are shown at as late as eleven o'clock at night. It is not surprising that these children show signs of fatigue the following morning.

One child who came to the attention of the University of Minnesota Psycho-Educational Clinic showed marked signs of fatigue during remedial reading periods. It was found, upon further study, that her parents attended bridge parties almost every week-day evening until as late as one o'clock in the morning. Because of the expense of baby sitters, this third-grade child was taken along each time. She slept in a strange bed each night and then was brought home early in the morning. The clinicians decided that this disturbed pattern of rest, rather than poor general physical condition, caused the child's fatigue.

The teacher's responsibility in regard to poor general physical condition is twofold. First, the teacher should be on the alert for evidence of physical illness, malnutrition, or defective glandular activity and recommend that the child be referred for medical attention if these symptoms are present. He should also be on the alert for other causes of fatigue and consult with the parents about ways in which lack of sleep or insufficient rest or overwork can be corrected. Second, the teacher must adjust instruction to meet the needs of the child with lowered physical stamina. The child should be given periods of rest and relaxation. Concentrated learning periods should be shortened for such children. The teacher should watch for signs of fatigue in the child and be sure that assignments are such that the child can accomplish them with comfort. It is unwise to ask a child who is suffering from a physical limitation to work beyond the point at which fatigue sets in. It is also unwise to place such a child under the strain of a too difficult or complex learning situation.

Motor Control

Children vary considerably in motor co-ordination and control. This is shown by the different degrees of co-ordination demonstrated in walking and running and in the finer co-ordinations called into play in writing.

Faulty motor control has been shown to be associated with reading disability and spelling defects. Whether motor control is actually a causal condition in reading or spelling disability, or a concomitant, has not been established. There is the possibility that marked degrees of deficiency in motor co-ordination may be the result of neurological disabilities which affect both motor co-ordination and the ability to learn to read and spell. It is quite apparent that lack of motor co-ordination would have a detrimental effect upon establishing effective handwriting skills, which in turn would influence achievement in other fields. For example, the child who finds it difficult to write numbers may find written exercises in arithmetic troublesome and frustrating. This is especially true if speed of calculation is emphasized. The child loses confidence not because he does not have knowledge of the arithmetical processes but because of the time consumed in writing the numbers. The same thing would apply to spelling, composition, or handwriting. However, whether lack of motor co-ordination is a cause of learning difficulty or just a concomitant, the teacher's role is clear and threefold. First, the teacher should avoid methods of instruction for these children which require fine muscular co-ordination. Second, the methods of instruction should be altered so that speed of manipulation is not emphasized. Third, an understanding attitude toward such an outcome as neatness of papers, and less emphasis on handwriting precision, should lead to the adjustment of goals to accord with the motor capability of the children involved.

It should be pointed out that children who are left-handed find it difficult to gain the speed and fluency in writing that the right-handed child can attain in the early grades. The left-handed child must learn to make rather marked adjustments of paper and writing position. Also he cannot see his work as well and is more apt to smudge his written work than is the right-handed child. This is not truly a motor co-ordination problem; nonetheless, it reflects the need for the same type of adjustment in the curriculum and in re-educative work as is necessary for the youngster lacking motor co-ordination.

Speech Defects

Speech defects of the motor co-ordination type have an important relationship to the deficiencies in learning being discussed in this book. The effect of speech difficulties upon reading success is determined by the way in which reading is taught. However, there is a greater tendency for children with speech troubles to get into reading difficulty. The strange thing is that it is not the severity of the speech difficulty that is important. For example, a stutterer will find it no more difficult to learn to read than children with normal speech. But some of the youngsters who stutter, have cumbersomeness of speech, or have articulatory difficulties of one sort or another are apt to get into difficulty if they are taught by a rather strict oral-phonetic method.

Children who are poor in speech, even though they are good silent readers, find oral reading difficult. A child who is a poor oral reader ordinarily is in trouble in reading, and this in turn may limit his silent reading. It is important for the teacher to note anything unusual in the child's speech so that the program can be adjusted to the child's speech limitation.

Visual Deficiencies

The relationship between visual deficiencies and learning difficulties is rather complex. There can be no question that the visual characteristics of a child in educational difficulty should be studied and every essential correction be made. Such corrections will add to the child's comfort in handling printed material and will thereby enable him to be a more effective learner. Considerable research tends to show that there is a slightly greater percentage of visual defects among children with educational disability than there are in the normal population, and that if one selects children with visual anomalies of one sort or another, he will find their educational development somewhat retarded. The studies seem to indicate that visual deficiencies make the child more likely to get into difficulty but they do not in any sense decisively determine that this will be the case, because for each child with a visual defect who is having learning difficulties there can be found another child with the same kind of visual defect who is getting along well.

Poor vision, then, appears to increase the hazard of becoming an educational disability case. It is true that poor vision is related to most learning difficulties. An adequate study of an educational disability in any field should always include an inspection of visual acuity and comfort. Poor vision need not be a limiting factor which inhibits learning to read, to spell, or to achieve in arithmetic. The average child's vision is usually good enough to learn well within these areas.

The child with poor vision apparently can accommodate to the task of reading print. At the time the average child begins to learn to read, he has a tremendously efficient eye; it is probably as flexible as it will ever be during his lifetime. It allows even the farsighted child to read print at reading distance. Nonetheless, he makes this accommodation under strain. It is likely the reason studies tend to show that poor vision is associated with learning difficulties, but is not a determiner of the difficulty, is that the child learns to read printed material in spite of his visual discomfort. Reading, for example, is probably so important to these children with visual limitations that they learn to read in spite of considerable strain. For many of them this strain accumulates until they begin to avoid reading and tend to stop after a shorter period of reading than does a child with normal vision. Such a child may read for only fifteen minutes and then stop because he actually is tired. Quite obviously, we should make him as comfortable visually as we possibly can.

The fact is that we should make every school child, good reader or poor reader, as visually comfortable as we can. Many children are not visually comfortable when they read. Fendrick,[5] for example, found that 30 per cent of the good readers had poor vision and 44 per cent of the poor readers had visual defects. Therefore the teacher should be on the alert for visual deficiencies among all the children.

Edson,[6] in studying the relationship between visual characteristics and specific silent reading abilities, found that a large number of visual anomalies are associated with reading difficulties but that no one anomaly seems to be of such significance that it determines reading disability. These findings are in keeping with those of Eames, Fendrick, Spache, Swanson and Tiffin, Robinson, Gates and Bond, Witty and Kopel, and other workers within the field. The more serious the defect, the more likely it is to have an unfavorable influence upon learnings which involve close scrutiny of the printed page.

Special Visual Deficiencies

Among the types of visual deficiencies found to be associated with learning difficulties are hyperopia and binocular difficulties of one sort or another. The child who is farsighted and finds it difficult to accommodate to near vision is more likely to get into difficulty than is the child who does not have such a deficiency. The nearsighted child, that is, the child who can see things more comfortably at reading distance than he can see things at far distance, is more likely to be successful in reading printed material than is the child with normal vision. However, if the teaching method leans upon the use of experience charts and considerable blackboard work, the nearsighted child will also be somewhat handicapped.

Muscular imbalance, fusion difficulties, and aniseikonia all cause a degree of strain and confusion on the part of the child when he is reading. The lack of muscular balance between the two eyes makes it difficult for the child to see a single image on the printed page. He may bring the two images together, but he does so only with some degree of muscular strain. From time to time the printed page will appear blurred or, in the more severe cases, the child will see two images. This condition is obviously confusing and the child must strain to avoid it. For the most part, he will be able to do this and thus be able to read printed material, do work with numbers, and spelling lessons, but it is not surprising if there is evidence of fatigue and irritability. The mere fact that children will work, and work effectively, even under strain and tension has made the problem of studying the relationship be-

[5] Paul Fendrick, *Visual Characteristics of Poor Readers,* Contributions to Education No. 656 (New York, Bureau of Publications, Teachers College, Columbia Univ., 1936).

[6] William H. Edson, *A Study of the Relationships between Visual Characteristics and Specific Silent Reading Abilities.* Unpublished Ph.D. thesis, Univ. of Minnesota, 1950.

tween muscular co-ordination and learning difficulties troublesome and has probably contributed to the variation in findings.

Another binocular characteristic apparently related to educational success is the precision of focus of the eye lenses so that the images may be fused into a single, clear picture. Eames [7] has reported that 35 per cent of 114 children with educational problems had fusion difficulties in comparison with 18 per cent found in unselected pupils. Speed as well as accuracy of fusion may have an influence in such exacting visual tasks as reading.

Aniseikonia, unequal ocular images in either size or shape in the two eyes, has been found by some research workers to be related to reading difficulties. Dearborn and Anderson [8] found that 51 per cent of poor readers that they studied and 23 per cent of unselected pupils had aniseikonia. They concluded that aniseikonia is one among the many factors which may contribute to reading and other learning difficulties.

How to Identify Visual Deficiencies

The teacher's responsibility in regard to visual limitations of children is great. First, he must recognize that such visual limitations as farsightedness, lack of co-ordination of the two eyes, and difficulties in fusion make the child's educational tasks more difficult and he is more likely to get into trouble. Therefore the teacher must be on the alert for any indication of visual discomfort among the children. It is his major responsibility to detect suspected visual problems and to refer them to a specialist. The following list of symptoms of visual discomfort given by Betts [9] is helpful:

1. Reddening and thickening of margins of lids.
2. Scales and crusts on lids.
3. Loss of eyelashes.
4. Tearing (or watering of the eyes).
5. Inflammation or reddening of the eyes.
6. Discharge around eyes.
7. Cloudiness of pupil.
8. Drooping of upper lid.
9. Widely dilated pupils.
10. Difference in size of pupils.
11. Deviation of one eye.
12. Forward thrusting of head.
13. Tilting of head.
14. Facial contortions, such as puckering face, frowning, scowling.
15. Continual rubbing of eyes.
16. Excessive blinking.
17. Excessive head movement while reading.

[7] Thomas H. Eames, "Improvement in School Eye Testing," *Education,* Vol. 56 (September, 1935), pp. 14 and 17.

[8] W. F. Dearborn and I. H. Anderson, "Aniseikonia as Related to Disability in Reading," *Journal of Experimental Psychology,* Vol. 22 (June, 1938), pp. 559-577.

[9] E. A. Betts, *Foundations of Reading Instruction* (New York, American Book, 1946), p. 182.

Providing Visual Comfort

A further responsibility of the teacher is to assure the visual comfort of the children during all activities that require careful use of the eyes. The room should be well lighted and free from glare. The children should have their seating arranged so that work done on the chalkboard is readily and comfortably visible to them. Children with visual anomalies should be assigned seats that enable them to pursue their visual work with comfort. The teacher should recognize that these children will work under some degree of strain and that they will need shorter periods of concentrated visual work. The teacher should also recognize that those children who are suffering from visual difficulties will need to be taught word recognition and spelling techniques that allow them to deal with larger elements rather than piecemeal, detailed analysis of the words. All of these adjustments, most of them readily made, will aid the child with poor vision to establish adequacy in the basic learnings without discomfort and the resulting hazard of educational failure.

In the case of those children who are already suffering from a specific disability, such as reading, the teacher must be aware that correction of vision alone will not correct the disability in reading. The visual problems of the child have caused him to acquire poor reading patterns or have made him neglect important learnings. After the visual correction is made, his reading pattern must be subjected to an educational diagnosis and appropriate remedial techniques must be applied for establishing adequate patterns for reading. It is obvious that visual defects should be corrected as soon as they are discovered in order to prevent disability or to plan the re-education of a disability case more readily.

Auditory Deficiency

Auditory deficiencies, under certain circumstances, may be a primary cause of reading difficulty. Research in this field shows that in general there is a direct, though very low, correlation between auditory characteristics and educational success. When children suffering from learning difficulties, especially in the fields of reading or spelling, are compared with children making average or better progress, auditory deficiencies are found slightly more frequently among the disabled group. By and large the studies show that this relationship, though rather consistent, is never high enough to be statistically significant. There seems to be an indication that acuity deficiencies alone do not determine that a child will get into learning difficulties. However, Bond [10] found that if the method of instruction leans heavily upon oral, sounding methods, then the child with hearing deficiencies is much

[10] Guy L. Bond, *The Auditory and Speech Characteristics of Poor Readers,* Contributions to Education No. 657 (New York, Bureau of Publications, Teachers College, Columbia Univ., 1935).

more likely to get into difficulty than is the child who is better equipped auditorily.

A study by Henry [11] indicated that children with a loss in the high tonal frequencies are more likely to get into difficulties in reading than are children without such hearing loss. The difference in school success between the children with hearing loss in the low frequencies and normal children is not so apparent. The study by Bond indicates also that certain functional aspects of hearing are related to success in reading, and particularly so when the method of instruction leans heavily upon oral, sounding approaches to word recognition. The conclusion Bond reached was that if the pupils are exposed to oral, phonetic types of instruction, auditory abilities appear to be important factors in reading disability. If, on the contrary, pupils are taught by a predominantly meaningful approach, with a broad attack on word recognition, auditory factors do not maintain their dominant position as causes of reading and spelling difficulties. It appears that the teacher should be on the alert to detect not only auditory acuity but also differences in auditory discrimination and auditory blending or ability to fuse letter sounds.

A careful and extensive study by Reynolds [12] supports the point of view that the extent to which poor hearing is associated with poor reading depends upon the method of instruction. He found one school in which there was a high correspondence between certain auditory characteristics and word-recognition ability and knowledge of common word elements. In three other schools where he measured the same elements of reading, this high correspondence did not exist. He concluded that the teaching methods used in the one school accounted for the difference. No adjustments were made in the other schools.

How to Identify Auditory Deficiencies

The teacher's responsibility is again one of detecting auditory deficiencies and recommending cases for referral to a specialist. There should be annual tests of hearing by means of individual audiometers. If such a program is not possible, the teacher may find it expedient to give "whisper" tests. One such test which has proved effective is to have four or five children line up across the front of the room, facing away from the teacher. Then the teacher, speaking in a soft voice, gives such directions as: "Walk four steps forward; put your hands behind your back; walk five more steps forward; show me two fingers; walk four steps farther; put your left hand behind your back; walk two steps farther; extend three fingers on your left hand." As the children get farther away, some of them may start looking at their neighbors,

[11] Sibyl Henry, "Children's Audiograms in Relation to Reading Attainment: III. Discussion, Summary and Conclusions," *Journal of Genetic Psychology,* Vol. LXXI (September, 1947), pp. 49-63.

[12] Maynard Reynolds, *A Study of the Relationships Between Auditory Characteristics and Specific Silent Reading Abilities.* Unpublished Ph.D. thesis, Univ. of Minnesota, 1950.

showing that they have not heard the directions. Such children are likely to be those with poorer hearing in the group tested.

The teacher should also be on the alert for other signs of poor hearing ability. The following list given by Betts [13] may prove helpful:

1. Monotonous or unnatural pitch of voice.
2. Faulty pronunciation and lack of clear or distinct speech.
3. Turning one ear toward the speaker.
4. Poor spelling.
5. Inattention.
6. Frequent requests for repeating questions or statements.
7. Difficult breathing, including mouth breathing.
8. Earache.
9. Discharging ears.
10. Catarrhal conditions.
11. Sinus infection.
12. Frequent colds.
13. Excessive accumulation of earwax.

The teacher has the additional responsibility of making adjustments for children with auditory limitations. He should seat children with hearing defects in favorable spots in the room. A favorable place is one that is located in the center of the room, no farther back than the third row. The custom of having small groups of children work closely with the teacher helps considerably the child who has an auditory defect. The teacher also should be sure that each child hears the specific oral directions and explanations. When doing remedial work with a child who has a known hearing loss, more dependence should be placed upon workbook exercises, silent reading, and visual analysis of words than upon an auditory approach.

Summary

To sum up, the physical and sensory characteristics of children bear a direct relationship to their educational success. Extensive research shows that the child who is somewhat limited in these respects is predisposed to learning difficulties. The child who lacks physical stamina is more likely to get into learning difficulties than is the child who is robust. The child who lacks good motor control will find those activities which require good motor control difficult to accomplish. The role of visual and auditory deficiencies depends, to a considerable degree, upon the extent to which the deficiencies are recognized and adjustments made to them, and on the suitability of the methods of instruction used. Physical and sensory limitations in the youngster make it more likely—but do not determine—that he will get into difficulty.

The teacher, in thinking about physical and sensory limitations, should realize that everything possible should be done to correct a child's physical

[13] E. A. Betts, *op. cit.*, p. 208.

or sensory limitations and also that he must adjust to those which still exist. The teacher must also be aware that the correction of a physical or sensory limitation will not automatically correct a specific educational disability. A careful diagnosis of the disability must be made and faulty approaches to learning corrected.

The teacher's responsibilities in the case of pupils with physical and sensory limitations are (1) detecting the limitation, (2) making the child comfortable in the learning situation, and (3) adjusting methods so as to lessen the effect of such deficiencies on the learning activity.

PERSONAL AND SOCIAL ADJUSTMENT

Relationship Between Learning and Personal and Social Adjustment

Clinical and classroom experience and systematic research indicate a close relationship between educational disabilities and personal and social maladjustment. The true character of this relationship is difficult to determine. We know that the behavior of a large proportion of children with learning problems demonstrates unfortunate personal and social adjustments. Reports from clinical workers who study marked educational disability cases tend to emphasize the role of these adjustment problems. Research has shown that those children who are in difficulty in educational learnings are also likely to be in difficulty in personal adjustment. The research indicates that there is a marked difference of opinion about the extent of this relationship and also whether failure in important educational learnings is the cause or the result of personality disturbances. It is to be expected, for example, that when a child is emotionally disturbed for any of a variety of reasons, his educational growth will suffer. On the other hand, it also can be expected that a child who is experiencing difficulty in such an important learning area as reading, upon which his success as a student depends, is likely to become confused and frustrated and to display emotional and social adjustment problems of one sort or another.

A careful study of the research will show several characteristics of the relationship. First, the incidence of cases that are said to exhibit both learning difficulty and personality problems varies with the severity of the educational disability. Clinical cases with severe educational problems tend to show a higher percentage of personality difficulties than do the less severely retarded cases. Studies made in a general school population, however, do not indicate nearly as strong a relationship. Second, the studies indicate that some children with severe personality and emotional problems may find rewarding success in educational achievement and, rather than becoming educational disability cases, they may become extremely competent students. Third, the studies tend to disagree on the extent to which emotional and social problems are the causes of educational disability and the extent to which they are the result of educational disability. Related evidence seems to support the contention that in the majority of cases of educational disability accompanied by personal and social disturbances, the educational disability was devastating enough to the child's personal adjustment to cause the disturbances. It is also true that in many cases emotional and social problems, brought about by other experiences, disturbed the child to such an extent that he became an inefficient learner. His educational success was impaired by such maladjustments. In certain cases the personality disturbance may for one reason or another be associated with a particular school subject. The child may react unfavorably in that area. At the same time, in some other area his psychological needs may be so well met that he performs successfully and happily there.

The problem of emotional and social adjustment is one that needs the attention of the educational therapist. We will examine rather closely three aspects of the problem:

1. The relationship between emotional maladjustment and educational disability.
2. Social maladjustment and its relation to learning difficulties.
3. Behavior and delinquency problems as related to learning difficulties.

Emotional Maladjustment as Related to Educational Disability

The close association between emotional maladjustment and educational disability is widely recognized by workers in the field of learning difficulties, and there has been an extensive body of research dealing with it. Undoubtedly the greatest concentration of effort has been aimed at the relationship between reading disability and emotional maladjustment. There have been three general types of studies conducted in this field. One series of studies has been made by clinical or psychiatric workers, that for the most part involved the study of children whose difficulties were considered serious enough to require special clinical attention. In other words, studies have been made by child study clinics of cases that were highly complex and seemingly unsolvable in the regular classroom situation. It is not surprising to find that these studies indicate an extremely high coexistence of emotional problems and educational disability. There is, however, considerable controversy as to whether the educational disability is the cause or the result of an emotional disturbance within the child. Certain clinical workers contend that emotional disturbances cause the educational disability. They maintain that the child comes to the learning situation with emotional maladjustments which make it difficult for him to be an effective learner, and that as a result he develops a serious educational disability.

Other workers, for example, Fernald, have a different point of view. Fernald,[14] after a careful study of the school histories of seventy-eight

[14] Grace M. Fernald, *Remedial Technique in Basic School Subjects* (New York, McGraw-Hill, 1943).

serious reading disability cases handled by her clinic, reports that only four cases indicated emotional instability preceding the reading disability. It was her opinion that children start out in school with satisfactory emotional adjustment and do not get into emotional conflict until after they have met educational defeat and its consequent feelings of confusion and frustration.

Robinson,[15] in a study of twenty-eight cases, came to the conclusion that the emotional maladjustment could be either the cause or the result of reading disability. She considered emotional maladjustment as a possible cause of reading failure in twelve cases, or 43 per cent of the cases studied. In a like number of cases, the emotional maladjustment was considered the result of reading faliure. Robinson listed emotional maladjustment as high in ascribing possible causality in her cases.

Gates and Bond,[16] after studying one hundred reading cases selected at random, came to the conclusion that approximately three-fourths of the cases demonstrated personality maladjustments of one sort or another. It was further estimated that the personality maladjustment was a contributing cause in approximately 25 per cent of the cases which demonstrated both reading disability and emotional maladjustment, or about 19 per cent of the total group. In the remaining cases, the personality disturbance was the result of the reading disability.

An interesting longitudinal study by Sornson [17] sheds light on the relationship between reading growth and emotional problems. She measured children entering the first grade with the California Test of Personality and had their parents fill out the Minnesota Parental Attitude Inventory. These measures were repeated at the end of the first year and again at the end of the second year. The Haggerty-Olson-Wickman Behavior Rating Scale was filled out for each child by his teacher at the end of the first year and at the end of the second year. After the two years of schooling, the children were separated into three groups according to their reading ability. The inventories for the beginning of the first grade, for the end of the first grade, and for the end of the second grade were then studied.

A comparison between good and poor readers tended to show that failure to achieve in reading upset the children and made them lose confidence in themselves. The teachers saw signs of increased emotional tensions among the poor readers, and the parents of the poor readers did not agree with expert opinion on child management as closely as did the parents of the good readers. The parents of the children who were poor readers were far

[15] Helen Robinson, *Why Pupils Fail in Reading* (Chicago, Univ. of Chicago Press, 1946).

[16] Arthur I. Gates and Guy L. Bond, "Failure in Reading and Social Maladjustment," *Journal of the National Education Association*, Vol. 25 (October, 1936), pp. 205-206.

[17] Helen Sornson, "A Longitudinal Study of the Relationship Between Various Child Behavior Ratings and Success in Primary Reading." Unpublished Ph.D. thesis, Univ. of Minnesota, 1950.

less lenient. The interesting fact is that these differences were not apparent when the children, who were later to become the good and the poor readers, entered the first grade.

The probable relationship between reading disability and adjustment can be summed up in three ways. First, severely emotionally maladjusted children may enter school and become educational disability cases The emotional disturbance, in these cases, would cause or at least be a contributing cause of the educational disability.

The second point important for teachers to recognize is that failure in the important educational learnings is a serious defeat to the child. He frequently exhibits unfortunate personal and social adjustments when he is frustrated by failure in a basic learning such as reading. Serious reading disability is likely to be a major catastrophe to many children. Teachers need to be aware of the types of adjustment children try to make in their attempts to meet the handicap of reading disability.

Gates and Bond [18] noted the following unfortunate types of adjustment:

1. Nervous tensions and habits such as stuttering, nail-biting, restlessness, insomnia, and pathological illness.
2. Putting up a bold front as a defense reaction, loud talk, defiant conduct, sullenness.
3. Retreat reactions such as withdrawal from ordinary associations, joining outside gangs, and truancy.
4. Counterattack such as making mischief in school, playing practical jokes, thefts, destruction, cruelty, bullying.
5. Withdrawing reactions including mind-wandering and daydreaming.
6. Extreme self-consciousness, becoming easily injured, blushing, developing peculiar fads and frills and eccentricities, inferior feelings.
7. Give-up or submissive adjustment, as shown by inattentiveness, indifference, apparent laziness.

The third point to remember is that emotional disturbance can be both cause and result of educational disability. The child may get into difficulty in reading, for example, and find that he is ineffective in the whole school enterprise. He may be highly disturbed because of this and become confused, frustrated, and upset. He may in turn reject reading and school in general, thereby becoming a less efficient learner than he would otherwise be. Thus a downward spiral is established. He becomes increasingly more disturbed about the situation in which he finds himself and as a result becomes an increasingly ineffective learner. Teachers need to be aware of this relationship so that the combined effects of school failure and emotional maladjustment can be overcome. The teacher must help the child out of this vicious circle, or better still, keep him from getting into it in the first place. His responsibility is to seek out any emotional conditions present among the poor readers and try to make adjustments to them. In the major-

[18] *Op. cit.*

ity of cases, reading difficulty is the source of the emotional disturbance and the best way to make the adjustment to such a problem is to remove the source of irritation, that is, to correct the reading problem.

Generally, then, the teacher's solution to these complex problems is to make a direct attack upon the learning difficulty, recognizing that the child is working under emotional stress, emphasizing success, adjusting the task so that the child can approach it with confidence, taking a personal interest in the child, and accepting him and his problem with a direct, confident attitude toward his personal worth. In some cases, the teacher will find that the problem is too complex to handle unaided. Under such circumstances, the child will need clinical help. The teacher need not feel that it is any reflection upon his capability to seek such help. The only cautionary remark is that the teacher should first try to solve the problem through regular classroom procedures.

Social Maladjustment and Learning Difficulties

The social adjustment of a child in serious learning difficulty is often poor. This may be the result of unfortunate emotional patterns which he has developed or it may be the result of his rejection by other members of the class. Current educational practices that segregate the good, average, and poor achievers within the classroom tend to exaggerate the child's social adjustment problem. It can be argued that if a class could be so organized that all children, irrespective of their reading or arithmetic capability, could work on the same general enterprises, the social relationship between the good and poor achievers would be less strained. It seems that the classroom is in some respects like a playground. When teams are chosen on the playground for playing baseball, the child who is inept at hitting, fielding, or pitching will find that he is chosen last. After a time, such a child will withdraw from the situation that always places him in an untenable position. A study by Buswell [19] shows that the same thing happens in classroom enterprises. When children are chosen to work on some topic, the choosing of a child depends in no small measure upon his ability to contribute to the group being formed. It is interesting to note that in Buswell's study, children of low reading ability preferred to work with the children of average reading ability, and those with average reading ability wanted to work with those children who had high reading capability, and the children with high reading ability tended to want to work with other children of similar ability.

The teacher's responsibility with regard to social adjustment for the children with educational disabilities is clear. Every effort should be made to find enterprises in which the child can demonstrate other types of capability. The class community should be working together on topics of importance

[19] Margaret Buswell, "The Relationship Between the Social Structure of the Classroom and the Academic Success of the Pupils." Unpublished Ph.D. thesis, Univ. of Minnesota, 1950.

to all the children within the class, whether they can read or calculate well or not. Materials should be designed which will allow the children to work together, and still be adjusted to the educational level of each child. The teacher should study the social structure of the children in the classroom. He should recognize that differences in achievement in the important learnings of reading, arithmetic, spelling, language usage, and the like are to be expected. When a child is found to have an educational disability, a direct attack should be made upon that disability and, in the meantime, the child must be made to feel comfortable within the classroom. He must be a participating member of the group with which he is associated for a large part of each day.

Behavior and Delinquency Problems as Related to Learning Difficulties

As in all cases of personal adjustment problems and educational disability, it is difficult to tell exactly what the causal relationship is between behavior problems, delinquency, and educational disability. The fact that they are associated is quite apparent. Fendrick and Bond [20] found that juvenile delinquents were, by and large, poor readers. Polmantier [21] found evidence supporting the theory that failure to adapt instruction to the needs of either poor readers of relatively low mental ability or of good readers of high mental ability was a possible cause of juvenile delinquency. He compared the reading attainments of delinquent and nondelinquent boys coming from the same socioeconomic class and delinquency areas. The boys of low mental ability who were delinquents were much poorer readers than their nondelinquent counterparts. The delinquent boys of high mental ability were better readers than the nondelinquent boys of equal mental ability. The boys in the low group may have been thoroughly discouraged because of inability to do school work, thus becoming behavior problems and truants and ultimately getting into legal difficulty. The bright boys who were very effective readers may have found that school had little to offer and consequently they may have sought relief from boredom through delinquent acts. Whatever the relationship, institutions for juvenile delinquents are finding it profitable to correct educational disability through remedial training programs. Of course, it may be that some of the boys tended to reject authority in general, school authority as well as legal authority, and became both educationally disabled and juvenile delinquents.

The school, under any circumstance, must assume the responsibility for making a direct attack upon educational disability as a possible means of preventing emotional, social, and behavioral problems.

[20] Paul Fendrick and Guy L. Bond, "Delinquency and Reading," *Pedagogical Seminary and Journal of Genetic Psychology,* Vol. 48 (March, 1936), pp. 236-243.

[21] Paul C. Polmantier, "A Comparative Study of Reading Interests and Abilities of Delinquent and Non-Delinquent Boys." Unpublished Ph.D. thesis, Univ. of Minnesota, 1941.

ENVIRONMENTAL AND INSTRUCTIONAL FACTORS

Factors Outside the Child That Contribute to Learning Difficulties

In our discussion of causes of educational difficulties to this point, we have considered factors within the child that make him more likely to get into learning difficulties. None of the conditions we have cited invariably determines that a child will develop an educational disability. They merely predispose him to that disability. If appropriate adjustments, suitable instruction, and good school and home environment are present, it is the rare child who is so limited within himself that he cannot be expected to progress in reading, arithmetic, spelling, and language usage in a way that is compatible with his intellectual capability.

Educational disability is usually brought about by environmental and instructional factors which in and of themselves are faulty or which fail to take into account limitations in the child. The child may get into a reading difficulty because he failed to learn an essential technique, or because the program overemphasized a phase of the reading program, or because he persisted in the use of an erroneous approach, or because he had conflicting interests and goals that did not make the learning seem worth the effort.

The contributions of environmental and instructional factors to educational disability and the complex nature of the learning involved are basically at the root of the vast majority of learning confusions which result in extreme disability cases. Among the environmental and instructional factors that are important to consider are:

1. Unfortunate home conditions.
2. Narrow community opportunities.
3. Conflicting interests.
4. Unfortunate emphases in the curriculum.
5. Faulty methods of instruction.
6. Undesirable school conditions.

Unfortunate Home Conditions

The development of adequacy in the basic school learnings is a co-operative enterprise shared by home, school, and other agencies concerned with the growth and development of children. The home has a very important role in educational progress. During the early years, the child's security, his ability to carry enterprises to a successful conclusion, his ability to follow directions, his basic language usage, and his background of understanding are developed in the home. If the members of the family group are quarrelsome, overexacting, overprotective, or inconsistent, the child is quite likely to come to the educational scene ill-equipped to acquire such complex learnings as reading, arithmetic, spelling, and written and oral expression.

During the school years, the home's responsibility for the educational success of the child is not lessened. The degree to which the home takes an interest in the child's school work has a distinct relationship to the child's success. If the child is encouraged to use the library, and if he has books purchased for his own collection, his chances of success in reading are considerably enhanced. If his parents show an active interest in the child's work in arithmetic, spelling, and other school subjects, the child is more likely to sense their importance. In all of this the parents have a rather clear-cut responsibility: that of showing interest in their child's school work and encouraging him to work, but at the same time avoiding unfortunate pressure or criticism. This is especially true when the child shows signs of having a learning difficulty. The parents must be aware of the learning difficulty when there is one, give the child encouragement, but avoid criticism, unfavorable comparisons with his brothers and sisters, and undue pressure. The home and school should consider the child's problem jointly and work out co-operatively a carefully planned program.

Narrow Community Opportunities

Communities in the United States vary considerably in their educational opportunities and in their attitudes toward education. The child who is fortunate enough to be raised in a community that is vitally concerned with the educational opportunities of its children will be more likely to have a highly successful educational career. The education of children is a community responsibility. Community support of education is reflected in the quality of the educational outcomes. There is a direct relationship between the amount of financial support a community gives to education and the freedom of the schools from educational disability cases, as well as the educational stature of the children who are getting along well. The attitude of the community should be one of constructive study of educational problems and needs rather than one of uninformed criticism.

The responsibility of the community, however, is broader than the adequate support of the schools alone. The recreational facilities, the library opportunities provided, and the degree to which other community resources are made available for the schools and the citizens all have a positive influence upon the educational growth of the children within the community.

The well-rounded development of children is a community responsibility. The school is one agency through which the community can live up to that responsibility. Community support of the schools, the churches, the child welfare agencies, and the other educational, recreational, and social enterprises will be evidenced in the emotional, social, and educational development of its children.

Conflicting Interests

Interests play an important role in the child's success with the basic skills and abilities. He may avoid learning how to spell if he does not see the importance of correct spelling. If he is not interested in writing, he may not be willing to put forth the effort necessary to learn to spell the words he would otherwise like to use. The child may avoid the necessary drill in learning his arithmetic facts if arithmetic is not made a vital part of his classroom enterprises. There must, therefore, be a careful balance between drill on the fundamentals in these basic learnings and the use of the skills and abilities in enterprises that are of importance to the child.

Development of interest in reading, arithmetic, and spelling must go along with development of ability. If the child gets into difficulty in any of these basic learnings, he may, and in many cases does, lose interest in them. On the other hand, if interest is not adequately maintained, he will not be willing to put forth the intellectual effort necessary to learn. For example, it is unreasonable to expect the high level of interest in reading or the language arts necessary to develop the skills and abilities in these areas without effective instruction in the fundamentals. On the other hand, it is unfortunate to require the child to learn, through restricted drill, procedures that deaden his interest in his school work. The child should be placed in purposeful learning situations where the importance of learning the skills and abilities in these basic school subjects becomes quite apparent to him.

The present-day world of the child is full of conflicting interests. He enters school able to share rather mature stories, for example, on television. However, in his reading program he must develop word-recognition abilities under carefully controlled conditions. The learning material will be immature compared to that which he can share through other means of communication. If the reading program does not take into account the fact that other media of communication more nearly match his intellectual development, the child is likely to get into serious difficulty in reading. It is not enough for us to say that the child must learn to read. We must make the necessity of learning to read important to the child's way of life. We should, as soon as possible, put the child in meaningful reading situations that allow him to use his creative capabilities in expressing what he has learned from that reading. What has been said about reading applies equally well to the mastery of all tools of learning.

Modern programs of reading instruction which enable the child to read to learn at the same time that he is learning to read are vital for the prevention of disability. This is equally true of the development of other basic skills. The child must use his spelling as he is learning to spell. Mere drilling on word lists will not insure the interest in spelling that is vital for success. Drill on number combinations will in no way show the child the importance of learning them. A program that allows the child to use number combinations and operations in classroom enterprises, that controls the learning situation so that the sequence of development of skills is maintained, and that provides the necessary drill to develop proficiency enables the child to grow effectively and comfortably and avoids creating disability cases.

Programs that fail to recognize conflicting interests will be inadequate.

Programs which lean upon interest alone will make for disabled readers, spellers, and calculators. Programs that overemphasize drill at the expense of purpose and interest will also create disabled learners.

Unfortunate Emphases in the Curriculum

The child's life in school is indeed a busy one. There are a great number of areas in which he needs instruction. In addition to developing the basic tool subjects of reading, arithmetic, spelling, and language usage, the child must broaden his concepts and understandings in each of the other content fields. He must gain the insights and facts offered in social studies and in science. He must develop skills and talents in the fields of art and music. He must learn to get along with and work with other children. All of these enterprises take time one from the other. If the educational program revolves around any one area, the others are sure to suffer. Until recently, there has been an unfortunate trend of emphasis in curriculum development. It has often been assumed that the child can learn the fundamental tool subjects as an incidental outcome of experiences designed to further social studies. This unfortunate emphasis has in many cases led to serious disability in reading, arithmetic, and other fields in which underlying skills and concepts must be systematically organized and developed. Unless adequate attention is paid to the development of the fundamental tool subjects, it can be expected that many children will get into learning difficulty. These complex learnings cannot be developed haphazardly or opportunistically; they must be developed through a systematic, orderly progression.

There is no real conflict between the areas of the curriculum. In reading, for example, the child needs many types of experience. He needs the basic program designed to show him how to go about reading. He needs experience within the various content fields so that he can adapt his skills and abilities to the needs in these areas. He needs recreational, personal reading so that he may extend his interests, develop appreciation, and the like. He sometimes needs re-educative experiences designed to straighten out learning difficulties before they become disabilities. In the other basic tool subjects he also needs systematic, organized programs of instruction. The neglect of any of these experiences will make for disability cases. Then he needs many opportunities to apply the basic tool subjects in the fields of social studies, science, and the other important areas within the curriculum.

Faulty Methods of Instruction

Of all of the causes of learning difficulties, faulty instruction is likely the most important. The complex nature of the basic tool subjects of reading, arithmetic, spelling, and language usage is at the root of the difficulty. Methods of instruction must be well defined and effective in order to insure success in these subjects.

Teachers cannot be expected to prevent all learning difficulties. The task of developing each of the basic tool subjects for the large number of children found in the typical classroom is great indeed and is fraught with hazard. The teacher cannot be a social welfare worker, a mental hygienist, and a psychiatrist. He needs to be a good teacher. All too often the classes are too large, materials too meager, and technical help not available. The surprising thing is not that some children fail to learn but that so many get along so well. Instruction which cannot develop each and every phase of all the basic tool subjects for these and other reasons actually may cause many children to get into difficulty. Individualized re-education will get them out. The sooner their trouble is discovered and correction is started, the more certain it is that success will follow.

The sequence in learning reading, spelling, and the like is quite different from other types of learning the child meets in other fields, such as the social studies and the fine arts. The learnings of arithmetic, reading, and spelling are cumulative. The child must learn to add and subtract before he can undertake the more difficult process of long division, for example. If he were to undertake to learn long division without first having mastered subtraction, he would be certain to encounter serious difficulties. The sequence of learning in the fields discussed in this book is a vital aspect of the educational program. The order in which the child is introduced to the new learnings within the skill subjects makes a good deal of difference in how well he will learn them. This is not true of other subjects he is dealing with in the curriculum. For example, it makes little difference whether he studies the way people live in Norway before he studies the way people live in Switzerland. But it makes a great deal of difference whether the child learns to recognize at sight certain root words before he learns how to add prefixes and suffixes to those basic words. Therefore, the use by the teacher of methods that insure readiness for each new learning in the cumulative development of the skills of reading, arithmetic, spelling, and language usage is of paramount importance.

The following list of essential characteristics of effective reading instruction given by Bond and Wagner [22] indicates appropriate methods of instruction in one of the basic tool subjects:

1. The reading program must be pleasant for the child.
2. The reading situation must be stimulating, but must free the child from undue pressure.
3. Once reading instruction is started, the child should not be allowed to experience repeated failure.
4. The methods should lend themselves to individualization of instruction.
5. The program should be one that recognizes the strengths and limitations of each child.
6. Reading instruction should progress by steps that the child can take readily.

[22] Guy L. Bond and Eva B. Wagner, *Teaching the Child to Read* (New York, Macmillan, 1950), pp. 57, 58.

7. Reading instruction should be organized instruction.
8. The processes should be made meaningful to the child.
9. The purposes for reading should be real to the child.
10. Procedures should foster both co-operative and individual reading.
11. Active use should be made of the results of reading.
12. Reading instruction should build favorable attitudes toward reading.
13. The methods should use and develop the child's interests.
14. The methods of reading instruction should use and encourage the child's initiative.
15. The methods of reading instruction should build habits of independence.
16. The methods should be carefully selected so as not to develop habits that will be detrimental to reading ability at a later time.
17. Materials should be plentiful and nicely graded.
18. Materials should be of many types.
19. Reading instruction should be efficient instruction.
20. Whenever possible, the methods should develop, in addition to reading ability, other educational outcomes.
21. Reading instruction should provide for systematic appraisals.
22. The child should be allowed to know his progress.
23. The reading program and the child's progress therein should be interpreted to his parents.

Similar principles underlying language arts and arithmetic are discussed in the respective chapters that follow.

In such complicated learnings as the basic tool subjects, the teacher must be alert to the onset of any difficulty. Immediate correction will avoid complex disability. The general methods of instruction that encourage learning will lessen, but cannot completely prevent, learning difficulties. Early diagnosis and correction will prevent minor learning difficulties from deterring future growth.

Undesirable School Conditions

There are certain conditions within the school that make difficult the task of utilizing adequate methods of instruction. Classes that are too large make it difficult for the teacher to study the individual members within the class. There are methods of appraisal, however, that make diagnostic studies of individuals possible; and there are materials that make effective adjustments to individual needs. If the teacher does not have good methods of appraisal and sufficient materials with which to work, the prevalence of learning difficulties will be increased. Modern methods of instruction require well-equipped classrooms. The teacher should study the materials that are available to aid him in adjusting instruction to the individual needs of children, and he should insist that the classroom be adequately equipped.

A poor physical plant is sometimes responsible for a child's learning difficulty. Inadequate lighting, poor blackboard facilities, poor seating arrangements, and other unfortunate conditions contribute to educational difficulty. Dull and drab surroundings are not conducive to effective learning. The school plant, equipment, and class size all are contributory causes of educational disability. Nonetheless, it should be recognized that the teacher's use of the facilities that are available, whatever their quality may be, is also important to the success of the pupils.

The causes of educational difficulties are legion. The major factor underlying all learning difficulty in the basic tool subjects is their very complexity. The conditions that have been discussed in this chapter are those that make the child more likely to fail to acquire an essential learning, to make a faulty learning, or to develop an overemphasized pattern of learning. The problem of those who would correct a learning disability is to find what is actually wrong with the child's approach. For example, if the child is a reading disability case, the most important phase of the diagnosis is to find out what is wrong with his reading. It then becomes necessary to decide in what respects instruction must be modified because of limiting conditions in the child or his environment in order to enable him to learn effectively. The teacher who would correct a learning difficulty should take the necessary steps to discover what is wrong with the learning and what adjustments in instruction must be made, rather than waste time looking for explanations of the learning difficulty in the child's previous personal and educational history.

SUGGESTED ACTIVITIES

1. Is there any similarity between medical and educational diagnosis? In what ways are they different?

2. Why is it difficult to determine specific causes of particular types of learning disabilities?

3. Illustrate from your own experiences the implications of the four general categories of factors related to learning difficulties that are listed on pages 31-32. Are there other factors that you could add?

4. If there is a local educational clinic, discuss with the staff problems that they face in trying to determine causes of learning disabilities. The consideration of one or more actual cases would be helpful.

5. What are the limitations of IQ's based on group tests as a basis of classification or diagnosis?

6. To what extent is brain damage due to injury or disease associated with learning disability?

7. How is it possible for a good reader to learn in spite of visual or auditory limitations?

8. Can you cite cases within your experience in which emotional maladjustment grew out of lack of success in school work? Can you cite cases in which it grew out of the development of learning difficulties? Can you cite cases in which emotional maladjustment disappeared when learning difficulties were corrected? Summarize the evidence related to this problem that is presented in this chapter.

9. Illustrate ways in which learning difficulties are contributed to by the curriculum; by faulty and inadequate instructional procedures and materials; by the personalities with whom the learner comes into contact; by the socioeconomic aspects of the total environment; by the characteristics of the school plant.

10. Why should the improvement of all aspects of the total teaching-learning

situation be regarded as a co-operative community undertaking? Can you give illustrations of school-community co-operation in improving the educational program?

11. Can all learning difficulties be prevented?

12. To what extent is juvenile delinquency associated with learning difficulties?

13. What is the value of parent conferences about the learning problems of children? What information should be given parents about the status of their children?

14. What are reasons why there are such wide variations in the quality of educational programs in our schools?

SELECTED BIBLIOGRAPHY

BARR, A. S., BURTON, W. H., and BRUECKNER, L. J., *Supervision* (New York, Appleton, 1947), Ch. 7. This volume contains a systematic discussion of methods of studying and improving instructional and social factors related to learning.

BRUECKNER, L. J., "Diagnosis in Teaching," in *Encyclopedia of Educational Research* (New York, Macmillan, 1950), pp. 314-321.

BURTON, W. H., and BRUECKNER, L. J., *Supervision: A Social Process,* 3rd ed. (New York, Appleton-Century-Crofts, 1955), Ch. 10.

BURTON, W. H., *The Guidance of Learning Activities,* 2nd ed. (New York, Appleton, 1952).

Educational Diagnosis, Thirty-fourth Yearbook, National Society for the Study of Education (Chicago, Univ. of Chicago Press, 1935), Chs. 4, 5.

4 TECHNIQUES OF DIAGNOSIS

IN THIS CHAPTER the following topics are discussed:

1. The nature of diagnosis.
2. The approach to diagnosis.
3. Levels of diagnosis, including (1) general diagnosis, (2) analytical diagnosis, and (3) case-study methods.
4. Techniques of analytical diagnosis.
5. Case-study methods.

THE NATURE OF DIAGNOSIS

Diagnosis Essential in Classroom Instruction

The diagnosis of learning difficulties may in general be regarded as an essential and integral phase of regular classroom instruction. Competent teachers always have taken steps to determine the nature and cause of learning difficulties of their pupils and to remedy them. In recent years teachers have become increasingly familiar with modern diagnostic procedures through contact with them in courses in teacher-education programs, and many are able to apply them quite effectively in dealing with ordinary learning problems.

Teachers, however, usually need special help in dealing with individuals who have complex learning difficulties whose nature and treatment require a more penetrating study and analysis than the regular classroom teacher can make because of lack of time or training. Sometimes it is necessary in making a diagnosis to use special equipment and apparatus ordinarily available only in a clinic. In some cases essential supplementary information must be secured from specialists such as physicians, psychiatrists, psychologists, and social workers. The more complex the problem, the more detailed its study should be, so that it can be satisfactorily diagnosed and therapy begun.

Because of the lack of clinical services in most of the smaller school systems of this country, it becomes the responsibility of classroom teachers to a large extent to attempt to diagnose learning difficulties of all kinds and to take steps to alleviate the conditions causing them. Fortunately, there are numerous simple diagnostic procedures that are easy for the teacher to apply, and many less complex learning difficulties that readily respond to therapeutic treatment. Analytical methods by which the pupil can evaluate his own achievements and discuss their shortcomings also have been devised and are used by many teachers. These diagnostic procedures are rapidly becoming an integral part of the learning activity and assist the learner to set up meaningful goals that he gladly attempts to achieve. In a number of curriculum areas—particularly in reading, arithmetic, written expression, and handwriting—modern textbooks and instructional materials often include valuable diagnostic tests and similar analytical devices that are thoroughly practical and usable by the teacher.

Competencies Essential for Skill in Diagnosis

The effectiveness of diagnosis depends on the extent to which the examiner, whether classroom teacher or clinical specialist, possesses the following competencies:

1. A thorough understanding of the learning process in the area being investigated and its components, of the ways in which these components normally grow and mature, and of symptoms that indicate that normal development is not taking place.

2. Knowledge of factors that contribute to learning difficulties in the area being investigated.

3. Skill in considering multiple hypotheses as to the causes of a child's learning difficulties.

4. Ability to apply intelligently and effectively the diagnostic methods and devices used in modern educational clinics, or to adapt them informally to the task at hand.

5. Ability to recognize symptoms of contributory conditions whose diagnosis requires the services of specialists in other professional fields, including medicine, psychology, psychiatry, physiology, endocrinology, and sociology.

6. The ability to synthesize the findings of the various agencies participating in the diagnosis and to identify the factors most likely to be contributory to the difficulty in the case at hand.

7. The ability to suggest the steps to be taken to bring about an improvement and to demonstrate the methods and materials of instruction to be used.

We shall now consider more in detail how diagnosis is applied to the study and treatment of learning problems by either the teacher or the clinician. The teacher will not be able to carry the diagnosis to the level of specificity to be expected of clinical workers, but the general approach is the same for both teachers and clinicians.

THE APPROACH TO DIAGNOSIS

Sequence of Steps in Diagnosis

The basic approach to diagnosis is similar for all areas of the curriculum and for all educational workers, including teachers, clinicians, and specialists. The sequence of steps in identifying, diagnosing, and treating learning difficulties and deficiencies is substantially as follows:

Step 1. The setting up of educational objectives which serve as guides for both learning and instruction. This is a basic point discussed in Chapter 2.

Step 2. The appraisal of the achievements and behavior of the learner by applying tests and evaluative procedures such as were discussed in Chapter 2, so as to determine his strengths and weaknesses and to provide a basis for evaluating his rate of growth and progress.

Although educational diagnosis is primarily concerned with actual learning difficulties or unsatisfactory growth in some curriculum area, treatment proceeds most effectively when it recognizes strengths that exist and builds on them.

Step 3. The recalling of previous experiences and of the results of scientific research with which the examiner may be familiar for ideas as to possible factors that may be contributing to unfavorable growth and progress.

The factors were discussed in Chapter 3. In general, they may be identified in elements of the learner's personality; in some phase of the educational program, such as the curriculum, classroom instruction, and the materials of instruction; in the personalities that he contacts in and out of school; and in socioeconomic conditions in his home and in the part of the community in which he lives. Usually a complex of factors is operative in serious learning problems. In the chapters that follow, specific factors contributing to disability in the various curriculum areas are discussed.

Step 4. A preliminary survey of the case under investigation leading to tentative judgments as to factors that should be systematically investigated to determine their possible contribution to the difficulty.

As a result of this preliminary survey, the scope of the investigation can be rather quickly limited to those factors that are thought most likely to be contributory to the disability. Sometimes the factors can be determined informally by the teacher; sometimes more penetrating diagnostic procedures clinical in nature must be applied, such as those to be described in this chapter.

Step 5. The systematic testing and analysis of the component elements of the area of learning involved to determine how extensive and serious the disability is and what the contributory factors probably are.

This step, which is the most important one in the entire diagnosis, requires the systematic use of analytical tests and clinical diagnostic procedures, the general nature of which will be discussed later in the chapter. The teacher or clinical worker also will gather all other available pertinent information from school records and elsewhere that may assist in making a diagnosis.

Step 6. The planning of the various measures to be taken that are most likely to bring about an improvement and a consideration of the ways in which they should be applied.

These measures may deal with any or all of the factors mentioned in Step 3 above, depending on the findings of the diagnostic study. The general principles of remediation are discussed in Chapter 5 and their specific application to the various fields of learning in the chapters that follow. In severe cases, teachers, specialists, and often parents should co-operatively plan the corrective measures.

Step 7. Finally, the determination of the validity of the diagnosis and the effectiveness of the corrective measures taken by making suitable evaluations of the growth and rate of progress of the learner.

Treatment should always proceed on a tentative, experimental basis and should be modified if it is not proving to be effective. At the present time, we lack definite information experimentally established on the specific steps that are most likely to correct many particular deficiencies and learning difficulties. The problem of treatment is further complicated by the fact that it is extremely difficult to identify specific factors that may be operative, because often the deficiencies have a long history and are subtle and not easily recognized, as was pointed out in Chapter 2.

The detailed methods of carrying out these steps in the various learning areas will be presented in the chapters that follow.

Informal Application of Diagnostic Procedures

It should be evident that the wide-awake classroom teacher informally applies diagnostic procedures which approximate these seven steps to the simpler learning difficulties that arise in every classroom. The more insight the teacher has into the nature and causes of learning difficulties, the more effective will be the diagnosis and treatment. Clinical workers obviously will follow these steps more systematically and methodically and to a deeper level of specificity than the teachers are able to do.

LEVELS OF DIAGNOSIS

For purposes of discussion, we shall consider in this chapter three levels of diagnosis. They may be identified as: (1) general diagnosis, (2) analytical or differential diagnosis, and (3) case-study procedures.

General Diagnosis

By general diagnosis we mean the use of comprehensive survey tests and other general evaluative procedures, such as were discussed in Chapter 2, which give the teacher and the staff of the school essential information about the general level of performance of the pupils in such fields as reading, arithmetic, and the language arts, the status of their health and development, their mental ability, their interests, and similar kinds of basic information needed in the operation of a well-managed school system. A summary of the information about the learners' school history, their behavior, their social background, and other data that a good school system cumulatively records is of value in surveying conditions that may affect the growth and condition the development of the children. The purpose of general diagnosis is to make a general appraisal of the characteristics and achievements of groups of children, not a detailed analysis of outcomes in any particular curriculum area or of the status of individual pupils.

Analytical Diagnosis

By analytical diagnosis we mean the use of systematic procedures for locating or identifying specific weaknesses or shortcomings in some curriculum area, such as reading, arithmetic, or composition, for the group as a whole or for some particular individual.

Case-Study Procedures

By case-study procedures we mean the application of clinical diagnostic techniques that will enable the teacher or clinical worker to study in detail the performance or achievement of an individual pupil with an evident learning problem, so as to determine as specifically as possible the nature and seriousness of the learning difficulty and the underlying causes.

Specific Illustration Showing the Place of Each Level of Diagnosis

The three levels of diagnosis can be illustrated by a brief statement of the procedures that were used to identify and diagnose the nature of a specific reading disability in the case of a fifth-grade boy:

Level 1. General Diagnosis. On a general achievement test it was found that George's scores were considerably below normal in reading and also relatively low in areas closely associated with reading. His scores in arithmetic computational skills were high, and his IQ was 118 as measured by an individual test. The general diagnosis was that George undoubtedly had a reading difficulty, but more information was needed to determine the nature of his handicap.

Level 2. Analytical Diagnosis. The results of an analytical reading test which included separate tests of word recognition, speed and power of comprehension, and various specific types of comprehension showed that George's speed was adequate, that his power of comprehension was his greatest strength, and that the profile of his scores on tests of types of comprehension was at a relatively uniform level, but that his scores on word-recognition tests were quite low. In this way, a rather specific area of deficiency was identified. However, the test scores did not reveal definitely what was wrong with his word-recognition techniques, nor did they indicate anything about George's personal reactions to his difficulties. More detailed information also was needed to determine what modifications of instructional procedures would have to be made to deal with George's reading problem.

Level 3. Case-Study Procedures. A thorough, individual diagnostic study of George's word-recognition techniques was then undertaken to determine how and where to begin the corrective program. This case-study approach involved a systematic examination of his word-recognition techniques, including his use of meaning aids, visual analysis of words, his knowledge of phonetics including visual and structural elements, his ability to blend or synthesize word elements, his degree of flexibility in handling all of these skills in recognizing new words, the extent of his sight vocabulary, and so on as the situation required. (See Chapter 6 for detailed diagnostic procedures in reading.) In addition, as a check on these results, it was believed desirable to measure his auditory capacities such as acuity, discrimination, and memory as well as similar aspects of his visual efficiency. Further information about his interests, drives, motives, and social background and his attitude toward his reading problem was of value in making the final diagnosis and planning the improvement program.

Using the Findings of Diagnostic Study

On the basis of such diagnostic findings the teacher must decide what changes from ordinary typical instructional approaches are necessary. If the problem presents complexities with which the teacher feels unable to deal effectively because of lack of experience or professional background, the case should be referred to the proper specialist if available.

Similar diagnostic procedures at these three levels that can be applied in the study and treatment of learning difficulties in spelling, written and oral expression, and arithmetic are described in the respective chapters that follow. The level to which a diagnosis is carried will depend on the particular circumstances and the ease with which the nature and causes of a learning difficulty can be established. Any diagnostic procedure that will help the teacher to understand the nature of a learning difficulty should be utilized. In cases of serious disability it becomes necessary to use the precise, objective techniques of a diagnostic clinic. (See pages 332-333 for a description of clinical diagnosis of a speech disability.)

THE TECHNIQUES OF ANALYTICAL DIAGNOSIS

Analytical Diagnostic Tests

By analytical diagnosis we mean the systematic analysis of achievement and performance in a number of the elements and subskills which are basic components of such major abilities as reading, spelling, language, or arithmetic. The purpose of analytical diagnosis is to locate and identify specific strengths and weaknesses in the performance of the individual learner through the use of tests which can be administered to the class as a whole or to a small group of pupils. Analysis of the test results reveals to the teacher the weak spots in the work of the pupils and thus establishes a basis for organizing instruction according to group and individual needs.

An excellent illustration of an analytical diagnostic test is the Iowa Silent Reading Test, which contains the following series of subtests of specific reading skills:

A. COMPREHENSION OF WHAT IS READ
  1. Paragraph meaning in
     a. Social Science
     b. Literature
     c. Science
  2. Word meaning in subject-matter vocabulary in
     a. Social Science
     b. Science
     c. Mathematics
     d. English
  3. Sentence comprehension

B. ORGANIZATION OF WHAT IS READ
  1. Sentence
  2. Paragraph
     a. Selection of central idea
     b. Outlining
     c. Organization

C. LOCATION OF INFORMATION IN PRINTED SOURCES
  1. Ability to use the index
     a. Use of index
     b. Selection of key words (alphabetizing)

D. RATE OF READING
  1. Silent reading rate

Parts I to III of this test provide a total comprehension score which can be broken down into separate scores for each section of the test, and Part IV gives a measure of rate of silent reading. This test will show specific areas of strength and weakness in reading. Low scores on one or more parts of the test indicate weaknesses that should be remedied by systematic instruction and directed practice. A general disability will require more detailed diagnosis.

More Specific Analytical Diagnostic Tests

More specific analytical diagnosis may be necessary when steps taken to bring about improvement in some area, such as reading, appear to be ineffective. Thus by means of the three Gates Primary Reading Tests it is possible to secure measures of ability to read words, sentences, and short paragraphs at the difficulty level of grades 1 to 3. An even more detailed diagnosis in reading can be made by applying the available standard individual reading diagnostic tests which are discussed in Chapter 6.

Similar analytical tests in written expression and arithmetic are described in the respective chapters. Thus by properly constructed tests, for example, in written expression, it is possible to determine in some detail how well the pupil knows the various uses of the different marks of punctuation and the rules for capitalization. Similarly, it is possible to break down into its component elements a major process in arithmetic, such as division of whole numbers (see pages 202-203), so that the teacher can test to determine whether or not there are deficiencies in one or more of these components which may be the underlying cause of poor achievement in division. When specific areas of deficiency are discovered, steps can be taken to remedy them. Ordinarily a direct attack on a specific difficulty will quickly lead to improvement. In cases where there is no evidence of growth, more penetrating diagnostic procedures must be applied.

There are numerous illustrations of informal diagnostic procedures in the chapters dealing with diagnosis of learning difficulties in reading, arithmetic, language, spelling, and handwriting.

Selected standardized tests that are analytical in nature are the following:

Analytical Scales of Attainment in Arithmetic (Educational Test Bureau).
California Achievement Tests (California Test Bureau).
Diagnostic Tests and Self Helps in Arithmetic (California Test Bureau).
Iowa Every Pupil Tests of Basic Skills (Houghton Mifflin).
Gates Silent Reading Tests (Teachers College, Columbia Univ.).
Van Wagenen Composition Scales (World Book).

CASE-STUDY PROCEDURES

Case-Study Procedures Are Clinical in Nature

The techniques used in case studies are clinical in nature. They involve the detailed study of an individual pupil's behavior and performance, usually in a test situation. However, many of the basic diagnostic techniques can be applied informally by the classroom teacher in the course of regular instruction whenever learning difficulties appear whose specific nature should be determined on the spot so that remedial steps can be undertaken at once.

In educational clinics, diagnostic procedures similar in nature to those that have been used by competent teachers for years are employed, but the test content and the diagnostic procedures are standardized and the information secured can be interpreted according to available standards. A clinical analysis and interpretation of the behavior and responses of the learner in the test situation and elsewhere and of pertinent related data of other kinds leads to a diagnosis. Clinical procedures perfected in psychological laboratories and research centers often are quite readily adapted for use by teachers in the course of instruction and thus lead to the improvement of teaching procedures. The difference between approaches to diagnosis by the teacher and the educational clinical diagnostician are analagous to the difference between the approaches of the general physician and specialists in a medical clinic. The procedures of the former are general in nature, whereas those of the latter are specific and highly analytical, often involving laboratory tests of various kinds. Teachers should make every effort to improve their use of diagnostic procedures.

Differences Between Analytical Diagnosis and Case-Study Procedures

The techniques of analytical diagnosis locate and identify specific areas of deficiency within a major ability, but more detailed diagnostic procedures must be used to determine the character and nature of the deficiency when there is evidence that casual observation will not suffice. For example, suppose that on an analytical diagnostic test in addition of fractions (such as the test on page 218) it is found that a pupil works all of the examples in row 4 incorrectly. A specific area of difficulty is thus located. However, the nature of the difficulty is not revealed by the test score. To determine its nature, several different methods of analyzing the work of this pupil can be used by the teacher, such as analyzing the errors that appear in the pupil's written work, having the pupil state orally his thought processes as he works the incorrect examples a second time so that faulty thought processes can be detected, or analyzing the pupil's answers to questions that are intended to bring out possible incorrect procedures and other causes of incorrect work, such as lack of understanding of some step in the solution. These techniques are all valuable, but the interpretation of the findings must necessarily be limited to the specific area of learning under consideration and cannot be generalized. However, inferences can be made as to the nature of the pupil's difficulty. More comprehensive and systematic procedures must be utilized when a severe general disability in arithmetic exists, such as would be utilized in making a detailed case study in a clinic.

Diagnostic Techniques Used in Case Studies

The techniques used in the case-study approach to the diagnosis of learning problems of individual pupils in all curriculum areas are of five major types:

1. Standardized clinical diagnostic tests.
2. Clinical diagnosis by less formal procedures.
    a. Observation of behavior or performance.
    b. Analysis of written work or responses.
    c. Analysis of oral responses or oral accounts of procedures.
    d. Interviews and questioning.
    e. Analysis of something produced by the pupil.
3. Use of special kinds of clinical equipment.
4. Medical, psychiatric, and psychological examinations.
5. Analysis of available records.

Standardized Clinical Diagnostic Tests

Standardized clinical diagnostic tests are available for reading, spelling, handwriting, and arithmetic. These tests are intended for the detailed critical study, under controlled conditions with standardized materials and by systematic procedures, of the work of individual pupils, and are employed when general survey and analytical diagnostic tests indicate that there are deficiencies serious enough to warrant systematic comprehensive diagnosis and treatment. Teachers should be familiar with these kinds of tests and the procedures utilized in applying them, as some of them can be adapted informally by the well-informed teacher whenever the need for diagnostic analysis arises from time to time in the classroom. The application of standard diagnostic tests and the interpretation of their results should be left to well-qualified examiners.

In a clinical situation, a case study ordinarily begins with study by the staff of pertinent information, supplied by the referring agency, including the reasons for the referral, data about the individual's achievements, behavior, attitudes, interests, activities, health, school history, and home conditions. The clinic ordinarily checks systematically the data about the pupil's mental ability, achievement in the area involved, physical development, visual acuity, loss of hearing, personality traits, and home background.

The diagnostic study of the achievement deficiency itself usually begins with the administration of some general survey test in the subject involved to get a measure of the pupil's level of achievement. When it is believed to be advisable, analytical tests also are administered to locate in more detail strength and weakness. Finally the clinical study of performance in the area under consideration is undertaken.

A well-constructed clinical diagnostic test usually consists of a group of test exercises, each of which gives a measure of a basic element involved in the total ability or of some factor that is known to be associated with inferior performance. As the diagnosis proceeds, the examiner notes carefully the pupil's attitudes, the effort he makes, his methods of work, the answers he gives to questions asked, and other significant kinds of information. Test results are evaluated by reference to available standards, and serious shortcomings are thus identified. For later detailed analysis, a careful record is kept of the pupil's responses when they are given orally—for instance, in diagnostic tests of reading or oral spelling. The responses on written tests of course lend themselves to direct analysis. All errors made are classified as to type and the results are interpreted in the light of available information as to their cruciality, as will be described later in appropriate sections of this book.

In short, in clinical diagnosis the examiner feels free to utilize any analytical or evaluative procedure and all available information that will give him an insight into the nature of the problem and its underlying causes. Most test manuals give specific directions on how to administer and score the tests. Specially prepared record forms also are usually provided by the publishers of tests, on which to record the basic data gathered. On the basis of all of the information thus assembled and the interpretation of the results of the diagnostic tests, the factors most probably contributing to the disability and the specific disabilities to be remedied can be tentatively established, and the steps most likely to lead to an improvement can be formulated.

The best-known standard tests intended for clinical diagnosis are the following:

READING

Bond-Clymer-Hoyt Silent Reading Diagnostic Test (Lyons & Carnahan).
Gates Reading Diagnosis Tests (Teachers College, Columbia Univ.).
Durrell Analysis of Reading Difficulty (World Book).
Monroe Diagnostic Reading Tests (Stoelting Co.).

SPELLING

Gates-Russell Spelling Diagnosis Tests (Teachers College, Columbia Univ.).

ARITHMETIC

Buswell-John Diagnostic Tests for Fundamental Processes (Public School Publishing Co.).
Brueckner-Diagnostic Tests in Whole Numbers, Fractions, and Decimals (Educational Test Bureau).

HANDWRITING

Freeman Chart for Diagnosing Faults in Handwriting (Houghton Mifflin).
Nystrom Self-Corrective Handwriting Charts (Minneapolis Public Schools).

To date there are no similar clinical diagnostic tests for written English. Several clinical tests for diagnosis in the field of oral speech are discussed in Chapter 10.

Simplified but quite adequate diagnostic tests suitable for use in classrooms in the course of day-to-day teaching are included in a number of present-day textbooks and workbooks, particularly in reading, arithmetic, spelling, and written composition. Probably more adequate developmental diagnostic tests, useful for continuous analysis of learning difficulties, have been developed for arithmetic than for any other curriculum area. When standard diagnostic tests are not available, suitable informal tests can be devised by the teacher according to specifications given in the following chapters.

Standardized clinical diagnostic tests can be applied by teachers who have had the necessary training. Less formal diagnostic techniques can be much more effectively and systematically applied than they are by many teachers at the present time. Their practicality and the value of their findings will be stressed throughout our discussion. Teachers should be aware of the valuable kinds of clinical equipment that are available for special types of testing, so that they will appreciate the possibilities of their use in clinical testing by specialists. Data supplied by medical and psychiatric examinations are sometimes essential in interpreting the results of other clinical procedures, and their implications should be carefully considered by the teacher under the direction of specialists.

Special emphasis will be placed on the adaptation of these diagnostic procedures for use by the classroom teacher in the chapters that follow.

Clinical Diagnosis by Less Formal Procedures

Many diagnostic procedures that are applied systematically under controlled conditions in clinical examinations can be applied informally to good advantage by the classroom teacher in diagnosing learning difficulties that arise from time to time in the work of pupils. Their application will give the teacher much valuable information about the pupil's thought processes, his methods of work, the nature of his learning difficulties, and other information significant for planning the learning activities necessary to correct unsatisfactory behavior and achievement. Diagnosis should be a continuing process to be applied by the teacher whenever a learning difficulty is evident.

a. Observation of the Pupil's Behavior and Performance. Through direct observation of the pupil at work in the classroom, the teacher can secure valuable information about the efficiency of his work habits and study skills; evidence of lack of control of basic skills, such as excessive lip movements in reading, counting and roundabout procedures used for computation; skill in the use of laboratory apparatus and measuring devices; posture of body in handwriting; social relations with other individuals in the group; interests, initiative, and similar information of significance in diagnosis. The teacher can also arrange informal but planned test situations in which to observe pupil behavior under fairly well-controlled conditions similar to those used with standardized diagnostic tests. Symptoms of difficulties and the underlying causes can often be determined by the classroom teacher in this way. It is important that the teacher be well informed about the significance of symptoms, so that observations will focus on critical aspects of learning.

b. Analysis of Written Responses. A careful analysis of a pupil's written work often will give the teacher valuable insight into the nature of his learning difficulties. For instance, the nature of his difficulties in arithmetic computation can often be inferred from an analysis of the errors in his written work. Similarly, a critical analysis of spelling errors in the pupil's daily written work, or on some specially prepared informal test exercise of knowledge of basic spelling rules, will give the teacher a clear notion as to possible points of attack to remedy a spelling deficiency. The same procedure also can be applied to the analysis of faults in written composition. Deficiencies in handwriting can of course be determined by systematic analysis of faults in the pupil's daily written work.

Specific applications of this informal diagnostic procedure are described in the various chapters that follow. It should be pointed out that because of the lack of comparable standards, it is much more difficult to make inferences as to the seriousness of conditions from the data secured by informal procedures than from the application of standard diagnostic tests especially prepared to secure a detailed description or measurement of deficiencies or faulty performance.

c. Analysis of Oral Responses or Oral Accounts of Procedures. The teacher's analysis of the pupil's oral responses is valuable for studying learning problems. The teacher sits down with a pupil and has him work aloud. Thus a fairly systematic analysis of the quality and characteristics of his oral reading and of the kinds of errors he makes in reading aloud gives the teacher much more information than ordinarily is secured through informal, unsystematic observations in the ongoing work of the class. Similar analyses may be made of the quality and faults of oral speech, and of the characteristics of oral spelling, such as lack of syllabification.

A very valuable procedure for discovering the underlying nature of difficulties in arithmetic computations is to have the pupil explain orally his thinking as he works an example of some type that persists in giving him trouble, so that the teacher can discover faulty thinking and roundabout methods of work. Similar analyses can be made of the pupil's oral description of his thinking in solving selected verbal problems in arithmetic.

Systematic studies have made available for teachers lists of the most common and continuing errors, which will assist them in analyzing the work of pupils. Some errors and faults are of minor significance, whereas others are indicative of serious learning problems. Thus frequent, random, and unique nonphonetic misspellings are a symptom of serious disability in spelling. Of special value are studies of the characteristic differences between the performance and errors of good and poor achievers in reading, spelling, and arithmetic.

d. Interviews and Questioning. Often it is necessary for the teacher to supplement information secured through observation or through an analysis of the pupil's oral responses and written work by an interview or by systematic questioning. For example, the teacher may wish to secure a clearer picture of the pupil's methods of studying spelling. This can be done by questioning the pupil systematically about his methods of study, after observing them during a study period. In a similar way, the teacher can determine how well the pupil understands the steps involved in some computation with which he has difficulty, and other possible causes of incorrect work. Interviews and questioning are especially suitable for the informal study of the pupil's interests, his activities outside of school, his attitudes, and similar types of information that usually cannot be secured effectively at the time by available paper-and-pencil tests.

Critical observation of the pupil's behavior and responses during an interview and in reply to questions often yields information that psychologists find exceedingly valuable in making a diagnosis. Interviews with the pupil's parents and associates often produce significant kinds of information.

e. Analysis of a Performance or of Something Produced by the Pupil. The informal analysis of the limitations of a pupil's performance in using a piece of laboratory apparatus, or in some sport, or of something that he has produced, such as a graph, chart, or table, or of some work of art, is undoubtedly valuable. This approach should contribute to the improvement of the pupil's achievements by making him aware of both strong points and possible weaknesses in his performance and in the quality of things he has produced, so that he can direct his attention to their improvement. This type of evaluation is greatly enhanced by the use of standard check-lists and comparison with standard models having varying degrees of merit, for instance, composition and handwriting scales and diagnostic charts such as are described in Chapters 10 and 12.

Use of Special Kinds of Clinical Equipment

The classroom teacher should be familiar with some of the essential kinds of clinical equipment used in diagnostic studies, although their administration should be left to competent technicians or specialists. For instance, the audiometer is a device useful for measuring loss of hearing. The Betts Ophthalmic Telebinocular is a screening device for making a qualitative diagnosis of nine different aspects of vision to detect visual defects which make it more likely that the child may get into reading difficulties.

Medical, Psychiatric, and Psychological Examinations

Special types of medical, psychological, and psychiatric examinations also yield specific kinds of information of diagnostic value, such as glandular imbalance, dietary deficiency, malnutrition, emotional maladjustment, brain injury, and abnormal mental conditions. Technical procedures are applied by specialists in the diagnosis of subtle conditions such as these that are believed to be of significance in particular cases.

Analysis of Available Records

A well-planned cumulative record system usually contains valuable information to be considered in a diagnostic study, including basic data about the individual's school history, his progress, attendance data, marks, social background, medical record, mental and achievement test scores of various kinds, his interests, his social relations, and often significant anecdotes about his actions. Records kept by other social agencies also should be consulted in diagnostic study, such as the library, juvenile courts, welfare organizations, churches, and established youth groups.

Informal records can also be kept by the teacher that are of value in appraising pupil progress, such as records of books read, scores on teacher-made objective tests and on informal tests included in textbooks and workbooks, specimens of day-to-day written work, and anecdotes of various kinds.

FINDING TIME FOR DIAGNOSIS

When diagnosis is regarded as an integral part of all teaching, the problem of finding time for diagnosing minor, less serious, learning difficulties that normally may develop at any time in any teaching situation is not of any particular significance. When the need for identifying and correcting some such learning difficulty arises, the teacher will ordinarily seize the opportunity at once to correct the condition.

Whenever the teacher finds it advisable to apply more systematic procedures in the diagnosis of a serious learning problem, he should try to find the necessary time, if possible, during the regular instruction period for the area involved. This may be when the other children are working on a variety of individual and group assignments. Or when the pupil's attainments in some other area are well advanced, some of the time allotted to that area may be used for making the diagnostic study. Time ordinarily allotted for activities of relatively little importance may also be used for diagnostic purposes.

In a similar way the teacher can find extra time for necessary remedial instruction. Additional periods should also be arranged if they are necessary.

THE SYNTHESIS OF DIAGNOSTIC FINDINGS

In many instances the teacher can in the course of regular instruction readily discover minor learning difficulties by applying informally the diagnostic procedures discussed in the preceding pages. Usually these difficulties can then be obviated at once by reteaching. Further analysis to determine underlying causes is not necessary under such conditions.

In cases in which there are serious learning problems which do not respond to treatment, all of the information bearing on the situation that has been gathered in the course of a systematic diagnostic study should be carefully scrutinized and evaluated. The skill with which the examiner and his associates can synthesize the findings and interpret the evidence will have an important bearing on the validity of the diagnosis that is made. Care must be taken not to stress unduly a particular bit of evidence but rather to approach the analysis on a comprehensive basis so that all aspects of the problem are fully considered. Any diagnosis of a serious learning deficiency should be regarded as tentative and more or less preliminary in nature. The validity of the diagnosis will be measured by the extent to which corrective measures taken to improve the condition are effective.

SUGGESTED ACTIVITIES

1. Discuss the competencies essential for skill in diagnosis that are given on page 61. Apply them specifically to some curriculum area.

2. How well prepared are teachers to utilize diagnostic procedures systematically in connection with daily instruction?

3. Trace in your own words the series of seven steps in the diagnosis and treatment of learning difficulties presented on pages 62-63. Is there any similarity between medical and educational diagnosis?

4. What provision is made for the diagnosis of learning difficulties in present-day textbooks and workbooks in the various curriculum areas?

5. Describe informal diagnostic procedures that teachers can utilize in connection with daily instruction.

6. Discuss the illustration of the three levels of diagnosis given on pages 63-64. Apply the three levels to some other area, such as arithmetic, spelling, or language. This is preliminary, only to make the student aware of the need of direct study of the procedures that are described in later chapters.

7. Describe informal clinical diagnostic procedures that teachers can easily apply. When should the services of experts be called on by the teacher? What experts are available for local teachers?

8. In what situations is analysis of written work an effective basis of diagnosis? When may analysis of oral responses be helpful? Outline the elements of an interview procedure that may be used to determine causes of difficulty in reading, spelling, and arithmetic.

9. What types of special apparatus should be available for use for diagnostic purposes?

10. What are the contributions to diagnosis of medical, psychiatric, and psychological examinations?

11. If there is an educational clinic in your community, several members of the class should visit it to find answers to questions raised by the group. It would be even better for the class as a whole to visit the clinic. Are there regional clinics? Who maintains them?

12. How adequate are local school records? How can they be improved?

13. Discuss with teachers plans they have worked out for finding time for diagnostic work and remedial teaching. Suggest plans that you think are workable.

14. In many educational clinics the staff as a whole discusses cases of serious learning problems in staff meetings. Why is this a good procedure?

15. Why may a diagnosis be incorrect, incomplete, or only partial?

SELECTED BIBLIOGRAPHY

BRUECKNER, L. J., and MELBY, E. O., *Diagnostic and Remedial Teaching* (Boston, Houghton, 1931).

Educational Diagnosis, Thirty-fourth Yearbook, National Society for the Study of Education (Chicago, Univ. of Chicago Press, 1935).

FERNALD, Grace, *Remedial Techniques in the Basic Skill Subjects* (New York, McGraw, 1943).

TORGERSON, T. L., *Studying Children: Diagnostic and Remedial Procedures in Teaching* (New York, Dryden, 1947).

WILLEY, R. D., *Guidance in Elementary Education* (New York, Harper, 1952).

It is strongly recommended that the list of diagnostic tests on page 70 be made available for study by the teacher and students, together with the manuals accompanying each test. Packets of these tests should be made available for purchase by students and schools.

In connection with the work to be done in later chapters it is highly desirable that a collection of up-to-date textbooks and workbooks in the various curriculum areas be placed in some convenient center for examination by students enrolled in workshops and college classes.

5 PRINCIPLES UNDERLYING TREATMENT OF LEARNING DIFFICULTIES

JUST AS no two cases of learning difficulty have completely similar causes, no two cases can be treated exactly alike. Every child is, in many respects, different from any other child. His difficulties in learning can stem from a wide variety of causes. Normal learners have difficulties that should be diagnosed and treated in the course of ordinary instruction. The unique kinds of learning that some children demonstrate indicate that no two problems of correction will be exactly the same. Nonetheless, there are some basic principles underlying the treatment of learning difficulties irrespective of the nature of the difficulty or the curricular area in which the difficulty resides. There are elements in common among the corrective programs whether we are considering reading, arithmetic, spelling, or language usage.

Among the more important general categories of principles underlying treatment of learning difficulties are the following:

1. Treatment must be based on a diagnosis.
2. The child's personal worth must be considered.
3. Corrective treatment must be individualized.
4. The program must be well motivated and encouraging to the child.
5. Materials and exercises must be carefully selected.
6. The entire environment of the child must be considered.
7. Continuous evaluations must be made.
8. Sound teaching procedures must be utilized in the treatment of learning difficulties.

TREATMENT MUST BE BASED ON A DIAGNOSIS

Locate Weaknesses That Require Correction

The purpose of a diagnosis is to formulate a remedial program for each child requiring it. The child who has trouble developing proficiency in the tool subjects often has an uneven profile in the area in which he is limited. Some phases of reading, for example, may be well learned, whereas other phases may be poorly learned. Still other phases may have been overemphasized to the point that they restrict the child's general development in reading. The diagnosis must ferret out the inconsistencies in the child's attack on reading printed material.

The child who is in difficulty will show irregular performances. He may know his addition facts well but be somewhat troubled by multiplication combinations. He may understand little about place value and still be adequate in his speed of simple calculation. Diagnosis is designed to locate faulty habits that preclude rapid and effective growth within a tool subject. The diagnosis locates areas of instruction that have been neglected, those which have been faultily learned, or those which have been overemphasized. It is impossible to start a remedial program until the nature of the instruction needed by the child has been established.

Establish the Type of Treatment Needed

A good diagnosis, in any area, tries to find the answers to these questions:

1. Is the child really a learning difficulty case or is he simply a slow learner?
2. Is the child's difficulty one that is more complicated than can be handled by the teacher alone? If so, what kind of technical help will be needed?
3. What specifically is wrong with the child's growth pattern in the tool subject in which he is deficient?
4. How can the corrective program be made as efficient as possible? At what level should the corrective work start? What motivational devices should be used for this child?
5. Are there any characteristics in the child that might impede learning? If so, how can they be corrected? How can the remedial program be adjusted to them?
6. Are there any conditions in the child's environment that must be corrected before the program can be expected to be effective?

Only after the teacher has the answer to these questions can a reasonable approach to the correction of an educational disability be made. Inasmuch as each case is different, there can be no bag of tricks nor universal approach to the solution of remedial problems. Many times remedial training which would be good for one child would be detrimental to another. For example, a remedial program in reading planned to develop more analytical ability in word recognition would be good for a child who had insufficient skill in independent word recognition. This same remedial program would be harmful to the youngster who was already overanalytical and saw each word as a set of phonetic elements. It would exaggerate the weakness he already had. Therefore, every remedial program must be based on a thorough appraisal of the child's needs, his strengths and weaknesses, and the environment in which he is to be nurtured.

Clearly Formulate the Remedial Program

After the diagnosis has been made and the plan of remedial instruction arrived at, it is necessary to formulate clearly the remedial program and to write out an analysis of what is to be done for each case. It is difficult to remember each child, his needs, the level of his attainments, and his limitations with the exactness that is necessary to conduct an effective re-education program. The written statement should indicate the nature of the disability and the level of material to be used in instruction. It should indicate the type of exercises to be used for improving the child's limited ability. The written report of the case should state any physical or sensory limitations of the child that should be corrected or for which the instructional adjustments should be made. A statement of the child's interests, attitudes, and personality adjustment also should be included.

Modify the Program as May Be Advisable

The original plan of remedial work will need to be modified from time to time as the child progresses toward the fulfillment of his potential. Frequently a child with a learning difficulty changes rapidly in his instructional needs. A child in reading difficulty, for example, may have failed to establish skill in the use of context clues in word recognition. He may be unable to employ the meaning of a sentence as an aid to solving independently a word problem and establishing the meaning of a word he does not recognize at sight. He may have considerable ability in employing the other word-recognition techniques but he does not readily anticipate what the word is likely to be. Therefore, although the phonetic, structural, and sight elements help him to approximate the correct pronunciation, he is unable to vary his solution slightly in order to get an accurate recognition of the word. After a short time, under good guidance, he will have established the use of context clues and his independent word-recognition techniques will come into focus. His problem no longer will be one of word-recognition. He may, however, be a slow reader because he has attempted for so long a time to employ analytical procedures that he has not built a large sight vocabulary nor gained fluency in reading. The program for such a child would have to be modified as his reading problem changed.

Inasmuch as the child's instructional needs change rapidly, it is unwise to plan a remedial program that simulates a production line. A production-line program would take the point of view that once the level of performance of the child was located, all that would be needed would be to put the child through a series of experiences designed to develop capability uniformly for all children. No one program is suitable for all children and even an individual child's needs change with great rapidity. A good remedial program must be based upon a continuous diagnosis and modification of the program as the child matures.

Use a Variety of Remedial Techniques

In basing a remedial program upon a diagnosis, there is frequently the tendency to use one specific exercise to overcome a known deficiency. However, there are many ways to develop the various skills and abilities in the basic tool subjects. An effective program will employ a variety of techniques and instructional procedures. The teacher should keep an account of those that appear to be effective in specific types of learning disability problems.

There are many sources of techniques available to the teacher. The professional books on remedial work within a field give suggestions for correcting specific types of learning difficulties. There are compilations of remedial techniques such as the one developed by Russell and Karp.[1] Perhaps the most fruitful source of specific teaching techniques is to be found in the manuals and workbooks accompanying basal programs in reading and arithmetic. If, for example, a sixth-grade child has difficulty with syllabication in reading, the teacher can find exercises designed to increase the child's auditory perception of syllables in third-grade manuals and workbooks accompanying basic reading programs. There also will be exercises designed to give the child experience in separating words into syllables in the manuals and workbooks that accompany fourth- and fifth-grade readers. It may be that this child has difficulty in reading because he has not progressed in his word-recognition techniques beyond the phonetic, sounding-out stage into the more mature structural and visual analysis of words. Other exercises designed to develop maturity in word recognition in general will be found in the manuals and workbooks accompanying the various readers in grades 3, 4, 5, and 6. While going through some of these materials, the teacher can accumulate a variety of teaching techniques and methods which will keep the program from becoming stereotyped and boring. Similar exercises for correcting specific faults are found in arithmetic and language textbooks and workbooks.

It should be remembered that in attempting to get variety in methods and techniques, complexity caused by too-frequent changes in technique should be avoided. The directions should be simple. The activities used should be like those used in the basic tool subject. The child should not have to spend his time following complicated programs or directions, but he should have enough variety so that the remedial program is stimulating and worth while.

It would be unfortunate if the child needing specific drill on sight words would meet nothing but the "fishbowl game." In this game the child fishes for words and sees if he can recognize them at sight. If he recognizes a word at sight, he counts the fish caught; if he does not recognize it at sight, he studies it so that he will be more likely to recognize the word the next day, but it is not counted in the "catch" for the second day. If the child is confronted with this same game day after day, it is likely that he will grow tired of it.

[1] David H. Russell and Etta E. Karp, *Reading Aids Through the Grades,* rev. ed. (New York, Bureau of Publications, Teachers College, Columbia Univ., 1951).

The Child Should Help Formulate the Program of Treatment

In planning a program of treatment for a child with a specific learning difficulty, the broad scope of the program should be carefully formulated. It should be modified when the need for alteration becomes apparent as the child progresses. A wide variety of techniques should be used. After the diagnosis is interpreted, the child should know the general plan of the remedial program. The child should be told the nature of his difficulty, and he should help plan ways of overcoming it.

If a child is in difficulty in spelling because he tries to remember all the words as isolated combinations of letters, rather than by systematically grouping the letters into syllables, the difficulties inherent in his approach should be pointed out to him. The teacher and pupil, working together, should formulate plans for solving his problem. The child may indicate that he has difficulty in hearing the syllables within a word. The teacher can then suggest ways of overcoming this difficulty. The teacher may show the child a number of exercises designed to increase his ability to perceive auditorily syllables within words. The child can indicate which among the exercises he enjoyed most. He can help select topics upon which he will write in order to apply his spelling techniques. He can help to set the time of day for individual help with his learning difficulty. It would be unfortunate to select arbitrarily certain times for remedial help, because other things of importance to the child might be going on then. The child must feel that this is his program and that he has a part in planning it.

Any program set up for the treatment of a learning difficulty must be based upon a thorough diagnosis of the difficulty, the instructional needs, and the child's strengths and weaknesses. If the basic principles of teaching discussed in this chapter are adhered to, approximately 65 per cent of the children having learning difficulties will improve even without diagnosis. However, there will be approximately 35 per cent of the children with learning difficulties who will require special attention. There is no way of knowing which among the disability cases will be the ones who will improve without diagnosis, and which will be among the 35 per cent whose difficulty will persist and who, as a result, will become even more stubborn cases. Even those children who improve without diagnosis would improve more rapidly if the program were designed to meet their specific needs.

The reason why most programs designed to correct learning difficulties have some degree of success is that the child is worked with individually, the area in which he is in difficulty is focused upon, and many good things are done. Many formalized remedial programs that are in fact basically poor demonstrate a modicum of success because the child is treated individually. Well-rounded programs, based on a careful and continuous diagnosis and using a variety of instructional techniques, prove to be more effective.

THE CHILD'S PERSONAL WORTH MUST BE CONSIDERED

The child who is having difficulty in one of the basic tool subjects frequently feels insecure and defeated in school. Any program that hopes to treat the learning difficulty must take into account the child's sense of personal worth. It often appears that the child in serious trouble is antagonistic toward the learning which is causing him difficulty. If, for example, he is in trouble in arithmetic, he tends to thoroughly dislike arithmetic; he sees little importance in learning it, and he has poor attitudes toward himself as a person. Programs designed to treat learning difficulties should avoid stigmatizing pupils by grouping them for treatment, should consider the child's emotional state, and should take steps to correct faulty attitudes. The contributions of both group and individual work should be recognized.

Avoid Stigmatizing Pupils in Classification and Grouping

The child having a learning difficulty builds a barrier between himself and the subject causing him trouble. For example, if the child is having trouble in spelling, he may persuade himself that spelling isn't worth while; that he will have a secretary anyway when he grows up; that his father couldn't spell well when he was a boy; that he does not have spelling aptitude; and the like. The same is true for other curricular areas.

Resistance to learning will be magnified if the program of treatment classifies the child in any unfortunate way. If the child is to be worked with individually in the classroom, the group separation should be made as free from stigma as possible. Names such as the "oaks," the "willows," and the "saplings" should not be used to designate reading groups, for example. If the children who are in difficulty can work on the same topics as the other children, the chances for the correction of a learning difficulty will be improved. Groupings designed to deal with specific learning difficulties are far better than a permanent group organization within the class that separates the able from the less able or the disabled learners.

If it is necessary to give a child special remedial help outside the regular classroom, care must be taken in instituting the procedure. Insofar as possible, remedial programs should be undertaken voluntarily and should be considered a privilege. Of course, there are certain youngsters who will avoid programs that are designed to meet their greatest need. If several children are formed into a remedial group, the youngster who is resistant will be easier to persuade. At the start, it is advisable to select for treatment the greatest discrepancy cases, that is, the brightest children who have the greatest disability. When a special remedial section is formed, children who are known to be bright and capable in other areas of the school curriculum should be selected first to get the special help that they need. Then other children will see that the program is designed to help capable children who have specific learning problems.

There is another reason for selecting the capable children first. The more able the child is generally, the greater is the chance for rapid and early improvement. In this way it becomes obvious to the children and the teacher that the remedial program has merit.

Consider the Child's Emotional State

Many of the children who are in educational difficulty are emotionally tense or are insecure and have little sense of belonging to their school or family groups. Whether the emotional disturbance is the primary cause or the result of the educational difficulty, the emotional state of the child must be considered in planning the program to treat the learning problem.

The child may demonstrate submissive or demanding attitudes; he may be resistant to help; he may have few interests; or he may have a tendency to withdraw into himself. The program must help to overcome the child's emotional tension and sense of failure if it is to be effective. The fact that a personal interest is taken in the child and that his learning difficulty is being solved often encourages him enough so that he recovers his sense of personal worth.

Evidence shows that a direct attack on the learning difficulty with a businesslike, though considerate, teacher will help the youngster overcome emotional problems. Children in difficulty frequently lean heavily upon the teacher for support. A first-grade teacher who places a child who is in difficulty next to him during group work understands the child's need for adult recognition. It is necessary to teach a disabled child at any age to rely more on his own resources as treatment of the learning difficulty progresses. This psychological weaning should be gradual. The child has felt support by the teacher's interest in him and the acceptance of his educational problem as one that can be solved. If his problem has been carefully diagnosed, and if effective and varied remedial techniques are used, evidences of success will appear early and the child's confidence will begin to be restored. If the child's emotional tensions are not relieved by the gradual improvement of his learning problem, outside technical help may be necessary. The child might then be referred to a Bureau of Child Guidance or a psychiatrist for further study and recommendation.

Correct Faulty Attitudes

Attitudes of indifference, dislike, rejection, and antagonism toward a learning difficulty are frequently encountered. Programs of treatment must devise means of overcoming these faulty attitudes if progress in the correction of the learning difficulty is to be made. In one sense, the teacher is a salesman and his first task is to develop in the child a need for learning the subject. If the child feels that spelling is of little importance, the teacher must show him the social value of correct spelling. It may be that the child wishes to place some of his creative writing on the bulletin board. The standards of acceptance will demonstrate to him the need for accurate spelling.

Whatever the means used, faulty attitudes toward the field in which the learning difficulty lies must be overcome.

Recognize the Importance of Group as Well as Individual Work

This is an important principle underlying all treatment of learning difficulties. The child who is having difficulty needs to share experiences with other children within the area in which he is in difficulty. It is beneficial for the child to see that there are other children who have similar difficulties. It is helpful for him to see how other children with a like difficulty progress in overcoming it. It aids the child to know that there are other children who are gradually learning to use their newly gained proficiencies in group enterprises. The child should never be made to feel that remedial instruction is a formal procedure in which he is separated from his kind and drilled until his disability is corrected.

It is important for the child who is in difficulty, as well as for the normal-growing child, to utilize the results of reading or other learnings in group activities. A child in reading difficulty can, for example, along with other children having similar difficulty, dramatize stories that they have shared. This will increase the child's sense of personal worth and also increase his learning efficiency. He will also need some individual attention and individual work. At periodic times the teacher should give him specific instruction that is important for correcting his learning difficulty.

A program designed to treat learning difficulties must take into account the fact that children in difficulty are very much like other children. They need to be recognized and appreciated. They need to be spared embarrassment. The child in difficulty must be reinforced as a person, because he may have feelings of insecurity and failure. His attitudes toward the work must receive consideration. In his regular classroom work, he should have the opportunity of sharing in the important activities. It is frequently the lack of consideration for the child's personal worth that starts him on the downward spiral which leads to educational disability.

CORRECTIVE TREATMENT MUST BE INDIVIDUALIZED

Many of the children who are in learning difficulties have failed to respond to programs designed to meet the needs and the characteristics of the majority of children. The child in difficulty has failed to progress in the customary fashion. He has developed unusual variation in his skills and abilities.[2] A program that is designed to treat learning difficulties must be based on the assumption that children learn differently and need programs which meet their individual requirements.

The program must be attuned to the child's needs within the area of limitation. It must alter the outcomes and the methods so that they are commensurate with the child's ability, and also it must be designed to be efficient for the particular child.

Outcomes and Methods Should Be Commensurate with the Child's Ability

The expected outcomes will have to be altered in some respects to meet the child's characteristics. If, for example, the child is a slow learner—that is, if he lacks general intelligence—he can neither be expected to grow as rapidly as children more favorably endowed nor can he gain their ultimate level of ability. He will need methods adjusted to the fact that his abstract reasoning capabilities are not quite as substantial as are those of the average child. He will need more first-hand contacts, more concrete experiences, more careful directions, and more emphasis on drill than will the youngster of higher general intelligence.

If the child has poor hearing ability, spelling and reading methods will need to be altered to take into account the fact that he cannot distinguish the differences in certain of the vowel sounds and will therefore have to depend more on the visual characteristics of words. If the child has motor co-ordination difficulties, the task of teaching him to write legibly will be greater. In some cases the teacher must be satisfied with legible although somewhat irregular handwriting. If the child is left-handed, the general approach to handwriting will need to be altered. These are just a few illustrations of the modifications that will be necessary in outcomes and methods if a reasonable approach to individualization is to be attained.

Treatment Should Be Specific and Not General

In treating a child with a learning difficulty, the teacher should focus upon his specific needs. Diagnosis will usually show something specifically wrong with the child's pattern of performance. The child may, for example, have many incorrect answers to division problems because he does not subtract correctly or because he makes errors in multiplication. In such cases the teacher should focus the remedial activities upon the steps in subtraction and multiplication used in long division.

By stating that the treatment should be specific and not general, we mean that the emphasis in instruction should be directed toward the child's specific needs. It is not meant that a certain phase of the developmental program is

[2] Mary Watkins, *A Comparison of the Reading Proficiencies Normal-Progress and Reading Disability Cases of the Same I.Q. and Reading Level.* Unpublished Ph.D. thesis, Univ. of Minnesota, 1953.

isolated and drilled upon. In the case of a child with a reading difficulty who needs to pay more attention to phonetic analysis, the teacher would be in error if he resorted to isolated drill upon phonetic elements. A better approach to the problem would be to place the youngster in a regular developmental program at a level at which he can read comfortably. The teacher would then have the child read for definite purposes and, when he encounters word difficulties, the teacher would emphasize the phonetic elements of the words as a means of solving his word-recognition problem.

In all exercises designed to develop basic reading skills and abilities, the teacher would emphasize for this youngster those that stress skill and ability in phonetic analysis. The teacher might add a few exercises of the same type as those in the manual accompanying the developmental reading program he is using and also some exercises from other manuals of developmental reading programs. Suitable workbook exercises accompanying basic developmental reading programs should be included in the work for the youngster who needs more experience in phonetic analysis. The teacher might also work out a few additional study sheets emphasizing word parts in contextual settings.

Evidence collected at the University of Minnesota Psycho-Educational Clinic shows that those children who are placed in a regular developmental program, modified to emphasize those skills in which a given youngster needs further training and to minimize those approaches which have been overemphasized for him, show far greater gain than do those children who are taught by isolated drill approaches. When it is stated that treatment should be specific and not general, it is meant that the child should be placed for remedial training in a systematic, controlled developmental program. The program should be modified, however, to meet the child's specific instructional needs.

Fatigue Should Be Noted and Practice Spaced

The child who has a learning disability frequently finds it difficult to attend to the learning task for any considerable length of time. His lack of attention may be the result of poor physical stamina, emotional reactions to the learning, or habits of escaping from uncomfortable situations. Whatever the cause, the length of the remedial period should be adjusted so that the child is capable of maintaining an energetic attack upon the subject being studied.

The case of Harold, a fourth-grade child who had rather marked difficulty in reading, illustrates the necessary approach. Harold was an energetic child who found the reading of second-grade material difficult and unrewarding. He had an IQ of 122 as measured by the Stanford-Binet and he was energetic on the playground and in other nonacademic school activities. In reading, however, this energy was not evident. After a careful diagnosis, daily remedial treatment was started for two thirty-minute periods, one in the morning and one in the afternoon each day. It was soon discovered that Harold could not profit from reading instruction of more than fifteen minutes at a time. He could work with a high degree of energy for ten minutes and then use the results of that reading in class discussion, in creative activities such as painting, construction, and the like. Then he was again ready for the remedial reading lesson. His remedial program was altered so as to space his reading periods, first having him read for about ten minutes, then having him create with the results of his reading, and then giving him drill designed to overcome his specific disability through activities requiring rereading of the material that he had read in the first ten-minute period. As he developed capability in reading, the length of consecutive reading time was increased. The remedial teacher was alert to the length of time that she could expect him to work energetically. When Harold discovered that he was reading better and that reading contributed something to his creative enterprises, it was possible to increase the length of the reading time until frequently he read for most of the thirty mintues. In the meantime, Harold gained confidence in himself and interest in reading to the point that he initiated additional reading activities.

In this case, there was nothing basically wrong physiologically that limited Harold's energy. If poor general health, malnutrition, a glandular condition, or emotional tension had limited his energy, it might have been necessary to hold to the shorter reading periods for a much longer time.

THE PROGRAM MUST BE WELL MOTIVATED AND ENCOURAGING TO THE CHILD

The effective learner is a purposeful, energetic, interested learner. He finds much pleasure in working toward a known goal. In order for a child with a learning difficulty to progress rapidly, comfortably, and consistently, it is necessary for him to work on something that is important and to see that he is progressing satisfactorily. There are several principles underlying the treatment of learning difficulties which stimulate the child's desire to learn and demonstrate his progress. Among the more important of these principles are the following:

1. The teacher must be optimistic.
2. Success of the student must be emphasized.
3. Errors should be pointed out in a positive way.
4. Growth should be made apparent to the child.
5. Treatment should not conflict with other enjoyable activities.
6. Purpose should always be established.
7. The results of the learning experience should be utilized and evaluated.

The Teacher Must Be Optimistic

Although at times children having learning problems seem to present insurmountable teaching problems, the teacher must approach them with confidence. The teacher must be not only optimistic, but he must "sell" that optimism to the child. A teacher who would help a child to overcome a learning difficulty should be buoyant and energetic himself. He should instill confidence in the child who is in difficulty. The teacher should have planned the program well enough in advance to know exactly what is going to be undertaken during each remedial lesson. It is through careful preparation on the part of the teacher, who knows exactly where the session is going, that confidence can be developed.

Fortunately, the teacher who is treating children with learning difficulties can approach them optimistically. If the child's problem and his capabilities and limitations have been appraised and if the program of treatment has been carefully formulated, success is almost assured. From time to time, it is true, the complexities inherent in treating a child with a learning difficulty will tax this optimism. Nonetheless, the optimism must be maintained even if sometimes things do not appear to be going well. They ultimately will go well except in a few rare cases of organic difficulty.

Success of the Student Must Be Emphasized

To be effective, programs of remedial treatment should emphasize the success of the student. Over a period of years the child has been discouraged about his ability to learn, and so even small achievements should be brought to his attention. There is a tendency for teachers to overlook many things that the child accomplishes successfully and to focus upon his errors until a sense of defeat overwhelms him.

At the start, it is wise for the teacher to put the child into learning situations that are relatively easy for him to handle successfully. As the work progresses, the difficulty of the tasks should be increased. At all times it should be remembered that one of the determiners of the effectiveness of the treatment is the degree to which the child experiences success within the field which has caused him difficulty.

Errors Should Be Pointed Out in a Positive Way

Even though the successes of the child should be emphasized, his errors must be detected and brought to his attention. Sometimes it is necessary to say that the answer to an arithmetic example is not quite right. Or, in the field of reading, it is often necessary to point out that a word has been incorrectly recognized. The teacher must point out the error, but while doing so, he might also point out that the child had most of the word correct. For example, if the child calls the word *house* for *home,* it can be pointed out that he had the word nearly right; it made sense; he got the other words in the sentence correct, but that in order to be exactly right he should have looked at the center of the word a little more carefully. Such an approach is quite different from one in which a teacher would say, "Why do you always make a mistake on that word?"; or, "You knew that word yesterday. Why don't you know it today?"

Frequently the child gets a large proportion of the work correct, and this should be pointed out to him as well as the nature of the mistakes that he may have made.

Growth Should Be Made Apparent to the Child

The child who is in learning difficulty needs to have his growth demonstrated to him. There are varieties of ways in which such growth can be shown. If the child is slow in reading or in number work, charts can be made to show how well he is progressing in the rate of doing his work.

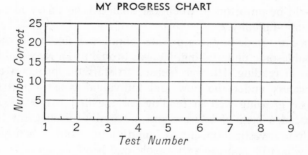

MY PROGRESS CHART

A child in difficulty in spelling can have the effectiveness of the new methods of studying his words demonstrated to him. For example, he can keep a list of words he has learned to spell and see them accumulate. The child who is working to build up a sight vocabulary can make a picture dictionary of words he is learning to recognize. Now and then a child who is trying to improve his reading should reread some of the material that was difficult for him the month before to show him the ease with which he can read it now. If the child is in difficulty in oral language, periodic tape recordings can be made and compared to show him that he is progressing. The same thing can be done for children who are having trouble with oral reading.

Now and then a child may bog down in his progress and then his learning chart will show a plateau. In such a case, the remedial program should be altered somewhat in order to demonstrate progress to the child. For example, with a word-recognition case in reading, instead of having the child read, "The man rode away on a $\frac{house}{horse}$," we might give the child a choice between two words which looked quite different, for example, *horse* and *chimney*. Then the decision would be easier for him to make. He would be kept at this easier level until he had re-established himself; then the difficulty of the work could be gradually increased again.

The child who has been in difficulty for a long time needs whatever encouragement can be given to him. He must be made to feel that he is making progress toward the desired outcomes. This does not mean that dawdling or ineffective approaches on the part of the child should be condoned. It does mean that the difficulty of the work should be controlled to such an extent that the child will not feel discouraged.

Treatment Should Not Conflict with Other Enjoyable Activities

Programs of remedial treatment should not be substituted for any enjoyable activity. Quite often, a busy teacher will try to find time to help a child who is in difficulty in one of the tool subjects when the other children do not need her attention. Such a time might be when the other children are in the auditorium viewing a movie, or when they are on the playground at recess time. It would be unfortunate to choose such a time to try to help a child with a learning difficulty.

George, a fifth-grade boy in a private school, was finding learning to read a rather troublesome undertaking. He was brought to a remedial teacher for special help in reading. He was pleased to start the program and he anticipated success under the new and individual type of instruction. He seemed to be growing well in reading for the first two weeks. Then the teacher noticed a lack of interest and a seeming distaste for the reading program. Upon investigation, it was found that the time when his class had swimming, which he enjoyed very much, had been changed. Now he could not go swimming because he had to go to the remedial teacher to get help with his reading. It was no wonder that George lost interest in improving his reading. It took only a rescheduling of the time for remedial teaching to re-establish his enthusiasm for the program.

The teacher must be on the alert to be sure that the treatment of a learning difficulty does not conflict with enterprises that are more important to the child.

Purpose Should Always Be Established

The child who is in difficulty, as well as any other child who is learning, should know why he is reading a story, writing a passage, or figuring the answer to an arithmetic problem. Modern programs of remedial treatment let the child understand what his problem is, direct his attention toward improving it, and use learning experiences that are important to the child. Corrective work in reading, for example, will prove much more effective if the child understands what he is expected to look for in a passage read. If the child is having trouble in comprehension, for example, he should have the expected outcomes of reading a passage well defined before he starts to read. This is equally true for a child not in difficulty.

It is often supposed that the development of interest alone will correct a learning difficulty. Such is not the case. The problem is really twofold. The child should know the purposes for which he is to use reading, arithmetic, writing, spelling, or language; that is, he should be making purposeful use of the tool subjects. In addition to this, he should understand what he is trying to improve in the basic learning itself. If the child is a poor oral reader because he is attempting to read the material too rapidly, he should work specifically upon that problem and try to develop a more reasonable rate, more accurate timing, better phrasing, and the like. If the child is in difficulty in spelling because he does not visually study the word part by part as he pronounces it, he should focus his attention on visual study. If a child has difficulty with zeros in subtraction, he should do special work in this area.

The child should know the purposes for employing the tool subjects and understand the modifications in the way that he is using the tool to meet those purposes.

The Results of the Learning Experience Should Be Utilized and Evaluated

This principle underlying the treatment of learning difficulties implies that the child is learning the skills and abilities in the basic tool subjects in activities that to him are of importance. He may be reading a story, for example, to find out about some animals for a chart he is making. After he has read it, he should enter the information he has gained on the chart. He may be writing an account of an experience to be posted on the bulletin board. After the account has been written, it should be posted if it meets the standards of quality required. The child may be using arithmetic to determine the true dimensions of a model boat to be constructed to scale. If he cannot make the boat, he can at least draw it to scale.

After the child has read, written, or calculated for purposes that to him are real, he should evaluate how much he has learned; how he would go about the task if he were to do it again; whether he employed the basic tool subjects effectively, and if not, how he could improve them. This is a good procedure for all children who are learning. It is essential, though often neglected, for children doing remedial work.

There are, then, wide varieties of ways in which a program can be well-motivated and encouraging to the youngster who is in difficulty. By and large, the program revolves around a teacher who is optimistic, who is eager to show the child his success, who is willing to take the time to establish purposes, who helps the children to use the results of the learning experiences, and who points out to the child improvement that is taking place.

MATERIALS AND EXERCISES MUST BE CAREFULLY SELECTED

The task of selecting appropriate material is not as easy as it would appear at first glance. Some teachers feel that the material is appropriate if it deals with a subject that interests the child. Other teachers feel that the material is suitable if it is at the level indicated by the child's ability as measured by standardized tests. The fact is, however, that there are several considerations to be borne in mind in the selection of material. The more important are the following:

1. Materials must be suitable in level of difficulty and type.
2. Materials must be suitable in interest and format.
3. Materials must be abundant and not artificial.

Materials Must Be Suitable in Level of Difficulty and Type

Exercises in arithmetic, for example, must take into account the difficulty of the operations involved and the nature of the learner's problems. The exercises must be carefully selected and retaught as may be necessary so that the child will have a reasonable chance of success.

In reading, the problem is even more complicated, because the proper level of difficulty depends upon the nature of the disability case for which it is being selected. The teacher must consider at least two factors about the nature of a reading disability case when selecting material at the appropriate level of difficulty.

First, the teacher must recognize that the child who is disabled in reading cannot read as well as would be expected of a child of his mental maturity. The problem of selecting material suitable in difficulty is complicated by this fact. Many teachers think that the approach would be to give a standardized reading test. They think that if a child measured, for example, 3.0 (beginning third grade), he should start his remedial instruction in material of beginning third-grade difficulty. Research and experience have shown that such an approach will, in many cases, prove ineffective. The disabled reader who measures 3.0 actually is in most cases not that far along in reading development. The child may have a mental grade of 6.0. So he is applying three years' more of mental maturity to the reading act than the typical child of 3.0 reading ability. The disabled reader with the mental maturity of 6.0 who reads only as well as a typical 3.0 child may be as much as a year lower in basic reading abilities, such as ability to recognize words or phrase them effectively for comprehension purposes. In judging the difficulty of the material suitable for initial remedial instruction, the teacher must consider, in addition to standardized tests, other evidences of the child's reading maturity. Such evidences as his comfort in reading the material orally, his skill in phrasing, his word-recognition ability, and his ability to answer various types of comprehension questions about the material read, help to locate the level of material with which he should start his remedial training.

A second consideration in selecting material for a child in difficulty in reading is the nature of the child's disability. The teacher must consider the instructional outcomes to be gained by the material. For example, if we want to try to develop fluency and speed of reading, then reading material should be used that is for him definitely easy, material in which he would not meet more than one new word in every one hundred running words. Such material would be suitable for increasing speed of reading. A child should no more be required to read difficult material to increase his speed of reading than a sixty-pound pack be placed on the back of someone who was being trained to sprint.

On the other hand, if the problem is one of developing word-recognition techniques, such as ability to analyze words effectively, the child would be given material in which he would meet a new word in approximately every twenty running words. He would meet enough words that he knows at sight so that the content would be meaningful, and yet he would be meeting a sufficient number of new words so that he would have to employ the techniques of word analysis that he needs to develop.

The first criterion, and likely the most important one in the selection of material or exercises to aid the child with a learning difficulty, is to use material and exercises appropriate from the standpoint of difficulty. Material and exercises must be suitable in type as well as in level of difficulty. The exercises designed to improve arithmetic, spelling, or language usage should similarly be selected because they give the child experience in the skills and abilities he needs to master. If, for example, the child who is having difficulty in spelling is deficient because he is using a restricted method of studying words, the exercises should be designed to give him practice in more effective word-study methods. If the child merely looks at the list of words and tries to memorize them without pronouncing or writing the words, the study exercises should be of a type that force him to pronounce the words syllable by syllable and check his knowledge by written recall.

In reading, the materials must be carefully selected so as to be suitable in type of content, to be compatible with the type of exercise and experiences needed by the child. For example, if the problem is one of increasing speed, the type of material should be short stories, where the plot unfolds rapidly and where the purpose is to get the general significance of what is read. If, on the other hand, the child is inaccurate because he is attempting to read too fast, it would be well to require him to read science material, factual material that demands a high degree of accuracy on the part of the reader. The purposes for which he would read it would require him to attend to the detail. If the problem is one of developing a high degree of efficiency in the ability to classify, the child should read material that lends itself to classification.

Materials and exercises used in the treatment of a learning difficulty in any of the basic tool subjects must be suitable to the type of outcomes and learnings to be acquired by the child, and they must be at the proper level of difficulty.

Materials Must Be Suitable in Interest and Format

An important consideration in selecting material to be used for remedial treatment is that it should be developmentally suitable to the child in both interest and format. This principle underlying the selecting of material presents a major problem, especially in the field of reading. Getting material in reading that is correct from the standpoint of difficulty and still suitable to the child's stage of development in regard to interest and format is a major undertaking. If a child who is 12 years old is only able to read with comfort material that is usually read in the third grade, the teacher is faced with one of the most difficult problems in the whole field of remedial treatment. Third-grade material is not suitable to a 12-year-old's level of interest. Such material deals with topics that have been demonstrated to be of interest to children of normal third-grade age. Nor is it suitable to the 12-year-old from the standpoint of format. The pictures are of smaller children and the print looks too large. In such a case, there can be no compromise with the need for using material suitable in difficulty. Third-grade material must be used. Therefore, the solution is to find material that looks less juvenile in format and deals with content that either has appeal to children of any age or is at a higher interest level than is its reading difficulty level.

There are available many suitable materials for re-educating a child with a reading difficulty. First, there are those that have been primarily designed for the less capable readers. Such books as the *Gates-Peardon Practice Exercises* and the *American Adventure Series* are of this type. Another source is to be found in basic reading programs that have parallel readers, such as the Regular and Classmate Editions of the *Developmental Reading Series*. The two editions are alike in all important aspects. They have the same covers, titles, pictures, content, and interest level. The difference lies in the fact that the Classmate Edition is written with a smaller vocabulary, shorter paragraphs, simpler sentences, and fewer words per page. The Regular Edition of the sixth-grade book, for example, requires sixth-grade reading ability, whereas the same stories can be read in the Classmate Edition by children of third-grade reading ability. Pamphlets put out by the Educational Press also meet this demand. The workbooks that accompany basic readers are another source of suitable material. Workbooks look considerably more mature than the basal readers they accompany. The pictures are in black and white; the drill exercises neither look nor sound immature to the child who is in reading difficulty. A third-grade workbook would be suitable for the child mentioned above.

In the treatment of learning difficulties in arithmetic, spelling, and language, the problem of correctness of interest level and of format is practically as difficult to solve as it is in the field of reading. Nonetheless, the topics to be talked about by a child who is in need of improvement in oral expression, for example, should be compatible with his developmental level. Similar adjustments should be made in the other fields.

Materials Must Be Abundant and Not Artificial

The problem of selecting material and exercises to meet the needs, the interests, and the over-all developmental level of the child is difficult indeed. The major consideration should be the selection of material of the proper difficulty level, but attention should also be given to the suitability of the material and exercises for the type of outcome that is being emphasized. They should be as nearly suitable as possible from the standpoint of interest and format. In addition, the materials and exercises should be abundant so that the child gets adequate experience in using the learnings he is trying to make. The materials and exercises should be similar to those that are used in developmental programs in all of the basic tool subjects. Remedial materials should not be artificial, routine, unusual, or mechanical in nature.

THE ENTIRE ENVIRONMENT OF THE CHILD MUST BE CONSIDERED

In developing a program of training for the correction of a learning difficulty, consideration must be given to the entire learning environment of the child both in and out of school. The discussion, so far, has indicated that remedial training programs must be based on a careful diagnosis, that consideration must be given to the child's personal worth, that the program should be suited to the individual child, that the program must be well motivated and encouraging to the child, and that abundant material, suited in difficulty, content, and style, is necessary. Such programs are designed to enable a child to improve rapidly. They are planned to control the learning environment during periods when disabilities are being treated.

Whether the treatment is conducted in the classroom or is handled by a special teacher or clinic, a small segment of the child's instructional time must be devoted to the specialized remedial program. If the disability is to be overcome and the remedial program is to prove successful, the use of the rest of the child's day must be properly adjusted as far as growth in the basic tool subject is concerned. It is necessary to study rather closely the program of the child throughout his school day, to be sure that it is compatible with the instruction he is getting in the corrective program. It is also necessary to study the child's home environment so as to be sure that no unfortunate pressures contribute to the child's learning problem nor unfortunate methods of correcting the learning problem are being tried at home. Conferences should be held with parents to identify these conditions.

Adjustments Must Be Made in the Child's School Program

The child who is in difficulty in any of the basic tool subjects is not in difficulty for only one hour in the day. He is in difficulty with those tools of learning at any time that they are being used in studying any of the content fields during the day. The child, for example, who is having difficulty with handwriting because of lack of motor co-ordination must have consideration given to his problem in all of his handwriting activities and not only during the corrective training period alone.

The growth accomplished during the remedial training period can be destroyed if unfortunate pressures and demands are placed upon the child during other times of the day. If, for example, a youngster is in a ninth-grade class and because of reading disability is able to read only fifth-grade material with profit, it does no good to offer him fifth-grade reading material during the remedial period and then confront him with material of ninth-grade difficulty for four or more hours during the day. Everything that is accomplished in the remedial period can be undone by what happens during the rest of the day.

The problem can be somewhat likened to that of a person who is threatened with pneumonia. An oxygen tent may be used to relieve the patient's breathing difficulty, but then if he is forced to go out in the cold winter air and work at hard labor for the rest of the day, the beneficial effects of the use of the oxygen tent will be destroyed. That is what often happens with children who are getting remedial help designed to correct their learning difficulty. In the remedial program proper adjustments are made, but then the children are placed in situations with which they cannot cope for the remainder of the school day. It frequently happens that the teacher makes a good adjustment to the child's reading needs during the reading period, but for the rest of the day expects the child to use basic texts appropriate for his age or grade group, but not for his reading capability, in all of his other school subjects. If the entire school day of the child is not attuned to the remedial program, then the remedial program is doomed to failure.

The Home Environment Must Be Favorable

There is ample evidence to show that if the home environment is unfavorable, the child's task of overcoming a learning disability is more difficult. Helen Robinson [3] has shown that 47 per cent of her reading cases failed to improve until faulty home conditions were corrected. It is difficult to conceive of parents who would not do everything within their power to help their child gain proficiency in a basic tool subject in which he is deficient. The parents of children in severe difficulty in reading, for example, have a right to be highly disturbed because of this disability. Frequently in

[3] Helen Mansfield Robinson, *Why Pupils Fail in Reading* (Chicago, University of Chicago Press, 1946).

such instances the parents attempt to teach the child to read. However, if the school is trying to correct the disability in one way and the parents instruct him in a way that is quite different, only confusion can result.

The parents of a child who is in difficulty in one of the tool subjects have an important role to play in correcting the disability.[4] In reading, for example, the parents should demonstrate an interest in their child's progress. They should encourage the child to read but they should avoid placing pressure upon him. The parents should listen to their child read, and they should read some of the material that he reads so that they can discuss it with him. They can take him to places of interest and discuss what they see in order to build backgrounds for materials that the child will read. They can give him a comfortable place in the house in which to read, where it is quiet and he will be free from distractions. They should go to the library with him and help him build a library of his own; and they should let the child see them read so that he knows that reading is important to adults.

If the child has too much work to do at home, this should be pointed out to the parents. If he is losing valuable rest time because of unwise use of television or because he is allowed to stay out too late at night, the proper recommendations should be made. The emphasis in home-school relationships for a youngster in serious learning difficulty should be placed on cooperatively working out what will be best for the child.

The entire school program of the child must be attuned to his educational problem. The efforts of the parents must be directed into activities beneficial to the child's re-education that they alone can perform. It must be certain that the child meets a consistent approach to the solution of his learning difficulty throughout his day.

CONTINUOUS EVALUATIONS MUST BE MADE

A fundamental principle of treatment for children with a learning difficulty which has been stressed is that remedial work must be the outgrowth of a careful diagnosis. It was pointed out in connection with this principle that the program must be altered from time to time as the child progresses toward successful achievement. In order to adjust the program to the child's changing needs as re-education progresses, it is necessary to keep a cumulative record of his experiences and attainments. It is also necessary to make the transition from the highly individualized program of treatment to the less personal regular classroom instruction as smooth as possible. Therefore a careful follow-up of the child's subsequent progress is necessary.

A Cumulative Record Must Be Kept

The need for constant study as he progresses through a program of remedial treatment necessitates a cumulative account of his progress. Such a

[4] Guy L. Bond and Eva B. Wagner, *Helping Children Learn to Read* (Chicago, Lyons & Carnahan, 1955).

record should include periodic test scores; the charts made to show the child his progress; a list of the exercises used, indicating the success of each; a list of the books he reads, indicating their interest to and suitability for the child; and an anecdotal account of any unusual incidents or of the child's reactions to the program.

As the work progresses, the teacher should review the cumulative record to study the successes and failures of the various approaches used. The teacher should relate the periods of rapid growth as shown on the charts to the learning experiences that were being employed at that time. Such periodic reviews make it possible to determine the type of teaching techniques that brought about the best results with a given child. Such a study will assist the remedial teacher to formulate a tailor-made program for the child in serious difficulty. For the child who has only a moderate amount of difficulty, a general impression of success or failure with the different teaching techniques used will suffice, but such impressions should be recorded and included in the child's cumulative folder for future reference.

A study of past case records will often recall techniques that proved successful in the treatment of similar learning problems. The remedial teacher can develop a set of case folders for various types of difficulties. In reading, for example, there could be a section of the file which deals with word-recognition cases, another section which deals with comprehension cases, and so on. The folders in each section should be tabbed to indicate the specific nature of the problems included. For example, the exact nature of a word-recognition difficulty should be specified because the treatment will vary markedly with the nature of the word-recognition problem involved. The teacher can refer to the file of cases that have been diagnosed similarly to those of the child with whom he is planning to work in order to help formulate a program for him. He will study the folder for suggestive approaches and make alterations he thinks necessary to meet the needs of the child.

A Follow-Up Is Necessary

A follow-up of the child must be made after he is no longer considered to be in learning difficulty. A child who has had a severe learning difficulty may regress if minor difficulties are not immediately corrected as they occur in his regular classroom work. The child who has overcome a learning difficulty is somewhat like a child who has recovered from a sickness. To readjust himself, a period of time must elapse between the direct treatment and the time when he again can be considered able to proceed independently. In the physical sense, this is called the period of convalescence. The child must be placed gradually on his own in the regular instructional program. His teachers should be aware that the child may become easily discouraged if his work does not progress well at the start. Therefore, special attention should be given in evaluating his adjustment and learning when he is no longer considered to be disabled. Any indications of loss of interest or of learning confusions should receive immediate attention during the readjustment period.

SOUND TEACHING PROCEDURES MUST BE UTILIZED IN THE TREATMENT OF LEARNING DIFFICULTIES

As has been implied in the entire discussion of principles underlying the treatment of learning difficulties, the teaching techniques used should be sound and directed toward meeting specific needs. Remedial techniques are not unusual in character. They should not include artificial devices and should be procedures like those found in the better developmental programs.

Organization of the learning activities is an essential element in the methods for improving a child's ability in the basic tool subjects. A remedial program must develop gradually and with care the skills underlying the tool subjects, so that the child does not encounter unusual hurdles or hazards. The directions which guide the learning activities need to be more explicit, the steps more gradual and uniform, the learning program more controlled than is the case in the regular developmental program.

A child in difficulty in spelling, for example, should not be introduced to so great a number of new words to learn that he is overwhelmed. In reading, certain aspects of the program will be emphasized and others minimized The skills are emphasized in actual reading and not in artificial drill. The same is true for arithmetic and language. Sound teaching procedures are employed such as are used for introducing the skill in the first place.

The procedures should be continued until the improved techniques have become as firmly established as in any sound instructional program. The difference between remedial programs and developmental programs lies in the degree of individualization rather than in uniqueness of method.

It must be kept in mind that a child in difficulty is likely to be insecure, so his sense of personal worth must be considered; his program must be highly individualized; it must be well motivated; it must be continuously evaluated; and the child himself must see that he is making successful progress. In addition, the treatment should not be limited to the specific time in which direct instruction is given but must be extended to include all related aspects of the child's entire learning environment both in and out of school.

SUGGESTED ACTIVITIES

1. Give illustrations of learning difficulties that normal children may have which can be diagnosed and treated in the course of regular instruction. Explain how.

2. Suppose that at the level of general diagnosis the results for a whole school system are considerably below standard in one or more of the areas tested but considerably above in others. Discuss the steps that should be taken to

determine possible causes of the unsatisfactory condition at the city level; at the level of the individual school; at the level of the classroom. Then discuss steps that may be taken to improve the situation. Draw on the local schools for illustrations of general improvement programs.

3. Suppose that at the level of analytical diagnosis the teacher discovers that certain pupils make many errors in capitalization in their written work. What may be the causes of these errors? What steps can the teacher take to improve the situation? Be specific. Illustrate also with other types of specific areas of difficulty.

4. Describe some case within your experience in which a serious learning difficulty was diagnosed by clinical procedures and then treated successfully. Apply the principles discussed in this chapter to the methods of treatment that were used.

5. Why must treatment of learning disabilities be based on a diagnosis?

6. Why must corrective treatment be individualized? How can this be done in the regular classroom?

7. What sources can the teacher draw on for corrective materials? How can they be adjusted to the needs of the individual learner?

8. What steps can the teacher take to make less likely the development of learning difficulties? Why is good teaching in fact "preventive" teaching?

9. Make a study of the methods and materials that are used by some classroom teacher to diagnose and treat learning difficulties. How can they be improved?

10. To what extent is it possible to prescribe specific remedial treatments of learning difficulties? Is there common agreement among various writers as to the methods of dealing with given learning problems? Illustrate.

11. How can the classroom teacher find the time needed for remedial instruction? Should remedial instruction be assigned to clinics or special teachers?

12. What experimental evidence is there that corrective and remedial treatment produces results?

13. What kinds of learning problems are relatively easy to correct? What types are difficult to correct?

14. Find out what local social agencies the schools can call on for assistance in the amelioration of unfavorable environmental factors. What are "co-ordinating councils"?

SELECTED BIBLIOGRAPHY

Educational Diagnosis, Thirty-fourth Yearbook, National Society for the Study of Education (Chicago, Univ. of Chicago Press, 1935), Ch. 4.

FENTON, Norman, *Mental Hygiene in School Practice* (Stanford, Calif., Stanford Univ. Press, 1943).

FERNALD, Grace M., *Remedial Techniques in Basic School Subjects* (New York, McGraw, 1943).

At the close of each of the following chapters dealing with the various areas of learning there appear special bibliographies in which are given references to methods of diagnosis and treatment of learning difficulties in these areas.

6

DIAGNOSIS IN READING

THIS CHAPTER will discuss the general background of reading outcomes and instruction necessary for an understanding of the purposes of diagnosis. It will also indicate the type of information the diagnosis is designed to ferret out and the methods of obtaining it. The following topics will be discussed:

1. The major objectives of reading instruction.
2. Principles of teaching reading.
3. Foundations of diagnosis in reading.
4. General diagnosis in reading.
5. Analytical diagnosis in reading.
6. Case-study diagnostic procedures in reading.

THE MAJOR OBJECTIVES OF READING INSTRUCTION

Reading instruction must be broader and more inclusive today than in the past if it is to meet the increased demands that are made on the reading abilities of every student. The reading program must do more than develop basic skills and techniques, although upon these the broader goals of the reading program will depend. It must develop more than the ability to group words into thought units, even though such grouping enables the reader to be a more fluent and understanding reader than would otherwise be possible. It must develop more than the ability to note details and follow directions, although such comprehension abilities allow the reader to use the printed page in a purposeful manner. Instruction must develop more than the basic study skills such as the ability to read maps, graphs, and charts to find information.

The program must, in addition, develop the attitude of wanting to find the references, establish broad interests in reading to gain information in many fields, and cultivate a taste for reading so the reader can choose material wisely. The program must develop an independent reader, one who can rely on his own resources, one who will initiate his own reading activities, and one who can appraise reading problems and adjust to the many purposes for reading. It must develop readers who can locate relevant and discard irrelevant material. It must develop readers who are able to see the relationships between things read and the problems they face. The program must develop individuals who can use many sources for getting information and who are able to organize the findings from these many sources. It must develop readers who can distinguish facts and opinions and detect propaganda or prejudice if critical judgments are to be made. It must develop readers who can draw conclusions from what has been read. It must develop readers who are able to sit down, relax, and enjoy reading and who gain from their leisure reading activities a degree of personal development and satisfaction. It must develop readers who can share interesting material with others through interpretative oral reading and discussion.

These, then, are some of the characteristics of the reader who can communicate effectively with authors. These objectives of the broader reading instruction of today give some guidance in setting up the more specific objectives of instruction that should be considered when organizing reading programs and when diagnosing a child in reading difficulty.

There is one other problem that confronts us in discussing objectives of reading instruction and that is the nature of reading growth itself. Fortunately for our discussion, reading growth is developmental in nature and takes two basic forms. First, the more mature reader is able to read material of increasing complexity which requires broader backgrounds, more mature knowledges, and more careful reorganization of these knowledges in order to get new concepts from reading. Second, the more mature reader is able to read material of increasing subject-matter specificity which requires greater adjustment of reading techniques, more highly specialized and well-defined vocabularies, and more diversified application of comprehension abilities. Fundamentally, however, he is employing reading in much the same manner as the child who is just beginning to learn to read. The characteristics of the mature reader have their start in the early reading experiences of the growing child.

The major objective of reading instruction is to aid each individual to become as able and as diversified a reader as his capabilities and the instructional time will allow. In order to meet this major responsibility, it appears that teachers at all levels must focus their attention on some specific goals, and these are the real objectives of reading instruction. Keen attention must be given to these objectives at every level of instruction if reading is to contribute to the educational goals to which all means of communication must relate.

A study of the objectives of reading instruction will show that they are formed during the child's early reading experiences and will continue to grow with each succeeding reading experience throughout the development of reading ability. It should be recognized that there is an interdependence among the objectives of reading instruction; that, for example, independence in word recognition makes comprehension abilities more possible; and that diversification of comprehension abilities makes adaptation to the materials of the content fields possible. The objectives will not be discussed in order of importance, since progress toward each is necessary for well-rounded, successful reading development. The following outline of major objectives may prove helpful:

A. MATURITY IN READING HABITS AND ATTITUDES
1. Appreciation of reading as a means of communication.
2. Habits of caring for books.
3. Intellectual curiosity and an understanding that reading can help satisfy this curiosity.
4. The attitude of demanding an understanding of all that is read.
5. The habit of attending to words and word meanings.
6. The habit of initiating reading activities.
7. The attitude of energetically attacking reading.
8. The attitude of relying on one's own resources.

B. INDEPENDENCE IN WORD RECOGNITION
1. To build a large vocabulary of words that can be recognized at sight.
2. To develop skills that enable the reader to recognize known words in their variant forms.
3. To develop proficiency in recognizing unfamiliar words by:
   a. Effective use of context and other meaning aids.
   b. Employing a systematic though flexible visual analysis of words to locate suitable recognition elements.
   c. Developing a large reservoir of visual, structural, and phonetic knowledges.
   d. Developing skill in rapidly blending or visually synthesizing the word parts into a word.

C. EFFICIENCY IN USE OF BASIC STUDY SKILLS
1. To develop skill in using various aids in locating materials to be read.
2. To build proficiency in using basic reference material.
3. To adequately interpret maps, graphs, tables, and other visual materials.
4. To develop techniques of organizing material read for retention or presentation.

D. MATURITY IN COMPREHENSION
1. To develop basic comprehension proficiencies.
   a. Word meanings including: extensiveness, descriptive words, figures of speech, and symbolic expression.
   b. Techniques for increasing vocabulary, such as use of author's definition, dictionary, structural aids to meaning, and context clues to meaning.
   c. Phrasing in thought units and to sense symbolic expressions and figures of speech in the thought units.
   d. Sentence sense.
   e. Paragraph meaning and organization.
   f. Story organization and story sense.
2. To develop ability in various types of comprehension.
   a. Retaining factual information read.

  b. Organizing information to follow directions, establish a sequence, sense relationships, and to summarize and generalize.
  c. Evaluating the information given to differentiate fanciful, fact, and opinion; to judge the reasonableness and relevancy; to sense implied meaning, and to establish cause and effect.
  d. Interpreting the information given to ascertain the main idea or general significance; to draw an inference or form an opinion; to predict the outcome or draw a conclusion.
  e. Appreciating the material read by sensing humor, plot, or action; by forming sensory impressions; and by understanding the feeling tone and the characters.

E. MATURITY IN ADJUSTING TO THE READING DEMANDS OF THE CONTENT FIELDS
  1. Adapting rate of reading to suit the content.
  2. Selecting purposes appropriate to content field.
  3. Reading interrupted content as found in geographies and arithmetic books.
  4. Reading cumulative content as found in science.
  5. Reading content designed to influence as found in the social studies.

F. BREADTH OF INTEREST IN READING AND MATURITY IN TASTES
  1. Interests in many areas of human experience.
  2. Intense desire to share experiences, ideas, and understanding with authors.
  3. Tastes that require accurate, realistic, and well-written presentations.

G. SKILL IN INTERPRETIVE ORAL READING
  1. To express an idea.
  2. To share an experience.
  3. To interpret an author.

Maturity in Reading Habits and Attitudes

The child starts early in his establishment of habits and attitudes and continues to grow in them as long as he is growing in reading capability. He soon learns to appreciate books and builds habits of caring for them. He develops the attitude of intellectual curiosity and the understanding that books can help him satisfy this curiosity. Such an attitude develops by using reading to solve individual and class problems, by reading to become an individual contributor to group enterprises, and the like. By these means, the child gradually achieves an understanding that reading is a part of written communication and he develops the attitude of wanting to share the author's experience, his factual information, his expression of point of view, and the stories that he has to tell. The habit of tending to words and word meanings is carefully nurtured in a well-rounded reading program. It starts early— when the child notices, for example, that a *trunk* is not only a part of an elephant but also part of a tree or something in which to put clothes for traveling. The habit of attending to words and demanding an understanding of their meanings is something that all teachers at all levels should encourage. The habit of relying on one's own resources and of energetically attacking material should be established early and nurtured throughout the reading program. These, then, are a few of the reading habits and attitudes that make up an important objective of reading instruction.

Independence in Word Recognition

That the reading program must build independence on the part of the reader is quite apparent. After the child ends his formal education, he must be able to continue his intellectual and personal growth. An independent reader is able to do this. One who is not so independent will not be able to use reading effectively for this growth. Independence in reading includes such attributes as adequacy in word recognition. The mature reader must have built a large sight vocabulary. In addition, the mature reader, quite obviously, must be able to recognize words rapidly and with a minimum of effort if he is to attend to the content. He must be able to work out the pronunciation and understanding of new words if he is to continue to grow in reading ability.

In order to gain independence in word recognition, it is necessary for the learner to develop a highly flexible and diversified set of word-recognition techniques. He must be able to use context and meaning clues so that he may anticipate the word, thereby making recognition rapid. He must also learn to use meaning clues as a check on the other word techniques used, so that if a faultily recognized word doesn't make sense he will re-inspect it. He must develop the ability to separate words into usable elements for recognition. The word *frighten,* for example, must be separated into *fr-ight-en* rather than *fri-ghten,* while the word *Friday* must be separated into *Fri-day.* Flexibility in visual analysis is essential to effective word recognition. The learner must establish a large reservoir of visual, structural, and phonetic knowledges so that he can recognize the parts of the words he locates by means of his visual analysis. Then he must acquire skill in reassembling the words by means of oral blending and visual synthesis so that the recognition will be complete. All of these word-recognition techniques must be developed in such a way that the more efficient and rapid approaches are used first and the more analytical are used when, and only when, needed.

Efficiency in the Use of Basic Study Skills

This set of objectives includes efficiency in locating information through the various aids such as tables of contents, indices, card catalogues, and the like. From the first day of reading instruction on, teachers are concerned with developing adequacy in the hierarchy of skills for locating information.

The teacher who says, "Our next story begins on page 8" (and writes the number 8 on the chalkboard), is starting the child on the long road that for some child will end in a degree of proficiency which will enable him to become a reference librarian in the Library of Congress. Independence in locating information includes the ability to select material adequately, to locate material in the library to meet the demands of the individual reader. After the student leaves school, he no longer has anyone to guide his reading. He must establish independence in selection, know of various sources for finding out about new material and adequate techniques for judging its suitability. The independent reader has developed the ability to initiate his own reading activities, to appraise the many reading problems, and to set his own reading purposes. Another group of basic study skills includes those required for adequate use of general reference material. The teacher who has a picture file of animals classified alphabetically, and who allows the child to locate in that file the picture of the animal he wishes to find out about, has encouraged the child's growth in efficient use of general reference material. At some points in the reading continuum, progress toward the goal is in the nature of readiness for more intensive training at a later date. At other times it is in the nature of further experience with things that have been previously introduced. But all teachers at all levels are concerned with more adequate use of general reference materials.

A third group of basic study skills concerns adequate interpretation of maps, graphs, charts, and other pictorial material. As in all other reading development, the start toward the goal of efficient use of this sort of material is begun early. The health chart in the kindergarten, indicating those children who have brought in dental certificates; a temperature graph on the bulletin board of a first-grade class that is following noonday temperatures for a given week; a map of the neighborhood showing where the police boys will be stationed for safety in crossing streets—all of these are early indications of the importance of this set of objectives of reading instruction. It would also indicate that progress toward the really important goals of reading are the concern of all teachers at all levels.

A fourth set of skills involves the techniques of organizing materials. These include such things as the mechanical aspects of outlining, the mechanical means of classifying material under a box subhead arrangement, the tabulation of class plans resulting from teacher-pupil planning, the writing of experience charts in sequential order, a time line around the room, the classifying of pictures into a sequence of stories in the prereading program; all of these are the initial indications of the fact that skill in organizing is one of the important basic study skills which are essential for well-rounded growth in reading capability. The wider use of reading as a tool of problem-solving and finding out about things gives efficiency in the use of basic study skills increased importance as an objective of reading instruction.

Maturity in Comprehension

Reading comprehension abilities which are major objectives of reading instruction can be roughly classified into five highly interrelated types: reading for specific information, reading to organize, reading to evaluate, reading to interpret, and reading for appreciation. We wish to look at only one of these types at this time. Nevertheless, all of these comprehension abilities are ever-present objectives of the teachers of reading and it would be unfortunate to leave any of them to be developed at more advanced school levels. Perhaps the group of abilities that can be wisely delayed is reading to evaluate, which includes ability to differentiate factual concepts from fanciful ones, fact from opinion; ability to judge the reasonableness of content; ability to determine the relevancy of content; ability to read critically.

If children at all levels are not working toward maturity in reading to evaluate, the printed page can easily become a tool of unscrupulous pressure groups; we know that the road to maturity in being able to detect propaganda or prejudice in the printed page or to be able to judge the reasonableness of content is a difficult one and it should be started early. The teacher, for example, who asks, "Do you think this could really happen?" when the children are reading a story about a fox who puts an ox in a bag, throws it over his shoulder, and walks away, is teaching the children to read to evaluate. Or again, the teacher who questioned whether the father was talking known fact or just informed opinion when he said that he believed the lost dog was at the neighbor's house, because he frequently went there to get a bone, is developing reading to evaluate. When the child finds that the father's informed opinion was wrong in the story, then the child begins to know the difference between fact and opinion. When children discover that authors disagree in their descriptions of homes in various countries, or disagree in their concepts of the bravery of wolves, and then follow up with the sources that we can place the most confidence in, reading to evaluate is being developed. When children appraise the meanings and overtones of words and the propaganda value of certain words and phrases, they are gaining the ability to read to evaluate. Growth toward the objective of adequate comprehension abilities of all sorts is equally developmental in nature and must be carefully nurtured throughout the reading program if adequacy of comprehension ability is to be achieved.

Maturity in Adjusting to the Reading Demands of the Content Fields

Each of the subject fields develops ways of writing suitable to the content to be handled by the authors within that field. It is necessary for the child growing in reading proficiency to learn to adjust his reading to the demands of the author and, therefore, to the demands of the type of material he is reading. Such adjustment grows out of a fine co-ordination between the various basic study skills and the various comprehension abilities. This adjustment must be taught and, therefore, is a goal of reading instruction. The child in the early primary grades, in his science reader or in reading a science unit in his basal reader, is starting his development of a differentiated attack upon various types of reading material. He should be helped to make these adjustments. As he proceeds through the reading program and as he becomes a more mature reader, he finds that one of the characteristics of maturity in writing is that of greater specificity in type of material. A differentiated attack, then, becomes an objective of reading instruction at all instructional levels.

Breadth of Interest in Reading and Maturity in Tastes

This is such an apparent objective that it needs little discussion. Quite obviously, there is little use in teaching efficient reading habits, attitudes, and abilities if the reader is to employ them on relatively inconsequential materials or if he is to employ them in completely restricted areas. Therefore, interests and tastes should be considered in the reading program.

Skill in Interpretive Oral Reading

An important objective of a well-rounded reading program is to build skill in oral reading. Skill in interpretive oral reading must rest upon the skills and abilities of the child in reading in general. A child cannot become an effective oral reader unless he is able to recognize words with great rapidity so that he can group them into thought units. He must be able to comprehend a passage before he can interpret it. He must develop an eye-voice span of several words before he can become a fluent sight reader; for, if he does not look ahead of the words he is actually saying, he is unable to interpret the meaning, feeling, action, or characterization with his voice. Therefore, most interpretive oral reading is taught in the creative activities that are part of a basic program and in the sharing of books in the recreational, personal development program.

Scope of the Reading Program

Progress through the reading program must be smooth but energetic, definite but adapted to individual rates of growth, stimulating but free from undue hazards. The child must be kept an inquisitive, energetic, and confident learner. The objectives of reading instruction are, then, to help the child to progress to greater maturity in each of the subgoals, and at the same time to so teach the use of printed materials that the broader objectives of education may be realized by youngsters confident that they have capability in this aid to intellectual and personal development.

The reading program designed to meet these broad objectives of education must itself be broad. Because of the developmental nature of reading and because of the difficulty inherent in learning to read, it is necessary for a well-rounded program to give the children four fundamental types of reading experience. One, those reading experiences designed to show the child how to read. This is frequently called the basic reading program. Two, those reading activities designed to give the child broad experience in using his growing reading abilities in all types of materials. This is frequently called the experience curriculum part of the reading program. Three, those reading experiences designed to make for personal growth and recreational appreciation. This is frequently called the children's literature or guided reading program. And, four, those reading activities designed to re-educate the child who has gotten into difficulty before that difficulty becomes involved with his personal adjustment and other types of problems. This is often called the remedial or corrective program. It is with this fourth type of reading experience that this chapter and the one to follow will deal for the most part.

PRINCIPLES OF TEACHING READING

Recently classroom teachers have been using methods of teaching reading modified by suggestions gained from studies on reading growth, studies of the general nature of learning, and those concerned primarily with child growth and development. Experience with the new methods, in the typical classroom, has shown that certain modern approaches to reading instruction have increased the rate of reading growth of children considerably. Experience has also shown it would be erroneous to suggest that traditional approaches had nothing to offer the program. Organization and concentration on the skills and abilities in a sequential order have proved necessary. However, skills and abilities must be evolved in a program that is problem-solving and creative. It must be done in a setting and done with material that is compatible with child growth and development. Such a developmental reading program has numerous important general characteristics which may be briefly summarized as follows:

1. *Modern reading programs recognize that reading growth is a natural, continuous development* rather than progress through a series of discrete steps or stages. The difference between the mature reader and the immature reader is not that one progressed through a series of stages and the other did not, but that the mature reader gradually attained clearer insights and was thereby able to solve more complex reading problems than was the less mature reader. This principle indicates that the program must be well rounded at all times, emphasizing comprehension abilities as well as the skills; emphasizing growth in interests and tastes as well as in word-recognition techniques. It implies that the teacher at the early levels is concerned with much the same problems as is the teacher at the higher grade levels.

2. *Reading programs must, in part, be well organized, sequential, and systematic.* An orderly reading program is necessary so there will be no omissions and less likelihood of overemphases. Sequential and systematic training is essential so that new skills and abilities may be introduced to the child when he has developed the prerequisites for learning them. The program recognizes that the child's maturing span of attention is gradual, so that the goals of reading should become increasingly more remote, more complex, and greater in number as the child grows older. The reading program recognizes the expanding interests and maturing tastes of the learners. It also recognizes the physical needs of a child and adjusts to the need for physical activity, especially in the early grades. It recognizes the essential need for scientific control of reading vocabulary so that the child is not overburdened. The reading program recognizes the need for the gradual introduction of word-recognition techniques, basic study skills, and diversity in comprehension abilities.

3. *Reading processes should be made meaningful.* This principle of teaching reading implies that trial-and-error learning or opportunistic learning is not effective in developing stature in reading nor is it effective in preventing reading disability. One of the teacher's major responsibilities is to help the child understand the usefulness of the skills and abilities he is learning. For example, in word recognition the structural clues to meaning are emphasized. The child is led to understand that prefixes, suffixes, and variant endings of words alter the meaning of those words. He is shown the utility of using meaning aids to check the accuracy of his word-recognition techniques. He is taught the importance of establishing a set of knowledges of word parts, such as visual, structural, and phonetic elements within words. He is taught how to adapt his reading to meet the demands of the content fields and is led to understand the importance of adjusting his rate of reading to varying purposes.

4. *The reading program should show the child how to read what he is expected to read throughout his curriculum.* This principle implies that the child is not only shown the importance of adjusting his reading skills and abilities to meet the demands of the content fields, but he is also shown how to make those adjustments. He is shown ways in which it is effective to organize materials for science, for example, as contrasted with the organization of materials for social studies. He is shown how to adjust his speed of reading to various types of materials. He is shown how to interrupt his reading. Interrupted reading is required, for example, in arithmetic, where problems are interspersed with the need for solving the problems; or in geography, where he must refer to tables or maps some pages removed from where he is reading. If reading disability is to be avoided, basic programs must systematically train the child to read all the various types of material he is expected to read.

5. *Reading instruction should anticipate reading problems the child will soon meet.* The reading program not only has the responsibility for showing the child how to read what he is expected to read throughout the curriculum, but it also has the responsibility for developing readiness for the new types of reading that he will soon meet. For example, the elementary-school program has the responsibility of developing readiness for the more systematic and specialized materials the child is going to read at the junior-high-school level. The primary program has the responsibility for developing readiness for the more systematic instruction in basic study skills which the child will meet in the intermediate grades. The kindergarten has the responsibility for developing certain attitudes, methods of work, and language facility that will develop readiness for initial instruction in reading.

6. *Reading materials should be interesting, attractive, and at the proper maturity level.* Growth in reading ability requires an energetic learner who is interested in sharing experiences, ideas, and facts with an author. Selections should be relatively short at the start and gradually increase in length as the efficiency of the reader increases. Format, pictures, and content must be suitable to the age level of the child.

7. *The material must be suitable to the reading capabilities of the child.* The materials must be nicely graded so that they can be read comfortably. If, on the one hand, the materials become too difficult, the child will lose interest in reading, make faulty approaches, and become confused in his development of skills and abilities. On the other hand, if the materials are such that they do not gradually increase in difficulty, the child will not gain stature. Modern reading programs are not *easy* reading programs. They are programs carefully planned so that the skills can be developed gradually in materials which increase in difficulty. It is likely that there is not a more effective way of creating reading disability cases than to give the youngster who has the desire to read on a certain topic material that is too difficult for him to read comfortably.

Many teachers feel that because a high level of interest in a topic will motivate a child to read material one or two grades higher than he can read comfortably, the child has gained stature. In the elementary grades quite the contrary is true. The immature reader in the early grades will use faulty approaches. If these faulty approaches become habituated and are left uncorrected, they will limit the child's reading capability for life. This does not mean that, from time to time, a child should not have material with which he has to "tussle," but it does mean that he should win the "tussle" and that most of his reading should be done in material that is comfortable for him. His recreation and other independent reading should be at a level considerably easier than that of his basic reading program. The child can be motivated to read material that is too difficult, but he will employ erroneous techniques in order to decipher it.

8. *Reading must be nurtured in a classroom environment that is friendly, is intellectually stimulating, and encourages creative work.* Because of the close relationship between reading disability and personality development, a special effort must be made to create a friendly environment, an environment that fosters feelings of security and belonging. The classroom should give evidence of intellectually energetic and creative work. Reading is best learned in a class environment that is intellectually stimulating, that provides problems to solve and creative work to do.

9. *Reading programs must adhere to the ten fundamentals of reading instruction.* Modern reading programs should be purposeful and goal-seeking. They should be in keeping with modern ways of organizing the curriculum. The child who has a real reason for reading is a more energetic reader and a more understanding reader. Modern reading programs encourage purposeful and goal-seeking reading by organizing the material in units which have a general theme to which the reading experiences contribute. The fundamentals of such instruction are:

a. Readiness must be developed at all levels of instruction for each topic studied. Effective instruction recognizes that reading is communication; that there is an author and a reader; that the author, when he wrote, made certain assumptions about the background of experience, word knowledge, and the reading capability of the children for whom he was writing. It is the teacher's responsibility to estimate the background needs of the children for each new reading unit and develop the concepts and word understandings necessary to interpret the printed page effectively.

If a third-grade class, for example, is to start reading a factual science unit in the basic reader about *Animals of the Zoo,* the teacher would help the children develop general backgrounds about zoos. The children would discuss the animals that might be seen there. They could pool their information by discussing facts they had heard, experiences they had had, or movies and television shows they had seen. Pictures of various zoo animals could be posted on the bulletin board. Labels indicating the names of the animals would introduce such new words as *elephant, giraffe, kangaroo, baboon,* and so on.

b. Pupil-teacher planning for the unit of instruction is imperative. The child who knows the purpose for reading will be a more understanding reader. He will attain the skills and abilities of reading more rapidly because he will be a more energetic reader. The teacher and children working together set up the long-range purposes for reading the unit. They also plan the constructive, linguistic, and creative work that will accompany the reading. Such careful preplanning, under the guidance and direction of the teacher, gives vitality to a reading program.

In the unit about *Animals of the Zoo* the children could inspect the pictures in their basic readers to get an overview of the topic. Then they could list some of the animals about which they will read. The children could raise study questions about these animals. These questions will set purposes for reading the factual science unit.

1. Where do these animals live?
2. How does the zoo get them?
3. What does each animal eat?
4. How do they protect themselves?
5. What unusual characteristics do they have?

The children should plan, in addition, how they will summarize what they have learned. They will consider possible creative activities to use the results of reading. They might, for example, plan to make a box television show indicating the natural environment of the animals, the foods they eat, and their means of protection. Tentative committees could be suggested but not yet formed, each to deal with a different group of animals.

c. The more immediate purposes for reading each selection within a unit must be established. In a selection about kangaroos the purpose of finding out the facts about the kangaroo given in the story could be suggested.

d. Suggestions of ways of adjusting reading to meet the purposes for reading a selection must be given. For example, in the selection dealing with kangaroos, it might be suggested that while reading, the child take notes on the facts about kangaroos so that he can make a chart which shows the physical characteristics of the animal, the foods it eats, and the various means by which the animal can protect itself.

e. The unusual or new words that the child will meet in reading the selection must be introduced prior to the reading. Such vocabulary should be introduced in meaningful content. The teacher might, for example, in discussing the pictures, prior to reading the selection, mention a new word in a sentence or a phrase and then write that word on the chalkboard in the sentence or phrase used in her conversation. Thereby the meaning of the new word and the recognition of it can be established. Also, at that time, the teacher can show the similarity of the new word to other words the children know. The teacher can develop some of the word-recognition techniques in a meaningful situation so that they will become a part of the youngsters' permanent reading equipment.

f. The selection should be read and discussed. During the silent reading of the selection, the teacher should be ready to help any child who gets into difficulty. Help can be in the form of a question that will aid the child to understand the content better or it can be in the form of helping him work out a word-recognition problem. Thus, the teacher can give instruction in the skills and abilities as the child is reading the selection silently. During the discussion, the children should be expected to go back to the story frequently to find the answers to questions raised. If a given child does not know the answer to a question, the teacher should help the child work out his reading confusion immediately rather than ask another child to give the answer.

g. The skills and abilities must be developed in connection with the selection read. The rereading and doing of exercises to develop skills and abilities must be a part of the reading. Exercises using the new words and words that have been previously introduced develop skill in seeing similarities and differences in words; develop visual analysis of words; develop the context clues; develop the structural, visual, and phonetic knowledges necessary to be effective in reading; and develop auditory and visual synthesis of words. Direct instruction is given in this phase of the program toward each of the objectives listed on page 103. Modern manuals which accompany basic reading programs offer the teacher many suggestions for this extremely important part of reading instruction. No teacher can keep in mind all of the skills and abilities necessary to facilitate growth in reading so that he can teach each in such a way that there will be no omissions or overemphases. The exercises suggested in the manuals are an essential part of the reading program. It is likely that of all the causes of reading disability, failure to recognize the importance of this phase of a reading program is the most frequent. Educators who assume that children can grow in reading by placing them in a wealth of interesting material, that the child under the guidance of the teacher will discover the ways of reading, do not fully recognize the complexities of learning to read.

h. The selections should be related to the unit as a whole. It is necessary that the individual stories and selections within a unit be related to the unit as a whole so that the child knows that each story he is reading is important. It should be recognized that the selections in a basic reader introduce the children to specific content and give the children a common background. They should then read extensively in other related materials. The purpose of the basic program is to allow children to build reading skills and abilities in an orderly fashion and in controlled situations. The skills and abilities must be practiced much more broadly than they can be in the basic reading program alone. The children thereby get the needed experience with their developing skills and abilities in the broader enrichment reading that is related to the topic introduced in the basic reading program.

After the class has read the selection on kangaroos in the unit on *Animals of the Zoo* in the basic reader, a committee to study the kangaroo and other marsupials should be formed. They will record facts given in the reader and then will explore related readings in other books to get additional information. They will also create their section of the television program that they and other committees are planning.

i. The unit must be culminated and creative use of the results of reading must be made. During the planning period which was discussed under subhead *b,* the children, under the guidance and supervision of the teacher, planned outcomes for the reading of the unit. The children should employ the results of reading in creative and linguistic activities so that the reading program has an importance in the school day and so that the children can learn to use reading as an aid to their own creative enterprises.

In the unit on *Animals of the Zoo,* the various committees will now bring together their findings, pictures for the box television, and their prepared dialogue to accompany the pictures. The television show will then be assembled and shown.

j. The learning experience should be carefully evaluated at the end of each unit. The evaluation should include the degree to which the children fulfilled their purposes; the effectiveness of their creative expression; a careful consideration of the skills and abilities learned; and an appraisal of the approaches and adjustments in reading that proved effective. The children should also estimate which books were of greatest interest and had the greatest utility for the unit.

10. *Units of instruction should include examples of a wide variety of reading activities.* There should be units that are concerned with social studies, some that are concerned with science, and others that are literary in nature. This is necessary because certain objectives of reading cannot be achieved in story material; other objectives cannot be achieved in factual material. The nature of the skills and abilities developed are closely related to the type of content.

11. *Reading instruction must be adjusted to individual rates of growth.* In order for reading instruction to be effective, the teacher must consider the individual needs and abilities of the children being taught. Diagnostic procedures are an essential element in the teaching of reading. For the most part, the teacher will use informal estimates of the needs of the children as shown in their reading of selections silently and orally, as shown by their performance in doing the exercises to develop skills and abilities suggested in the manuals, and as shown by their errors in workbook activities.

Functional groups will be formed for various types of work that is being done within the classroom. Instructional groups for teaching the basic reading program will be formed. It would be well if these groups could be reading basic readers that dealt with the same topic so that the class as a whole could share in the creative enterprises, the planning, the discussion, and the culmination of units of instruction. Committees and other interest groups will be formed to explore more fully the topic introduced in the basic reader. For example, if the children are reading about *Animals of the Zoo,* one committee might explore the life, characteristics, food, and so on, of elephants; another committee would do the same for monkeys and apes; another one for lions and tigers; another for deer, buffaloes, and antelopes; and so forth. Groups will be formed for re-education and remedial training.

For example, when it is found that some of the children have not learned to use guide letters and numbers on maps for locating places, they can be called aside for special instruction not needed by other members of the class.

12. *Oral reading should be an objective rather than a method of teaching reading.* Effective programs should develop interpretive oral reading, but oral reading as a device for teaching reading should be used sparingly. The "round-the-room" oral reading of a story, pupil after pupil, is detrimental to reading growth. On the other hand, oral reading to prove a point or to answer a specific question after silent reading is a good method of teaching effective oral reading and of developing accuracy in silent reading. A balance must be maintained between oral and silent reading, and it is likely that in the early grades a child should not be expected to read something orally that he has not read silently first.

13. *Reading situations should be pleasant and free from undue pressure.* The child who feels that he is getting along well and can use reading effectively as a tool of learning will be a far better learner than is the child who is overly anxious or fearful about his reading progress.

14. *The reading program must be broad.* The reading program includes all of the reading activities that come during the day. It includes the basic reading program which introduces the child to the skills and abilities and gives him sufficient practice in them so that there is a reasonable chance he will be able to use them throughout his school day. It includes all of the activities in which the child is using reading as an aid to learning in the content fields. In assigning materials, attention should be given to the level of the child's reading capabilities. In addition, the program should include a rich program of children's literature for his personal development in reading. Lastly, the program should make provision, at all levels, for the diagnosis and correction of reading difficulties.

A thorough understanding of the basic principles of teaching reading is necessary for both the developmental program in reading and the remedial instruction. The importance of applying these principles to remedial instruction cannot be overemphasized. The tendency to think of remedial programs as isolated drill programs is unfortunate. Effective remedial instruction must be even more carefully based upon the principles of effective reading instruction than is necessary in the developmental program. The children need a more carefully graded approach; more attention to the systematic, orderly sequence; more emphasis on the fundamentals of reading instruction than is necessary with the child of normal reading growth. It is difficult to conceive of any instruction in reading, whether developmental or remedial, that can possibly be effective if it neglects any of these principles.

FOUNDATIONS OF DIAGNOSIS IN READING

A reading diagnosis is always directed toward formulating methods for improving a given child's reading ability. The chapter on "Factors Related to Learning Difficulties" indicated that there are many conditions that may contribute to ineffective learning. The task of a diagnosis is to find out what is wrong with the child's reading and what conditions are present that must be taken into account in formulating an effective program of treatment.

A remedial program should be the outcome of a careful diagnosis. This is true whether it be a teacher who is going to formulate a corrective program for overcoming an initial confusion in the classroom, or a clinical worker dealing with a complex disability case of long duration. The difference in the two situations is one of degree and the extent to which diagnostic appraisals will need to be made. The classroom teacher and the clinician will need to develop the same understandings of the child's problem.

Reading diagnosis, just as diagnosis in any field, must meet the following standards:

1. The diagnosis must determine the general nature of the problem.
2. The diagnosis must indicate where the child can be best treated.
3. The diagnosis must clearly isolate the specific nature of the reading problem.
4. The diagnosis must indicate how improvement can be brought about most efficiently.
5. The diagnosis must detect any limiting conditions within the child that need correction or for which the program must adjust.
6. The diagnosis must locate any environmental conditions that need correcting before improvement can be expected.

The Diagnosis Must Determine the General Nature of the Problem

Not all children who are considered in difficulty in learning to read are actually in such difficulty. The first decision that the teacher or a clinician must make is whether the child is really a reading disability case or not. There are many children who are poor readers who in no way are in learning difficulty as far as reading is concerned. A child who has low verbal intelligence may, for his age level, be an inefficient, ineffective reader. Nonetheless, he may be reading even somewhat better than could be normally expected of him. This book would do a disservice to children if it did not point out that it is quite normal to expect children to grow in reading at different rates. Just because a child of low intelligence is unable to establish reading skills and abilities as rapidly as another child of higher intelligence in no way means that he is having a learning problem. A child is not considered in learning difficulty in reading unless there is a discrepancy between his general verbal and abstract reasoning capability and his reading performance.

A child in reading difficulty is one who has something wrong with his reading growth patterns, something so fundamentally wrong that it limits his reading capability and, in many instances, precludes continued progress. The teacher in the classroom must decide whether the learning difficulty is one that will correct itself with more experience, whether it is one that is negligible from the standpoint of impeding future learning, or whether it is one of such importance that it needs to be corrected in order for the child to maintain normal, balanced growth in reading.

The clinician must decide whether reading difficulty is the basic problem or whether the problem is basically something else. If the child is not basically a reading problem, but is basically a problem of low mentality, certain adjustments in instruction must be made. Those adjustments will be discussed in a special section of Chapter 7. If the child suffers from a basic emotional disturbance that precludes successful work in any field, appropriate treatment must be undertaken to relieve it. It should be pointed out, however, that children in difficulty in reading quite frequently display emotional tension. Special adjustments to the child with concurrent emotional and reading problems will be discussed in a special section of Chapter 7.

The decision as to whether or not a child who is poor in reading is basically a reading problem is not always easy to make and should be made only after a careful study.

The Diagnosis Must Indicate Where the Child Can Best Be Treated

There are three ways in which the child in reading difficulty can be treated. First, the vast majority of children having difficulty can and should be treated in the classroom by the regular classroom teacher as a part of instruction in reading. The classroom teacher must always, however, decide how much time can be spent helping one child at the expense of the other children in the class. If learning difficulties in reading are discovered early, treatment can be handled by the classroom teacher as part of his regular group work. Second, another approach is to have a remedial teacher in the school who works with groups of children needing special instruction. The remedial teacher is one who has had additional training in reading and reading disability. He has time to handle cases that need more individual attention than the classroom teacher can give. Third, another way in which the child can get remedial treatment for a reading difficulty is to be taught at an educational clinic or a reading clinic. In such a case, the child is excused from a part of his regular class work and given careful, individual clinical attention.

In order to decide where the child in reading difficulty can best be treated, the diagnostician—classroom teacher or clinical worker—needs to determine in which of the following three categories a disabled reader appears to be. It should be remembered that there is no clear line of demarcation between the categories to be discussed. They should be considered as descriptive designations. The three categories are simple retardation, specific disability, and complex disability.

Simple retardation is the descriptive category which includes children who are growing less rapidly in reading than are other children of their own age and general capability. The distinguishing feature of simple retardation is that there is nothing basically wrong with the reading pattern of the child. The child may be generally low in all types of reading because he is inexperienced. A child with interests other than those of reading might be in this category. A child who is devoting all of his spare time to playing baseball might be a case of simple retardation. He lacks experience in reading because of conflicting interests. Or a child who recently came from another country might be generally low in reading ability. He would need to gain experience in reading. Such a child might be in the sixth grade; he might have the mental capability of the other sixth-grade children, but he might have only developed the skills and abilities of the usual third-grade child. Such a child might well be a perfectly competent third-grade reader. The classroom teacher can be expected to make the adjustments necessary for the continued growth of this child. Another kind of simple retardation might be that the child is basically a capable reader, but he is inexperienced in a certain kind of reading ability. For example, he might have good general comprehension ability but he may never have learned to read to organize. His competencies in word recognition and in basic comprehension might be high, yet he would be inexperienced in this one type of reading. In this case, what is needed is to place the child into reading situations that demand greater attention to the interrelationship among the facts presented so that he can organize them. Such a child can, and should, be corrected by the classroom teacher.

If a child, then, is coming along more slowly in reading than the other children, but if his pattern of reading shows a high degree of consistency, his problems should be solved with the aid of his regular teacher. If the child is limited in one type of reading but is generally competent in other aspects of reading, his problem can and should be handled in regular classroom instruction.

Specific disability is a descriptive category which includes children who have something fundamentally wrong with their reading. There is always an interfering habit, or unfortunate emphasis, or ineffective approach present in this type of disability. The child may be using faulty word-recognition techniques. He may be either overanalytical or underanalytical. He may use excessive articulation, which limits his speed. He may lack some of the basic comprehension abilities, such as adequacy in phrasing. His entire reading growth may be stunted because of some basic reading limitation. Such a child is in serious learning difficulty which, if left uncorrected, will limit his future success in reading. Specific disability cases are frequently low in all types of reading and there is always something wrong with their general reading pattern. If the diagnosis shows that the re-education necessary to correct the specific disability case is not too time-consuming and will not require an unusually great amount of individualization, the regular class-room teacher can be expected to conduct the treatment. If, however, the condition has been allowed to persist until the faulty habit or ineffective approach has become well established, it will be necessary for the child to get his instruction from a remedial teacher in a special reading group.

Complex disability is a descriptive category that includes the more subtle cases of reading disability. Such cases are always severely retarded. They are frequently bright, capable youngsters in situations other than reading or in subjects that require reading. Approximately three out of four of them are boys. Complex disability cases are low in all types of reading. Faulty reading habits, overemphases, or gaps in learning are always present. These children have developed blockings and tensions that make them ineffective learners. They are in a downward spiral that causes increasing tensions and ever greater inefficiency in learning. These children demonstrate worry and fear in any reading situation and they frequently demonstrate a lack of desire to learn to read. They have an antagonism toward reading and they are embarrassed about reading. They are frequently lower in oral reading than in silent reading, because their insecurity increases when they must demonstrate their inadequacy in reading. This group of children needs careful, individual clinical attention.

The Diagnosis Must Clearly Isolate the Specific Nature of the Reading Problem

Locating the nature of the reading limitation is the most important phase of a diagnosis for formulating a program of correction. The remedial teacher's basic problem is that of finding what, in the reading pattern of the youngster, is retarding his growth. The study of what is really wrong with the child's reading, what faulty techniques he is using, what abilities he lacks, is essential for the formulation of a remedial program. The child may be unable to read the materials of science and the social studies or he may not have proficiency in some of the basic study skills. These limitations can be located and effective work instituted so as to overcome the specific deficiencies. However, these are not factors that limit a child's entire reading growth.

There are other limitations in the reading patterns of disability cases that have more devastating effects. Failure to establish certain skills and abilities, or the overemphasis of certain skills in the reading act, or the use of faulty approaches may interefere with the entire reading development of the child. The following classification of the more prevalent reading difficulties which seriously limit growth in reading includes the types of limitations that must be located if the diagnosis is to clearly indicate the nature of instruction that is needed:

CLASSIFICATION OF THE MORE PREVALENT READING DIFFICULTIES

A. FAULTY WORD-STUDY TECHNIQUES
1. Failure to use context and other meaning clues.
2. Ineffective visual analysis of words.
3. Insufficient knowledge of visual, structural, and phonetic elements.
4. Lack of ability in auditory blending or visual synthesis.
5. Overanalytical.
   a. Analyzes known words.
   b. Breaks words into too many parts.
   c. Uses spelling attack.
6. Insufficient sight vocabulary.
7. Orientational confusions.

B. POOR COMPREHENSION
1. Small reading vocabulary.
2. Small meaning vocabulary.
3. Lack of phrasing ability.
4. Insufficient sentence sense.
5. Lack of sense of paragraph organization.
6. Inability to adjust rate to different types of comprehension.
7. Inability to read for certain types of purposes.

C. INEFFICIENT READER
1. Excessive articulation.
2. Habits of pointing and head movements.
3. Word-by-word reader.
4. Overanalytical reader.
5. Insufficient sight vocabulary.
6. Dawdling over reading.
7. Lack of ability to attend.
8. Attempting to read too fast.

D. POOR ORAL READER
1. Insufficient eye-voice span.
2. Trying to maintain too great an eye-voice span.
3. Poor timing.
4. Poor phrasing.
5. Unnatural voice.

The Diagnosis Must Indicate How Improvement Can Be Brought About Most Efficiently

A corrective program must be very efficient, since it must develop reading capabilities at an accelerated rate. The purpose of the re-educative program is to overcome unfortunate approaches to reading that have limited or are likely to limit the child's reading growth. In order to make the program as efficient as possible, several decisions must be made as a result of the diagnosis. First, a decision about the level of difficulty of the material to be used must be made. The selection of the appropriate level of difficulty must be determined by the child's general reading capability and also by the nature of his limitation. As has been previously stated, if the child is a slow reader because he is overanalytical, material that has few, or no, word difficulties should be used to increase his speed. If the child is in difficulty because he lacks word-study techniques, then he should have material that contains a sufficient number of new words so that he will get practice in applying word-study techniques. In all types of remedial reading, the child should be offered material he can read comfortably. The exact level of the material, within the range of comfortable reading, must be decided by the outcomes that are expected from reading that material.

Topics that are highly interesting to the child must be selected because interest is the motivating force and the driving power. Frequently, children who are in serious trouble in reading have grown intellectually so far away from their reading capability that it is difficult to find material that is interesting and suitable in format and at the low reading level required. Gerald, a 12-year-old boy with an IQ of 122, was rather uncomfortable when he was reading beginning second-grade material. His diagnosis showed that he needed more adequate word-study techniques. The pattern of word-study techniques showed that he was relatively high in visual analysis of words; he had a knowledge of visual, structural, and phonetic elements equal to the usual fifth-grade child; but he had a very limited sight vocabulary and a marked tendency to analyze even the few words he knew. He was depending upon independently recognizing each word he met in print as though it were entirely new. It was felt that Gerald should be offered reading material that was suitable to the usual first-grade child. The suggestion was made to the boy that he could be helpful to the clinical workers. He was told that often other boys who were as old as he came to the clinic to get help in learning to read. It was suggested to Gerald that he could help in surveying some reading material to find out if he thought the other boys who were having difficulty could read it and if they would be interested in it. He was also asked to find what facts the materials contained. This extrinsic approach was used because there were no interesting materials available to this boy who had rejected reading.

In order to make instruction more efficient, methods of showing a child his growth in reading should be worked out. If the problem is primarily one of speed, a chart showing gain in rate can be made. If the problem is one of building sight vocabulary, a card file of words learned may be kept. If the problem is one of comprehension difficulties, accuracy charts will be planned. If the problem is one of poor oral reading, a periodic series of tapes is suggested. Lastly, an estimation of the approximate length of time for each training period should be made.

The Diagnosis Must Detect Any Limiting Conditions Within the Child That Need Correction or to Which the Program Must Be Adjusted

For the re-education program to be effective, any limitations in the child which might influence reading growth detrimentally must be isolated. If the child has poor vision, such a limitation should be noted. If there is any indication of poor hearing, speech defect, or lack of blending ability, that, too, should be noted. Whenever possible, such limitations should be corrected prior to the start of a remedial program. Where no correction is possible, the program must be altered to adjust to known limitations.

The Diagnosis Must Locate Any Environmental Conditions That Need Correcting Before Improvement Can Be Expected

There are certain limitations within a child's environment that have an influence upon the success of a remedial program. If the home and school are not working together consistently, the child's growth in reading will be impaired. The entire program must be co-ordinated if the child who is in difficulty is to progress satisfactorily. Sometimes, in their zeal to help their child, parents create emotional tensions that do not help his reading and disturb the child greatly. A child in difficulty dislikes immensely to have to demonstrate it to his parents. At times, the approaches used by parents are unfortunate for the child. At times, the school situation is not conducive to effective development of reading. The diagnosis, then, must attempt to locate any irritants within the environment of the child that will impede his progress in learning to read.

GENERAL DIAGNOSIS IN READING

Diagnosis in reading should start with the more simple, general, and more common differentiations and progress to the more complex, specialized, and unusual. A diagnosis should go no farther than is necessary to formulate educational adjustments that will correct the difficulty. The first level of diagnosis can be called general diagnosis. By general diagnosis is meant the securing of general information about level of performance in the more common aspects of reading growth. To secure information of this sort, many schools give periodic achievement tests. From these, a comparison of the child's performance in various subject-matter fields can be made. The teacher can see the relative stature of a given child in reading, arithmetic, science information, social studies, and so on. A general diagnosis should also include an estimate of the child's general intelligence.

By comparing the child's mental grade status, his reading grade status, and his level of performance in other fields, it is possible to make an estimate of whether or not a child is having difficulty with reading. That is, is he or is he not a reading disability case? If his reading performance is approximately in line with his mental level and his success in other fields of learning, the child can be considered as suited to the regular developmental program. He is not in need of further specialized diagnosis in reading. Of course, the teacher of the developmental program must be a constant student of each child whose reading growth he is directing. In regular class work the teacher must constantly make a systematic study of every child's performance in an analytical, diagnostic fashion.

If the child is lower by a significant amount in reading ability than he is in mental stature or in the subject-matter fields that are not dependent upon successful reading, such as arithmetic computation, there is indication that a further diagnosis is needed. The general diagnosis, then, helps the teacher to locate, among the children in the class, those few who are educationally handicapped by ineffective reading.

The teacher has available three types of information for making a general diagnosis.

1. Standardized tests.
2. Informal objective tests.
3. General observation.

Standardized Tests

The standardized tests useful in general diagnosis in reading are the survey or achievement-type tests. These tests should be given periodically, preferably at the beginning of the school year. There are many values in surveying the reading attainments of children. The results can be used by administrative officers in planning the year's program. As an outgrowth of such initial surveys, the administrators might encourage the teachers to make a study of reading and reading improvement during the year. Knowledge of the number of children who need special attention would indicate whether or not a remedial teacher was necessary. A study of the results might indicate the need for the purchase of additional material to meet the wide range of reading capability with which the teacher must cope.

Probably the greatest use for standardized tests is in estimating the instructional needs and adjustments to individual differences that must be made by the teacher, and in identifying those students who need a more detailed diagnosis.

Perhaps an examination of a typical fourth-grade class will demonstrate the use a teacher could make of general diagnosis in her class. The table below indicates the results of a survey of reading capabilities and mental ability given at the beginning of the school year. The tests used were the 1937 revision of the Stanford-Binet for measuring intelligence and the Gates Reading Survey for measuring reading ability. The Gates Reading Survey measures three general reading characteristics: level of comprehension, vocabulary, and speed of reading. The grade scores in reading are arrived at from the table of norms given in the test booklet. The grade score indicates the performance of the average child at a given grade level. For example, if a child in the fourth grade receives a reading grade score of 2.5, it means that he reads as well as the average child midway through the second grade. The mental ages, as measured by the Stanford-Binet, have been changed into grade scores as have the chronological ages of the children. This makes possible a direct comparison between chronological grade, mental grade, and reading grade.

TEST INFORMATION ABOUT A BEGINNING FOURTH-GRADE CLASS

| | CHRONO-LOGICAL GRADE | MENTAL GRADE | GATES READING SURVEY | | | |
			Power of Compre-hension	Vocabu-lary	Speed	Average Reading Grade
Above 8.0					1	
7.5-7.9			1	1	1	
7.0-7.4				2	2	2
6.5-6.9		1	2	1	1	1
6.0-6.4		1	1	2	2	2
5.5-5.9		3	3	3	2	3
5.0-5.4		4	3	2	3	2
4.5-4.9	6	5	6	5	4	6
4.0-4.4	21	6	6	4	5	5
3.5-3.9	8	6	5	4	3	4
3.0-3.4		5	3	3	4	3
2.5-2.9		2	1	4	2	3
2.0-2.4		1	2	2	2	2
Below 2.0		1	2	2	3	2
AVERAGE	4.1	4.2	4.3	4.2	4.4	4.3

N = 35

An inspection of the table above by the teacher will give much useful information. First, the teacher knows that he has a rather typical class. The average mental grade of his group is 4.2, which indicates that the class is only slightly in advance of an average class. The average reading grade of his group is slightly higher, being 4.3; this means three months through the fourth grade. This indicates that his class, on an average, is doing fairly well in reading. A further inspection would indicate that the class is rather uniform in its attainments in reading. The average power of comprehension is 4.3, average vocabulary is 4.2, and average speed of reading is 4.4. It would seem then, on the basis of the above-average performance of his class, that this teacher was confronted with no reading problem.

A further study, however, would reveal some important information. First, that he has a rather large problem of adjusting materials and methods to individual differences. A child at the fourth-grade level is well suited to a typical fourth-grade book if he is within a half-year in his general reading ability of that book. If we inspect the average reading ability of these children, we will see that there are fifteen children within the class who are instructionally suited to a fourth-grade basal reader.

There are ten children who are below 3.5 in reading ability and are therefore unsuited to a typical fourth-grade reading book. There are ten children who are above fifth-grade in reading ability and they will therefore need an expanded reading program. Actually, it would be well to let these latter children read the fourth-grade reader to develop the skills and abilities it is designed to teach, and then they should be expected to be resource readers for the units of instruction and should do a great deal of personal development reading, in excess of that which is expected of the typical members of the class.

There are seven children within the class who are reading a year or more lower than a typical fourth-grade child. The test scores of these seven children should be studied further to find out if they are in learning difficulty or are getting along as well as can be expected of children of their mental capability. The seven children retarded over a year in reading growth do not necessarily constitute all of the children who are in need of further analysis. As a matter of fact, in order to locate the children who are in reading difficulty, the teacher will need to inspect the profiles of all members of the class.

Such a study of this fourth-grade class indicated that five children were in reading difficulty and needed further diagnosis. Of these five children, three came from the group of seven who were reading over a year below their grade placement. Four of the children who were reading more than a year below their grade placement were found to be doing a reasonably effective job. Their reading ability was either at, or above, their mental level. They could not, therefore, be considered in reading difficulty.

The figure below shows the results of the further inspection of the general diagnosis in the case of three children, two of whom would be considered in reading difficulty and one who was not. The figure shows that Mary was a child with much less than average mental ability. Her chronological grade of 4.9 shows that she was one of the older children in the class. She had been retarded one year. A study of the figure shows that her mental grade places her next to the lowest in the room. Her IQ of 70 was the lowest in the class. Mary was doing a rather remarkable job of learning to read. She was reading approximately a half year higher than would be expected from a child of her mental level. Mary needs an adjusted curriculum and a reappraisal of expected outcomes. An appropriate adjustment for Mary will be discussed in the next chapter.

Peter is in rather serious difficulty in reading. A comparison of his mental grade and average reading grade indicates that he is more than a year and a half retarded in his reading development. Peter is a boy of average intelligence who is exceedingly low in reading power of comprehension and vocabulary. He needs to be studied further in order to determine the nature of his instructional needs.

PROFILES OF THREE CHILDREN BEGINNING FOURTH-GRADE

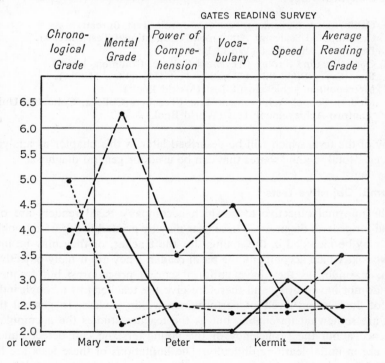

GATES READING SURVEY

Kermit is an extreme reading disability case, although he is reading only one half-year below his grade placement. He is reading two and a half years lower than is expected of a child of his mental capability. Kermit is one of the younger members of the class, but his IQ of 120 indicates that he should be reading at approximately the sixth-grade level instead of 3.5, his average reading grade. A thorough analysis of Kermit and his reading strengths and weaknesses will need to be made in order to locate the specific nature of his disability so that appropriate remedial training can be given.

A general diagnosis shows the teacher the instructional needs in his class, indicates some of the adjustments that are necessary to take care of individual differences, and helps him locate children who are in need of further diagnosis. Standardized tests are desirable in making a general diagnosis because the norms which accompany them enable the teacher to make the necessary comparisons with a high degree of accuracy.

The tests used for general diagnosis in the field of reading must, to a degree, be analytical. This is true because the complex nature of reading growth and development makes it imperative that no single type of test be used as the full criterion for judging a child's stature. The following survey and achievement tests are suitable for general diagnosis. They also have some analytical value:

1. California Achievement Test (California Test Bureau).
2. Co-ordinated Scales of Attainment (Educational Test Bureau).
3. Detroit Reading Test (World Book).
4. Gates Reading Survey (Teachers College, Columbia Univ.).
5. Iowa Every Pupil Silent Reading Test (Houghton Mifflin).
6. Metropolitan Achievement Test (World Book).
7. Modern School Achievement Test (Teachers College, Columbia Univ.).
8. Stanford Achievement Test (World Book).

Many of the tests which will be described later in this chapter as analytical tests give total reading scores that can be used for general diagnosis.

Informal Objective Tests

The informal objective tests which accompany basal readers are often useful for general diagnosis. These tests may be printed in separate booklets, they may be included in the manual for the teacher, or they may be in the workbooks which accompany the basal reader. They are usually objective in form, inasmuch as they have uniform scoring procedures, but frequently they do not have norms and therefore give the teacher just a rough indication of the varying levels of performance within a class. In general these tests are somewhat unreliable, but as the teacher studies the accumulating evidence about the proficiency of the youngsters, he can detect children who are in initial learning difficulty. The limitations of these tests are their unreliability and the lack of norms. The advantages are that they are measuring outcomes directly related to the instructional program, using the same vocabulary, and are interspersed so that a continued diagnosis is possible.

Another type of informal objective test is that constructed by the teacher. Quite frequently teachers find it expedient to construct tests of their own to measure specific outcomes of instruction. These teacher-made objective tests have the advantage of being directly related to the teacher's instruction. Results of these tests augment the information derived from the standardized tests and the tests accompanying basal reading programs. Information about the construction of teacher-made tests and sources of information on general evaluating procedures is contained in Chapter 2. It is necessary to mention here only that the use of teacher-made tests to appraise the child's learning of immediate objectives is an important phase of continued diagnosis. It is the use of such tests that enables the teacher to detect the onset of a reading difficulty so that immediate correction can be made, thereby preventing more serious trouble.

General Observation

Among the most important methods of general diagnosis is the day-by-day observation of the children by the teacher. Many outcomes of reading instruction cannot be measured effectively by standardized procedures. Such observations as the interest displayed by the children, the application of their reading to the solution of their own or class problems, the degree to which the children initiate reading activities of their own, the extent to which they contribute to class discussions from their own reading, the effectiveness of their oral reading before an audience, the sense of responsibility shown in class reading enterprises, and other indications of reading habits, interests, and attitudes are best made by the teacher in his day-by-day contacts with the children. Suggestions for making systematic observations are given in Chapter 2. The day-by-day observations of the teacher contribute to his understanding of the children's growth and development in reading, their attitude toward reading, and their interest in reading.

The teacher should enter the results of his systematic observations in the cumulative record of each child. The teacher should note any loss of interest in reading on the part of a child, any inefficiency in his reading activities, or any inaccuracies in his contributions derived from reading. Any of these conditions are indicative of the need for a more analytical diagnosis.

ANALYTICAL DIAGNOSIS IN READING

The purpose of analytical diagnosis in reading is to detect the areas in which a child's limitations exist so that a more exact understanding of his learning difficulty may be derived. An analytical diagnosis would show whether the child's difficulty is in word-recognition techniques, comprehension, reading efficiency, oral reading ability, or in the basic study skills. An analytical diagnosis might also give information as to how well the child is able to adapt his reading capabilities to meet the demands of the content fields. An indication of his reading success in science, social studies, literary materials, and mathematical materials might be sought through analytical diagnosis.

In order to make an analytical diagnosis, the teacher should have information on the child's relative level of performance in the general areas of word recognition, comprehension, speed, basic study skills, and oral reading. In addition, the teacher should have information about the child's status in reading within these general areas. For example, it is important for the teacher to make a comparison between the child's sight vocabulary and his independent word-recognition techniques. In the area of comprehension, the teacher, for example, should know a child's ability to retain factual information read, his ability to organize information, his ability to evaluate and interpret information, and his ability to read for appreciation. In the same area, the teacher should have some evidence of the child's ability to read the materials of science, literature, and social studies. As a result of the analytical diagnosis, the teacher can find the nature of instruction that is required for many of the disability cases and the diagnosis need go no further.

In watching the growth of children in the regular developmental program in reading, the teacher must also study the relative extent to which each child is developing in these basic areas and the major parts within the areas. This sort of analytical diagnosis is important for studying the child who is in marked reading difficulty and for studying the pattern of growth of children in the regular developmental program. The teacher has available two types of appraisal for making analytical diagnoses: standardized tests and informal appraisals.

Standardized Tests

There are available many standardized tests that will help the teacher make a systematic, analytical diagnosis of the child's growth in reading. By administering well-selected standardized tests, the teacher can determine instructional needs within his class. He may find that entire areas of reading instruction have been neglected to the point that the class in general is low in a specific ability. Or he may find that while the class in general is progressing rather uniformly in the various reading areas, there are certain individuals within the class who have deficiencies in some specific phases of the reading program. The teacher may also find, from a careful appraisal of his analytical diagnoses, that certain children need further study of their reading problems through case-study techniques.

The tests that are suitable for analytical diagnosis are group tests which give the teacher a set of scores upon which to make judgments about the relative stature of each child. The standardized norms enable the teacher to make comparisons among the various subtests, thereby enabling him to locate the areas of need for the class as a whole or for individual members within the class. The following tests are suitable for analytical diagnosis:

TESTS SUITABLE FOR ANALYTICAL DIAGNOSIS

Name of Test	Suitable for Grades	Abilities Measured	Publisher, Year
Developmental Reading Tests, G. L. Bond, T. Clymer, C. Hoyt Primer, Upper Primary, Lower Primary	1-3	Part I. Basic Vocabulary. Part II. General Comprehension. Part III. Specific Comprehension.	Lyons and Carnahan, 1955
Intermediate	4-6	Part I. Basic Vocabulary. Part II. Reading to Retain Information. Part III. Reading to Organize. Part IV. Reading to Evaluate-Interpret. Part V. Reading to Appreciate. Part VI. Basic Study Skills.	
Diagnostic Examination of Silent Reading Abilities, M. J. Van Wagenen and A. Dvorak	4-12	Rate of comprehension. Perception of relations. Vocabulary in context. Vocabulary in isolation. Range of gen. information. Central thought ability. Ability to note clearly stated details. Interpretation. Interpretation of dispersal ideas. Ability to draw inferences.	Educational Test Bureau, 1940
Garvey Primary Reading Test, H. S. Read and M. V. Seagel	1-3	Recognition of words and phrases. Vocabulary. Comprehension of details. Comprehension of simple facts.	California Test Bureau, 1936
Gates Primary Reading Test	1-2	Word recognition. Sentence reading. Paragraph reading.	Teachers College, Columbia Univ., 1943
Gates Advanced Primary Reading Test	2-3	Word recognition. Paragraph reading	Teachers College, Columbia Univ., 1943
Gates Basic Reading Tests	3-8	Appreciate general significance. Predict outcomes. Understand directions. Note details.	Teachers College, Columbia Univ., 1943
Gates Reading Survey	3-10	Vocabulary. Power of comprehension. Speed. Accuracy.	Teachers College, Columbia Univ., 1939
Greene-Noar Self-Diagnostic Reading Test	3-8	General significance. Ability to select facts. Ability to understand directions.	Heath, 1931

TESTS SUITABLE FOR ANALYTICAL DIAGNOSIS (Continued)

Name of Test	Suitable for Grades	Abilities Measured	Publisher, Year
Instructional Reading Tests, M. J. Nelson	4-6	Level of reading ability. General significance. Note details. Logical outcomes. Vocabulary.	Houghton Mifflin, 1938-1939
Instructional Test in Reading, P. V. Sangren and M. C. Wilson	1-4	Many abilities, such as: Word recognition. Phrase recognition. Recognition of meaning of word. Association of rhyme or sentence with illustration. Following directions. Noting details. Understanding sentences. General significance. Anticipating meanings. Using judgment. Organization of ideas.	Public School Publishing Co., 1932
Iowa Test B—Basic Study Skills—Elem. Battery, E. Horn, M. McBroom, H. A. Greene, E. F. Linquist	3-5	Reading maps. Use of references. Use of index. Use of dictionary. Alphabetizing.	Houghton Mifflin, Yearly
Iowa Test B—Basic Study Skills— Advanced Battery, E. Horn, M. McBroom, H. A. Greene, E. F. Linquist	5-9	Reading maps. Use of references. Use of index. Use of dictionary. Reading graphs, charts, tables.	Houghton Mifflin, Yearly
Iowa Silent Reading Test, H. A. Greene and V. H. Kelley	4-9	Rate of reading at a controlled level of comprehension. Comprehension of words, sentences, paragraphs, and longer articles. Alphabetizing. Indexing.	World Book, 1943
Primary Reading Every Pupil Test	2-3	Sentence recognition. Word recognition. Directions. Details. Larger meanings.	State Department of Education, Columbus, Ohio, Yearly
Progressive Reading Tests, E. W. Tiegs and W. W. Clark	1-2	Word recognition. Word form. Meaning of opposites. Following directions. Directly stated facts. Interpretations.	California Test Bureau, 1937

TESTS SUITABLE FOR ANALYTICAL DIAGNOSIS (Continued)

Name of Test	Suitable for Grades	Abilities Measured	Publisher, Year
Progressive Reading Tests, E. W. Tiegs and W. W. Clark	3-6	Word form. Word recognitions. Meaning of opposites. Meaning of similarities. Following directions. Interpretations. Organization.	California Test Bureau, 1937
Progressive Reading Tests, E. W. Tiegs and W. W. Clark	7-9	Vocabulary—mathematics, science, social science, literature. Following directions. Organization. Interpretations.	California Test Bureau, 1937
SRA Reading Record, Guy T. Buswell	7-12	Rate. Comprehension. Paragraph meaning. Directory reading. Map, table, graph reading. Advertisement meaning. Index reading. Sentence meaning. Vocabulary—technical and general.	Science Research Associates, 1947
Silent Reading Test, E. Horn, M. Mc-Broom, H. A. Greene, E. F. Linquist *Elementary Battery*	3-5	Vocabulary. Paragraph comprehension. Noting detail. Organization of ideas. Grasping total meaning.	Houghton Mifflin, 1945
Advanced Battery	5-9	Vocabulary. Paragraph comprehension. Noting detail. Organization of ideas. Grasping total meaning.	Houghton Mifflin, 1945

The figure on page 134 shows the results of an analytical diagnosis for three members of a fourth-grade class at the start of the school year.

General diagnosis had revealed that Kermit and Peter were in difficulty in learning to read. Helen had not shown such an over-all deficiency. However, an inspection of Helen's relative scores on the analytical diagnosis in the figure shows that she is a case of simple retardation in one phase of comprehension. In general, Helen is a perfectly competent reader. Her average reading grade on the Gates Reading Survey is slightly in excess of her mental grade. This indicates that, in general, Helen is doing a good job of learning to read. Her profile shows, however, that she is low in one type of reading—reading to predict outcomes, in which she is more than a year lower than would be expected of a girl with her mental ability and general

AN ANALYTICAL READING DIAGNOSIS OF THREE CHILDREN BEGINNING FOURTH GRADE

B = indicates the lowest score possible.
Helen ----- Peter ——— Kermit ------

reading ability. It is likely that Helen is inexperienced in this type of reading and that a short, concentrated period of instruction on the predicting of outcomes will make Helen as proficient in this type of reading comprehension as she is in the others.

In the figure on page 134, Kermit's score shows a very uneven profile. The analytical diagnosis of Kermit shows that he is low in the more general types of comprehension, Types *A* and *B* on the Gates Basic Reading Test, and somewhat higher on the more detailed types of comprehension, Types *C* and *D*. On Tests I and II of the Silent Reading Diagnostic Tests, Kermit was considerably higher on recognizing words in isolation than he was on recognizing words in content. In fact, Kermit's highest reading score was in recognizing isolated words. He also showed as his highest score on the Gates Reading Survey the vocabulary test. Kermit needs further study by case-study diagnostic approaches.

In the figure, Peter is seen to be low in all types of reading and must be studied further. The analytical diagnosis of Peter shows that further information is necessary to solve his problem. There is only one score that even approaches his mental capability and that is the score on speed. An inspection of the speed test, however, shows that there was a high degree of inaccuracy and therefore even Peter's speed score should not be considered a good performance because speed without accuracy is a questionable attribute.

It can be seen from these three illustrative cases that an analytical diagnosis will give enough information to the teacher to formulate an instructional program for certain children. Helen, in the above illustration, is such a case. She has been diagnosed sufficiently to know her reading needs. In the case of other children, the analytical diagnosis enables the teacher to isolate the areas of reading that must be studied further. Kermit, for example, needs careful study in the area of comprehension. However, there is a rather distinct possibility that his high score on words in isolation, along with his low score on speed of reading and the more general types of comprehension, indicates that Kermit may be an overanalytical reader. He has not maintained a balance between analyzing words and building sight vocabulary. It is likely also that he has failed to discover that certain types of reading can be done rapidly and other types should be done with more care. A further study of Kermit is necessary in order to find out the specific nature of his difficulty. In still other cases, as in the case of Peter, analytical diagnosis will indicate to the teacher that the child is extremely poor in reading but gives no clue to the area in which he is poor.

An estimate might be made at this time that Helen is a case of simple retardation, that Kermit is a case of specific disability, and that Peter is a case of complex reading disability which necessitates careful, clinical, remedial instruction. Standardized test procedures enable the teacher to make systematic comparisons which are impossible by informal procedures.

Informal Appraisals

Informal approaches to analytical diagnosis are most effective in the day-by-day study of the children's growth in the developmental reading program. Through informal appraisal techniques of the analytical sort, the teacher may detect the onset of such difficulties as were described in the cases of Helen, Peter, and Kermit.

The teacher may also use informal analytical approaches in the study of individuals who are in as advanced a stage of difficulty as are Peter and Kermit. The most discriminating informal approaches to analytical diagnosis are found in the use of workbook exercises and of exercises described in teacher's manuals which accompany basic readers for developing basic skills and abilities. In the back of most modern basic reading-program workbooks will be found an index of exercises that are included to develop the very skills and abilities that should be appraised in an analytical diagnosis. The teacher can detect readily a child who tends to miss an unusual number of items in any specific type of exercise. Using the workbook, then, as a work sample of the child's skills and abilities, the teacher may diagnose the child's instructional needs. A sample of such an index will illustrate this source of procedures useful in informal appraisal.[1]

INDEX OF READING PROFICIENCIES *

I. COMPREHENSION ABILITIES

   A. *Reading to retain information*
       1. Isolate details: 6, 10, 27, 38, 59, 62, 72, 75, 85
       2. Recall specific items: 16, 26, 29, 39, 59, 64, 75, 90
       3. Retain fundamental concepts: 7, 8, 26, 28, 39
       4. Using facts to answer specific questions: 26, 39, 59, 62, 74

   B. *Reading to organize*
       1. Classify: 16, 20, 63, 66, 67, 80, 81, 83, 89, 91, 92
       2. Establish sequence: 16, 55, 68, 71, 77
       3. Follow directions: 18, 33, 37, 55, 76, 83
       4. Sense relationships: 4, 14, 15, 28, 63, 87, 91
       5. Summarize and generalize: 51, 55, 92

   C. *Reading to evaluate*
       1. Fact from opinion: 2, 3, 78
       2. Judge reasonableness and relevancy: 23, 28, 60, 72, 78
       3. Sense implied meaning: 12, 77
       4. Establish cause and effect: 14, 15, 50

   D. *Reading to interpret*
       1. Main idea: 11, 30, 31, 40, 44, 51
       2. Draw inference or conclusion: 4, 6, 7, 8, 12, 26, 28, 29, 40, 41, 43, 58, 60, 74, 77, 79, 86, 89

* Numbers after headings give pages on which specific experience is given.

[1]Guy L. Bond and Marie C. Cuddy, *Fun to Do Book for Meeting New Friends,* Teachers Ed. (Chicago, Lyons & Carnahan, 1954).

3. Predict outcome: 6, 7, 8, 10, 31, 34, 49
4. Form an opinion: 7, 8, 41, 60, 73, 79, 86, 90

E. *Reading for appreciation*
   1. Sense of humor and plot: 48, 50
   2. Form sensory impressions: 25, 33, 52, 58, 61, 70, 88, 93, 94
   3. Understand characters: 2, 3, 33, 48, 64, 73

II. BASIC STUDY SKILLS

A. *Location of information*
   1. Table of contents: 1
   2. Alphabetized references: 9, 95
   3. Skimming: 10, 12

B. *Using general references*
   1. Dictionary and glossary: 9, 13, 17, 19, 35, 56, 76
   2. Encyclopedia: 38, 91

C. *Using visual material*
   1. Maps: 18, 22, 53, 82
   2. Pictorial and tabular: 16, 25, 48, 64, 71, 72

D. *Organizing*
   1. Outlining: 16, 68, 77, 87
   2. Grouping or catagorizing: 20, 63, 77, 80, 83, 89, 91, 92

III. BASIC MEANING DEVELOPMENT

A. *Paragraph meaning and organization:* 30, 40, 44, 45, 46, 64, 72

B. *Sentence sense:* 66, 67, 81

C. *Word meaning*
   1. Context clues to meaning: 5, 8, 24, 35, 36, 37, 52, 54, 56, 57, 58, 76
   2. Dictionary and glossary: 17, 56, 76
   3. Antonyms, synonyms, and homonyms: 5, 7, 24, 37, 54, 56, 57, 58, 76
   4. Extensiveness of meaning (semantic variations): 17, 35, 37, 54, 58, 76
   5. Enriching meanings (descriptive words, figures of speech, symbolic expressions): 4, 8, 25, 36, 47, 52, 58, 61, 70, 93, 94

IV. WORD-RECOGNITION TECHNIQUES

A. *Meaning aids*
   1. Context clues to recognition: 5, 7, 8, 24, 35, 37, 56, 76, 89
   2. Expectancy clues: 4, 20, 52, 87

B. *Visual and structural aids*
   1. Root words: 21, 32, 42, 69
   2. Prefixes and suffixes: 21, 32, 42, 69
   3. Syllabification: 19, 32, 52, 69, 84

C. *Auditory and phonetic aids*
   1. Vowel and consonant sounds: 13, 19, 83, 84, 96
   2. Diacritical markings and pronunciation aids: 13, 17, 19, 32, 34, 70, 76
   3. Blends and digraphs: 96
   4. Synthesis (blending and accent): 13, 19, 32, 34, 40, 70

V. CREATIVE WORK
   A. *Writing and speaking:* 17, 23, 25, 29, 31, 34, 45, 46, 65
   B. *Drawing:* 33, 85, 88
   C. *Constructing:* 55

Similar lists of exercises designed to develop reading skills and abilities will be found in the index of proficiencies in the teacher's manuals that accompany basic readers. These can be used as work samples for diagnostic purposes. In addition, the teacher can informally study the child's capability by means of teacher-prepared objective tests as well as by means of noticing his successes and failures with specific types of reading assignments.

CASE-STUDY DIAGNOSTIC PROCEDURES IN READING

A thorough case-study diagnosis includes the use of the standardized tests employed in general and analytical diagnosis, individual standardized tests, detailed silent reading diagnostic tests, and informal study of the child's approaches to the various aspects of reading. It also includes an analysis of the child's strengths and limitations as an individual—his sensory capacities, his emotional reactions, and his attitudes toward reading. A case-study diagnosis must satisfy the general requirements of the principles of diagnosis listed on page 78.

The first principle is that the diagnosis must determine whether or not the child is a reading case. This is answered by the general diagnosis and the analytical diagnosis for the most part. However, from time to time, a case-study approach will indicate that the child's major problem is something other than an extreme disability in reading. For example, the case study may show that the child is actually an emotionally disturbed child and that his reading is handicapped for this reason. Usually, in such a case it is best to attack the two problems simultaneously, but in certain instances the emotional disturbance is so acute that a start on the solution of that problem needs to precede the solution of the reading problem. This situation is very unusual but should be recognized when it occurs. It may be found that the child is suffering from a neurological disorder, such as petit mal epilepsy, and that because of recurrent seizures, the child is unable to read efficiently.

The second principle, that the diagnosis must indicate where the child should be treated, is frequently served by the analytical diagnosis. The analytical diagnosis indicated that Peter, described above, needed clinical attention.

The third principle, that the diagnosis must clearly isolate the specific nature of the reading problem, is sometimes answered by the general diagnosis, as in the case of Mary. The specific nature of her problem was isolated as being one of low mentality, with the child reading about as well as could be expected. The adjustment indicated was a change to methods suitable to children of less than normal abstract and verbal capability, and an alteration of the expected outcomes from that instruction.

Helen's reading problem was indicated by the analytical diagnosis. Helen was a case of simple retardation. She was perfectly competent in most types of reading but needed attention in reading to predict outcomes. In her case, it was possible to formulate the corrective program from the analytical diagnosis.

The cases of Peter and Kermit are somewhat different. Although there were indications of Kermit's needs as a result of the analytical diagnosis, the specific nature of those needs could not be determined without a detailed case study. The analytical diagnostic tests gave no indication of Peter's instructional needs.

The fourth principle, that the diagnosis must indicate how improvement can be brought about most efficiently, could have been fulfilled in the cases of both Helen and Mary as a result of the general and analytical diagnosis. Mary should be given material at approximately the middle of the second-grade level. She needs encouragement, success, and many opportunities to use the results of her reading in constructive activities, such as building models, or helping make displays, and things of that sort. She needs concrete illustrations of the things she is reading about. Because she has low intelligence, Mary should read for only one well-defined purpose at a time. Helen ought to be started with material at about the last half of the third grade in level of difficulty, with emphasis on reading to predict outcomes. The Gates-Peardon Practice Exercises at the third-grade level might be good material with which to start Helen's instruction. It would be well to keep a chart indicating her speed and accuracy in doing the exercises. As she increased in speed and accuracy, she could be advanced to the same type of exercise at the fourth-grade level. In addition to the practice exercises, in her recreational and personal development reading Helen can be expected to read half of a story and then estimate how the story is going to end. She can then check her completion of the story with that of the author. In her basic reading instruction, Helen can read the fourth-grade reader without difficulty and the teacher should emphasize, for Helen, the exercises designed to develop the ability to predict the outcome of given events.

In order to answer the problem of how improvement can be brought about most efficiently for Kermit and Peter, a case-study diagnosis is necessary.

The fifth principle, that the diagnosis must detect any limiting condition within the child that needs correction or for which the program must be adjusted, needs to be fulfilled in the cases of Kermit and Peter. The study of such severely retarded readers as these two boys must include a thorough appraisal of their sensory characteristics, their emotional reactions, their attitudes toward reading, and their social adjustment.

The sixth principle, that the diagnosis must locate any environmental conditions that need to be corrected before improvement can be expected, also must be fulfilled in the cases of Kermit and Peter. Parent consultations will be necessary to find out whether there are any conditions in their homes which might impede the progress of the boys. But, more important, consultations are necessary to formulate the co-operative approach that the home and school will make in order to solve each boy's reading problems. If reading growth is to be expected, the teacher will have to appraise the entire curriculum of these two boys at school in order to eliminate any interfering conditions that they might meet throughout the school day.

If the case-study diagnosis is made in a reading clinic or a child-study center, a consultation with the classroom teacher will be necessary. In making a case-study diagnosis of a reading disability case, both standardized and informal procedures must be employed.

Standardized Procedures in Case-Study Diagnosis

Among the more useful standardized, detailed, case-study diagnostic tests [2] of the skills and abilities in reading are the following:

1. *Durrell Analysis of Reading Difficulty.* This consists of a series of individual tests in oral and silent reading and in word perception as well as systematic observations of the child's approaches to reading. It includes a study of oral and silent reading, word analysis, phonetic pronunciation, difficulties in writing and spelling. The tests give a good background for formulating a remedial program.

2. *The Monroe Reading Diagnosis.* This individually administered method of reading diagnosis is described in Monroe's *Children Who Cannot Read.*[3] It consists of a compilation of testing procedures, including the Gray's Oral Reading Examination, Monroe's Iota Word Test, and Monroe's Word Discrimination Test. There are two outstanding features of the Monroe method of diagnosis. The first is the use of a reading index which indicates the amount of retardation in reading. The index is determined by

---

[2] A more detailed description of these programs of diagnosis can be found in Guy L. Bond and Miles Tinker, *Fundamentals of Remedial Reading* (New York, Appleton-Century-Crofts, in press).

[3] Marion Monroe, *Children Who Cannot Read* (Chicago, Univ. of Chicago Press, 1932).

using the child's reading age, his chronological age, arithmetic age, and mental age. A child's reading index can be found by using the following formula: Reading Index equals Reading Age divided by the average of the Chronological Age, Mental Age and Arithmetic Age,

$$\text{or R.I.} = \frac{\text{R.A.}}{(\text{C.A.} + \text{M.A.} + \text{A.A.}) \div 3}.$$

The second feature of Monroe diagnosis is the classification of oral reading errors. All errors made by the child are carefully recorded and classified as follows: faulty vowels (*dig* for *dug*); faulty consonants (*send* for *sent*); reversals (*dig* for *big, was* for *saw*, or *he said* for *said he*); addition of sounds (*track* for *tack*); omission of sounds (*bind* for *blind*); substitution of words (*was* for *lived*); repetition of words (*the horse the horse was big* for *the horse was big*); addition of words (*the big horse was* for *the horse was*); omission of words (*the cat* for *the small cat*); refusal and words aided. If a child does not pronounce a word, it must be supplied by the examiner at the end of fifteen seconds. The reading index and classification of types of errors given by Monroe are of considerable use in making a case-study diagnosis.

3. *The Gates Reading Diagnostic Tests.* The Gates Reading Diagnostic Tests and their use are described in *The Improvement of Reading.*[4] The Gates Reading Diagnostic Tests are systematic, standardized appraisals which are very useful in making case studies of children who are in reading difficulty. These tests must be given individually. The front page of the pupil's record booklet, shown on page 142, indicates the extensiveness of the standardized portion of the tests.

In addition to the information given on the cover of the record booklet, there are several check-lists which are valuable to the diagnostician. Check-lists of the analysis of errors; of difficulties; of word pronunciation in oral reading; of word pronunciation in isolated word lists; and of spelling characteristics are included. There are also spaces furnished at the back of the pupil's record booklet for entering related information such as tests of vision and of hearing; observation or test of speech; indications of unfortunate silent reading characteristics, such as faulty eye movements, use of finger, lip movements, head movements, and so on; evidences of emotional tension, fear, irritation, lack of confidence; evidence of special interests and distastes; influence of home, parents, and out-of-school factors; school history; and then there is room for a summary of the diagnosis and for recommendations for remedial procedures. This instrument undoubtedly is the most complete and useful individual appraisal program available for case-study diagnosis.

[4] Arthur I. Gates, *The Improvement of Reading,* 3rd ed. (New York, Macmillan, 1947).

GATES READING DIAGNOSTIC TESTS
PUPIL'S RECORD BOOKLET
By ARTHUR I. GATES, *Professor of Education*
Teachers College, Columbia University

Pupil's Name...School.............................Date.............................

Pupil's Age...............Birthday.......................Grade.............Examiner.......................Teacher...........................

	1 Raw Score	2 Grade Score	3 Rating		1 Raw Score	2 Grade Score	Rating
AGE, GRADE, INTELLIGENCE				**PHRASE PERCEPTION**			
1. Chronological Age				1. Number Phrases Correct			
2. Grade Status				**WORD PERCEPTION, ANALYSIS, ETC.**			
3. Binet I.Q............M.A.				1. Flash Presentation			
4. ...............I.Q..........M.A.				2. Untimed Presentation			
SILENT READING TESTS				**SPELLING**			
1.				1. Gates Test			
2.				**VISUAL PERCEPTION TECHNIQUES**			
3.				1. Syllabication			
4.				2. Recognition of Syllables			
5.				3. Recognition of Phonograms			
Average of Reading Tests				4. Blending Letter Sounds			
ORAL READING				5. Giving Letter Sounds			
1. Gates Oral — Total Score				6. Reading Capital Letters			
a. Omissions, Words				a. Speed			
b. Additions, Words				b. Errors			
c. Repetitions				7. Reading Small Letters			
d. Mispronunciations				a. Speed			
e. Full Reversals				b. Errors			
f. Reversal of Parts				**AUDITORY TECHNIQUES**			
g. Wrong Order (e+f)				1. Blending Letter Sounds			
h. Wrong Beginnings				2. Giving Letters for Sounds			
i. Wrong Middles				3. Giving Words—Initial Sounds			
j. Wrong Endings				4. Giving Words—Ending Sounds			
k. Wrong Several Parts				**OTHER TESTS**			
VOCABULARY							
1. Gates Oral Vocabulary							
2.							
REVERSAL TEST							
1. Total Errors							
2. Per Cent Reversals							

BUREAU OF PUBLICATIONS, TEACHERS COLLEGE, COLUMBIA UNIVERSITY
Copyright, 1945, by Teachers College, Columbia University

4. *The Silent Reading Diagnostic Test* by Bond, Clymer, Hoyt.[5] This set of diagnostic tests differs from those previously discussed in two respects. First, it can be given as a group test as well as an individual test. Second, it measures the child's characteristics in silent rather than in oral reading. The graphic profile, shown on page 143, indicates the scope of this standardized set of diagnostic tests.

[5] Guy L. Bond, Theodore Clymer, and Cyril Hoyt, *The Silent Reading Diagnostic Test* (Chicago, Lyons & Carnahan, 1955).

SILENT READING DIAGNOSTIC TESTS—EXPERIMENTAL FORM
Graphic Profile

Name **Steve Martin** School **Blake** Grade **3** Date **May 8, 1954**

Grade Equivalent scale: 1.5 2.0 2.5 3.0 3.5 4.0 4.5 5.0 5.5 6.0 6.5 7.0 7.5 8.0

BASIC DATA

	Pupil Score
Chronological Grade	4.7
Mental Grade	4.9
Grade in School	3-8

READING ABILITIES

	Pupil Score
Vocabulary	3.8
Factual (General)	3.6
Organize (Specific)	3.4
Evaluate-Interpret	
Appreciate	
Average Reading	3.6

RECOGNITION PATTERN

	Pupil Score	Grade Equivalent values
Total Right (1+2)	71	1,0 2,4 3,4 4,8 6,6 7,2 7,7 7,9 8,0 8,2
Total Errors (1+2)	9	5,4 4,5 3,8 2,6 1,5 ,9 ,4 ,4 ,2 ,0
Total Omitted (1+2)	1	2,0 1,5 1,2 1,0 ,7 ,3 ,3 ,2 ,0 ,0
Words in Isolation (1)	51	,9 1,6 2,2 3,2 4,4 4,8 5,1 5,2 5,3 5,4
Words in Context (2)	20	,5 ,8 1,2 1,6 2,1 2,4 2,6 2,7 2,7 2,8
Orientation (3)	17	,4 ,6 1,0 1,6 2,0 2,1 2,1 2,2 2,2 2,3

Perfect Score

ERROR ANALYSIS (1+2)

	Pupil Score	Grade Equivalent values
Initial Errors	3	1,2 ,9 ,7 ,5 ,2 ,1 ,0 ,0 ,0 ,0
Middle Errors	2	1,5 1,3 1,1 ,8 ,6 ,4 ,2 ,1 ,1 ,0
Ending Errors	1	1,4 1,2 1,1 ,7 ,5 ,3 ,2 ,2 ,1 ,0
Orientation Errors	3	1,3 1,1 ,9 ,6 ,2 ,1 ,0 ,0 ,0 ,0

RECOGNITION TECHNIQUES

	Pupil Score	Grade Equivalent values
Visual Analysis (4+5+6)	33	1,0 1,4 3,0 4,3 5,3 6,3 6,6 6,9 7,2 7,4
Locating Elements (4)	16	,6 ,8 1,6 2,3 2,8 3,4 3,4 3,5 3,6 3,6
Syllabication (5)	7	,2 ,3 ,5 ,7 ,9 1,0 1,1 1,1 1,2 1,2
Locating Root Word (6)	10	,2 ,3 ,9 1,3 1,6 1,9 2,1 2,3 2,4 2,6
Phonetic Kn. (7+8+9+10)	68	2,3 3,9 5,5 6,9 7,8 8,8 9,5 102 106 111
Word Elements (7)	18	,5 ,8 1,3 1,7 1,9 2,1 2,3 2,4 2,5 2,7
Beginning Sounds (8)	17	,8 1,2 1,6 2,0 2,2 2,4 2,5 2,6 2,7 2,8
Rhyming Sounds (9)	13	,0 ,3 ,6 ,8 1,3 1,8 2,2 2,5 2,7 2,8
Letter Sounds (10)	20	1,0 1,6 2,0 2,4 2,4 2,5 2,6 2,7 2,8 2,8

WORD SYNTHESIS (11)

	Pupil Score	Grade Equivalent values
Word Synthesis (11)	9	,1 ,2 ,4 ,7 1,3 1,8 2,0 2,2 2,3 2,4

Lines of Importance

MISCELLANEOUS DATA

Hearing _____ Other _____

Vision _____

An estimate of the severity of a child's reading difficulty can be made by a comparison of his mental grade and his average reading grade as measured by the Developmental Reading Tests.[6] The results of these tests are listed at the top of the profile. The extent to which a child has a diagnostically significant difference in performance on any of the various comprehension abilities can be readily seen by comparing each with his average for all the types of comprehension. A diagnosis of the child's word-recognition characteristics follows on the profile and includes the following subtests: recognition of words in isolation, recognition of words in context, recognition of reversible words in context, locating elements, syllabification, locating root word, knowledge of word elements, knowledge of beginning sounds, knowledge of rhyming sounds, knowledge of letter sounds, and word synthesis. The resultant profile quickly enables the teacher to locate those areas of reading in which the child has limited ability and also the areas of over-emphasis. A study of the profile gives the diagnostician an indication of the type of error the child makes in recognizing words. It shows the extent of orientational confusions; it indicates the efficiency with which the child uses context clues; it indicates the relationship between word recognition and comprehension; it gives an indication of the child's ability to visually analyze words into usable parts; it gives an accurate measurement of the child's phonetic knowledge and locates the areas of weakness; it gives an indication of the overanalytical as well as underanalytical cases; and it measures the ability of the child to synthesize word parts auditorily and visually. This battery of tests has proved of value to classroom teachers in diagnosing the needs of the children in reading difficulty, as well as to the clinician studying severe reading disability cases.

The classroom teacher and the clinician making case-study diagnoses frequently use a combination of the systematic approaches described above and informal appraisals.

Informal Methods of Case-Study Diagnosis

Informal procedures can give the teacher or the clinical worker valuable information about the reading patterns of children in difficulty. Informal procedures are, in reality, an extension and refinement of the day-by-day observations of teachers in the classroom.

A fairly systematic and accurate estimation of a child's reading strengths and limitations can be made by using a graded series of readers. The teacher or clinical worker arranges a series of basal readers in the order that a child would normally progress through them as he goes up through the years of reading instruction. The child is asked to read at a level that the diagnostician estimates he can read with few errors. If the content appears to be

[6] Guy L. Bond, Theodore Clymer, and Cyril Hoyt, *Developmental Reading Tests* (Chicago, Lyons & Carnahan, 1955).

very easy for the child to read, he is asked to read the next higher book in the series. If the initial trial book appears to be too difficult, the diagnostician will give him the next lower book in the series until he reaches one he can read comfortably. For example, if a child in the fourth grade who is in difficulty is estimated to have the reading ability of approximately a beginning second-grade child, he would then be asked to try to read in a second-grade reader. If this was found to be too difficult for him, he would be asked to read a first-grade reader. If this was still too difficult, he would be asked to read a primer. If the child were 95 per cent accurate in the words recognized as he read orally, that is, if he did not make more than one error in every twenty running words, that material would be considered useful for instructional purposes. It should be pointed out, however, that if the child's reading difficulty has been determined to be rate of speed, this material would be too difficult for effective remedial work. If his reading difficulty is in word recognition, this material would be at approximately the correct level. If his reading difficulty is in comprehension, he should be offered material at a level in which he would make one error in about every forty running words. The material that a child is expected to read independently should be considerably easier.

When a child's level of reading ability has been determined by this oral sampling of a series of basic readers, he should then read some passages silently to answer various types of comprehension questions. At the same time, his rate of reading should be measured, that is, how many words per minute does he read. While he is reading silently, the teacher should look for signs of lip movements, faulty eye movements, or other unfortunate habits. In addition to to these estimates, the diagnostician should collect a list of the words the child missed and the errors made. These words can then be classified to find out the nature of the errors the child is making. The classification used in the Gates Diagnostic Tests or the Monroe Diagnostic Test could be employed for this purpose.

It would also be of benefit to note how the child tried to solve his word problems; how efficient was his visual analysis of words into useful elements; how effectively did he use context clues; did he seem to know the structural, visual, and phonetic elements within words; and how effective was he in synthesis. In other words, the classification of word-recognition techniques used in the Silent Reading Diagnostic Tests by Bond, Clymer, and Hoyt could be applied, in the informal diagnosis, to his oral study of words when he was in difficulty.

A case such as Kermit, described above, would be seen to analyze too many words, although he would likely come to a successful conclusion in working out many of them. His speed of reading would be at a low level; his comprehension for exact sorts of reading would be higher than his reading to get the general significance of a passage read. As a result of the informal diagnosis, Kermit would be adjudged an overanalytical reader. It

BOND INFORMAL DIAGNOSIS BLANK

Name_____

Grade Placement_____

Chronological Grade_____ Mental Grade_____ I.Q. _____

Silent Reading From Book	Grade	
	Lip Movement	
	Vocalization	
	Regressions	
	Speed	
	Finger Pointing	
	Head Movements	
	Other Faulty Habits	
Oral Reading From Book	Grade	
	Reversals	
	Initial Beg.	
	Middle } ---Word Elements Missed	
	End.	
	Wrong Sev. Pts.	

	Habits
	
	  Word-by-word reading
	  Lack of contextual reading
	  Comprehension	

Word Pronunciation From Book	Grade	
	Phonetic Attack	
	Spelling Attack	
	Syllabification	
	Known Parts	
	Little Words-in-Words	
	Suffixes	
	Prefixes	
	Faulty Vowels	
	Faulty Constructions	

Word Pro-nunciation From Book	Omits Sounds	
	Adds Sounds	
	Repeats Sounds	
	Blending	

Blending	
Hearing	
Vision	
Speech Defects	

Interests	

Work Habits	
Concentration & Persistence	
Emotional Reaction	
Attitude Toward School	
Attitude Toward Reading	
Handedness	
Eyedness	
Physical Defects	
Home Environment	

Other Important Observations

should be pointed out that the more systematic, standardized diagnostic procedures are more reliable and will result in a more meaningful and thorough diagnosis. However, the informal procedures can supplement the more formal diagnosis. The diagnostician can explore areas not treated in the standardized procedure.

If a blank such as the Bond Informal Diagnosis Blank is used (pages 146-147), informal procedures have merit and can be applied in the regular classroom as well as in the clinic.

It is recommended that the diagnostician, whether classroom teacher or clinician, use both standardized and informal appraisals to study children's reading patterns in order to formulate programs of remediation. The three levels of diagnosis—general diagnosis, analytical diagnosis, and case-study techniques—must be used by both the classroom teacher and the clinical worker. The diagnostician should start with a general diagnosis and proceed as far as is necessary to formulate a remedial program.

Additional Characteristics Should Be Studied

In order to have a clear picture of a child who is in difficulty in reading, it is necessary for the teacher or clinical worker to appraise the child's vision and hearing. It is also necessary for the diagnosis to include appraisals of the child's emotional reactions to reading and his interest in reading. The diagnostician's responsibility here is to detect those children who will need further study by a specialist. The Keystone View Telebinocular and the Eames Eye Test have proved to be effective screening devices for detecting any limitations in a child's vision. As a result of the findings, the diagnostician will know whether or not to refer the child to a specialist for visual diagnosis. Watch-tick tests, whisper tests, and group and individual audiometer tests have been successfully employed as screening measures of hearing ability. The diagnostician will refer the child to a specialist in otology if any limitation is suspected.

By means of interviews and questioning, the teacher can ascertain the child's dominant interests, his hobbies, and his attitudes toward reading. The determination of a child's emotional adjustment is difficult and technical. It is suggested that suitable tests of this are limited and should be interpreted with caution even by a trained psychological or psychiatric worker. The reading diagnostician, unless thoroughly trained in interpreting such measures, should secure the services of a competent specialist in this area. Many children who appear to be emotionally maladjusted are, in reality, reflecting their insecurity in reading.

SUGGESTED ACTIVITIES

1. Examine instructional guides and local courses of study to see if they provide experiences that develop all of the major objectives of reading instruction given on page 103.

2. Describe classroom procedures that would aid in developing "diversified readers" as discussed on page 102. What types of reading programs would hinder growth in this regard?

3. Why should basic study skills, such as use of references and use of maps, be considered reading skills? How do they differ from such reading skills as reading to retain information or the ability to evaluate? How are they alike?

4. Examine each of the principles for the teaching of reading, given on pages 109-116, and indicate how a classroom teacher could organize both developmental and remedial instruction to conform to these principles.

5. Indicate the reasons why a remedial program should conform to the six principles given on page 117. What would be the result if the program did not conform to one or more of these principles?

6. Describe local reading disability cases illustrative of each of the three types discussed in this chapter. Tell how you would provide a program that would conform in each case to each of the six principles. Illustrate with specific procedures.

7. What possible explanations can be advanced for the fact that three out of four complex reading disability cases are boys? How can reading programs be set up so as to adjust to the needs of the boys?

8. Compare the range of ability of the fourth grade class given in Table 3 on page 39 with the results for some other fourth grade class. What similarities and differences do you find? What implications for the reading program are evident from the table on page 125?

9. Obtain copies of several of the tests useful for general diagnosis listed on page 128. Compare them to see what different elements of reading they test. What might you expect to find if one child were to take all of these tests? Would you expect the same results for all the tests and subtests? Why?

10. Obtain copies of teacher-made tests used for informal diagnosis. What are the advantages and disadvantages of these tests?

11. Consult Buros' *Mental Measurements Yearbooks* for evaluations and further descriptions of the tests listed on page 128. If you were to set up a diagnostic testing program, which of these tests would you use? Remember that different types of difficulties may require different analytical tests.

12. What are the advantages and disadvantages of the application of standardized tests such as those listed on pages 131-133?

13. Set up a tentative remedial program for the three children whose test data are given in the figure on page 134. Give specific examples of materials and procedures you might find useful. What further information would you need on the case-study level before you would be ready to proceed?

14. Describe how a remedial worker may utilize reading workbook exercises to diagnose and correct reading difficulties.

15. Examine and evaluate the tests recommended for case-study diagnosis. What are the advantages and disadvantages of each? What differences in remedial instruction might you expect if one rather than another of these tests were used to make the diagnosis?

16. Using the Bond Informal Diagnosis Blank, attempt to diagnose a reading disability case. What are the advantages of using a prepared blank such as this?

17. If possible, observe the administration by a specialist of a clinical diagnostic test in reading. The observers should have copies of the test and should record pertinent information as the test is given. The specialist should then assist the observers to analyze the findings and to make a diagnosis. Find out the kinds of information that health records and reports of physical examinations give that may be helpful in a diagnosis in reading. What types of supplementary information should be reported to an educational clinic when cases are referred?

SELECTED BIBLIOGRAPHY

BETTS, E. A., *The Prevention and Correction of Reading Difficulties* (Evanston, Ill., Row, 1936).

BOND, Guy L., and TINKER, Miles A., *Fundamentals of Remedial Reading* (New York, Appleton-Century-Crofts, in press).

BOND, Guy L., and WAGNER, Eva Bond, *Teaching the Child to Read,* rev. ed. (New York, Macmillan, 1950).

DOLCH, E. W., *A Manual of Remedial Reading,* 2nd ed. (Champaign, Ill., Garrard Press, 1945).

DURRELL, D. D., *Improvement of Basic Reading Abilities* (New York, World Book, 1940).

FERNALD, Grace, *Remedial Techniques in Basic School Subjects* (New York, McGraw, 1943).

GATES, Arthur I., *The Improvement of Reading,* 3rd ed. (New York, Macmillan, 1947).

HARRIS, A. J., *How to Increase Reading Ability,* rev. ed. (New York, Longmans, 1947).

KIRK, S. A., *Teaching Reading to Slow Learning Children* (Boston, Houghton, 1940).

MCCULLOUGH, C. M., STRANG, Ruth, and TRAXLER, A. E., *Problems in the Improvement of Reading* (New York, McGraw, 1946).

MONROE, Marion, *Children Who Cannot Read* (Chicago, Univ. of Chicago Press, 1932).

Reading in the Elementary School, Forty-eighth Yearbook, Part II, National Society for the Study of Education (Chicago, Univ. of Chicago Press, 1949).

WITTY, Paul, and KOPEL, David, *Reading and the Educative Process* (Boston, Ginn, 1939).

7

TREATMENT OF LEARNING
DIFFICULTIES IN READING

A PROGRAM of treatment for reading difficulties is based on an understanding of the causes of the difficulties, the outcomes of diagnosis, and the application of basic principles of remedial treatment. Although it is true that a basic understanding of the individual characteristics of each learner is essential for effective programs of treatment, the fundamental problem is that of locating what is wrong with the child's reading and re-educating him. A remedial program, then, must be based upon a thorough understanding of the nature of reading growth and upon a thorough appreciation of the many subsidiary and interrelated learnings that are necessary in acquiring skill in reading. The basic reasons for the vast majority of reading difficulties are to be found not in the characteristics of the child nor in inappropriate methods alone, but in the complexity of reading itself.

In order to learn to read, the child must develop a whole hierarchy of abilities. These are developed gradually and simultaneously through the years as the child grows toward reading maturity. Such a comprehension ability as critical evaluation, for example, may start in a prereading program when a picture of a squirrel keeping house is recognized as fanciful rather than real. This ability develops further, later on, when a child decides it is quite unlikely for a fox and some rabbits to be engaged in conversation, to be dressed in clothes, and to be living in houses. The ability develops further when the child distinguishes fact from opinion and judges the accuracy of supposedly factual accounts. The child approaches maturity in reading to critically evaluate when he understands that words, their overtones and specialized meanings, are used to influence the thinking of people. All of the skills in reading grow in a similar fashion, with the child gradually gaining maturity in each. Any failure or faulty learning along the way can impede or halt the progress.

A prime requisite for reading growth is the maintenance of balance among all of the skills that are gradually developing. An overemphasis on any one of the skills may halt the learning in another. For example, if the child depends too much on the analytical approaches to word recognition, he may fail to build a large sight vocabulary. Without a large sight vocabulary the child cannot use context clues effectively; he cannot comprehend his reading; he cannot gain fluency.

Diagnosis in reading is designed primarily to locate arrested development in any of the skills and abilities, or a lack of balance between the skills and abilities necessary for effective reading. After a thorough diagnosis has been made, the instructional needs of the child have been located, and his characteristics have been studied so that any necessary modifications in the approaches to reading can be made, the teacher is ready to start treatment of the difficulty.

In treating children who are having difficulty in learning to read, the teacher must be guided by the following principles, which were discussed in detail in Chapter 5:

1. Treatment must be based on a diagnosis.
2. The program must be clearly formulated.
3. The program should be modified as needed.
4. A variety of remedial techniques should be used.
5. The child should help formulate the program of treatment.
6. Consideration of the child's personal worth is necessary.
7. Stigmatism in classification should be avoided.
8. The child's emotional state must be considered.
9. Faulty attitudes should be corrected.
10. The child should participate in group work as well as in individual work.
11. Corrective programs must be individualized.
12. The outcomes and methods should be commensurate with the child's ability.
13. Treatment should be specific and not general.
14. Fatigue should be noted and practice spaced.
15. The program must be well motivated and encouraging to the child.
16. The teacher must be optimistic.
17. Success of the student must be emphasized.
18. Errors should be pointed in a positive way.
19. Growth should be made apparent to the child.
20. Treatment should not be in conflict with other enjoyable activities.
21. Purposes for reading should always be established.
22. The results of reading should be utilized and evaluated.
23. The materials for reading should be carefully selected so as to be at the proper level of difficulty.
24. Materials should be suitable in interest, format, and type.
25. The materials must be abundant and not artificial.
26. Adjustments must be made in the child's entire school program.
27. The home environment should be favorable.
28. Continuous evaluation must be made and a cumulative record kept.
29. Attention should be given to the child until newly formed skills and abilities are firmly established.

Fulfillment of all of these principles of remedial treatment is essential if effective re-education is to ensue.

It must be remembered in applying these general principles that every child in difficulty in reading constitutes a somewhat different problem. There are many types of faulty learnings possible in reading growth and development. Each of the resultant deficiencies may be accompanied by one or more other deficiencies in the reading pattern of a child. It is therefore unreasonable to suppose that a uniform approach to the correction of learning difficulties in reading can be established. The program of re-education must be tailor-made to fit any given child's own characteristics and the nature of his reading disability.

This chapter cannot hope to cover all of the specific faulty learnings that can constitute basic problems. Only the more prevalent and the more crucial categories of reading difficulties and their correction will be discussed. The following have been selected as being essential for discussion in this chapter:

1. Faulty word study.
2. Poor comprehension.
3. The inefficient reader.

In addition, some of the special adjustments that must be made for the slow-learning child will be discussed.

FAULTY WORD STUDY

The child who has difficulty in word study cannot hope to become an effective reader unless this problem is corrected. Word study encompasses two types of instructional problems. First is the development of clear, precise, and extensive meanings of words. There is little use in being able to recognize and pronounce printed symbols if those symbols have no meaning. So the child, as he develops his reading capabilities, must continually expand his meaning vocabulary by word study. He must develop clear and precise understanding of word meanings. He must also realize that words in the English language can have many meanings. The word, *set,* for example, even in a dictionary used in the fourth grade, has fourteen distinct meanings—all the way from *"the cement set"* to *"they sailed at the set of the tide."* The child must learn to use context to help him select the correct meaning from the numerous meanings for any given word. This is one among many reasons for developing word-study techniques in contextual settings.

The second problem in word study is the establishment of independence in word recognition. If the child is unable to independently work out the pronunciation of a word he has not previously seen in print, or if he is unable to recognize it visually, he will stand little chance of understanding its meaning.

In developing the word-recognition techniques needed to enable the child to recognize new words visually or phonetically, there are several balances that must be maintained. The first of these is the balance between word-recognition techniques and the development of meaning vocabulary. It is not enough to be able to recognize the word; the meaning of the word must also be established.

Second, there is a need for a balance between the development of a sight vocabulary, words the child can recognize without detailed inspection, and the development of word-recognition techniques. If the child is led to emphasize one more than the other, disability in word study will result. The child who places too much emphasis upon developing a sight vocabulary may fail to establish some of the essential word-recognition techniques. The child who is led to emphasize analytical word-recognition techniques too early or too intently may neglect to develop the essential sight vocabulary.

Third, there must be a balance between the use of context clues and the application of the more analytical word-recognition techniques. If, on the one hand, the child places too much dependence on context clues, he may not develop sufficient word-recognition techniques to enable him to recognize words that cannot be anticipated from the context. On the other hand, if the child is led to depend too much upon isolated techniques of word recognition, he may not establish capability in using context to speed the recognition and to check the accuracy of that recognition.

Fourth, there must be a balance among the analytical techniques taught. Too much emphasis on the sounding out of words may force the child into piecemeal observation at the expense of using the larger, more effective, structural and visual analysis of words. On the other hand, too much emphasis on the structural and visual analysis of words may force the child to neglect the detailed study necessary in recognizing unusual names, for example.

In word recognition there is an additional factor that makes it essential that we equip children with broad, versatile attacks on words rather than emphasizing one approach at the expense of another. Suitable methods for recognizing words vary because the words themselves vary in the ways in which they can best be recognized. Some words are best recognized through their phonetic elements; other words are nonphonetic and must be recognized through their structure. An element that may be useful in recognizing one word may be detrimental in recognizing another word. For example, noting *on* in the word *upon* would likely be helpful, but noting *on* in the word *action* would make the recognition much more difficult or even impossible.

Word recognition is complex and there are many related learnings. They can probably be classified into the following five basic learnings:

1. The association of meanings with the words recognized.
2. The use of context clues and other meaning aids as a means of anticipating the word to be recognized and as a check on the accuracy of the recognition.
3. The ability to visually separate the word into usable recognition elements.
4. The development of knowledges of visual, structural, and phonetic elements (knowledge, for example, of what the visual element *ight* in the word *right* says).
5. The ability to auditorily blend or visually synthesize the word parts.

Failure to establish any of these basic learnings or overemphasis on any of them constitute the major sources of word-recognition difficulty. It should be pointed out, however, that in a study in which approximately four thousand youngsters were measured on their capabilities in each of the above skills, it was found that a child could not be a good reader if he had insufficient capability in any one of them. But the mere fact that he was competent in any one of these, or even in all of them, was no guarantee that the child would be a good reader. The following types of faulty word study appear frequently and hamper the child's reading growth:

1. Insufficient sight vocabulary.
2. Failure to associate meaning with words.
3. Ineffective use of context clues.
4. Ineffective visual analysis of words.
5. Insufficient knowledge of visual, structural, or phonetic elements.
6. Lack of ability in auditory blending or visual synthesis.
7. Overanalysis in word recognition.
8. Orientational confusion.

Insufficient Sight Vocabulary

The child who has not formed the habit of trying to recognize words as words at sight and who has not built a group of basic sight words will be limited in all aspects of reading growth. There are many words that are so frequently met in stories that developing the ability immediately to recognize them is essential to fluency and capability in reading. The more important words have been listed by Dale, Dolch, Gates, and Thorndike. These lists represent careful studies of the words that have a high degree of utility in reading. Modern basic reading programs develop carefully these important words so that the introduction is gradual and repetition well spaced. It is supposed that the child will learn the basic vocabulary used in his reading program. If the child fails to master the sight vocabulary introduced in his basic reading program, the load of words that must be analyzed and recognized as new words becomes unbearable, and before long the child's reading development collapses.

The most effective way to increase the sight vocabulary of a disabled reader is to instruct him in a basic reader at a level of difficulty where he has sufficient sight vocabulary to read and read comfortably. He should be given more experience through additional exercises so that he may learn the sight vocabulary the basal reader is designed to teach. The workbooks accompanying the reading program should be used and special emphasis should be placed on the word-building exercises described in the teacher's manual. Extensive reading of related materials that are definitely easy for the child will encourage rapid sight recognition of words.

The following types of exercises, using basic sight words being developed in the reader, will encourage rapid recognition:

1. Exercises in which the content so nearly tells the word that recognition is possible with only slight inspection.

    a. He put the hat on his _____.
        ran   head   drink

    b. Mother put the cake in the _____ to bake.
        oven   lake   tree

2. Words that answer leading questions or statements.

    a. Draw a line around the right word.
        (1) Where do we buy food?
            apple   flag   store

        (2) On what does a cowboy ride?
            chicken   cow   horse

3. Exercises that require the meaningful scanning of lists.

    a. Draw a line around all the animals that have four feet.
        pony   goat
        chicken   horse
        duck   cat

4. Word card games can be used that call for immediate responses, such as a pack of cards, some of which have the names of animals printed on them, and others, clothing. Two children working together can flash the cards for each other to respond to. Such words as the following could be printed on the cards:

        pony   donkey   dress
        hat   goat   shoes
        cat   coat   elephant

One child would be expected to tell the cards that had the names of animals on them as they were flashed. The next time, the other child could tell those that named clothing.

Another set might contain action words and the child tells which cards have words on them that tell movement. These cards might include:

        run   slide
        jump   was
        know   walk
        flew   are

Exercises designed to develop sight vocabulary should be such that the child is not required to inspect the words in great detail and they should always be used in situations that require understanding of the word meanings.

The rapid reading of material with few word difficulties to find answers to specific questions helps the child to build sight vocabulary. The reading of highly interesting material that is relatively easy encourages rapid inspection of the words. In all attempts to build sight vocabulary, the words being learned should be repeated often and at well-spaced intervals. The exercises should be such that understanding the meaning of the words is required and the pronunciation of words is held to a minimum.

Failure to Associate Meaning with Words

Frequently the child's major difficulty in word recognition is that he has had oral pronunciation of the words emphasized to the point that he fails to sense the importance, or has not established the habit, of rapidly associating meaning with the printed symbol. The exercises given above for the development of sight vocabulary have kept the meanings of the words in the forefront. Exercises of that nature, then, will be effective in establishing the habit of associating meaning with printed words. These types of exercises are quite different from flashing a group of isolated word symbols at the child and having him pronounce them.

If the child is to be encouraged to associate clear and vivid ideas with the printed symbols for those ideas, he must at all times be developing his word-recognition techniques in meaningful settings. In addition to the exercises given above, the following will prove helpful:

1. Exercises that call for clear visualization.

   a. A horse with large, colored spots on it.
       pony   pinto

2. Having children find words that have the opposite meaning.

   a. In each row make a box around the word that means the opposite of the first word.
       (1) short   long   pint
       (2) good   bad   nice
       (3) night   now   day

3. Finding synonyms.

   a. In each row find the word that means the same as the first word. Draw a line around it.
       (1) glow   starts   shine   coal
       (2) bumped   mistake   welcome   knocked

4. Exercises that develop extensiveness of meanings.

   a. Tell the difference in the meaning of *cross* in the following sentences.
       (1) A duck can cross a puddle.
       (2) Willy is not cross now.
   b. Tell the difference in the meaning of *trunk*.
       (1) The girl packed the trunk for the trip.
       (2) The elephant put the peanut in his trunk.

Such exercises as those above will help the child develop the ability and the habit of associating meanings with words. There are more intrinsic methods of building these habits. If the children are requested to draw pictures illustrating stories they have read, attention to the meaning of descriptive words will be greater. If the children are to dramatize a story, they will pay attention to action words and attention to other word meanings will be encouraged. Having the child retell a story in his own words after he has read it will encourage him in the habit of associating meaning with the words read.

Ineffective Use of Context Clues

Failure to use context clues can seriously hamper the growth of reading ability. It can also limit the development of accuracy in using the other word-recognition techniques. Context clues and other meaning aids give an indication of the word that is likely to come, so that it can be more readily recognized. Instead of the word being any one of some 800,000 words in the English language, it is only one of the few that it could possibly be in the contextual setting in which it is found. Contextual and meaning aids make for greater rapidity in word recognition.

The reader who applies contextual aids is more apt to get the word correct than if he is using no such aids. He will get a close approximation to the actual pronunciation of the word from other clues. The context clues will then enable him to recognize the word even though his more analytical techniques only approximated the correct pronunciation.

Contextual and other meaning aids have an equally, if not more, important use. They are checks on the accuracy of all the other word-recognition techniques. In word recognition, when a child figures out what the word is, he must see then if the word makes sense in the context in which it is found. If it does not make sense, he must reinspect that word. Many children who seem to be limited in word-recognition techniques are in difficulty because they are not using context clues effectively.

Training in the use of context and other meaning clues is effected by having the child read material that contains one new word in about every forty running words. The child should be reading for real purposes. It may be useful in the case of children who are severely handicapped in the use of context clues to establish a purpose for each paragraph or sentence the child reads. This will keep reading for meaning at a high level and will enable the child to recognize enough words that he knows at sight so that any new word will stand a reasonable chance of being recognized from the context.

In addition to reading for immediate purposes, such as finding the answer to a specific question, there are more formal exercises which will encourage the use of context clues. Among useful exercises are the following:

1. Sentences that indicate the word to be recognized.

    a. It made a noise as it flew over the road.
       store   airplane

    b. The man saw a car on it.
       road   kitten

2. Sentences that must be completed by a choice among two words.

   a. Mother made the cake so Billy could have it for his _____.
   birthday   picture

   b. He went for a walk in the snow one cold _____.
   window   winter

3. Exercises requiring the use of expectancy clues.

   a. If you were reading about a dog, which words would you see? Draw a line under them.

window	bark	tail
wings	bone	eggs
feet	ears	trunk

4. Exercises developing the use of picture clues.

   a. What do you see in the picture?
   a donkey   a boat

   b. Draw a line around the animals you see in this picture of a farm.

pig	elephant
horse	lion
giraffe	cow
chicken	kangaroo

5. Exercises that have children classify according to expectancy.

   a. Draw a circle around the animals that are wild. Put *X* on the ones that are tame.

lion	horse
dog	baboon
cat	tiger

Ineffective Visual Analysis of Words

In order for the child to become a good reader he needs to develop an effective visual analysis of words. He must be able to select visually, within the word being recognized, those elements that are going to be effective in the solution of that word problem. If his original analysis does not work, he must be able to reject it rapidly and reinspect the word until he finds the elements that will work. The child, then, must develop a high degree of flexibility in visually inspecting words that he does not recognize at sight. He must analyze words when, and only when, he is unable to recognize them at sight. He must learn to analyze words only so far as is necessary in order to recognize them. He must also achieve flexibility, so that if one method does not work, he reappraises the word, reanalyzes it visually, to locate elements that lead to recognition. The need for flexibility can be shown in the following illustration. A child had learned that in certain compound words a useful visual analysis was to locate the two smaller words from which the compound word was made. For example, he had found that recognizing the words *in* and *to* was helpful in recognizing the word *into*. Then he was confronted with the word *because*. He knew the words *be* and *use* very well, but when he tried to work out the word as *be ca use,* he got nowhere. Until he rejected the initial visual analysis of the word, and then analyzed it into *be cause,* he could not solve the problem.

The child who is having difficulty in visual analysis of words should be given help in locating structural, visual, and phonetic elements that will be useful in solving the word. He also must be given exercises that develop flexibility in word analysis. The teacher, in the regular reading program, gives the child considerable instruction in visual analysis of words. Instruction for the child who is in difficulty is the same as that given to the child in the regular reading program, but greater emphasis is placed on this ability for the child who is deficient.

Such help as finding similarities in words like *right* and *night* gives the child training in finding usable elements within words. The teacher who presents a new word by pointing out its similarity to other words the child knows, is giving direct instruction in visual analysis of words. The teacher who has the children listen to words that start with the same sound and then writes them on the chalkboard, pointing out that they not only sound alike but start with the same visual element in print, is aiding the child to develop skill in visual analysis. Exercises such as the following can be used to give direct instruction in visual analysis of words:

1. Finding the root word in words having variant endings, such as: *look* in *looking, play* in *played, jump* in *jumped.*

2. Having the child make a choice between two variants of a word in a sentence, such as:

   a. The boy was $^{\text{look}}_{\text{looking}}$ at them.

   b. Let me $^{\text{play}}_{\text{played}}$ with you.

   c. I was $^{\text{going}}_{\text{go}}$ there.

   d. Cows $^{\text{like}}_{\text{liking}}$ to eat grass.

3. Exercises that emphasize initial blends.

   a. You see the picture of a street, say *street.* Look at the words here. Put an *X* on the ones that begin like *street.*

string	strap
tricks	stop
strong	stir
sleep	strange

4. Contextual exercises that emphasize word parts.

   a. Put a box around the right word.

   (1) *That* rabbit jumped _____ bushes.

shell	those	then

(2) Ea*ch* boy may _____ with a flag.

    march   walk   catch

b. Put the right word in a box.

   (1) The doll _____ off the chair.

      tell   smell   sell   fell

   (2) The apples will _____ very large.

      grow   slow   row   crow

5. Locating an element in any part of the word.

   a. Say *chimney*. Notice the sound of the first part of *chimney*. Draw a line around the part of these words that makes that sound.

      chatter   peach

      kitchen   beach

      branch   chase

6. Exercises designed to teach syllabication.

   a. Say the words below and think of how many parts there are in each word. Write the number of parts after each word.

      noon ____   recess ____   Columbus ____   discovery ____

      grade ____   agreed ____   opposite ____   dictionary ____

   b. Divide these words into syllables, like Oc/to/ber.

      d a r k n e s s

      E n g l i s h m e n

      c o n t i n e n t

      s t o c k a d e

      c e l e b r a t i o n

7. Exercises that emphasize seeing the two parts of compound words.

   a. Find a word under *B* that goes with a word under *A* to make a new word. Write the new word under *C*. The first one has been done for you.

A	*B*	*C*
1. bath	berries	bathtub
2. straw	tub	
3. snow	prints	
4. foot	storm	

   b. Find the two small words in each big word. Tell how they help you know what the big word means.

      football   afternoon

      birthday   blackbird

      snowball   groundhog

      playground   hillside

8. Exercises designed to develop the ability to see prefixes and root words in affixed words.

   a. Draw a circle around the part of each word that says *not*.

      unhappy   unknown   uneven

      unkind   untied   unable

9. Exercises designed to teach the child to locate root words and suffixes in affixed words.

   a. When something is done *bravely,* we mean *in a brave way.* Find the part of the word that tells us that something is done *in a certain way.* And then tell what each word means.

gladly	wisely	kindly
quickly	poorly	softly

   b. The syllable *ful* at the end of a word means *full of,* or *lots of.* If something is *beautiful,* it is *full of beauty.* Look at the words below and find the root words. Then tell what the whole word means.

faithful	thankful
truthful	wonderful

10. Finding the root word in affixed words, with both prefixes and suffixes.

    a. The root word is the word from which a larger word is made. Draw a line around the root word. Tell what the root word means and then tell how the added parts change its meaning.

unlikely	distrustful	unhealthful
unfriendly	disagreeable	unsuitable

In all of the exercises designed to show the child how to visually analyze words into usable elements, the child should be led to understand that rapid inspection is necessary. He should separate the words into the largest elements that he is able to recognize. As nearly as possible, the exercises should be done in meaningful settings. In all of the exercises given above, the child should use the words immediately in sentences, tell the derived meaning of the words, or use them in the completion of incomplete sentences. They should be words that are soon going to be used or that have been introduced recently in the child's basic reading program.

Insufficient Knowledge of Visual, Structural, and Phonetic Elements

There is little use in being effective in finding usable parts within words unless the child knows what the parts say. For example, there is no use being able to recognize initial blends, as *str* in *street,* unless the child knows what *str* says. The child must attain the knowledge of visual, structural, and phonetic elements if he is to become a capable, effective, and independent reader. The larger the elements the child uses in recognizing a word, the more rapid will be his recognition of that word. From time to time, it is necessary for a child to break a word down into small parts in order to recognize it. The mere breaking of a word into small parts will not aid him in the recognition unless he knows the small elements.

The teacher or remedial worker, when introducing the child to new vocabulary for a given story, frequently gives instruction in word-element knowledges. When the teacher points out similarities between two words, in such an introduction, the child is being given help in developing the necessary knowledges in order to apply analytical techniques. When the teacher has a child substitute initial sound elements in words, such as making *fall* from *ball,* she is teaching the child word elements. By showing the child how to change words by adding variant endings, such as *sing* to *singing,* or *walk* to *walks, walked* or *walking,* the teacher is building the child's background of knowledges of visual, structural, and phonetic elements.

All of the exercises given in the section above for the development of visual analysis of words aid in teaching the knowledges of visual, structural, and phonetic elements. Additional exercises such as the following will add to the word-element knowledges of the child.

1. Exercises to develop knowledge of initial consonant sounds.

   a. Write a word in the space that ends like the two sample words.
   1. The man was t_____.
      call   ball
   2. The boat was in the b_____.
      say   day

   b. Say the words *do* and *day*. Put X on all the words that start like *do* and *day* and that name animals.
      donkey   dig
      down   dog
      head   bear
      duck   pig

2. Exercises that develop knowledge of initial blends.

   a. Put in the blank the right word that begins like the underlined word.
   1. The step led to the door of the _____.
      store   house   stone
   2. The train was on the _____.
      trick   track   boat
   3. The string was very _____.
      strong   street   long

3. Exercises designed to teach knowledge of digraphs.

   a. Put in the right word. It should sound like the samples.
   1. Th____ dog is big.
      hat   cat
   2. Wh____ will we have dinner?
      hen   men
   3. The ch____ has four legs.
      fair   hair
   4. See the light sh____.
      mine   fine

4. Exercises designed to teach vowel sound.

    a. In many words the vowels *a e i o u* have a long sound, that is, they say their name. Write the letter that is long after each word. Then use the word in a sentence.

safe _____	eat _____	home _____
gate _____	kite _____	hope _____
these _____	hide _____	use _____

    b. Draw a line under each word that has long *a* in it.

fat	man	take
face	cake	rain

    c. Draw a line under each word that has long *e* in it.

feet	each	set
tree	bed	bean

Other exercises of this sort may be used to develop a knowledge of long and short vowel sounds.

5. Exercises that can be used to develop the ability to distinguish between long and short vowel sounds.

    a. Mark the long vowel sounds like this _ .
    Mark the short vowel sounds like this ◡ .

take	get	tell
can	but	use
five	mule	cat
cake	mine	let

6. Exercises that can be used to develop the ability to distinguish between hard and soft sounds of consonants.

    a. When the letter *c* has the same sound as *s*, it has the soft sound. When it sounds like the letter *k*, it has the hard sound. Put *S* after the sentences in which *c* has the soft sound. Put *H* after the sentences in which *c* has the hard sound.

    (1) We stayed in a cabin. _____
    (2) It was a good act. _____
    (3) It sold for twenty cents. _____
    (4) It was a fast race. _____
    (5) We went to the city. _____
    (6) We saw a cowboy. _____

Similar exercises can be used for other hard and soft sounds.

7. Exercises emphasizing variant endings of words.

    a. Draw a line around the right word. The sentences should be read using the correct word.

Now she $\begin{matrix} \text{want} \\ \text{wanted} \end{matrix}$ to run.

The boy was $\begin{matrix} \text{look} \\ \text{looking} \end{matrix}$ for the ball.

The dog $\begin{matrix} \text{like} \\ \text{likes} \end{matrix}$ the meat.

When developing knowledges of visual, structural, and phonetic elements, the elements should be taught in words, in contextual settings, and the printed symbols should be associated with the oral pronunciation. More detailed knowledges can be taught by methods of instruction that emphasize sounding and tracing. Such methods as those recommended by Grace Fernald [1] will build knowledge of word elements.

Lack of Ability to Auditorily Blend or Visually Synthesize Words

After the child has separated a word and recognized the parts, he must reassemble the word. The effective synthesis of words is important in word recognition. Many children get into trouble in word recognition because they are unable to put words together again effectively after they have separated them into parts. This ability is sometimes called auditory blending. However, it is likely that in actual reading, the parts of a word are not thoroughly sounded nor auditorily blended. The reader usually locates elements within the word visually and then reassembles the word visually. For example, if the word *something* was being inspected for recognition, the reader might see the words *some* and *thing* in the larger word. He probably would not pronounce the parts of the word nor the word as a whole, but simply see that it is a compound word made up of two well-known words and would recognize the word *something* by visually synthesizing the two known parts.

The mature reader, while reading silently, does not sound the hyphenated words at the end of a line. He just looks at the part on one line and then quickly glances down to the remainder of the word on the next line and recognizes the word in its entirety. Too great a separation of the parts when studying a word orally causes the child to get into blending difficulty.

Many children have difficulty in blending because the word parts were learned in isolation rather than in real words, or they were learned in drill exercises rather than in contextual settings. The remedial work that should be done with a child who is poor in the synthesis of words is to have him recognize the parts by rapid visual inspection of the words.

For a child lacking ability in auditory blending, any sounding out of words should be done in a smooth rather than in an interrupted fashion. For the child who is in difficulty because he has learned to separate the words so distinctly that he is unable to reassemble them, more attention should be given to exercises to develop sight vocabulary, to associate meaning with the words, and to use context clues.

The Overanalytical Reader

Overemphasis on oral-phonetic instruction leads to one of the most prevalent types of reading disabilities—an overanalytical reader. The child

[1] Grace Fernald, *Remedial Techniques in the Basic School Subjects* (New York, McGraw, 1943).

who has been taught word-recognition techniques in artificial or isolated exercises is likely to develop overanalytical characteristics. Overanalysis takes two forms. First, the child may have the tendency to analyze words that he knows as sight words. This is not only a slow process but it interrupts the thought as well. Basically, in word recognition, we want the child to be able to do three things. One, to recognize known words without detailed study. Two, to recognize words that he knows as sight words in any of their variant forms. For example, if a child knows *walk,* then *walked, walking,* and *walks* should cause him no difficulty and should require only a hasty inspection to note the slightly altered characteristics and meanings of the word. Third, we want the child to be able to work out the pronunciation of words that he has not previously met in print. The characteristics of an effective reader are that he allows detailed inspection and sounding out of words to become part of his reading pattern when and only when needed. The overanalytical reader has, in a way, reversed this process. He approaches every word, or the majority of words, as though they were new. He studies them in detail, isolates the elements within them, applies his knowledge of word elements, and then blends the word only to find that it is a word with which he is already familiar. Such a pattern of reading is detrimental to reading fluency and comprehension. The child is so concerned with analyzing words that he has no time to attend to the content. It takes him so long to recognize each word that fluency in reading is impossible.

The second type of overanalytical reader is the child who breaks words into too many parts. Instead of recognizing new words by isolating large elements known to him, he resorts too early and too often to a piecemeal inspection of the word and letter-by-letter sounding of it. Such a habit of recognizing words is inefficient and is often confusing. It would be foolish, for example, for a child who knew the word *walk* to resort to a letter-by-letter sounding of the word *walking.* It would be equally foolish and totally ineffective for a child who knew the element *ight* in *night,* to try a letter-by-letter sounding of that element.

Children who are overanalytical sometimes go to the extreme of a spelling attack on words, wherein they try to remember each word by spelling it out. This approach to word recognition is very inefficient and soon impedes growth in reading. It is impossible for a child to remember all of the words he is expected to learn in the first grade by trying to recall the sequence of letters through spelling. The breaking of a word into too many parts is often encouraged by methods which first teach the children the letters of the alphabet and then has them recognize the word, such as, learning *cat* by saying *c a t* is *cat.*

The method of treatment for children who tend to analyze words that are already known as sight words is to give more attention to the types of exercises that were discussed above for the development of sight vocabulary, the association of meaning with words, and the effective use of context clues. Flash techniques, such as the use of a tachistoscope as described by Durrell,[2] are helpful. Rapid exposure cards will be useful in overcoming the tendency to analyze words that are well known. Reading of material with few word difficulties for purposes that allow rapid reading, such as finding a specific bit of information, reading to get the general significance, or reading to predict outcomes will tend to overcome this type of overanalytical difficulty. It is indeed unfortunate that artificial programs of word recognition which bring about such overanalysis are still being used at the present time.

The second type of overanalytical reader, the one who breaks words up into too many parts, is corrected by giving more emphasis to structural analysis and knowledge of the large visual elements within words. Breaking a word into syllables is much more effective than sounding out each independent letter. Noting the root word, prefixes, suffixes, and variant endings is much more effective than is letter-by-letter or phonetic sounding of the words. This is not meant to imply that the child should find it unnecessary to develop a knowledge of phonetic elements and the ability to use them in recognizing words which he cannot recognize by the less analytical methods. It does indicate that instruction in word recognition should encourage the child to select within the word as large elements as he can in working out the pronunciation of words that he does not know at sight. The method for overcoming the characteristic of breaking the words into too many parts is to emphasize the exercises given above under ineffective visual analysis, so as to teach the child to isolate the larger structural and visual elements within words.

Tendency to Make Specific Types of Errors

Frequently children in difficulty in word recognition tend to mispronounce the words in consistent error patterns which can be analyzed. These errors are analyzed in many ways by different workers in the field of reading. In general, the classifications deal with the location in the words in which the error occurs. For example, the error may take place in the initial part of the word, in the middle of the word, or toward the end of the word.

Beginning errors indicate that the child is neglecting to notice the initial part in his inspection of words. He tends to make errors such as *his* for *this,* which would be classified as an error in the initial part of the word. Another type of initial error would be calling the word *house, mouse.* To illustrate the type of error that occurs in the middle of a word, the child might call *house, horse.* An ending error would be one such as *speech* called *speed.*

Another group of specific types of errors would deal with phonetic errors, such as faulty vowels, faulty consonants, or the addition or omission of

[2] Donald D. Durrell, *Improvement of Basic Reading Abilities* (Yonkers, N. Y., World Book, 1940), pp. 177-178.

sounds. *Hot* called *hat* would be an example of a faulty vowel error; *cat* called *sat* would be a faulty consonant error.

The third major type of errors would be the orientational errors which include reversals and axial rotations. An example of a reversal error would be *ton* called *not*, or *was* called *saw*. Reversal errors would also include the transposition of letters, such as *left* called *felt*. Axial rotation errors would include such things as *b* and *p*, as in *pig* called *big;* or *u* and *n*, or *w* and *m;* any rotation of the letters within the words would be classified as orientational confusion.

The remedial techniques used to overcome the tendency to make specific types of errors are similar to those described above. The difference lies in the matter of emphasis. For example, if the child tends to make errors in the initial part of words, all the exercises would be designed to focus his attention more directly and systematically on the initial part of the word. The building of a picture dictionary by the child would force him to look at the initial element in order to alphabetize the words correctly. Multiple-choice exercises that forced the child to look systematically at the words from start to finish would help him. Sorting labeled pictures for filing would force the child to look closely at the initial part of the words. The child should be shown the nature of his errors and a comparison should be made of the way the child read the word and the way it actually was in print. For example, if the child read the word *moon* as *noon,* he should be shown the slight difference. In the study of his error, it should be pointed out that he had the word nearly right but that he must pay more attention to the beginnings of words. All the exercises on initial consonants, initial blends, initial diagraphs will aid in correcting the child's tendency to make an undue proportion of errors in the initial part of words. The following type of exercises might prove effective:

1. Multiple-choice questions in which the child's attention is focused upon the beginning element.

    ball.
    a. The boy plays with a call.
    fall.

2. Classification exercises that emphasize beginning sound and meaning.

    a. Find the words that start like *call* and name an animal.

come	that
home	cow
cat	eat

3. Multiple-choice exercises in which the initial consonant is given.

    a. Mary dresses her d_____.
    cat   goat   doll

Middle errors call for a closer inspection of the words. These errors are brought about by two factors. First, the child may be hurrying his inspection of words to the point that he overlooks the middle. Second, a frequent cause of middle errors in words is to be found in faulty knowledge of vowel sounds. Exercises that teach the phonetic sounds of vowels will be helpful. Methods that encourage the youngster to inspect words in a systematic orderly fashion will aid in eliminating errors in the middle of words. The use of context as a check on accuracy will encourage the child to make the inspection necessary to avoid middle errors. The need for closer inspection of the middle of words should be pointed out to the child. Multiple-choice exercises will prove helpful. The following type of exercise, for example, will aid in forcing attention to the middle part of the word:

> home.
> 1. The man rode on the house.
> horse.

Final errors are quite frequent, and it will be found that a higher percentage of the errors of good readers will appear in the endings of words than in the errors of poor readers. All of the exercises designed to give training in variant endings, suffixes, and families of words will aid in eliminating errors in the ending of words. A cautionary remark should be made about emphasis on the final element within words. The mature recognizer of words starts at the beginning of the word and goes systematically along it from left to right until the word is completely inspected. Exercises designed to increase attention to the endings of words frequently have the detrimental effect of forcing the child to neglect the beginning of the words. However, if the exercises are put in contextual settings, where both the beginnings and endings of words must be studied in order to answer the question or problem, the child can be taught to pay more attention to the ending of words without losing the inspection of the essential initial element. Multiple-choice exercises such as the following demand that the child notice both the initial and the final elements and will prove helpful:

> came.
> 1. The dog is running after the fat.
> cat.

Or ask the child to find in a list the word that belongs to the *all* family and with which he would like to play.

> call   tall
> sail   with
> doll   ball

Faulty vowels or consonants. Frequently a child appears to make most of his errors either in mispronouncing vowels or in mispronouncing consonants. In such cases, there can be any one of several interfering characteristics within the child. First, he may have a speech defect that makes articulation of the vowel or consonant difficult. If so, speech correction is indicated. Second, the child may have difficulty in discriminating between speech sounds. He may be hard of hearing and cannot differentiate fine distinctions between short sounds of *i* and *e,* for example. Or it may be that he has failed to learn to listen carefully and accurately.

If the child is having difficulty in hearing, the best approach to improving his general word-recognition ability is to avoid strict phonetic training and teach him by methods that emphasize the visual elements within words. Such methods as the non-oral approach to teaching reading will prove beneficial to the child who has hearing limitations. Of course, he should have his hearing checked by an otologist and he should be seated in a favorable location in the classroom.

For the child who has failed to learn to attend to speech sounds, ear training emphasizing rhymes and other auditory elements within the spoken word will prove beneficial. After the child has been taught to listen to words and word parts, he should be given direct instruction on phonetics and sounds, such as were indicated in the section on insufficient knowledge of visual, structural, and phonetic elements.

Orientational confusion is another type of error which warrants special attention. The left-handed child is slightly more apt to have orientational confusions than is the right-handed child. This is especially true because he brings to reading the habits formed during his early preschool years. The left-handed child has found it easier to work from right to left because his hand will not then cover his work and he can see what he is doing better if he works in that direction. His visual perception has tended to go from right to left as he followed the work he did with his left hand. Likely the cause of orientational confusion, then, is the transfer of eye-movement habits from preschool work into reading. Careful initial instruction can prevent the formation of habitual orientational confusion. The classroom teacher should constantly be on the alert to detect orientational confusions at the onset and give the appropriate instruction.

Reversals and axial rotations are brought about by prolonged word study due to a heavy vocabulary burden, prolonged study of words due to visual defects, or as a result of too analytical an observation of words so that by the time the child gets to the end of the word, he forgets how it began and tends to look back at the beginning. Reversals and axial rotations are also brought about by too early attention to word endings or word families before the child has established the habit of attending to the initial elements of words. Many children having axial rotation difficulties are immature in their mastery of word-recognition techniques. The remedial instruction for the child who makes an unusual number of reversal or axial rotation errors should be done with material that has few unknown words. It has been found that the child who makes this type of error is much more likely to reverse the parts of a word with which he is less familiar than he is with its reverse form. For example, the child is much more likely to call *ton, not* than he is to call *not, ton*. Therefore the teacher should be careful to introduce all new words to the child suffering an orientational confusion prior to the reading of a selection.

Frequent demonstrations, by the teacher, of left to right progression are helpful, especially in the early grades. When the teacher is writing on the chalkboard, he should be sure he is observed by the child who has reversal tendencies. He should give manual direction by sweeping his hand under the print as he has the children read chalkboard or chart work. If the child has a rather severe case of orientational confusion, exercises prepared with single lines of print to be read are helpful. The child should be allowed to follow under the print with the eraser end of his pencil. The child who suffers orientational confusion is often overwhelmed by a page of compact print. It is advisable to use material that has wide spaces between the lines for these children. It has proved helpful with this type of case to show the child the correct word and its reverse form. He should be given time to study the two words, with one written above the other, such as $\frac{was}{saw}$. Multiple-choice and completion exercises that require the child to distinguish between such words as *stop* and *pots* or *tops* are helpful. Having the child distinguish between such words as *dig, big,* and *pig* in multiple-choice or completion exercises would also prove beneficial.

If the orientational confusion persists after a few weeks in which corrective aids such as those suggested above are used, sounding and tracing methods such as recommended by Fernald [3] should be used. Having the child write the word and its reverse form may prove helpful. Likely the best approach for correcting orientational confusion errors is by teaching the child to study words systematically, sounding them part by part, always making a clear-cut regression to the beginning of the word if he gets into difficulty. Employing exercises designed to force the child to look at the beginning of the word will tend to eliminate orientational confusions.

Word recognition is a difficult learning. It implies the development of a highly integrated and flexible set of skills and abilities. In order to avoid some of the more serious types of word-recognition difficulties, systematic and orderly instruction must be given at all levels. The child must start by having instruction that builds the habit of attempting to recognize words as words through the use of context clues, picture clues, and teacher aids. Then the child should be led to note similarities in the beginnings of words. He should start to learn some of the easier consonant sounds. As the child is building a sight vocabulary, he should be led to an understanding of variant endings and the knowledges necessary to be effective in the recognition of them. Gradually, he will develop a knowledge of all of the consonant sounds and will be introduced to the long and short sounds of vowels. He will gain the ability to syllabify words and to use root words, prefixes, suffixes, and

[3] Grace M. Fernald, *op. cit.*

other structural elements. It is only through a gradual, orderly program of reading instruction that very troublesome faults in word study can be avoided. The classroom teacher should constantly be diagnosing the needs of the children in word recognition and should be on the alert to detect the onset of any of the word-recognition difficulties which have been described. Most of these are easy to overcome if they are detected early. If they are allowed to persist, they can lead to the most difficult problems found in a clinic. The child cannot be an effective reader if he develops faulty techniques of word study which are allowed to persist. He can become a stubborn reading disability case.

POOR COMPREHENSION

The objective of all reading is to communicate with authors. The development of comprehension abilities is the major objective of all reading instruction. The child should at all times be reading for definite purposes which demand an understanding of the material read. At one time, the child may be reading to enjoy the plot of a well-told tale. At another time, he may be skimming through material to locate the answer to a specific question. At still another time, he may be reading to organize the facts of science. In each of these instances, the child is using the printed page to understand the ideas of the author or to get information from that author. The child, then, in all reading is in some way attempting to let the author communicate with him.

To encourage the establishment of a variety of comprehension abilities, modern reading programs develop background and word-meaning readiness so that the child can understand what he reads. In this way verbalism, that is, reading the words and recalling them without understanding, is avoided. Modern programs suggest that pupils and teachers set the goals for reading. Purposes for reading are well established before the selections are read. In this way, the child is able to learn to adjust his comprehension abilities to meet the demands of the purposes.

Basically, there are five major categories of comprehension ability.

1. *Reading to retain information* is an exacting sort of reading. It includes such things as being able to isolate detail, to recall specific items, to retain the larger, fundamental concepts, to use facts to answer specific questions, and to find statements to prove a point or answer questions.

2. *Reading to organize information* includes such abilities as being able to sense relationships, establish a sequence, classify or list facts into reasonable organization, to follow the step-by-step directions given to perform a specific task, to summarize and generalize, to plan major headings and to relate to those major headings the supporting information.

3. *Reading to evaluate* is the general category of comprehension abilities that involves making critical judgments of the information given. This includes such abilities as judging the reasonableness or relevance of content,

sensing the meaning that is implied but not directly stated, establishing cause- and-effect relationships and making comparisons, judging the authenticity of material read, and critically appraising it.

4. *Reading to interpret* includes recognizing the main idea or general significance of the passage, drawing inferences and conclusions, predicting outcomes of information given, and forming an opinion or judgment about the topic being discussed.

5. *Reading for appreciation* includes such abilities as sensing the humor of the plot and action of the story, the ability to form sensory impressions, the ability to establish the feeling tone, and the ability to interpret and appreciate the characterizations.

In addition to these comprehension abilities, which form the major objective of reading instruction, the child must develop the ability to adjust his comprehension to meet the demands of the specific content fields. All of these abilities and adjustments in comprehension depend upon the child's skill and capability in deriving meaning from the printed page.

The child may be poor in comprehension for the following three reasons:

1. Limited development of basic comprehension proficiencies.
2. Immaturity in the specific types of comprehension ability.
3. Lack of ability to adjust to the nature of the material read.

Limited Development of Basic Comprehension Proficiencies

With the possible exception of skill in word recognition, the most prevalent limitation in children's reading abilities is lack of development of basic comprehension proficiencies. The ability to get meaning from the printed page rests upon the child's familiarity with word meanings. He must have extensive knowledge of the variations in meanings of words so that he can select the appropriate meaning for the passage in which the word appears. He must have the ability to sense visually and auditorily the meaning of descriptive words. He must be able to interpret figures of speech and symbolic expressions.

When a limitation in word meanings is found, an immediate attack must be made on that problem if the child is to gain stature in reading. There are varieties of exercises designed to develop word meanings. Probably the most important approach to increasing the meaning vocabulary of children is through first-hand experiences. In order for first-hand experience to be effective in building vocabulary, the child must be made ready; the vocabulary must be connected to the experience, and the vocabulary must be utilized in discussion after the experience. The second approach is through vicarious experiences, such as motion pictures and other visual aids. The child can gain in meaning vocabulary through such vicarious experiences if the vocabulary is emphasized by readiness for the vicarious experience and reinforced by discussion after the experience takes place. The third avenue available for building meaning vocabulary is through extensive reading. Reading will increase the child's vocabulary if he has established the habit of attending to words and word meanings. This habit is developed by the teacher who places importance upon the use of new words, figures of speech, symbolic expressions, descriptive words, and colorful speech in the discussions about what has been read. The types of exercises for developing word meanings suggested in the discussion of word study will prove helpful.

Another basic comprehension proficiency is the development of techniques for increasing vocabulary. Such skills as the ability to use authors' definitions, to use the dictionary, to use structural aids to meaning, and to use context clues are essential techniques for acquiring an adequate vocabulary.

A third basic comprehension proficiency is skill in reading thought units within the passage read. This includes the ability to isolate the thought units, to understand their literal meaning, and to sense symbolic expressions and figures of speech.

A gradual increase in sentence sense is another area in the basic comprehension proficiencies. The child likely has little difficulty in understanding simple sentences if he knows all the words involved. Sentences become more complex as conjunctives are added and as qualifying phrases are inserted. The task of understanding the idea presented in a complex sentence becomes more difficult.

Understanding paragraph meaning and organization is important in the hierarchy of basic comprehension abilities. The child must sense the various ways in which paragraphs can be written, and he must be able to detect the central idea and the supporting information if he is to comprehend adequately printed material.

The basic comprehension proficiencies are gained by reading the materials in basic reading programs for specific purposes. They are reinforced by reading the material of the content fields and in the personal development reading of the children. It is recommended that for remedial work, basic readers be used to teach the basic comprehension proficiencies. The better manuals of instruction accompanying basic readers list exercises designed to encourage an understanding of basic meanings. Such exercises as the following have proved helpful:

1. Exercises emphasizing word meaning.

    a. Read the words. Then read the phrases opposite them. Put the number of the word in front of the phrase that has the same meaning.

(1) lagged	_____	makes soft whispering sounds
(2) clatter	_____	walked in a shaky way
(3) staggered	_____	fell behind the others
(4) rustles	_____	ran quickly away
(5) bolted	_____	sharp, rattling sounds

2. Exercises designed to teach children how to use author's definitions.

   a. The person who writes the story helps you know many of the words he uses. Look at the word at the left. Then underline the part in the sentence that lets you know what that word means.

     (1) combat   The combat was hard until the fighting stopped.

     (2) sombrero   He put on his sombrero, and the big hat hid his black eyes.

     (3) levee   The levee, walls of dirt, kept the river from flooding the land.

3. Exercises designed to show the child how to select the appropriate dictionary definition.

   a. Find the number of the right meaning for each underlined word and write that number in front of the sentence.

_____ The cutter fired a shot to stop the smuggler.   cutter 1. person who cuts; 2. small sleigh; 3. small sailboat; 4. small armed ship

_____ It was fun to see the bird light on the mast of the ship.   light 1. that by which we see; 2. easy to carry; 3. come down upon

4. Exercises designed to teach phrasing in thought units and figures of speech.

   a. Read the sentence and look at the underlined phrase. Then put X before the number of the one that means the same.

He would run like the wind.

     1. He ran in the air.
     2. He ran softly.
     3. He ran fast.
     4. The wind has legs.

When John saw the new sled, his face *seemed to shine.*

     1. A bright light was shining on John's face.
     2. His face was well-scrubbed.
     3. The light from the sled was on his face.
     4. The boy looked happy.

5. Exercises designed to develop sentence sense.

   a. Read the sentences and put the right letter in front of them to show what the underlined phrase tells us.

     (A) Who   (B) Did What   (C) Where   (D) Why

_____ 1. We have many goats on our farm.

_____ 2. We saw some little eggs in the nest.

_____ 3. The big horse pulled the wagon up the hill.

_____ 4. A boy came to the farm to see the horse.

6. Exercises designed to teach paragraph organization.

   a. Read the paragraphs and underline the topic sentence in each.
   The little dog was happy at last. He had traveled all night trying to find a home. The night was cold and wet. He was sad as he looked for a warm place to sleep. At last he had seen a small boy. The boy called to him and patted his head. The dog followed the boy to his house. The boy opened the door and called to the dog. The little dog's tail showed how he felt.
   An old man walked toward his home. He had a package under his arm. The old man smiled to himself as he thought about the package. Soon he would be home. He knew that his grandson would like the birthday present he had in the package.

Exercises such as those given above are available to the teacher. In the manuals of modern basic readers there is a wide variety of such exercises. The workbooks accompanying modern readers also have many exercises similar to the ones given above. Unfortunately, these workbook materials and the exercises suggested in the manuals are not used extensively enough in education. If they were used more widely, many of the comprehension disability cases would be prevented. It is suggested that the classroom teacher study the children, diagnose their needs, and use these exercises so that the child can be taught the basic comprehension proficiencies. For the child who has been allowed to get into serious difficulty, exercises given in workbooks and in the manuals accompanying the basic readers are the best for correcting his deficiencies. The manuals and workbooks have indexes of proficiencies which indicate the pages upon which such exercises can be found.

Immaturity in Specific Types of Comprehension Abilities

Even though the child has ability in word recognition and has grown adequately in basic comprehension proficiencies, he may be in difficulty in comprehension because he has failed to establish some of the specific types of comprehension abilities.

If the child has faulty word-study techniques, or if he is limited in basic comprehension abilities, he will be low in all types of comprehension. Even if the child is adequate in these two areas, he may still be inexperienced or inadequate in reading for a specific purpose or a specific type of purpose. The child, on the one hand, may be overexacting in his reading comprehension. He may become so concerned with the details within a passage that he fails to sense the implications or the general significance of the passage. On the other hand, a child may be so concerned with the general idea the author is trying to get across that he fails to note sufficient details.

There are some children who are so concerned with noting every detail in a selection that they read with an exactness not warranted by the material. There are other children who are so fearful of losing the detail within a passage that they search for information not contained in the selection. Such compulsive, overanalytical reading makes for slow, laborious readers who frequently fail to comprehend the ideas the author is presenting because of their intense concern about the minutia he is using to develop his ideas. These children need reading experiences that will develop flexibility in their reading approaches. The well-rounded program, that introduces the children to the various types of comprehension indicated on pages 172-173, will create such diversified readers.

When a child is found to be overexacting, he should be encouraged to read relatively easy material for purposes of enjoyment or of getting the general significance of the passage, or of predicting the outcomes of the events given. The child who, on the other hand, is not attending to the details within the passage, when such attention is demanded by the purposes for reading, should be given reading experiences that require the listing or organizing of factual information. Such experiences will require him to locate the answers to specific questions, and they will require him to retain factual information. Such a child should be given material that has considerable factual content—science material is exceptionally good for developing the patterns of exact reading.

The child who is unable to read for certain types of purposes should be placed in reading situations where the purposes, for which he has limited capability, are established. The best approach in teaching specific types of comprehension is to set the purposes for reading carefully, select passages and materials the children read that fit those purposes, and plan for creative use of the results of such reading. If, for example, a child of first-grade reading capability has limited ability in retaining factual information, a suitable purpose would be to read first-grade material to find facts about animals of the forest. He should plan to read to locate these facts, and he should list them. He should plan to organize his facts in a table that has the names of the animals listed along the left-hand margin and facts about them listed across the top. Such facts as what they eat, how they protect themselves, how they get ready for winter, any unusual characteristics, and where they live should be included in the table. Then, for each animal, the child can fill in the information in the appropriate box. This reading will demand careful attention to the detailed information within the passage. Other types of comprehension should be developed in a similar manner.

The major approach, then, to the correction of specific types of comprehension disabilities is to have the child work with a well-graded set of materials at a level at which he can read comfortably. The type of material to be read should be suitable to the type of comprehension being emphasized. The purposes should be established and then the material read. After the material has been read once, the child should reread it for new purposes to get further experience in the type of comprehension in which he is limited. Manuals of instruction that accompany basic readers have numerous suggestions for developing all skills and abilities including the various types of comprehension.

The following sample page [4] from such a manual will show the help that the teacher or the remedial worker can get from using such manuals:

DEVELOPING SKILLS AND ABILITIES

COMPREHENSION

Summarizing and Generalizing: The story should be reread carefully and a list of all the means of controlling floods should be made. The children may then formulate plans for controlling the floods of the Mississippi Basin. At this time their generalized plan will not be complete, but it should include such control measures as dams and reservoirs in the contributary rivers and streams, straightening of the channel, building of levees. They should get the general idea that flood control in the Lower Mississippi Basin depends upon: 1. Slowing the onrush of water in the upper tributaries by storing it and in other ways; 2. Speeding of water through the lower channel by straightening the channel and by making it deeper with levees.

BASIC MEANING DEVELOPMENT

Using Author's Definition or Explanation of Technical Words: The children should be made aware of the author's definition or explanation of technical words as he introduces them. It should be pointed out to the children that frequently, when a technical word is used, the author explains the meaning of that word. The examples which follow may be used to illustrate the author's definition or explanation of technical words.

Page 357, "The channel of a river is the river bed—the place where the river runs."
"The river basin is all the land from which the waters come to the river."
"Erosion means wearing away."

Page 360, "A reservoir is a storage place."

WORD RECOGNITION

Seeing Similarity in Word Form and Meaning: Write *fertile* and have it identified; then have it defined as meaning rich or productive. Write other words in which *fertile* appears, have them identified and give help with meaning and use, as:

fertile—rich; productive
fertileness—richness, productiveness
     The fertileness of the soil was shown by the fine crops.
fertilize—make productive
     After the farmer fertilized the soil of the cornfield he got a better crop.
fertilizer—something which makes soil productive
     Each year Jack put fertilizer in the soil of his garden.
Carry on the same type of exercise with the word *erosion,* as:
erosion—wearing away
erode—to wear or to eat away
     The metal was eroded by rust.

[4] Guy L. Bond and Marie C. Cuddy, Manual for *Days of Adventure* (Chicago, Lyons & Carnahan, 1954), p. 549.

erosive—tending to wear away
>Rivers usually are most erosive in the spring because then they are large from melting snow.

BASIC STUDY SKILL

Using a Map: The map on page 359 should be inspected in detail. The watershed of the Mississippi River should be studied. The children might find their own locality on the map and ascertain if it is in the Mississippi River Basin. They should discuss the effects of the mountain ranges on the water flow. They might speculate as to how the water from the Great Lakes gets to the sea (another map may be used to show that it goes through the St. Lawrence River). While the children are looking at a large map of North America, the teacher might explain that the water in Northern Minnesota and in parts of Canada flows into Hudson Bay. The flow of the water into Hudson Bay will help give the children the understanding that north is not necessarily uphill. They may have that notion from always seeing the north at the top of two-dimensional maps. They may also have the notion that it is quite natural for the Mississippi River to flow down the map toward the bottom because that is seemingly downhill on two-dimensional maps. As a matter of fact, the Mississippi River does flow south but it is because of the lower elevation of the land and not because south is at the bottom of the map. These concepts of elevation should be made clear at this time and the true generalization established: *Water always flows downhill unless affected by some other force and downhill may be toward the north as well as toward the south.*

WORKBOOK ACTIVITIES

Fun to Do Book, pages 80-81, may now be used.

The index in the back of the manual will show that on this page, for example, there is a comprehension exercise dealing with summarizing and generalizing. There is a basic meaning development exercise dealing with the author's definitions or explanations of technical words. There are word-recognition exercises dealing with word forms and structural analysis including root words and variants. There are exercises designed to teach the basic study skill of using a map. Such materials give the classroom teacher or clinician a whole pool of exercises and reading experiences for developing all of the essential elements necessary to establish reading in the first place or to correct disabilities. The workbooks accompanying basic readers also are a fruitful source of remedial exercises in the specific comprehension abilities.

Some teachers and clinicians prefer to select passages from the wealth of children's books that are available. They then formulate purposes that will stress the type of reading in which the child has shown inadequacy and prepare comprehension questions to check on the accuracy with which he has read for the purposes set. Whatever the materials used for training in the specific types of comprehension, the purposes must be well established before the child reads. There is a second necessary condition—the child must be reading material that is suitable, both from the standpoint of difficulty and from the standpoint of type of content. There is little use in trying to develop comprehension with material that is too difficult for the child to read with understanding. There is also little use in trying to develop the ability to outline, for example, in material that should be read for a general impression. There is little use in trying to develop the ability to read critically in material that is designed to amuse or entertain.

Lack of Ability to Adjust to the Nature of the Material Read

The writers in each field of human experience have evolved their own distinct ways of writing to best handle the content in their fields. The geographer, for example, writes in one way; the historian writes in another; the scientist writes in still another way. The child must learn to read all types of material. A thorough program of diagnosis reveals the child's capability in reading materials of the various content fields. If the child is overly weak in reading material of one field, he should be given instruction in that type of material. The child should learn that each field has its own technical and specialized vocabulary. In order to be able to read in science he must attain an understanding of scientific words. In order to read in the social studies, the child must develop the ability to interpret the technical words, the abstract words, and the specialized meanings of words. For example, the child must learn the meaning of a definite term such as *referendum,* which can be clearly defined. He must gain through wide experience an understanding of such an abstract word as *democracy,* which is difficult to define. He must learn specialized meanings, such as the *head* and *mouth* of a river.

In addition to vocabulary differences, there are differences in the ways the materials are organized and there are differences in the basic study skills needed in the various fields.

If the child finds it difficult to sense the organization of ideas within a field, he should be given specific instruction to correct the deficiency. If, for example, a child confuses sequences in history, he should be taught to use time lines. If he has trouble in formulating generalizations in science, he should be given instruction in the steps involved in arriving at generalizations.

If a child demonstrates weakness in a specific study skill, the nature of his weakness within the skill should be studied and appropriate instruction given. Many children, for example, fail to recognize the symbolism on maps, which represents mountains, rivers, roads, and so on. If a child is found to have such a limitation in the reading of maps, he should be given instruction in the symbolism of map reading. If he is found to be limited in location of information in the field of science, and if further diagnosis shows that his limitation is inability to sense key words, he should be given exercises designed to show him the likely words under which to find the topic on which he wants information. The study skills should be evaluated and the indicated instruction given. The child must also develop the ability to estimate which type of material is being read and to learn how to adjust his speed to that type of material. In addition, he must learn the types of comprehension which are compatible with the content area in which he is reading.

THE INEFFICIENT READER

The slow, inefficient reader is usually one who has a deficiency in some of the skills and abilities previously discussed. Quite often a child who is a slow reader does not read rapidly because he is deficient in word-study techniques. Some other children are not reading rapidly because they overvocalize while they are reading silently. They read everything aloud to themselves. Still other children are word-by-word readers; they must look at every word separately. These children lack phrasing ability. Other children are slow readers because they are ineffective in the use of context clues and therefore do not readily anticipate the content they are going to read, nor the words that are likely to appear in that content. Other children are slower than they should be in certain types of reading because they set inappropriate purposes. Still other children are slow, inefficient readers because they have established unfortunate habits. In other words, there are many reasons why people are inefficient readers.

The efficient reader is one who reads as rapidly as he can understand the passages being read, bearing in mind the purposes for which he is reading. The inefficient reader is one who reads slowly and with poor comprehension. A child is also inefficient if his comprehension is good but his speed is slow. At all times, the child should comprehend what he is reading. Good speed with poor comprehension is not a desired outcome of a reading program. The true measure of speed, then, is how rapidly a child can read material of a given difficulty with good understanding, taking into account the purpose for which he is reading. It would seem unwise, for example, to teach a child to read science material or mathematical problems at a rapid rate. On the other hand, it is unfortunate if a child cannot read relatively easy material to get the general significance at a good rate of speed.

There are some general suggestions for increasing speed of reading, irrespective of the exact nature of the speed limitations.

1. The material used in developing speed should be highly interesting and easy. Short-story material is exceptionally good for increasing general rate of reading.

2. The more exacting types of comprehension exercises should be avoided. Those which require the retention of factual information or organizing that factual information should be avoided. Comprehension exercises which demand evaluative, reflective reading should be avoided, too. The types of reading which encourage an increase in speed are: reading

to get the general significance, reading to predict outcomes, reading to appreciate the plot or action, and reading to appreciate the humor.

3. The practice period should be introduced with vigor. The child should know that he is expected to read as rapidly as he can for the purposes involved and that a check is to be made on time spent as well as on his comprehension. A good approach is to have the first part of a period used for independent silent reading. The pupils are to practice reading as rapidly as they can interpret the material. The last part of the period may be used for timed reading under the direction of the teacher. While the children are reading independently, the teacher may watch them for signs of faulty habits which would retard reading rate. Such faulty habits as excessive articulation, head movements, keeping the place with the finger, and so forth, can be easily seen. If evidences of some faulty habit are found, the child should be told about it. When the attention of the pupil is called to a specific faulty habit, he may overcome it without further assistance.

4. Charts of the child's progress in reading should be kept. Records of the rate of reading of each child during the timed reading period should be kept and plotted so that each child can see how his work is progressing. A chart such as the one shown below is effective for demonstrating an increase in speed of reading. If the child reaches a plateau, such as is shown in the child's fifth practice period, the teacher should ease the material so that continued growth can be demonstrated.

WEEKLY SPEED CHART

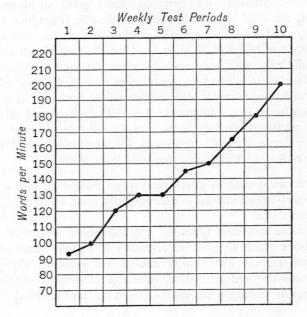

Weekly Test Periods

5. Fatigue and boredom should be avoided. The child should not try to increase speed of reading if he is tired, and the material should be changed if it is uninteresting to him. It is important, in improving speed of reading, to have the child read for purposes that are useful in a subsequent creative enterprise. The child will read much faster if he is trying to get information that, to him, is important.

6. Practice periods for increasing speed should be regular and at well-spaced intervals, rather than spasmodic. It is better to give speed exercises after the child has had a little time to warm up, but he should know when his rate of reading is being measured.

7. In all cases, except in the case of a child who is a slow reader because of his inability to phrase, oral reading should be avoided. A large proportion of slow readers are inefficient because they are either overanalyzing or over-vocalizing. Oral reading and oral word study tend to develop slow, inefficient readers. So, in the vast majority of cases, any oral reading or any detailed word study should be avoided. The teacher should anticipate any word difficulties the child is likely to encounter and should present the words to the child before he starts his reading.

The following types of inefficient readers will be discussed:

1. The slow reader having deficiencies in word study.
2. The slow reader who is overvocalizing.
3. The word-by-word reader.
4. The reader who is unable to adjust his speed to suit the purpose.
5. The reader who is slow because of unfortunate habits.

Deficiencies in Word Study

Many of the slow, ineffective readers are in difficulty because of inappropriate word-study techniques. The child who, because of an overemphasis upon analytical approaches to word recognition, has formed the habit of breaking into parts words that he knows at sight will obviously be a slow reader. The child who lacks sufficient sight vocabulary will be slow and inefficient. The child who fails to use context clues to anticipate the meaning of the sentences he is reading will be unable to recognize the words with the speed that is necessary to be a continuous, smooth, fast reader. The reader who resorts to piecemeal observation of words is one of the most difficult types of slow readers to treat.

The best means of correcting children who are ineffective readers because of deficiencies in word study is to make a direct attack on the word-study problem rather than to try to increase their speed of reading through pacing devices, time tests, or mechanical apparatus. If the child's speed of reading is hampered by faulty word study, mechanical or other artificial devices will enhance the difficulty rather than correct it. Frequently, the child who is a slow reader because of unfortunate word-study techniques has become thus because the more analytical approaches to word recognition were introduced too early, or the vocabulary burden of the reading material was so great that the only way he could comprehend it was by analytically decipher- ing the words. The child in such difficulty should be given instruction with material that is easy for him, and the training should be on word recognition rather than on speed.

Overvocalization

Vocalization is usually the result of too much use, during early teaching, of oral reading as a method of instruction rather than an outcome of instruc- tion. Oral sight reading, pupil after pupil, leads to overvocalization in the child's silent reading. Many adults are slow readers because they find it necessary to vocalize most of the words. The reader who must read aloud to himself usually finds it difficult to read faster than 150 or so words a minute for any purpose. The degree to which the person must vocalize what he is reading determines, in many cases, the rate at which he can read. The methods for overcoming vocalization are to explain the nature of the prob- lem and to indicate that excessive articulation is being used. It should be pointed out that vocalization can be overcome and that to gain speed the speech organs should be kept inactive. The child should try to read faster, to see the words ahead so that he can anticipate them and will not have to vocalize them.

In such cases, emphasis on use of context clues is highly desirable. No oral reading should accompany the silent reading. Rapid exposure methods, such as the Science Research Associates Rate Controller, may prove of some benefit in treating this type of slow reader.

Word-by-Word Reader

Some slow readers are word-by-word readers. They lack the ability to locate thought units within a sentence and to read the sentence thought unit by thought unit. All of the exercises suggested above for developing phrasing ability will be helpful. In the case of the word-by-word reader, interpretive oral reading is recommended as a means of teaching the child to phrase. If he prepares a selection to read aloud, he must phrase, in order to interpret the material to his audience. Such preparation, then, teaches the child to select the appropriate phrases and thereby increases his speed of reading. This is the only type of slow reader for whom oral reading is recommended. In addition, such exercises as the following may prove beneficial. It should be remembered, however, that the fundamental difficulty of the youngster is that he is unable to isolate phrases. Therefore, these exercises have only limited usefulness.

1. Read each group of words at one glance, and then go on to the next group of words.

> The big boy/ was going/ to the fair. On the way/ he saw/ a race horse. The race horse/ was one/ from the farm/ next to his./ He wanted/ to see/ the horse run/ in the race.

2. Mark out the units that tell who, did what, where, why.
    The dog chased the rabbit over the hill trying to catch it.
    The fast train whistled loudly on the bridge to warn the boys.

The Reader Who Is Unable to Adjust His Speed to Suit the Purpose

Some slow, inefficient readers are, in reality, overconscientious readers. They approach all reading as though it were a legal document or a chemistry laboratory manual in which every bit of information should be carefully studied, evaluated, and digested. Frequently, some of these children are so concerned with the factual detail within a passage that they look for information not included. An efficient reader displays a high degree of flexibility in the speed at which he reads material. There are times when it is important to read for factual, detailed understanding of the passage. It is unlikely that a good reader would read a passage again and again to find information that the author did not include in his writing. It is unfortunate for the reader to be constantly in search of all the factual detail, when the purpose of the particular reading is to derive a general understanding. If the child has the habit of setting too exacting purposes for reading, the teacher should demonstrate to him that for certain types of outcomes his reading can be more rapid than it can for others; that for certain purposes he need not note all of the factual detail. The child must learn to appraise his reading; he must recognize the purposes for which he is reading, and he must adjust his speed accordingly. The ability to choose the appropriate speed of reading comes about through broad experience in reading for many types of purposes. The teacher, before each reading, can tell the child how to adjust his rate. For example, if the material is to be read to get the main idea of the story, the child can be told to read rapidly without too much concern about the details. If the material is to be read in order to discover the steps necessary to conduct an experiment, it should be read slowly, paying attention to the detailed instructions that are given. Such instruction will enable the child to adjust his reading to the outcomes he expects from the reading.

Inappropriate Habits

There are certain faulty habits that have detrimental effects upon speed of reading. Some children have formed the habit of dawdling over their reading. They do not energetically attack the problem of reading the selection at hand. If they are reading a story for appreciation of the plot, they may approach the reading in a somewhat less than energetic attitude. Such an attitude will obviously slow the reading. If a child were reading a story to see if he wanted to suggest it to the class for dramatization, he might read it somewhat more rapidly. The suggestion is made, then, that the purposes should be real to the child, important to him, and that he should not be allowed to dawdle.

The second type of inappropriate habit is that of pointing at the page while reading. The person who points at the page is likely somewhat insecure about his ability to understand the content. The material being read may be too difficult. The child may have had too many experiences with material with which he had to struggle; under such circumstances, the only way that he could read effectively was to point. It is not unusual to see a capable adult reader point when he is faced with a difficult problem in mathematics or a difficult piece of reading in a test situation. Two things can be done for the child who points while he reads. One is to give him material he can read with ease. The other is to have him hold the book in both hands so that pointing is difficult and this habit is thereby broken.

An unusual number of repetitions or other types of faulty eye movements may cause slow reading. Faulty eye movements are usually the result of some other deficiency in reading. For example, if the child encounters a word that he is unable to recognize, frequently he must go back to pick up the content of the material read. Poor comprehension also makes the child regress. If his attention wanders, he has to go back over the printed material to pick up the meaning. There are certain children, however, who have faulty eye movements because they are attempting to read too rapidly. They skip ahead too far in their reading and then have to regress in order to re-establish the understanding. In each of these cases, the remedial instruction should be directed toward the cause and not toward the symptomatic faulty eye movements.

SPECIAL ADJUSTMENTS FOR THE SLOW-LEARNING CHILD

There are many children who are developing in reading at a slow rate who are actually not disabled in reading. They do not have a learning difficulty. For such children, poor reading is really a part of a more general limitation. These children lack abstract, verbal intelligence and they cannot be expected to develop in reading capability as rapidly, nor can they be expected to develop as much capability as can the average child. The children under consideration are not mentally defective but are classified as slow learners. Their IQ's range from 70 to 95. They make up approximately 27 per cent of the population. Some of these children may be both mentally retarded and reading disability cases. The usual program is not adjusted to their specific needs, and therefore they may get into difficulty because the program advances too rapidly for them and the objectives are not compatible with their abilities.

The following table indicates the reading ability that can be expected of such children under average instruction when they reach the age of 16.

READING GRADE OF SLOW-LEARNING CHILDREN AT 16 UNDER
AVERAGE AND SUPERIOR INSTRUCTION

IQ as Measured by the Stanford Binet Scale	Expected Reading Grade at 16 Under Average Instruction	Estimated Reading Grade at 16 Under Superior Instruction
95	8.6	9.5
90	7.7	8.3
85	7.0	7.5
80	6.2	6.7
75	5.4	5.8
70	4.8	5.2

The table also shows the estimated reading grade at the age of 16 under instruction adjusted to the needs of the slow-learning child. This estimation is made on the basis of follow-up studies which have shown that children who were given special instruction could not maintain reading ability very far in advance of their mental age. On the other hand, it was interesting to note, in the individual follow-ups of slow-learning children, that they were able to maintain reading ability somewhat in excess of their mental level.

Slow-learning children have certain characteristics which influence the nature of instruction that is suitable for them.

1. They like work that is repetitive in nature and they profit from drill and rereading.
2. They lack initiative and therefore must be carefully guided in the reading program, their purposes must be carefully set, and suggestions for constructive use of reading must be carefully directed.
3. They are not good planners. They need careful direction in their reading work, more detailed instructions, and more immediate goals for their reading.
4. They are easily discouraged in reading activities. Therefore, materials should be easy enough so that they can feel successful achievement. They should not read for many purposes at one time.
5. They are not able to handle some of the abstract reasoning necessary to read critically, to evaluate, and to interpret beyond the statement made in the reading selection.

The goals of instruction must be modified to meet the needs of these children. Reading instruction can effectively teach the practical types of reading. Such abilities as reading advertisements, much of the newspaper, and factual types of reading are suitable. In addition to these types of reading, the children should learn to read to follow directions. Such directions as are found in shop manuals, instructions on how to assemble equipment, cookbooks, and other materials giving specific directions and instructions should be the objectives of their reading instruction. Therefore, the emphasis for these children should be on factual reading and reading to follow directions. They can also read to understand the general significance of newspaper articles and certain magazine articles.

The following statement of principles for reading instruction will prove helpful in working with the child who has an IQ between 70 and 95:

1. Reading instruction should begin later. Because of limited intelligence, the slow-learning child has not developed the background necessary for initial instruction in reading quite as rapidly as has the average, or the more superior, child. It is not necessary to delay the introduction of reading instruction until these children have a mental age of 6 years and 6 months, as is sometimes implied, but care should be taken to help these children attain the educational readiness for initial instruction in reading. The child with an IQ of 70, for example, will not be 6 years and 6 months old mentally until he is 9 years and 4 months old chronologically. It would be unwise to delay reading instruction until that time. A better course of action would be to delay initial instruction as long as is necessary to establish the prerequisite learnings.

2. It should be recognized that these children develop reading ability in much the same way as do other children but at a somewhat slower pace. They need to develop similar capability in word recognition and must have readiness in the form of vocabulary introduction and the setting of purposes just as do other children. There are, however, modifications in instruction that should be made, but these modifications are more in the nature of emphasis rather than a drastically different program.

3. They need a great amount of carefully controlled material. The usual program introduces words too rapidly for these children to make them a permanent part of their sight vocabulary. Therefore, they need material that is more gradual in its vocabulary development.

4. They need more review of the basic words. The slow-learning child will profit from use and reuse of workbook material. He will profit from reading a selection several times because it gives him the opportunity of reviewing the basic vocabulary he is trying to establish.

5. The slow-learning child needs more detailed and more simplified explanations of the techniques. Reading, at best, is a complicated learning, and children with less than average verbal intelligence find some of the directions in workbooks or in teachers' exercises difficult to understand. The teacher must be sure the child understands what is expected of him in all reading assignments.

6. He needs more concrete illustrations of the things about which he is reading. The average child is able to generalize his experiences and he can interpret the printed page more readily from experiences that are only somewhat similar to the one about which he is reading. The slow-reading child is handicapped in abstract thinking and therefore should be given every opportunity to come in direct contact with things about which he is studying.

7. The goals for reading should be relatively immediate. The child who

is a slow learner cannot work upon projects of long duration. He needs purposes that can be fulfilled in a relatively short time.

8. This child needs more rereading for different purposes. For example, if a slow-learning child is to read about a buffalo hunt, he may read it the first time to find out whether or not the little Indian boy shot a buffalo. He may read it the second time to find out how the Indians got ready for a buffalo hunt and how they actually conducted the hunt. He may read it a third time to find out all of the equipment that was necessary for the buffalo hunt; and he may read it a fourth time to find all of the uses that were made of the buffalo by the Plains Indians. The child who is less well equipped intellectually than other children cannot read with several purposes in mind. The gifted or more able child can read the story once for all of the purposes listed. He might reread it to list some of the uses made, but he would have achieved most of the purposes for which the slow-learning child would need to reread. The slow-learning child does not mind rereading, for it enables him to gain a fuller understanding of the material, it gives him an opportunity to review the ideas expressed in the story, and it also furnishes an excellent review of the basic vocabulary he is developing.

9. More experience and more guidance in discovering visual and auditory characteristics of the words are needed by the slow-learning child. In order for the word-recognition skills to operate effectively in all reading, they must become a generalized learning. This is a difficult type of learning for slow-learning children. Therefore, they profit from additional drill in analyzing words and in learning the sounds of word elements. These children will not find it necessary to read at the rapid rate that the average or superior child will need to read. Therefore, there is not so much concern about a moderate degree of overanalysis for slow-learning children. As long as the analytical techniques do not interfere with their understanding of what they read, the fact that it slows speed should cause little concern to the teacher.

10. More use of oral reading and oral prestudy is advisable in the instruction of the slow-learning child. Many of them need to vocalize what they are reading in order to comprehend it well. It may be that the material they are reading is frequently somewhat difficult for them because of the abstract reasoning involved and therefore pronouncing the words helps them to comprehend. The fact that vocalization slows the reading rate is not a matter of great concern in the case of the slow-learning child. The reading of detailed directions need not be done at a rapid rate. The reading of a recipe in a cookbook should not be done rapidly. A little longer time spent in reading a recipe in no way limits a person's effectiveness. Reading the recipe constitutes a very small proportion of the time devoted to the entire act of preparing a meal. This is true even if the reading is done at a very slow rate.

11. More physical and motor activity, in connection with the reading, is recommended for slow-learning children. Often they can read and make

models from the content of their reading. For example, if they are reading about the farm, it would be well for them to build a miniature farm, using a pasteboard box for the barn, a round rolled-oats box for the silo, and so on. The major point in having them doing constructive work is that they learn more effectively if they can manipulate material.

If suggestions such as the above are used in teaching reading to the slow-learning child, he can be expected to grow in reading comfortably and effectively. If the slow-learning child is in the same classroom with average and superior youngsters, material should be made available that will enable him to read on the same topics as his more able classmates. It is wise for children of all mental capabilities to learn to work together. It is unfortunate if the structure of the classroom segregates any specific intellectual level within that classroom and so organizes the instruction that any child will feel as one apart. The slow-learning child must be given material that he can read comfortably. He must have purposes that are quickly fulfilled. He must have more concrete experiences, and he needs a greater amount of drill and repetition than does the average child. Although he will not be able to read much above his mental level, in other respects his learning experiences may be, for the most part, similar to those of other children. Under such conditions, he can be expected to profit from reading instruction.

SUGGESTED ACTIVITIES

1. Give specific illustrations of classroom practices that adhere to the principles of remedial instruction given on page 152. Outline a remedial program adjusted to the needs of pupils who have reading difficulties falling under any one of the four categories on page 153. Be specific.

2. Describe learning situations which might lead to failure to associate meanings with words. How can these situations be avoided? How can the teacher organize instruction so as to find the time needed to treat learning difficulties in this area?

3. What classroom procedures will aid in the development of a large sight vocabulary? What place do basic readers have in developing sight vocabulary?

4. Examine the manuals and readers of several basic series. What evidence do they present of vocabulary control? How does this control contribute to the development of sight vocabulary?

5. Examine the teacher's manuals of several series of basic readers. What aids do they present the teacher for developing word recognition? How could the materials in these teacher's manuals aid in remediation of the various types of faulty word study discussed in this chapter? Give specific illustrations.

6. Examine the workbooks that accompany basic reading series. Show how they could aid in the remediation of the faulty word-study techniques discussed in this chapter.

7. Make a list of criteria for word-recognition exercises. Then evaluate the various word-recognition exercises given in this chapter.

8. If there are word-recognition exercises in the chapter that do not meet this list of criteria, write other exercises that teach the same recognition skills and meet the criteria you have set up.

9. Describe word games you have used or know about that contribute to word recognition skills. What might be the result of overuse of word games?

10. Describe remedial procedures that are useful with a child who has over-learned certain word recognition techniques, such as overanalysis of word parts.

11. Show why it would be possible for a child to be very good in one of the comprehension abilities but poor in the others. Describe a teaching situation which would help the child overcome inability to evaluate. How would this teaching situation differ from one designed to overcome disability in reading to retain information?

12. Describe a reading program suitable for slow-learning children in the primary grades; in the intermediate grades. How will this program differ from a program for rapid learners?

13. What provision should be made for developing the reading skills that are peculiar to the various areas of the curriculum?

14. Why do certain children develop a distaste for reading? What can be done to correct a bad attitude toward reading?

15. Outline provisions a school can make for dealing with cases of complex reading disability.

SELECTED BIBLIOGRAPHY

See bibliography at end of Chapter 6.

8
DIAGNOSIS IN ARITHMETIC

IN THIS CHAPTER the diagnosis of difficulties in arithmetic is discussed under the following headings:

1. The fundamentals of effective instruction in arithmetic.
2. Foundations of diagnosis.
3. General diagnosis in arithmetic.
4. Analytical diagnosis in arithmetic.
5. Case-study diagnostic procedures.
6. Diagnosis in problem-solving and quantitative thinking.

Chapter 9 deals with the treatment of learning difficulties in arithmetic.

In thinking about diagnosis in arithmetic the teacher should bear in mind the factors associated with learning difficulties which were discussed in Chapter 3. Since the ability to read is of fundamental importance in arithmetic, it is obvious that much of the discussion of the diagnosis and treatment of reading difficulties in Chapters 6 and 7 applies to the study of arithmetic difficulties. However, arithmetic also is a hierarchy of special knowledges, skills, and understandings that are peculiar to the subject. The basic problem of diagnosis in arithmetic is the discovery of deficiencies in the many subsidiary and interrelated learnings that must be corrected in order to acquire proficiency in the subject. For instance, to succeed in arithmetic the child must master several hundred basic number facts so that he can give their answers quickly and correctly. The logic of arithmetic requires that the number operations be taught in a sequential order, since skill in more difficult processes such as long division requires prior mastery of underlying skills which are its components. Thus a child cannot divide by a two-place number unless he already knows how to divide by one-place numbers, can multiply the divisor by the quotient, and subtract to find the remainder. Weakness in any one of these underlying skills may be the source of incorrect work in division. Later the child must learn to use division in even more difficult work with common and decimal fractions.

The basic reason for the vast majority of difficulties in arithmetic is the complexity of the operations themselves. When they are not understood by the child and when underlying skills are not mastered, deficiencies are sure to develop. The continuous application of diagnostic methods to ferret out the difficulties pupils may be having with arithmetic is vital. Just as is true of reading, there will be found cases of simple retardation, specific disability, and complex disability in arithmetic. However, there will also be many instances of minor difficulties for normal pupils which can be corrected easily in the course of regular instruction. Because arithmetic skills rapidly deteriorate with disuse, the teacher must provide the practice necessary to maintain them.

THE FUNDAMENTALS OF EFFECTIVE INSTRUCTION IN ARITHMETIC

The Major Objectives of Arithmetic Instruction

The two major objectives of the modern arithmetic program are (1) to develop the ability of the learner to perform number operations skillfully and intelligently, and (2) to provide a wide variety of learning experiences that will assure the ability of the learner to apply quantitative procedures effectively in social situations both in and out of school.

In recent literature two phases of the arithmetic program have been discussed under which more specific objectives can be grouped, namely, the mathematical phase and the social phase. For purposes of evaluation and diagnosis, the following classification of outcomes will be helpful:

1. *The mathematical phase of arithmetic,* which includes

   a. Understanding of number and of the relationships in the number system
   b. Knowledge of basic number facts in the four fundamental processes and their interrelationships
   c. The meaning of the various operations and the relationships among them, including the essential technical vocabulary
   d. Skill in computational procedures
   e. Ability to apply computational techniques in life situations, also in solving verbal problems

2. *The social phase of arithmetic,* which involves

   a. Skill in using measurement and measuring devices
   b. Ability to read and interpret quantitative data in tables, charts, graphs, maps, diagrams, and other forms used for the systematic presentation of information
   c. Knowledge about social institutions through which number functions, such as money, banking, bonds, taxation, insurance, and the like
   d. Understanding of basic economic concepts underlying production, distribution, and consumption, or stated more briefly, consumer education
   e. Ingenuity and resourcefulness in dealing with quantitative aspects of social situations and problems encountered in daily life

Learning difficulties and deficiencies fall into categories which correspond in general to the various subheadings listed above. Those that are grouped under the mathematical phase include deficiencies in the basic elements involved in the computational skills and the ability to use them in problem-solving. These are the primary concerns of this book. However, the learning activities grouped under the social phase make the study of arithmetic skills purposeful, vital, and significant to the learners, and in a well-rounded program of arithmetic, both phases are dealt with in a well-integrated manner.

The Intercorrelations of Arithmetic Abilities and General Intelligence

Sometimes it is assumed that arithmetic is a general ability composed of a group of closely related knowledges and skills. The limitations of this point of view are revealed by the intercorrelations given below between scores on standard tests of the four aspects of arithmetic indicated and the IQ's of 453 pupils in grades 4 and 5, having a median IQ of 93.[1]

INTERCORRELATIONS OF ARITHMETIC ABILITIES
AND GENERAL INTELLIGENCE

	Computation	*Problem-Solving*	*Vocabu-lary*	*Quantitative Relationships*
IQ *	.350	.506	.766	.602
Computation		.631	.361	.417
Problem-solving	.631		.522	.576
Vocabulary	.361	.522		.661
Quantitative relationships	.417	.576	.661	

* Mental ability based on Van Wagenen *Unit Scales of Aptitude.* Mean IQ of group, 93. Arithmetic scores based on *Analytical Scales of Attainment in Arithmetic.*

All of the correlation coefficients given in the table are positive, but they range from as low as .350 to as high as .766. Both of these correlations are between IQ and test scores, the lowest for computation, the highest for vocabulary. The intercorrelations among the four arithmetic tests range from as low as .361 between computation and vocabulary to as high as .661 between vocabulary and quantitative relationships. The latter is essentially a test of knowledge of social aspects of arithmetic. It is perhaps significant that the correlation between computation and quantitative relationships is positive but low, only .417. The correlation of .631 between computation and problem-solving is one of the highest given in the table, showing the relatively close relationship between skill in computation as such and ability to per-

[1] Data from an unpublished Master's thesis by Virgil Walker, graduate student at the Univ. of Minnesota.

form the number operations needed in solving verbal problems. The correlations of knowledge of vocabulary with problem-solving and quantitative relationships are both over .50.

The nature of profiles of arithmetic ages of four typical 11-year-old fifth-grade pupils based on the results of the four parts of the test is shown by the data in the table below:

Pupil	Mental Age	Computation	Problem-Solving	Vocabulary	Quantitative Relationships
1.	9.6	9.8	9.4	9.4	9.6
2.	15.3	11.9	13.4	14.5	12.3
3.	10.0	11.4	8.4	8.0	7.6
4.	11.0	13.0	10.4	9.8	11.04

The chief conclusion to be drawn from the above data is that arithmetic is not a general ability, and that a high level of proficiency in one aspect of arithmetic is no guarantee of a correspondingly high level in any other area. To secure an adequate picture of a pupil's ability in arithmetic, it is necessary to study his profile based on tests of a number of traits. Usually such profiles are very irregular, indicating considerable differences in the levels of the various traits tested. It is evident that arithmetic instruction must provide for the development of all desirable outcomes through well-selected learning experiences adapted to the pupils' mental ability, needs, and interests. If undue emphasis is placed on any one of the major objectives, for example, computational skill, it is quite likely that the other desirable outcomes will not be developed to a satisfactory level at the same time. The only way in which the school can, so to speak, guarantee the various outcomes in the mathematical and social phases of arithmetic is to provide a balanced well-rounded program in which all of the desirable outcomes are given careful consideration.

Fundamental Principles Underlying All Arithmetic Instruction

The basic principles underlying an effective developmental program that is most likely to assure power and to prevent disability in arithmetic may be briefly summarized as follows:

1. A rich, functional program should be provided in which number and the arithmetical skills are applied in a wide variety of social situations so that a genuine interest in arithmetic will be aroused and also a desire on the part of the learner to master the various number operations.

2. Number operations should be made mathematically meaningful to the learner so that he will understand the procedures he is expected to learn and be successful in his efforts to master them. Insight is fundamental in learning.

3. The discovery of facts, meanings, generalizations, and relationships

by the learner through experimental procedures and investigations, involving first the manipulation and arrangement of concrete objects, then the analysis of the steps in processes visualized in diagrams, charts, and illustrations, and finally the study of explanations of abstract procedures such as textbooks and workbooks contain, leads to understanding and insight, thereby facilitating the retention of what is being learned.

4.   Learning arithmetic is a gradual growth process which requires expert guidance to assure the development of efficient performance. Readiness tests should be used to determine readiness of pupils for new work, and individual differences in rates of growth should be provided for in the gradation and organization of the curriculum. It is realized that ordinarily there is a gradual growth in the level of maturity of pupil performance from the immature reactions of the beginners to the point when efficient procedures used by adults are mastered.

5.   Diagnostic procedures are an essential element of teaching arithmetic and should be continuously applied in the course of the learning activity so that difficulties will be promptly detected and corrected. Self-diagnosis by the learner should be emphasized so that he can take increasing responsibility for improving his performance.

6.   A wide variety of vital, realistic, interesting learning activities should be provided to enrich and extend meanings and to assure needed experience in practicing and applying what is being learned. Intensive, systematic, planned practice to develop proficiency is necessary, but "drills" should never be assigned until the learner understands the steps in processes he is learning and they are meaningful to him. The slogan should be: Meanings first, then practice to attain proficiency.

It is beyond the province of the present volume to show in detail how these principles are to be applied in the course of regular instruction. However, their significance for the diagnosis and treatment of arithmetic difficulties will be made clear in the descriptions of diagnostic and remedial procedures contained in the following pages. General discussion of basic principles of teaching arithmetic are to be found in such books as the following:

Leo J. Brueckner and F. E. Grossnickle, *How to Make Arithmetic Meaningful* (Philadelphia, J. C. Winston, 1947).
———, *Making Arithmetic Meaningful* (Philadelphia, J. C. Winston, 1953).
B. R. Buckingham, *Elementary Arithmetic: Its Meaning and Practice* (Boston, Ginn, 1947).
P. L. Spencer and M. Brydegaard, *Building Mathematical Concepts in the Elementary School* (New York, Holt, 1952).
H. F. Spitzer, *The Teaching of Arithmetic* (Boston, Houghton, 1954).
The Teaching of Arithmetic, Fifty-first Yearbook, Part II, National Society for the Study of Education (Chicago, Univ. of Chicago Press, 1951).

Illustration Showing How to Apply the Basic Principles

For illustrative purposes we shall show how the basic principles just discussed can be applied in teaching a single new step in the addition of like fractions. To make the description as concrete as possible, we shall show how they are applied by analyzing the steps in teaching how to add 1½ and 1½, as presented on the typical textbook page given on page 198. The development of the step is detailed and gradual, complete enough so that even slow learners can grasp the procedure.

1. The new step is presented on the page in a social setting so as to make it realistic. The pupils are expected to write out the example to be worked. The teacher can use instead classroom situations that arise in the course of regular instruction.

2. The answer to the example is then found by using manipulative materials, namely, circle cutouts and whole circles. The answer found is checked by reference to the row of pictures at the top of the page. (See problem 1.)

3. Next the sum is found by using the diagram at the left of the worked-out example given in exercise 2. The diagram visualizes the solution for the children.

4. Then the work given at the right of the diagram is studied. Reference to visualization in the diagram clarifies the discussion which is guided by the statements given below the diagram.

5. Next the pupils study and explain worked-out models. The examples may also be worked out at the blackboard by pupils. (See exercise 3.) If necessary, slow pupils can work them out with their fractional cutouts.

6. To check understanding of the new step the pupils copy the worked-out model examples, work them, and compare their solutions with those given under exercise 3. At this point any pupil difficulties are revealed and steps can be taken to correct them. (See exercise 4.) Further and perhaps even simpler manipulative and visual experiences may be necessary.

7. Finally "bunched" practice on the new step is provided in exercise 5, to be followed by mixed practice containing the new type of examples as well as other types previously learned. On subsequent days mixed practice should be provided so as to maintain the new skill.

ADDITION WITH IMPROPER FRACTIONS IN THE SUM

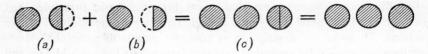

1. On the table there were 1½ apple pies and 1½ cherry pies. How many pies were there altogether?

    a. Write the example we must work on the blackboard.
    b. First show the pies with your cutouts of circles.
    c. Join the half circles. How many circles are there in all?
    d. Use the pictures at the top of the page to check your answer.

2. We can add 1½ and 1½ as shown below.

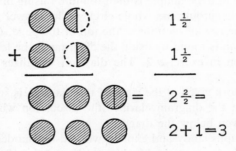

$$1\tfrac{1}{2}$$
$$+\;\;1\tfrac{1}{2}$$
$$2\tfrac{2}{2} =$$
$$2 + 1 = 3$$

First find the sum, using the drawings.
Now let us study the example.
First add ½ and ½. This is ²⁄₂.
Then add 1 and 1. This is 2. Is 2 ²⁄₂ the same as 2 + ²⁄₂?
Explain why 2 + ²⁄₂ = 2 + 1.

3. Now explain each step in the work in the examples below:

    a.   2½   *b.*   2¼   *c.*   1⅜
        +1½   +2¾   + ⅝
        3²⁄₂ = 3 + 1 = 4   4⁴⁄₄ = 4 + 1 = 5   1⁸⁄₈ = 1 + 1 = 2

4. Now copy the three examples and work them with your book closed. Then open your book and see if your work is correct. If you had errors, ask your teacher for help if you think you need it. If you had no errors you are ready for the practice below.

5.

	a	*b*	*c*	*d*	*e*	*f*
	1½	3⅔	5¼	⅞	2⅙	2⅖
	2½	1⅓	6¾	2⅛	⅚	1⅗

6. Now do the mixed practice exercises on the next page.

The above steps can be summarized briefly as follows:

1. A social setting is provided for the new step.
2. Manipulative materials are used to discover the answer.
3. Visualization of procedure follows.
4. Procedure with symbolic materials is studied, involving diagnosis.
5. Practice is provided to develop and maintain skills.

These steps should be followed in teaching any new element of a process. If they are followed, the teacher can be reasonably sure that pupils of all levels of maturity and mental ability will understand the procedures involved. Judicious questioning of pupils who have difficulty will usually enable the teacher to discover the source. These steps should also be used in corrective teaching in connection with the review work in the fall of the year.

FOUNDATIONS OF DIAGNOSIS IN ARITHMETIC

The Structure of Our Number System

An understanding by the teacher of the basic concepts underlying the Hindu-Arabic number system is essential to the diagnosis of difficulties in all number operations. These concepts can be identified by reference to the number 703, as follows:

1. Each place in the number has a value or base of 10, since our number system is a decimal system. ("Decem" means ten.)

2. Ten symbols, 1, 2, 3, 4, 5, 6, 7, 8, 9, and 0 are used to express the frequency of any base. Thus in 703 there are 7 hundreds, no (0) tens and 3 ones.

3. In the Hindu-Arabic system 0 serves as a place-holder when there is no frequency to record in a given place, thus making complete use of place value possible. The Romans did not have a 0 in their system and made only a limited use of the idea of place value, for instance, in such numbers as IX and VII.

4. The ratio of the bases from left to right in the Hindu-Arabic system is 10 to 1, and from right to left 1 to 10. For example, in 22 the 2 at the right has one-tenth times the value of the 2 at the left. Similarly the 2 at the left in 22 has ten times the value of the 2 at the right.

The last of these principles is fundamental in changing the forms of numbers as when carrying 10 ones or 1 ten to tens' place in example *a* below or as when regrouping 72 as 6 tens and 12 ones in example *b*.

$$
a. \quad \begin{array}{r} 1 \\ 27 \\ +34 \\ \hline 1 \end{array}
\qquad\qquad
b. \quad \begin{array}{r} 72 = 6 \text{ tens } 12 \text{ ones} \\ -28 = 2 \text{ tens } 8 \text{ ones} \\ \hline 4 \text{ tens } 4 \text{ ones} \end{array}
$$

Common fractions are expressed with the symbols that are used to write whole numbers but the figures are used in a different way. Common fractions represent an *addition* to our number system, used to express quantities of less than 1.

Decimal fractions are based on an *extension* of our number system by making use of the places to the right of *ones'* place to represent values of less than 1 whole. The function of the decimal point is to identify ones' place. Thus in 302.01 the 1 has a value of 1 hundredth since it is in hundredths' place which is two places to the right of ones' place; correspondingly the 3 is in hundreds' place, or two places to the left of ones' place, and has the value of 3 hundreds, or 30 tens, or 300 ones. We can also write 302.01 as $302\frac{1}{100}$, thus showing the relationship between the two kinds of fractions.

Complexity of Operations with Whole Numbers

The learning of the four fundamental operations with whole numbers requires not only a clear conception of the nature and structure of the number system itself but also a mastery of the underlying skills through which the number system operates. First, the basic number facts for all processes must be known to assure efficiency of performance. Research has discovered that a major cause of incorrect work in all processes is lack of knowledge of basic number facts, as revealed by incorrect responses, slow rate of work, the use of roundabout procedures, counting, and the like. Diagnosis, therefore, should begin with the study of how well the pupil knows the various basic number facts involved in any process in which he is encountering difficulty. Methods of diagnosis will shortly be described.

Number operations with whole numbers vary in complexity from the relatively simple group of skills involved in addition of whole numbers to the highly complex group of related skills involved in division by two-or-more-place numbers.

The addition of whole numbers is comparatively simple because similar, closely related skills are involved, together with a knowledge of the 100 basic addition facts. This can be seen in the analysis of the series of addition examples below which involve steps of increasing complexity:

a. 32
   +24   No carrying is required.

b. 27
   +36   It is necessary to regroup 13 ones as 1 ten and 3 ones and to carry the 1 ten from ones' place to tens' place.

c. 253
   +370   It is necessary to regroup 12 tens as 1 hundred and 2 tens and to carry the 1 hundred from tens' place to hundreds' place.

d. 287
   +365   Regrouping is necessary in both ones' and tens' places and carrying from both ones' and tens' places.

c. 6 Adding by endings is involved here, as $13 + 5 = 18$. In this
    7 case the 13 is not seen, and no bridging of decades is required.
    5 However, in finding 18 and $9 = 27$, not only is the 18 not seen
    9 but also "bridging" the tens from teens to twenties is required to
   ── get the 27.

Subtraction of whole numbers is also a relatively simple operation. The major difficulty is the regrouping required in order to subtract, as explained in the examples below:

a.   48
      −28   No regrouping required, since both the figures in 28 can be sub-
      ──   tracted from corresponding figures in 48.
       20

       6 12
b.   7̶ 2̶   To subtract in ones' place, it is necessary to regroup 72 as 6 tens
      −3 4   and 12 ones, as shown in the example.
      ───
       3 8

       6 11
c.   7̶ 1̶ 6   To subtract in tens' place, it is necessary to regroup the 71 as 6
      −6 5 3   hundreds and 11 tens, as shown in the example.
      ─────
        6 3

        11
       5 1̶ 17
d.   6̶ 2̶ 7̶   Here it is necessary to regroup in more than one place to subtract,
      −1 5 9   in both ones' and tens' places.
      ─────
       4 6 8

When the learner has mastered the above steps in subtraction, he can subtract any two whole numbers by applying these underlying concepts of regrouping. Sometimes zeros in the minuend present special difficulties to children.

Multiplication by one-place whole numbers requires not only a knowledge of the 90 basic multiplication facts and of the process of multiplication, but also the ability to add, as is done when carrying to places to the left is necessary. This is shown in each of the examples below. Addition is also used in finding sums of partial products, as in example *d* below.

a.   32
       ×3   No carrying is required in the solution of this example.
      ───
       96

b.   68   The steps are: multiplying 8 ones by 2, then changing 16 ones
       ×2   (2×8) to 1 ten and 6 ones; writing 6, and remembering the 1
      ───   ten to be carried to tens' place; then adding this 1 to 12 (2×6);
      136   simple addition by endings.

c.
$$\begin{array}{r} 651 \\ \times 8 \\ \hline 5208 \end{array}$$
Here there is no carrying in ones' place, but it is necessary to carry 4 hundreds, from 8×5 tens = 40 tens, to hundreds' place. It is necessary to add the 4 to 8×6 hundreds = 48 hundreds, which involves bridging of decades.

d.
$$\begin{array}{r} 49 \\ \times 34 \\ \hline 196 \\ 1470 \\ \hline 1666 \end{array}$$
Multiplying by two-or-more place numbers requires not only ability to multiply by one figure, but also an understanding of the procedure of placing partial products correctly and the ability to find the sum of the partial products, a step in which addition is used.

Judging from the illustrations above, multiplication is a more complicated process than either addition or subtraction, since it is a complex of both simple multiplication and addition.

The ability to divide by two-place numbers requires mastery of a much more complex hierarchy of skills than those described above for the other processes. This can be seen by the following analysis of the skills involved in working the difficult division example given below. It will be observed that actually all four processes are required.

$$\begin{array}{r} 35 \\ 27\overline{)953} \\ 81x \\ \hline 143 \\ 135 \\ \hline 8 \end{array}$$

1. Obviously a knowledge of certain of the 90 basic even division facts and of the 360 uneven division facts is necessary to estimate the quotient figure ($2\overline{)9}$, $2\overline{)14}$), as well as of the series of steps used in working easy division examples.

2. Also required is the ability to test and correct the estimated (trial) quotient figure to find the true quotient, which in the first step in the example is 3, or 1 less than the estimated quotient (4) and in the second step is 5, or 2 less than the estimated quotient (7), and also the ability to place the first quotient figure correctly.

3. The ability to multiply is necessary, but in the different form found in division, as in multiplying the divisor 27 first by 3 and then by 5.

4. The ability to add is required in the carrying involved in multiplying 27 by both 3 and 5.

5. The ability to subtract is necessary when subtracting 81 from 95 and 135 from 143. In the first subtraction regrouping is not necessary, whereas in the second subtraction regrouping is required.

Wiest [2] reported the following series of correlations between the scores on a comprehensive 32-example test in division by two-place numbers and scores made on each of five special tests of skills underlying that process.

Special Tests Related to Division	r's	
1. Division by one-place numbers (25 items)	.79	
2. Estimating first quotient figure (24 items)	.74	3
3. Multiplication as used in division (24 items) ..	.67	(Example: $39\overline{)126}$)
4. Finding errors in worked out examples (24 items)	.60	
5. Subtraction used in division (30 items)	.48	

[2] Unpublished study, College of Education, Univ. of Minnesota, 1952.

Evidently the skill used in division by one-place numbers has the highest relationship to the ability to divide by two-place numbers; the next highest relationship is for ability to estimate quotient figures, one of the major learning difficulties in this process; the ability to multiply in the form used in division also correlates fairly high with the general ability to divide, as does the ability to detect and correct errors embedded in worked-out division examples. Ability to subtract does not correlate very highly with the ability to divide, perhaps because by grade 6 most pupils make relatively few errors in subtraction, as is indicated by the fact that the mean number of examples correct was 27.8 out of 30 examples, or about 93 per cent accuracy. However, Wiest found that a considerable number of children had extremely low scores in subtraction, a fact to be borne in mind in diagnosis.

The implications of the above analysis of skills for the diagnosis and treatment of difficulties in division by two-place numbers are obvious. Deficiencies in any of the five basic abilities described above may be the cause of unsatisfactory work in this difficult operation. They can be identified by suitable diagnostic methods. Research has shown that there are significant differences between the performances of good and poor achievers in division in all of these basic skills.[3] To improve performance in division, deficiencies in any or all of these areas must be diagnosed and remedied. Fortunately, it has been shown that in many instances pupils require corrective work in only one or two of these underlying skills and not in all of them, thus simplifying the problem of bringing about an improvement in their work in division.

It is evident from the above discussion that in order to compute efficiently with whole numbers the pupil must understand the relationships involved in the number system so as to be able to transform and regroup numbers in working examples as shown above; he must have mastery of the basic number facts; he must have insight into the steps in the process of working any example; and he must be able to integrate the various component skills outlined above for each of the operations. Incorrect work and actual deficiencies in any process may be due to shortcomings in one or more of the elements which comprise a total skill.

Complexity of Operations with Common Fractions

Operations with fractions can be analyzed into component skills in a similar way. Analysis of the example at the left shows that certain basic skills are involved in working it; inability to apply any of them may be the cause of difficulty in working the example. The basic skills in the above example may be listed as follows:

$$5 \tfrac{1}{2} = 5 \tfrac{3}{6}$$
$$+2 \tfrac{5}{6} = 2 \tfrac{5}{6}$$
$$\overline{ 7 \tfrac{8}{6}} = 7 + 1 \tfrac{2}{6} =$$
$$8 \tfrac{2}{6} = 8 \tfrac{1}{3}$$

[3] R. L. Koenker, "Certain Characteristic Differences of Good and Poor Achievers in Long Division," *Journal of Educational Research,* Vol. 35 (April, 1942), pp. 578-587.

1. Ability to change the two fractions which are in the same family to a common denominator.
2. Ability to find the sum of two mixed numbers.
3. Ability to change the improper fraction $\frac{6}{8}$ in the sum to a mixed number.
4. Ability to add a whole number and a mixed number when expressed in horizontal form to find the final sum.
5. Ability to reduce the fraction $\frac{2}{8}$ to lowest terms.

Similar analyses of the basic skills involved in other addition examples can easily be made by the reader. The combinations of skills may vary from example to example, as will be seen by an examination of the work shown in the six addition examples below:

a.
$$3\tfrac{1}{4}$$
$$+2\tfrac{1}{4}$$
$$5\tfrac{2}{4} = 5\tfrac{1}{2}$$

b.
$$4\tfrac{1}{2}$$
$$+6\tfrac{1}{2}$$
$$10\tfrac{2}{2} = 10 + 1 = 11$$

c.
$$6\tfrac{3}{8}$$
$$+5\tfrac{7}{8}$$
$$11\tfrac{10}{8} = 11 + 1\tfrac{2}{8} = 12\tfrac{1}{4}$$

d.
$$6\tfrac{1}{2} = 6\tfrac{2}{4}$$
$$5\tfrac{1}{4} \quad 5\tfrac{1}{4}$$
$$11\tfrac{3}{4}$$

e.
$$7\tfrac{3}{4} = 7\tfrac{15}{20}$$
$$+2\tfrac{4}{5} \quad 2\tfrac{16}{20}$$
$$9\tfrac{31}{20} = 9 + 1\tfrac{11}{20} = 10\tfrac{11}{20}$$

f.
$$7\tfrac{5}{6} = 7\tfrac{20}{24}$$
$$+6\tfrac{3}{4} = 6\tfrac{18}{24}$$
$$13\tfrac{38}{24} = 13 + 1\tfrac{14}{24} = 14\tfrac{7}{12}$$

Notice that in examples *a, b,* and *c* there is in each case involved the ability to add like fractions and to express proper or improper fractions in sums in simplest form; in *a* simple reduction alone is required, while in *b* and *c* reduction of improper fractions is necessary, a step complicated in *c* by a required second reduction of $\frac{2}{8}$ to $\frac{1}{4}$. In examples *d, e,* and *f,* three different difficulties in changing unlike fractions to like fractions are involved: (1) in *d* the common denominator 4 is present; (2) in *e* the common denominator is not present and is the product of the two given denominators 4 and 5, or 20; and (3) in *f* there is a common factor of the two denominators 6 and 4 and the smallest common denominator is 12. Example *f* is the most complicated type of addition example possible, and it also is the most difficult type for pupils to learn to solve. The mastery of all these procedures is certain to present difficulties to many pupils, especially if they are not taught meaningfully.

$$9\tfrac{5}{6} = 9\tfrac{20}{24} = 8\tfrac{44}{24}$$
$$-4\tfrac{7}{8} = 4\tfrac{21}{24} = 4\tfrac{21}{24}$$
$$4\tfrac{23}{24}$$

The subtraction example at the left is known to be the most difficult and complex type in that process, as can easily be seen by an analysis of the work shown. First a common denominator must be found. How? Because $^{21}\!/_{24}$ cannot be subtracted from $^{20}\!/_{24}$, the minuend $9\,^{20}\!/_{24}$ must first be regrouped as 8 and $1\,^{20}\!/_{24}$, and then expressed as $8\,^{44}\!/_{24}$. This regrouping step in which 1 one is taken from the 9 is similar to the regrouping needed in subtracting 17 from 43.

Similar analyses should be made by the reader of the increasingly complex steps in working each of the following examples:

a. $3\frac{3}{8}$
  $-1\frac{1}{8}$

b. 4
  $-1\frac{1}{2}$

c. $3\frac{1}{8}$
  $-1\frac{7}{8}$

d. $2\frac{1}{2}$
  $-1\frac{1}{6}$

e. $4\frac{2}{8}$
  $-1\frac{3}{4}$

Regrouping the minuend as in b, c, and e is the only new skill involved in subtraction of fractions other than regrouping as explained above.

$2\frac{1}{2} \times \frac{1}{4} \times 6 =$
$\frac{5}{2} \times \frac{1}{4} \times \frac{6}{1} = \frac{30}{8} =$
$3\frac{6}{8} = 3\frac{3}{4}$

The work in this multiplication example at the left illustrates the new steps in that process, namely, the method of expressing mixed numbers and whole numbers as improper fractions, the method of multiplying the numerators and the denominators to find the terms of the product, and finally expressing the improper fraction in the answer in simplest form, in this case reducing $\frac{30}{8}$ to $3\frac{6}{8}$, and then to $3\frac{3}{4}$. Errors in multiplication and division, which are the same steps as with whole numbers, are major causes of incorrect work in this operation with fractions. Errors in reducing fractions to lowest terms occur very frequently.

The only new step involved in division of fractions is inverting the divisor; aside from this step the process is similar to multiplication of fractions, as is shown in the work in the solutions below which should be analyzed in detail by the reader to note the different steps in the solutions shown:

a. $4\frac{1}{2} \div \frac{3}{4} =$
  $\frac{9}{2} \times \frac{4}{3} = \frac{36}{6} = 6$

b. $4 \div 6\frac{2}{3} = 4 \div \frac{20}{3} =$
  $\frac{4}{1} \times \frac{3}{20} = \frac{12}{20} = \frac{3}{5}$

c. $3\frac{1}{2} \div 2 = \frac{7}{2} \div \frac{2}{1} =$
  $\frac{7}{2} \times \frac{1}{2} = \frac{7}{4} = 1\frac{3}{4}$

Complexity of Operations with Decimal Fractions and Per Cents

Operations with decimal fractions are the same as those for whole numbers, the only new learnings involved being the meaning of decimal fractions, the management of the decimal point in arranging the numbers in addition and subtraction examples, and its proper placement in products and quotients. Per cents may be regarded as a special usage of decimals.

Level of Difficulty of Arithmetic Processes

One of the most important causes of difficulty in learning arithmetic processes is the lack on the part of the pupil of the mental capacity required to learn them at the time they are presented. On the basis of available evidence it is possible to prepare a graded sequential arrangement [4] of the various processes by levels of difficulty as in the table on pages 206-207. The phases of each process are arranged in the table in columns by levels of mental ability required to master them, each step representing approximately two years of mental age beginning with the mental ages of 6 to 7 years in level 1, which approximately corresponds to grade 1, the mental ages of 7 to 8 years in level 2, and so on for all of the levels.

[4] The background data on which this analysis is based is given in Chapter 3 of Leo J. Brueckner and F. E. Grossnickle, *Making Arithmetic Meaningful* (Philadelphia, I. C. Winston, 1953).

RECOMMENDED GRADATION OF ARITHMETIC PROCESSES

Mental Age *	Whole Numbers	Fractions	Decimals	Per Cent
6-7	1. Counting. 2. Identifying numbers to 200. 3. Writing numbers to 100. 4. Serial idea. 5. Using numbers in activities of all kinds.	1. Contacts in activity units and in simple measurements.	1. Tens as basis of number system.	
	1. Reading and writing numbers to 1000. 2. Concept development. 3. Addition and subtraction facts to 6.	1. Recognizing fractional parts.	1. Place value. 2. Zero as a place holder.	
8-9	1. Addition and subtraction facts and simple processes. 2. Multiplication and division facts through threes. 3. Multiplication by one-place numbers. 4. Related even division by one-place numbers.	1. Extending uses of fractions in measurement. 2. Finding part of a number.	1. Reading money values. 2. Addition and subtraction of dollars and cents. 3. Multiplication and division of cents only.	
9-10	1. Completion of all multiplication and division facts. 2. Uneven division facts. 3. All steps with one-place multipliers and divisors.	1. Extending use and meaning of fractions. 2. Easy steps in addition and subtraction of like fractions by concrete and visual means. 3. Finding a part of a number.	1. Computing with dollars and cents in all processes.	
10-11	1. Two-place multipliers. 2. Two-place divisors—apparent quotient need not be corrected. 3. Zeros in quotients.	1. Addition and subtraction of like fractions; also the halves, fourths, eighths family.	1. Addition and subtraction through hundredths.	

Mental Age *	Whole Numbers	Fractions	Decimals	Per Cent
11-12	1. Three and four place multipliers. 2. Two-place divisors, apparent quotient must be corrected.	1. Addition and subtraction of related fractions; as ⅓ and ⅙; also of easy unrelated types, ½ and ⅓. 2. Multiplication. 3. Division of whole numbers and mixed numbers by fractions.	1. Addition and subtraction extended to thousandths. 2. Multiplication and division of decimals by whole numbers.	
12-13	1. Three-place divisors.	1. Addition and subtraction of types: ¾ + ⅝; 4⅝ − 3⅝. 2. All other types of division examples.	1. Multiplication and division of whole numbers and decimals by decimals. 2. Changing fractions to decimals, and vice versa.	1. Cases I and II in percentage using whole per cents.
13-14	1. Extending uses of whole numbers.	1. Extending uses of fractions.	1. Extending uses of decimals.	2. Case III of percentage 2. Fractional per cents.

* Arithmetic age can be substituted in the first column.

The table enables the teacher quickly to tell the steps in each process that a pupil of a particular mental age should find easy, those that he should be able to learn with regular instruction, and those that will be difficult for him to master even under the best of teaching. Thus, a 10-year-old fifth-grade pupil, with a mental age of 8 years and an IQ of 80, will ordinarily find it difficult to master the skills given in level 5 because he lacks the necessary mental ability; however, he should have relatively little difficulty with the skills in levels 3 and 4. Similarly a 10-year-old fifth-grade pupil with a mental age of 12 years and an IQ of 120 has the mental capacity easily to master the skills given in levels 6 and 7. It is the teacher's problem to adjust the content of the arithmetic curriculum to the child's mental capacity. There is no reason why pupils of a given chronological age should all do the same work even when they are grouped as a single class and have a grade designation. The important thing for the teacher to realize is that in most classes there is a wide range in arithmetic ability which must be considered in planning the instructional program. Within a given class, all of the pupils can work together as a group on experience units dealing with the social phase of arithmetic, such as "How we tell time," while in learning the computational skills pupils should be grouped according to stage of progress so that each one will be learning number skills which he is able to master. This requires a differentiated program. Individual pupils will probably be at work at different points in the textbook, perhaps even in different textbooks, much as is commonly done in adjusting instruction in reading classes to individual differences in reading ability. This approach is especially necessary in the diagnosis and treatment of serious disability in arithmetic.

The Teacher's Responsibility for Diagnosis

Diagnosis in arithmetic may proceed at different levels when done either by the teacher in the classroom or by diagnostic specialists in clinics established to deal with severe disability cases. In most places, the teacher is the key person in the diagnosis and treatment of learning difficulties, since special clinical facilities are seldom found outside the larger cities. Diagnosis should in fact be regarded as an integral element of classroom instruction in all curriculum areas.

GENERAL DIAGNOSIS IN ARITHMETIC

If the purpose of diagnosis is to make a general evaluation of the effectiveness of the instructional program in arithmetic, the most satisfactory procedure is the administration of a standard test which measures outcomes that are in line with the objectives accepted by the schools and with the content of the subject matter that is taught.

The list below contains the names of a number of the most widely used tests in arithmetic. The scope of their contents is indicated in each case as well as the grade levels at which the test is administered:

1. Iowa Every Pupil Tests of Basic Skills—information, problems, and computational skill, grades 3 to 9.
2. Stanford Achievement Test—problems and processes, grades 3 to 12.
3. California Achievement Tests—problems and processes, grades 3 to 9.
4. Co-ordinated Scales of Attainment—computational skill and problem-solving, grades 3 to 8.

The Essentials of a Survey Testing Program in Arithmetic

A testing program that will supply the essential information needed to evaluate outcomes in the field of arithmetic should include at least the following:

1. Test of computational skills.
2. Test of ability to solve verbal problems.
3. Test of arithmetic vocabulary.
4. Test of knowledge of social applications of arithmetic.
5. Test of ability to read graphs, tables, charts, and similar arrangements of quantitative data.

Information about the interest of children in arithmetic would be exceedingly valuable supplementary data.

The results of these standard tests can be compared with standard scores so that strengths and weaknesses of the school system as a whole, of individual schools and classes, and even of individual pupils can be determined. When standard tests are administered early in the school year, the resulting information is of undoubted value in planning the year's program. The effectiveness of the year's work can be determined by the administration of a second form of the tests near the end of the school year and comparing the results with those of the first tests.

When standard survey tests are not available for any reason at the beginning of the year, teachers should administer informal inventory tests, such as are available in some textbooks or that they may themselves prepare covering the essentials of the work of preceding years. A typical sixth-grade inventory test of the chief arithmetic skills in operations with whole numbers taught in preceding years is given below. A quick analysis of the total scores and of the scores on each section of this test will not only afford a fairly satisfactory measure of the general level of ability of individual pupils but also indicate for the teacher in a general way the processes in which they are strong and those in which carefully planned review and in some cases special help may be necessary.

Graded series of progress tests in processes and problem-solving that can be administered at regular intervals throughout the year also are available in textbooks and in separate pamphlets. They afford both teacher and pupils valuable information as to the success of the class in mastering the work of the year and serve as an excellent motivating device.

INVENTORY TESTS IN ARITHMETIC—WHOLE NUMBERS

1. ADDITION

a.	b.	c.	d.	e.
96	875	845	305	895
41	+967	9	90	977
+32		56	600	738
		+78	+5	528
				+957

2. SUBTRACTION

a.	b.	c.	d.	e.
876	982	8254	6003	90805
−351	−709	−4596	−2736	−24785

3. MULTIPLICATION—A

a.	721	*b.*	624	*c.*	958	*d.*	6050	*e.*	$90.01
	×4		×3		×7		×8		×9

MULTIPLICATION—B

a.	75	*b.*	86	*c.*	68	*d.*	785	*e.*	987
	×10		×20		×47		×906		×850

4. DIVISION—A

a. 3/159 *b.* 5/85 *c.* 7/493 *d.* 6/3659 *e.* 8/5427

DIVISION—B

a. 20/979 *b.* 35/1750 *c.* 64/3217 *d.* 17/1087 *e.* 28/2443

Readiness Tests in Arithmetic

Tests are available for measuring the readiness of pupils in grades 1 and 2 for systematic work in arithmetic. There are two parts to the Brueckner Primary Arithmetic Readiness Test, one dealing with the mathematical phase of arithmetic, the other with the social phase. Twenty selected items of this test are shown below. The complete test, which contains forty items, is administered individually by the teacher. Test items are read by the teacher and pupil responses are recorded and evaluated. The mean score for grade 1 is 15 answers correct for grade 1 and 25 correct for grade 2. However, there is a very wide range in the scores made on the test by individual pupils, indicating large differences in their experiential backgrounds and in sensitiveness to number in their daily life activities. The predictive value of this test is very high, since the correlation between the results of this test and achievement tests administered at the end of the year has been shown [5] to be .87, one of the highest predictive coefficients for any existing readiness tests of any kind. Adjustments of instruction must be made to the needs of pupils, especially those who score low on the readiness test.

READINESS TEST IN PRIMARY ARITHMETIC (MATHEMATICAL PHASE)

NAME _____ AGE _____ GRADE _____

1. Number sequence (oral—read by teacher):

_____ *a.* (90) When I say 1, 2, 3, 4, what comes next?
_____ *d.* (70) What number is left out? 1-2-3-4-5-7-8-9?
_____ *f.* (45) What number is left out? 10-20-30-50-60.

[5] L. J. Brueckner, "The Development and Validation of an Arithmetic Readiness Test," *Journal of Educational Research*, Vol. 40 (March, 1947), pp. 496-502. The complete test is given in L. J. Brueckner and F. E. Grossnickle, *Making Arithmetic Meaningful*.

2. Reading numbers:

    ———— *a.* Read these numbers for me: 5, 8, 9

3. Fractions (oral—read by teacher):

    ———— *a.* (80) What part of this pie is eaten?
    ———— *b.* (5) What part of the pie is not eaten?
    ———— *d.* (30) How many eggs in a half-dozen?

4. Use of numbers in solving problems (oral—read by teacher):

    ———— *a.* (90) Bob had 5 pennies. He spent 1 penny. How many pennies did he have left?
    ———— *c.* (60) How many 5-cent ice cream cones can you buy for a dime?
    ———— *f.* (20) Carol was invited to a 3 o'clock party. She got there at 3:30. How late was she?

READINESS TEST IN PRIMARY ARITHMETIC (SOCIAL PHASE)

1. Uses of precision instruments:

    ———— *a.* (90) What is the thing we use to tell what time it is?
    ———— *c.* (80) What is the thing we use to tell what day of the month it is?
    ———— *d.* (65) What is the thing we use to tell how warm or cold a room is?
    ———— *f.* (25) What is the thing we use to tell how heavy a child is?

2. Units of measure:

    ———— *a.* (80) How many cents in a nickel?
    ———— *c.* (30) How many cents in a dollar?
    ———— *f.* (10) How many quarts make a gallon?

3. General uses of number:

    ———— *a.* (70) How many sides has a square?
    ———— *c.* (40) What is the name of the last day of the week?
    ———— *e.* (30) We buy tea by the pound. How do we buy eggs?

Note: The figures in parentheses are the percentages of correct response on the items by children in Grade 1 on whom the test was standardized.

Readiness tests are also available for each of the major processes with whole numbers, fractions, and decimals. Their function is to enable the teacher to determine strengths of a pupil and those weaknesses that are likely to interfere with optimum growth in learning a new skill, such as division by two-place numbers, addition of like fractions, or subtraction of decimal fractions. In this instance, the function of a readiness test is both diagnostic and predictive. It has been found [6] that well-constructed readiness tests not only will identify deficiencies in specific underlying skills that will interfere with future success but at the same time will predict fairly well the pupil's level of performance on an end test.

[6] L. J. Brueckner, "The Development of Readiness Tests in Arithmetic," *Journal of Educational Research,* Vol. 34 (September, 1940), pp. 15-20.

Those who may be interested in readiness tests for all grade levels should examine the readiness tests in *The Winston Arithmetics,* grades 3 to 7 (Philadelphia, J. C. Winston, 1952).

The elements of an illustrative readiness test for new work in division by two-place numbers are given below. The test consists of five sections: (1) a short test of knowledge of difficult division facts, (2) a short test of ability to divide by one-place numbers, (3) a test of the subtraction used in long division, (4) a test of the multiplication used in division, and (5) a short test of knowledge of place value required in regrouping numbers in division and in placing quotient figures. Strange as it may seem, it has been demonstrated that many pupils who were about to begin the work in division by two-place numbers made very low scores on one or more parts of this test, indicating complete lack of readiness for the new work. Even if a particular pupil has the mental ability needed to learn this difficult process, it is obvious that deficiencies in important underlying skills, such as division by one-figure numbers or the subtraction and multiplication needed in the new operation, will cause much incorrect work and thus interfere with successful mastery. When the results of a readiness test indicate that there are serious weaknesses in underlying skills, these deficiencies should be carefully analyzed by the teacher and corrected insofar as is possible before the new work is taught. The pupil should also be made aware of shortcomings when the new work is begun and taught to guard against them by carefully going over all of the steps involved in his work to check each computation made.

ILLUSTRATIVE READINESS TEST FOR DIVISION BY TWO-PLACE NUMBERS

1. Knowledge of even division facts

   a. $9\overline{)72}$ $8\overline{)56}$ $6\overline{)42}$ $7\overline{)63}$ $8\overline{)64}$ $9\overline{)54}$ $6\overline{)48}$

   b. $8\overline{)71}$ $7\overline{)60}$ $9\overline{)42}$ $6\overline{)58}$ $7\overline{)41}$ $9\overline{)80}$ $8\overline{)78}$

2. How well can you divide by one-place numbers?

   a. $4\overline{)384}$ $9\overline{)8649}$ $3\overline{)2625}$ $5\overline{)4720}$ $6\overline{)5406}$

   b. $5\overline{)400}$ $7\overline{)424}$ $8\overline{)2448}$ $6\overline{)4211}$ $9\overline{)7202}$

3. How well can you subtract?

   a.
328	804	750	173	900
−296	−782	−746	− 96	−783

   b.
600	387	402	80	110
−600	−386	−386	−76	−95

4. Write the products:

   a. $30 \times 9 =$ $32 \times 7 =$ $49 \times 7 =$ $53 \times 8 =$
   b. $47 \times 8 =$ $81 \times 8 =$ $58 \times 9 =$ $49 \times 6 =$
   c. $58 \times 7 =$ $82 \times 6 =$ $58 \times 5 =$ $79 \times 9 =$

5. Write the missing numbers below:

   a. 37 = ____ tens ____ ones, or ____ ones.
   b. 186 = ____ tens ____ ones, or ____ ones.
   c. 307 = ____ hundreds ____ tens ____ ones, or ____ tens ____ ones, or ____ ones.

When readiness tests are not available in textbooks and workbooks, the teacher should prepare informal test exercises of underlying skills similar to those included in the test for division. For instance, it is rather obvious that success in subtraction of unlike fractions depends in large part on mastery of the skills needed in subtracting like fractions. The administration of an abbreviated diagnostic test in the subtraction of like fractions will reveal to the teacher the pupils who are likely to have difficulty with the new work, and the points that should be reviewed before the more difficult steps with unlike fractions are presented.

The value of readiness tests for diagnostic purposes has been shown by Souder,[7] who has found that the diagnostic use of readiness tests in teaching the addition and subtraction of fractions led to results that were superior to those secured where the information supplied by readiness tests was not available to guide the work of the teacher. Readiness tests are clearly an essential element of effective arithmetic instruction at all grade levels.

ANALYTICAL DIAGNOSIS IN ARITHMETIC

When the purpose of diagnosis is to determine with greater exactness the specific phases or elements of some process in which a weakness or deficiency exists, diagnostic tests of an analytical type should be utilized. For instance, to locate weak spots in addition of whole numbers the following elements should be tested as shown in the illustrative test below.

1. Knowledge of basic addition facts.
2. The process of carrying in adding whole numbers.
3. Adding by endings
4. Bridging the tens
5. Addition of longer columns

DIAGNOSTIC TEST IN ADDITION OF WHOLE NUMBERS

1. Knowledge of basic addition facts (to be dictated)

a.
9	7	4	8	6	7	9	5
8	6	9	7	5	9	3	7

b.
8	6	8	4	9	7	6	9
5	9	8	8	5	4	8	9

2. Find the sums (carrying)

a.
43	23	160
25	30	200

b.
53	27	56
38	33	28

c.
364	290	438
153	184	291

d.
296	387	892
258	253	279

[7] Hugh C. Souder, "The Construction and Validation of Certain Readiness Tests in Common Fractions," *Journal of Educational Research*, Vol. 37 (October, 1943), pp. 127-134.

e. 806	9005	7060	*f.* 3156	6153	5904
207	7005	8092	2798	2938	3096

3. Addition by endings:

   a. $16 + 3 =$ $22 + 7 =$ $21 + 8 =$ $13 + 6 =$
   b. $25 + 2 =$ $24 + 5 =$ $32 + 6 =$ $34 + 3 =$

4. Bridging the tens:

   a. $19 + 7 =$ $14 + 9 =$ $18 + 9 =$ $13 + 8 =$
   b. $15 + 8 =$ $22 + 9 =$ $26 + 8 =$ $29 + 5 =$
   c. $17 + 8 =$ $29 + 6 =$ $33 + 7 =$ $37 + 6 =$

5. Addition of longer columns:

   a. 4   *b.* 5   *c.* 83   *d.* 5   *e.* 8   *f.* 59
       2   2   20   9   7   83
       3   7   14   2   9   64
                                   1   6   59

In analyzing the results of such tests of specific skills as those listed above, special consideration should be given to the pupil's rate of work, the accuracy of his responses, the level of difficulty at which a skill tends to break down, and evidence of any serious difficulty which clearly requires further investigation. The relationship between rate and accuracy is shown in the diagram below.

		ACCURACY		
		High	*Average*	*Low*
	High	I High in both rate and accuracy	II High in rate— average in accuracy	III High in rate— low in accuracy
RATE	*Average*	IV Average in rate— high in accuracy	V Average in both rate and accuracy	VI Average in rate— low in accuracy
	Low	VII Low in rate— high in accuracy	VIII Low in rate— average in accuracy	IX Low in both rate and accuracy

The characteristics of pupils who fall into each group can readily be described. Pupils in Group I clearly are the most able ones. Pupils in Group IX clearly are the least able ones; it would undoubtedly be extremely difficult to bring about any considerable improvement in their work. Pupils in Group III are speedy but inaccurate workers, possibly because of careless or indifferent work, possibly because of a lack of basic knowledge and skills requiring further diagnostic study. Pupils in Group VII are efficient, accurate workers whose rate of work is slow; it is quite probable that their rate of work can be increased by well-directed practice, but accuracy should not be sacrificed to increase rate of work. Pupils in Groups II, IV, V, and VII probably do not require any special assistance other than guidance of regular instruction, whereas the work of pupils in groups VI, VIII, and IX should be carefully analyzed to determine underlying difficulties and deficiencies.

It is known that rate of work is an important factor conditioning accuracy of responses on the basic number facts. The correct responses for three pupils on a test of 25 difficult multiplication facts administered in five different ways that are given below show this.[8]

Method of Testing	*Pupil I*	*Pupil II*	*Pupil III*
A. Unlimited time to find answers	25	25	18
B. Facts dictated at intervals of:			
(1) 5 seconds	25	23	15
(2) 4 seconds	25	18	10
(3) 2½ seconds	25	12	1
C. Facts on test paper read at 3-second intervals . . .	25	21	11

The answers of Pupil I were all correct on the five tests; results were not affected at all by differences in the rates at which the products were written. The rates given under *B* were controlled by using recordings of facts and having the pupil write the products on squared papers as rapidly as the facts were dictated. The results for Pupil II show that he was able to give or work out all of the answers when he had unlimited time; however, under time pressure his responses became much less accurate, indicating lack of mastery and a tendency to guess at answers. The results for Pupil III indicate inaccurate work even when under no time pressure, increased inaccuracy under moderate time pressure, and an almost complete breakdown when the rate of writing answers was increased to intervals of 2½ seconds.

Ideally, all pupils should strive initially for accuracy and then gradually increase their rates of work without sacrificing accuracy. The rate at which different individuals will work will depend on each one's personal traits and characteristics and on his willingness to make the efforts needed to achieve a high level of performance through intelligent, effective practice. It must be remembered that rate of work will increase with maturity and therefore speed should not be unduly emphasized early in the learning process. Proficiency will increase when purposeful, systematic practice of meaningful skills is provided. The teacher's problem is to help children increase the efficiency of their thought habits and methods of work, which will automatically lead to more rapid responses.

In some of the more complex phases of arithmetic, such as division by two-place numbers, it is possible to administer a series of diagnostic exercises to determine the specific elements in the total process that may be

[8] Data supplied by William Gemeinhardt, graduate student, Univ. of Minnesota.

contributory to an apparent deficiency in it. These diagnostic exercises can be constructed so as to test each of the basic skills included in the analysis of the division example given on page 202 as follows:

1. Ability to divide by one-place numbers, as an indication of knowledge of basic even and uneven division facts and of the steps in the division process itself.

2. Ability to estimate and place quotient figures correctly, first those in which the estimated quotient is the true quotient, as in $21\overline{)93}$, and then those in which the estimated quotient must be corrected so as to find the true quotient, as in $34\overline{)231}$, $27\overline{)253}$, and $17\overline{)114}$.

3. Ability to multiply, as in finding products of divisor and quotient figures.

4. Ability to subtract, as in finding remainders.

The following diagnostic exercises illustrate the approach for identifying weaknesses in division by two-place numbers. If there are two or more incorrect answers on any of the four parts of the test, a difficulty that should be carefully studied may be suspected.

DIAGNOSTIC TESTS TO LOCATE WEAK SPOTS IN DIVISION

A. Division by one-place numbers:

a	b	c	d	e
1. $7\overline{)525}$	$8\overline{)3672}$	$6\overline{)5909}$	$9\overline{)7238}$	$8\overline{)6839}$

B. Estimating and placing quotient figures:
Find the first quotient figure only. Be sure to place it correctly.

a	b	c	d	e
1. $20\overline{)1376}$	$43\overline{)1498}$	$83\overline{)5027}$	$25\overline{)792}$	$96\overline{)5803}$
2. $25\overline{)728}$	$34\overline{)93}$	$26\overline{)1376}$	$39\overline{)3144}$	$17\overline{)1486}$

C. Multiplying as needed in division:

	2	5	6	9	8
1.	$39\overline{)81}$	$85\overline{)430}$	$76\overline{)456}$	$87\overline{)798}$	$96\overline{)786}$
	8	7	5	4	9
2.	$49\overline{)402}$	$73\overline{)523}$	$18\overline{)97}$	$38\overline{)160}$	$59\overline{)541}$

Note. Check products; check then on subtraction.

D. Subtraction as needed in division:
Find the remainders only in these examples:

	7	9	8	6	8
1.	$43\overline{)3106}$	$75\overline{)702}$	$86\overline{)7110}$	$39\overline{)27011}$	$53\overline{)427}$
	301	675	688	234	424

Note: Those who may be interested in diagnostic tests in arithmetic of this kind will find it worth-while to examine the diagnostic tests in Winston Arithmetics, grades 3 to 8, and the accompanying workbooks, *Guided Thinking and Practice*, one for each grade.

Analytical diagnosis should also closely parallel the development of new work. At regular intervals, preferably at the end of each new unit of instruction, a suitably constructed developmental diagnostic test should be administered to a class to locate weak spots in the new work that has been presented so that they can be promptly diagnosed and corrected. For example, a complete series of developmental diagnostic tests in addition of fractions should parallel the following series of instructional units:

Unit 1. Addition of like fractions, no carrying required, as in $\frac{1}{3} + \frac{1}{3}$, $2\frac{1}{4} + 3\frac{1}{4}$, and $3 + 1\frac{1}{2}$.

Unit 2. Addition of like fractions, reduction of improper fractions and carrying required in finding sums, as in $\frac{1}{2} + \frac{1}{2}$, $\frac{3}{4} + \frac{3}{4}$, $1\frac{1}{2} + 2\frac{1}{2}$, and $4\frac{5}{6} + 3\frac{5}{6}$.

Unit 3. Addition of unlike fractions with denominators in the same family, as in $\frac{1}{2} + \frac{1}{4}$, and $3\frac{5}{8} + 1\frac{3}{4}$.

Unit 4. Addition of unlike fractions with denominators not in the same family, as in $\frac{1}{3} + \frac{1}{4}$, $4\frac{3}{4} + 2\frac{4}{5}$, and $5\frac{3}{4} + 6\frac{5}{6}$.

Analytical diagnostic tests are sometimes found in textbooks and workbooks. Where they are not available, the teacher can quite easily construct them according to the following specifications:

1. Select an integrated instructional unit, for example, Unit 2 in addition of like fractions as defined above.

2. Break down this major unit into a series of the subtypes taught in the course of the unit. For example, the series of examples given below illustrates the increasing complexity of the basic subtypes, all of them taught in the course of this unit.

$\frac{2}{3}$	$\frac{3}{4}$	$\frac{1}{2}$	$4\frac{2}{3}$	$6\frac{7}{8}$	$6\frac{1}{4}$
$+\frac{2}{3}$	$+\frac{3}{4}$	$+\frac{1}{2}$	$5\frac{2}{3}$	$+7\frac{5}{8}$	$+4\frac{3}{4}$

3. In the diagnostic exercise itself there should be a row of at least three, preferably four, examples representing each of the six subtypes.[9] An illustrative developmental diagnostic test on Unit 2 of addition of fractions is shown on page 219. One incorrect example in a single row of the examples may be regarded as an accidental error; if there are two or more incorrect examples in a single row, a persistent difficulty is indicated whose nature should be determined by what we have defined in Chapter 4 as methods of individual diagnosis, shortly to be described for arithmetic.

4. To facilitate remedial treatment, developmental diagnostic tests should be keyed to special remedial helps and learning aids included in textbooks, workbooks, or suitable supplementary materials prepared by the teacher.

Similar tests can be prepared for all operations with whole numbers, fractions, and decimals. The major problem is to break down the developmental work in each process into a number of instructional units and then to identify the subtypes of examples presented in each unit. The following

[9] L. J. Brueckner and Ella Hawkinson, "Optimum Order of Arrangement of Items in a Diagnostic Test in Arithmetic," *Elementary School Journal*, Vol. 34 (January, 1934), pp. 351-357.

analysis of the subtypes in three major instructional units in estimating quotient figures illustrates the procedure:

Unit 1, dividing by even tens

20/40	20/63	20/74	40/120	50/257	60/402

Unit 2, dividing by other two-place numbers, no correction of the estimated quotient required.

21/63	22/68	21/70	24/75	34/136	34/142

Unit 3, correction of the estimated quotient necessary

21/80	24/92	24/146	28/156	29/235	17/135

The reader should work the examples in each of these three sets and note the increasing complexity and difficulty of the examples within each set and from set to set. It may be of interest to know that on the basis of the data given in table on page 219, approximately two years more of mental age are required to achieve 80 per cent mastery on the subtypes included in Unit 3 than those in Unit 2, while the subtypes in Unit 1 approximate the difficulty of examples with one-place divisors. As was shown in the analysis on page 202, the process of division is very complex and involves all of the other number operations. A pupil may be able to find quotients correctly but still fail to make progress in mastering the operation because of deficiencies in other processes that cause him to make errors in some phases of the work other than in actual division as such.

DIAGNOSTIC TEST IN ADDITION OF LIKE FRACTIONS—TYPE 2

	a	*b*	*c*		*a*	*b*	*c*
1.	2/3 + 2/3	3/8 + 6/8	4/5 + 3/5	4.	4 2/3 + 5 2/3	4 7/8 + 2 6/8	4 3/5 + 2 4/5
2.	3/4 + 3/4	7/8 + 5/8	5/6 + 5/6	5.	6 7/8 + 7 5/8	8 3/4 + 7 3/4	6 7/10 + 4 9/10
3.	1/2 + 1/2	1/4 + 1/4	5/8 + 3/8	6.	6 1/4 + 4 3/4	5 1/2 + 7 1/2	6 1/3 + 5 2/3

A comprehensive series [10] of analytical diagnostic tests in arithmetic operations with whole numbers, fractions, decimals, per cent, and denominate numbers is available. The series includes the following tests:

1. Four screening tests for locating general areas of disability.
2. Five tests of knowledge of the basic number facts.
3. Five tests of operations with whole numbers, one for each operation.
4. Seven tests in operations with common fractions.
5. Four tests in decimal fractions, one for each operation.
6. One test in the three cases of per cent.
7. One test in operations with measures.

[10] *Diagnostic Tests and Self-Helps in Arithmetic,* devised by L. J. Brueckner, and published by the California Test Bureau, 5916 Hollywood Blvd., Los Angeles, Calif., 1955.

RELATIVE DIFFICULTY OF MAJOR TYPES OF EXAMPLES WITH TWO-PLACE DIVISORS
BASED ON PERCENTAGES OF CORRECT RESPONSES BY MENTAL AGE GROUPS
(GRADES 5-B—6-A COMBINED)

TYPES OF EXAMPLES	MENTAL AGES IN YEARS							
	8	9	10	11	12	13	14	15
1. Apparent quotient is true quotient	48	71	76	85	82	85	88	90
2. Apparent quotient must be corrected	21	26	33	48	54	67	74	86
3. Zeros in quotients	14	43	46	58	60	71	80	71
4. All types	24	48	52	64	66	75	81	83
Number of cases	4	24	92	120	121	73	31	9

To facilitate treatment of the learning difficulties revealed by each of these diagnostic tests, each test is geared to *Self-Helps* on the reverse side of the test which are so adjusted and constructed as to provide a means of self-directed study by pupils. An illustrative test in the series is given on pages 220-221.

CASE-STUDY DIAGNOSTIC PROCEDURES

The diagnostic testing techniques described in preceding pages will help the teacher and pupil to locate specific areas of weakness in number operations, but more penetrating methods must be used by the teacher to determine the exact nature of a serious difficulty and, if possible, the causes of unsatisfactory performance so that the proper kind of corrective treatment can be applied.

Case-study procedures are clinical in nature and are most suitably applied in the study of the work of individual pupils or small groups of pupils who have difficulty in the same area. The general nature and methods of case studies have already been described in Chapter 4. We shall now describe their application to the diagnosis of weaknesses in arithmetic operations and problem-solving.

Illustrations of Case-Study Procedures Applied to Arithmetic Diagnosis

Illustrations of methods of applying to arithmetic the various techniques used in individual diagnosis to determine shortcomings of various kinds are given below. We shall begin with informal procedures that any teacher can apply and end with standardized tests, suitable for clinical purposes, whose administration requires special training:

1. Analysis of written work to discover such faults as:
   Numbers written incorrectly, for example, reversals of 3 and 5.
   Incorrect answers to number facts.
   Omitted answers to number facts.
   Incorrect procedures or faulty format of work.
   Misconceptions of steps in solutions.

Diagnostic Tests and Self-Helps in Arithmetic
DEVISED BY LEO J. BRUECKNER
Diagnostic Test in Multiplication of Whole Numbers

TEST NO.
8

Name.. Grade or Course.................... Age..............

School..................... Teacher.................... Room........... Date...............

I. One-Place Multipliers

	a	b	c		a	b	c
1.	3 4 ×2	2 1 3 ×3	1 1 1 ×6	2.	3 0 ×6	4 0 1 ×4	2 0 0 ×5
3.	4 7 ×2	1 6 ×4	2 9 ×3	4.	8 4 ×4	5 7 ×6	8 9 ×9
5.	2 1 6 ×5	8 5 1 ×7	6 5 9 ×8	6.	8 0 5 ×4	9 0 6 ×7	6 0 7 0 ×9

No. Correct
I.

1_____
2_____
3_____
4_____
5_____
6_____
Total_____

II. Two- and Three-Place Multipliers

	a	b	c		a	b	c
1.	1 8 ×10	3 0 ×10	2 4 7 ×10	2.	1 2 ×20	2 6 ×30	4 8 ×40
3.	4 6 ×36	8 4 ×95	2 5 7 ×84	4.	7 6 0 ×59	8 0 6 ×48	9 0 0 ×67
5.	3 9 7 ×300	5 0 9 ×603	6 0 5 0 ×950	6.	7 2 8 ×259	9 3 2 ×487	

No. Correct
II.

1_____
2_____
3_____
4_____
5_____
6_____
Total_____

Related Tests: 1, 3, & 6

220

Self-Helps in Multiplication of Whole Numbers

1. Study the work of one row of examples at a time to see how the answers were found.
2. Cover the answers of a row of examples with a slip of paper. Then multiply, and write the answers on the paper. Go over your work a second time to check it. Then slide down the slip of paper to see if your answers were correct.

I. One-Place Multipliers

	a	b	c		a	b	c
	No Carrying				Zeros in Multiplying		
1.	34 ×2 = 68	213 ×3 = 639	111 ×6 = 666	2.	30 ×6 = 180	401 ×4 = 1604	200 ×5 = 1000
	Carrying to Tens' Place				More Difficult Carrying		
3.	47 ×2 = 94	16 ×4 = 64	29 ×3 = 87	4.	84 ×4 = 336	57 ×6 = 342	89 ×9 = 801
	Carrying in One or Two Places				Carrying to Zeros		
5.	216 ×5 = 1080	851 ×7 = 5957	659 ×8 = 5272	6.	805 ×4 = 3220	906 ×7 = 6342	6070 ×9 = 54630

II. Two- and Three-Place Multipliers

1.

a

18
×10
180

b

30
×10
300

c

247
×10
2470

2.

a

12
×20
240

b

26
×30
780

c

48
×40
1920

3.

a

46
×36
276
1380
1656

b

84
×95
420
7560
7980

c

257
×84
1028
20560
21588

4.

a

760
×59
6840
38000
44840

b

806
×48
6448
32240
38688

c

900
×67
6300
54000
60300

5.

a

397
×300
119100

b

509
×603
1527
305400
306927

c

6050
×950
302500
5445000
5747500

6.

a

728
×259
6552
36400
145600
188552

b

932
×487
6524
74560
372800
453884

Errors in computations within examples.
Zero difficulties.
Incomplete solutions of examples.

2. Analysis of oral responses, as:
   Having pupil state orally the thinking done in working examples so as to discover faulty thinking, roundabout methods, and so on.
   Oral reading of verbal problems to discover reading difficulties.

3. Interview with pupil (also teachers, associates, and parents)
   Questioning pupil about thought processes used.
   Questioning pupil to test understanding of computations.
   Questioning pupil about procedures used in working examples.
   Testing ability to state generalizations and relationships.
   Securing information about interest in arithmetic, etc.

4. Questionnaire
   Securing pupil rating of interest in arithmetic.
   Ranking arithmetic among areas of curriculum.
   Uses of arithmetic in life outside the school.

5. Free observation in course of daily work
   Evidence of counting.
   Evidence of roundabout, inefficient procedures used.
   Evidence of difficulties due to short attention span.
   Evidence about interest, attitudes, satisfactions.
   Evidence of physical factors affecting performance, health, fatigue.
   Rate of work.
   Study habits.
   Efficiency of work habits, dawdling.
   Emotional and social adjustment.

6. Controlled observation of pupil when he is at work on set tasks
   Methods of working examples given to locate suspected faults.
   Rate and accuracy of work under controlled conditions, such as time.
   Methods of solving a problem involving some factor such as a formula, unit of measurement, vocabulary, etc.
   Methods of using a measuring device.
   Answering questions based on table, graph, chart, etc.

7. Analysis of available records for helpful data
   Scores on intelligence tests and achievement tests.
   Health and medical records; social data.
   School history—attendance, behavior, promotion, school marks, etc.
   Anecdotal records.

8. Administration of informal diagnostic tests given in textbooks or workbooks, or prepared by the teacher to secure essential information

9. Administration of standardized diagnostic tests intended for clinical diagnosis by some available expert or by a teacher familiar with the procedure

Standard Diagnostic Tests for Individual Study

The systematic use of special diagnostic tests is highly desirable when a pupil has such serious difficulty that the regular teacher requires special assistance in identifying deficiencies and in developing an appropriate remedial program. The manuals for the following tests describe in detail how they are applied in making a diagnosis. Each test consists of a carefully graded series of examples of increasing complexity which enables the teacher to make a systematic canvass to determine when the major skill breaks down and the specific weaknesses that require special treatment. Record forms listing the most frequent faults are provided for recording the information secured through the diagnostic study:

1. Brueckner Diagnostic Test in Whole Numbers.
2. Brueckner Diagnostic Test in Fractions.
3. Brueckner Diagnostic Test in Decimals.
4. Buswell-John Diagnostic Test in Processes in Whole Numbers.

The Brueckner tests are published by the Educational Test Bureau, Inc., Minneapolis, Minnesota. The Buswell-John test is published by the Public School Publishing Co., Bloomington, Illinois.

One page of the record form for the Brueckner test in fractions is given on page 224. Note the faults listed.

With study and careful following of directions in the manuals, most teachers can easily learn to apply any of the above tests.

Steps to Be Followed in Making Case Studies

A pupil whose test scores or day-to-day work indicate serious deficiencies in arithmetic should be examined individually by the teacher in some inconspicuous place while the other pupils work at their seats on some assignment, or at some other convenient time during the day.

The following outline lists the sequence of steps to be taken in making a diagnostic study to establish the nature of a deficiency:

1. Administer an informal screening test containing a graded series of examples in the operations being studied to locate areas of deficiency and to determine the pupil's level of development.
2. Administer a properly constructed analytical diagnostic test (see page 217) in each process in which the screening tests indicate a real deficiency.
   a. Readiness tests for underlying skills are available in some textbooks and workbooks.
   b. Process analytical tests are sometimes available in textbooks and workbooks, keyed to remedial exercises.
3. When the work in these tests reveals weak spots, apply the following case-study procedures to discover the underlying difficulties:
   a. Examine the written work in the test to determine faults, errors, incorrect procedures, poor form, etc.
   b. Have the pupil work the incorrect examples again on another paper to see if the fault persists. Observe also his methods of work, his attitudes, and symptomatic behavior.
   c. In case of doubt as to the thought processes used, have the pupil do the work aloud and observe his thought processes. Record illustrations of his procedures. The Brueckner and Buswell tests will be useful in this connection.

BRUECKNER DIAGNOSTIC TEST IN FRACTIONS
INDIVIDUAL DIAGNOSTIC RECORD SHEET—ADDITION

Name_____Grade_____Room_____

School_____Date_____

Diagnosis	Summary	Diagnosis	Summary
I. Lack of Comprehension of Process		IV. Computation Errors	
a. Adds numerators and denominators_____		a. Addition_____	
b. Adds numerators, multiplies denomin-		b. Subtraction_____	
ators_____		c. Division_____	
c. Numerator added without changing to		V. Omitted_____	
common denominator. Either denomin-			
ator used in sum_____		VI. Wrong Operation_____	
II. Reduction to Lowest Terms			
a. Fraction not reduced_____		VII. Partial Operation	
b. Denominator divided by numerator_____		a. In adding mixed numbers adds only	
c. Denominator and numerator divided by		fractions_____	
different numbers_____		VIII. Changing to Common Denominator_____	
III. Difficulties with Improper Fractions_____		IX. Other Difficulties_____	
a. Not changed to mixed numbers_____			
b. Changed but not added to whole num-			
ber_____			

First indicate by number opposite each row the types of errors made on each example that was missed. For example Ia means that the pupil adds numerators and denominators.

Then summarize under "Summary" the total number of times each difficulty was found.

Examples

Row	1	2	3	4	5
I					
II					
III					
IV					
V					
VI					
VII					
VIII					

Copyright, 1931, by Educational Test Bureau

Published by

EDUCATIONAL TEST BUREAU
EDUCATIONAL PUBLISHERS, Inc.
Minneapolis - Nashville - Philadelphia

d. In case of doubt, ask the pupil questions to get at subtle, hidden difficulties that the pupil may not be able to express orally, also to test his understanding of a step.

e. If you identify an apparent weakness in an underlying process, for example, in the subtraction used in long division, administer a diagnostic test in subtraction to see how serious the problem is.

4. Repeat the above steps for any or all operations where there is difficulty.

Incidentally, it should be mentioned at this point that similar diagnostic procedures should be used by the teacher at any time in teaching new steps when errors in the written work of a pupil show that a difficulty exists that should be diagnosed promptly and corrected. Faults should not be permitted to accumulate until they overwhelm and discourage the learner. Practice will merely establish faulty habits and make them more difficult to correct.

The Most Common Faults and Errors in Number Operations

1. *The Most Common Faults in Operations with Whole Numbers.* In order to make teachers aware of the many faulty methods of work and the wide variety of causes of errors in operations with whole numbers, the complete list of faults in multiplication discovered by Buswell and John in their well-known diagnostic study of pupils' methods of work in grades III to VI is illustrated on page 226. The descriptive titles in the table are self-explanatory. Later we shall give lists of the ten most common faults discovered by Buswell and John in the three remaining operations.

An analysis of the list shows that the most frequent source of error in multiplication in the work of the 329 pupils examined was lack of knowledge of the basic multiplication combinations. There was special difficulty with the zero facts. The methods of counting to get the products of combinations, described in the third group of errors, were often used by pupils, all of them roundabout, inefficient methods of work. Many of the faulty procedures that are listed in the fourth group should be carefully reviewed by the reader item by item to get a clear notion of the strange ways in which children proceed when working examples; they can only be discovered by painstaking analysis of the pupil's methods of work by diagnostic methods. Note also the further evidence of zero difficulties. A large number of errors were due to carrying difficulties, both in the additions to be made and in the carrying procedure itself. Other errors were made in the addition of partial products. This list should be consulted by anyone making a diagnostic study of difficulties in multiplication so as to have clearly in mind the kinds of faults to expect to find or to explore through questions and observation.

The ten most common faults in the three remaining operations that were identified by Buswell and John are listed on p. 227 for illustrative purposes and to facilitate diagnosis.

THE MOST COMMON FAULTS IN MULTIPLICATION OF WHOLE NUMBERS

	GRADES	III	IV	V	VI	Total
1. Combinations:						
a.	Errors in combinations	36	59	60	41	196
b.	Errors in single zero combinations, 0 as multiplier	11	20	23	27	81
2. Carrying:						
a.	Error in adding carried number	6	40	58	45	149
b.	Carried wrong number	5	28	40	22	95
c.	Forgot to carry	10	30	27	22	89
d.	Counted to carry	4	20	28	9	61
e.	Wrote carried number	8	16	14	9	47
f.	Error in carrying into zero	1	6	7	1	15
g.	Multiplied carried number	2	1	0	1	4
h.	Added carried number twice	0	1	1	0	2
i.	Carried when nothing to carry	0	0	1	0	1
3. Counting:						
a.	Counting to get combinations	15	11	9	5	40
b.	Repeated table	3	11	11	6	31
c.	Multiplied by adding	6	11	8	4	29
d.	Wrote table	0	0	4	1	5
4. Faulty Procedures						
a.	Wrote rows of zeros	2	33	40	34	109
b.	Used multiplicand as multiplier	18	33	23	15	89
c.	Errors due to zero as multiplier	5	26	30	17	78
d.	Omitted digit in multiplier	1	15	20	16	52
e.	Omitted digit in multiplicand	2	17	12	12	43
f.	Errors due to zero in multiplicand	4	14	15	9	42
g.	Error in position of partial products	0	15	15	9	39
h.	Confused products when multiplier has two or more digits	1	13	9	9	32
i.	Did not multiply a digit in multiplicand	5	9	7	7	28
j.	Omitted digit in product	0	5	7	5	17
k.	Forgot to add partial products	0	3	7	2	12
l.	Split multiplier	0	1	6	4	11
m.	Wrote wrong digit of product	0	3	4	2	9
n.	Used multiplier or multiplicand as product	1	1	1	1	4
o.	Used digit in product twice	0	1	2	0	3
p.	Began at the left side	1	0	0	0	1
q.	Multiplied partial products	0	1	0	0	1
5. Lapses, etc.:						
a.	Used wrong process	18	22	16	10	66
b.	Derived unknown combination from known	3	11	6	6	26
c.	Errors in reading	6	5	11	3	25
d.	Errors in writing products	2	4	8	2	16
e.	Multiplied twice by same digit	1	1	3	2	7
f.	Reversed digits in products	1	1	2	2	6
6.	Errors in addition	5	31	41	21	98
7.	Illegible figures	0	3	5	7	15
	Total cases	47	98	102	82	329

The table is adapted from data in G. T. Buswell and L. John, *Diagnostic Studies in Arithmetic*, Supplementary Educational Monograph, No. 27 (Chicago, Univ. of Chicago Press, 1926), pp. 138-140.

It should be clear from an examination of the above lists that certain kinds of faults are common to all of the operations, namely, errors in number combinations, counting in various ways, faulty procedures, and lapses. There also are special kinds of faults that are peculiar to each process, such

THE TEN MOST COMMON FAULTS IN ADDITION, SUBTRACTION, AND DIVISION

	GRADES			
	III	*IV*	*V*	*VI*	*Total*

ADDITION

	III	*IV*	*V*	*VI*	*Total*
1. Errors in combinations	81	103	78	58	320
2. Counting	61	83	54	17	215
3. Added carried number last	39	45	45	26	155
4. Forgot to add carried number	37	38	34	17	126
5. Retraced work partly done	26	34	39	22	121
6. Added carried number irregularly	26	30	28	18	102
7. Wrote number to be carried	34	25	18	12	89
8. Carried wrong number	28	19	26	14	87
9. Irregular procedure	16	29	23	18	86
10. Grouped numbers	25	22	21	16	84

SUBTRACTION

	III	*IV*	*V*	*VI*	*Total*
1. Errors in combinations	62	75	69	40	246
2. Did not allow for having borrowed	19	50	57	36	162
3. Counting	43	44	39	10	136
4. Errors due to zero in minuend	25	39	26	15	105
5. Said example backward	21	38	29	12	100
6. Subtracted minuend from subtrahend	47	33	12	4	96
7. Failed to borrow; gave zero as answer	21	20	14	4	59
8. Added instead of subtracted	18	9	19	1	47
9. Error in reading	14	5	13	10	42
10. Used same digit in two columns	18	15	3	4	40

DIVISION

	III	*IV*	*V*	*VI*	*Total*
1. Errors in division combinations	35	55	59	42	191
2. Errors in subtraction	4	25	47	37	113
3. Errors in multiplication	1	20	48	36	105
4. Used remainder larger than divisor	1	17	39	29	86
5. Found quotient by trial multiplication	1	8	49	24	82
6. Neglected to use remainder within example	5	27	25	13	70
7. Omitted zero resulting from another digit	0	20	22	24	66
8. Omitted digit in dividend	4	15	27	18	64
9. Used wrong operation	17	17	24	6	64
10. Counted to get quotient	5	25	24	4	58

as carrying in addition and multiplication, regrouping in subtraction, and remainder difficulties in division. Some of the faults may be regarded as due to immaturity rather than disability. The teacher should observe closely the procedures used by all children and analyze by suitable diagnostic methods the thought processes of those who are encountering unusual difficulty in learning some step in some process or in a whole process. It is not possible to plan corrective measures intelligently until the faults to be corrected have been identified by the diagnostic methods that are described in this chapter.

Identifying Faulty Methods of Work. Because they do not know the basic number facts or because they do not understand the processes involved in working examples, children often devise roundabout, inefficient methods that are uneconomical and wasteful. These methods may work with small numbers but they are too difficult to use with larger numbers. Several illustrations of faulty methods of work follow:

81
−37

Case A. A fourth-grade boy reported as failing in arithmetic found the answer to the subtraction example at the left by counting back from 81 to 37 by ones. He had devised a way of keeping a mental record as he counted. He used this method in all cases when regrouping was required. When asked to subtract two larger three-place numbers, he balked and refused to attempt to find the answer.

72
−26

Case B. A fourth-grade girl persistently worked subtraction examples in which regrouping in the minuend was necessary by subtracting the smaller number in ones' place in the minuend from the larger number in ones' place in the subtrahend. This seemed to her to be a procedure logically correct.

64
×8
722

Case C. This sixth-grade boy added the carried numbers to the figure to be multiplied before he multiplied. Thus he found $8 \times 4 = 32$; he wrote the 2, and added the 3 carried to the 6; then he found $8 \times 9 = 72$. This is a case of transfer from carrying in addition.

6 7 r5
6/3647
36
47
42
5

Case D. This pupil does not understand the role of 0 as a place holder, as is shown in the incorrect work in the division example.

Case E. This boy, grade 4, IQ 118, 1.4 years below grade in arithmetic, had devised many ingenious but awkward methods of finding answers to problems, as illustrated by the following:

He was asked to read the problem below and to give the answer:

If 2 loaves of bread cost 42¢, how much does 1 loaf cost? Quick as a flash he said, "21¢." When asked, "How did you find the answer?", he replied, "Well, 20 and 20 are 40, and 1 and 1 are 2, so 21."

The example 2/42¢ was written on the blackboard, but he was unable to work it.

Dozens of similar cases could be described, but these five will suggest the nature of faulty work in arithmetic which can be diagnosed by suitable methods. The first four are specific disability cases, the fifth a complex disability case who had difficulties with all phases of arithmetic operations.

The statement below reports the results of a systematic survey by diagnostic methods of the kinds of faults that were found in the work with whole numbers of a group of children all of whose test scores were considerably below standard for their grade. The data are typical of results for practically any school.

The types of difficulty disclosed were most interesting. The most common fault proved to be the habit of counting. The teachers had worked faithfully to secure automatization of all combinations, but in spite of their efforts, twenty-three counters slipped through. They counted in the most amazing ways, with lips, tongue, toes, and fingers. Sometimes the counting was scarcely perceptible. Fourteen had a short attention span. They could readily add a column of four or five figures but beyond that they were lost. Fourteen moved lips constantly, vocalizing every step, ten had a bad habit of guessing, eight failed because of faulty procedure, and six failed because of slowness.

Addition difficulties. Twenty-two skipped around, selecting combinations that seemed easy to them; eighteen hunted about for addends of 10; eighteen inspected the example to find a starting point; eleven had trouble with carrying; five added all the large numbers first to get them out of the way, and nine used curious roundabout methods.

Subtraction difficulties. Fifteen showed weakness in the fundamentals; fourteen had trouble with borrowing; twelve used roundabout methods; three always subtracted the smaller numbers from the larger whether it was in the minuend or the subtrahend; four added to obtain results, and three counted backwards, using the fingers to keep track of the count.

Multiplication difficulties. Ten showed weakness in fundamentals; seven had carrying difficulties; nine used the multiplicand as the multiplier, and two had zero difficulties.

Division difficulties. Nineteen had trouble with divisions having remainders; twelve had zero difficulties; eleven repeated the tables to secure results; eight used roundabout methods; twelve had difficulty with trial division, and six couldn't remember the number to carry in the multiplication involved.

It took from forty-five to ninety minutes to complete an individual diagnosis, the time depending upon the number and kind of difficulties encountered. We were fortunate in having the assistance of student examiners, but if we had not had their help, we could readily have made our own diagnoses. Anyone who is supplied with the necessary diagnostic material can do the work. As a matter of fact, it is a distinct advantage for a teacher to make her own diagnosis, and some of our teachers preferred to do so.

The children, themselves, were keenly interested in the analysis and co-operated willingly with the teachers in their effort to improve the situation. It sometimes happened that a child had only one or two special difficulties. When these were known it was a comparatively easy matter to clear up the trouble. On the other hand, one boy in 5A grade had a total of twenty-three separate kinds of trouble. No wonder his teachers considered him extremely "careless" in the handling of figures! [11]

2. *The Most Common Difficulties in Operations with Fractions.* The six most common faulty responses in each of the four operations with common fractions are given below. The list is based on an analysis by Brueckner and his students of 21,065 errors in comprehensive tests of each process administered to about 600 pupils in grade 5 and 6 in six elementary schools in a large Midwestern city.

[11] Adapted from a report by Ella M. Probst, formerly principal of Longfellow School, Minneapolis.

THE MOST COMMON DIFFICULTIES IN OPERATIONS WITH FRACTIONS

	Per Cent of Total
1. Addition	
a. Lack of comprehension of process indicated, e.g., added numerators and denominators	20.2
b. Difficulty in reducing fractions to lowest terms	17.5
c. Difficulty with improper fractions in the sums	17.1
d. Computational errors as such	13.8
e. Partial operation only	2.2
f. Errors in changing fractions to common denominator	1.5

Number of errors in process analyzed—6202

2. Subtraction	
a. Difficulty when regrouping is involved, as in $10\frac{1}{4} - 4\frac{3}{4}$	24.3
b. Difficulty in reducing fractions to lowest terms	14.6
c. Lack of comprehension of process indicated, e.g., $4\frac{3}{4} - \frac{3}{4} = 40$	14.6
d. Errors in changing fractions to common denominator	8.3
e. Computational errors as such	8.2
f. Partial operation only, e.g., $3\frac{3}{4} - 1\frac{1}{4} = 2$	4.0

Number of errors in process analyzed—7511

3. Multiplication	
a. Computational errors as such	28.7
b. Lack of comprehension of process indicated	17.3
c. Difficulty in reducing fractions to lowest terms	17.3
d. Failure to reduce improper fractions	8.8
e. Errors in copying figures	3.5
f. Difficulty in changing mixed numbers to improper fractions	2.8

Number of errors in process analyzed—2477

4. Division	
a. Used incorrect process, e.g., failed to invert divisor	31.1
b. Computational errors as such	13.8
c. Lack of comprehension of process indicated	12.1
d. Difficulty in reducing fractions to lowest terms	8.9
e. Changing mixed numbers to improper fractions	8.6
f. Changing improper fractions to mixed numbers	7.2

Number of errors analyzed—4875

In all operations a major source of error was an indicated lack of comprehension of the process. Evidently the processes were not meaningful to the pupils. There were also numerous purely computational errors in each process, especially in multiplication and division. The prevalence of this type of error undoubtedly could be greatly reduced by encouraging the checking of all computations by going over the work a second time. Difficulty with reduction of fractions to lowest terms and with improper fractions were two major errors in all processes. In both multiplication and division a major source of error was difficulty in changing mixed numbers to improper fractions. Regrouping the minuend caused the most errors in subtraction.

In addition to the types of errors listed above, which can be quite easily detected by an analysis of the pupil's written work, there were many peculiar types of errors which could not be classified, especially in the work of pupils who were clearly deficient in processes with fractions. Investigations show that these children sometimes simply juggle the figures in examples almost at random so as to arrive at an answer which therefore actually is meaningless, indicating complete lack of comprehension by the pupil of the process involved. Where such errors appear in the pupil's work, the necessity of a complete reteaching of the steps by use of simpler more direct methods is indicated. These will be described in the next chapter.

3. *The Most Common Faults in Operations with Decimals.* The three or four most common faults in each of the four operations with decimal fractions are given below. The data are based on an analysis of errors made by 168 pupils in grade 7 on a comprehensive series of four tests, each test including a wide variety of relatively simple examples in the process involved. Computations as such in the tests used were very easy, since the purpose of the investigation was to determine how well the children could manage the decimal point in performing the operations. The number of errors analyzed in each process is given in the table below.

THE MOST COMMON FAULTS IN OPERATIONS WITH DECIMALS

	Per Cent of Total Number
1. Addition of decimals	
a. Misplacing decimal point in the sum	47.4
b. Computational errors as such	27.4
c. Errors in adding common and decimal fractions	7.4
Number of errors analyzed—580	
2. Subtraction of decimals	
a. Computational errors as such	73.8
b. Misplacing decimal number in the subtrahend	15.9
c. Misplacing decimal point in remainder	1.7
Number of errors analyzed—465	
3. Multiplication of decimals	
a. Misplacing decimal point in product	34.8
b. Computational errors	25.6
c. Annexing and prefixing zeros	8.4
d. Omission of decimal point in product	6.6
Number of errors analyzed—1814	
4. Division of decimals	
a. Misplacing decimal point in quotient	38.3
b. Computational errors	16.4
c. Handling of zeros in dividend or quotient	14.7
d. Omission of decimal point in quotient	9.5
Number of errors analyzed—3751	

The number of errors discovered was least for subtraction and addition, larger for multiplication, and by far the greatest in division. In each operation there were numerous purely computational errors which in many cases would have been corrected if the pupils had checked their work or gone over it a second time. In both multiplication and division, the placement of the decimal point in products and quotients was the most frequent kind of error. Difficulty in prefixing and annexing zeros in the various parts of multiplication and division examples also was a major source of error. For example, the most common kinds of errors in division of decimals were the following:

a. Failure to prefix necessary zeros in the quotient, as in $7\overline{)\,.049}^{\,.7}$

b. Failure to annex zeros in dividend, as in $.4\overline{)\,8}^{\,2}$

c. Failure to annex zero to quotient, as in $.3\overline{)\,6.0}^{\,2}$

d. Placing extra zeros in quotient, as in $5\overline{)\,2.5}^{\,.05}$

Many of the errors listed above are obviously due to lack of understanding of the meaning of decimal fractions and of relationships involved in the processes. Every effort must be made to make clear the meaning of decimal fractions as such and to help the pupils use the relations among the numbers in examples to check the reasonableness of answers. Methods of approximation to be described in a section of the next chapter are especially helpful.

4. *Practice in Analyzing Errors in Written Work.* Some of the most common kinds of errors that are made by pupils in working examples in the various operations are embedded in the work given below. Make a list of the errors and faults you can find in each example based on an examination of the written work that is given. In some cases you will find that the answer is incorrect but that you must have additional information before you can tell what the actual source of the error was. Indicate in your analysis how you would proceed to secure this information. Use the lists of errors in preceding pages to guide you in making your analysis.

a.	$3\,\tfrac{1}{2} = 3\,\tfrac{2}{4}$ $\underline{+2\,\tfrac{1}{4} = 2\,\tfrac{1}{4}}$ $\tfrac{3}{8}$	b.	4 $\underline{-1\,\tfrac{2}{3}}$ 30	c.	$\tfrac{3}{4} \times 4\,\tfrac{1}{2} =$ $\tfrac{1}{3} \times \tfrac{5}{2} = 2\tfrac{6}{6}$
d.	$2\,\tfrac{1}{2} \div \tfrac{1}{4} =$ $\tfrac{3}{2} \times \tfrac{1}{4} = \tfrac{3}{8} = 2$	e.	2.4 $\underline{+13.8}$ 16.3	f.	3.75 $\underline{\times 1.2}$ 640 375 $\overline{91.5}$

g. 62   h.   860   i. 24/980 ⎺⎺⎺⎺⎺
   −27   ×5   31 r 20
   ⎺⎺⎺   ⎺⎺⎺⎺   72
    45   4005   ⎺⎺
                                      26
                                      24
                                      ⎺⎺
                                      20

DIAGNOSIS IN PROBLEM-SOLVING AND QUANTITATIVE THINKING

General Diagnosis

To measure the ability of pupils to solve problems and to think quantitatively, tests of the following types should be administered: (1) the ability to solve verbal problems, one of the major skills measured by available standard tests; (2) the ability to read graphs, charts, tables, and similar materials and to answer questions based on them; (3) knowledge of vocabulary; (4) knowledge about social applications of arithmetic fundamental in problem-solving; and (5) quantitative understandings. Comparison of pupil scores with standard scores will enable the teacher to estimate the seriousness of any apparent deficiency. This information must also be supplemented by measures of ability to compute, as well as of reading ability.

None of the available standard tests in arithmetic provides measures of all of these elements. All of the general survey tests listed on page 208 contain tests in problem-solving. The Analytical Scales of Attainment contain tests of problem-solving, vocabulary, and quantitative relationships. Data concerning these tests are given on page 194. The Iowa Test of Basic Study Skills contains a test of the ability to interpret graphs, tables, and charts. The New Stanford Achievement Test also contains a similar test of study skills. Sueltz has developed a Test of Quantitative Understanding (Educational Test Bureau) which measures an important aspect of the comprehension of mathematics and social concepts in arithmetic.

When standard tests are not available, the teacher should use the informal tests of problem-solving and quantitative thinking often included in textbooks or workbooks. Teacher-made tests can also be used. For example, the short informal test of ability to solve easy problems given on page 273 is a simple informal test of the pupil's understanding of the rudimentary computational skills and of his ability to use them in easy problem-solving situations. Similar tests can be devised by the teacher to determine the ability of the pupils to apply formulas, to use measures and measuring devices, to read tables, charts, and graphs, and similar fundamental skills and abilities. The yearbook, *Measurement of Understanding,*[12] contains numerous illustrations of items that can be included in informal tests of understandings of mathematical and social aspects of arithmetic.

[12] Forty-fifth Yearbook, Part I, National Society of Education (Chicago, Univ. of Chicago Press, 1946). Ch. 7.

Analytical Diagnosis in Problem-Solving

There are several analytical tests in problem-solving which break down this general ability into component elements. For example, the Compass Diagnostic Tests in Problem-Solving include the following subtests, each of which gives a specific measurement of the element named:

1. Comprehension (a reading test).
2. What is given?
3. What is called for?
4. Probable answer (estimation).
5. The correct solution (choice of five that are given).

The arithmetic reasoning portion of the National Achievement Test is a similar test and contains the following subtests.

1. Comparisons (based on data in problems).
2. Problem analysis (steps in problem-solving).
3. Finding the key to problems (the question asked).
4. Problems to solve (solutions).

The problem-solving test in the Coordinated Scales of Attainment is a special type that provides a measure of how well the pupil can select from among four given methods of solving a problem the correct procedure. He is not required to perform the computations involved, in which errors so often are the major cause of incorrect answers to problems. This test therefore provides a measure of only one element in problem-solving, the ability to select the correct method of solution.

Sample item:

1. John bought an apple for 6 cents and a loaf of bread for 18 cents. He gave the clerk 50 cents. How much change did he receive?
   a. Add 6¢, 18¢, and 50¢.
   b. Subtract 18¢ from 50¢, and then add 6 cents.
   c. Add 6¢ and 18¢. Subtract sum from 50¢.
   d. Divide 18 by 6. Subtract result from 50¢.

Some teachers find it helpful to examine the written work on tests in problem-solving to determine (1) whether or not the correct method of solution was used, and (2) whether or not the computations were performed correctly. Two scores are given for the work done. This method of scoring gives full credit for correctness of method even when errors are made in computations, thus isolating each element.

A valuable analytical procedure for locating special difficulties is to tabulate the number of times each problem in a test was worked incorrectly by the pupils. In this way, problems that caused the greatest difficulty can be identified.

Case-Study Procedures in Problem-Solving

The same kinds of diagnostic procedures that are used in the diagnosis of computational deficiencies should be applied to determine the nature and causes of poor quantitative thinking in general and poor performance on tests of problem-solving. There are no standard diagnostic tests in problem-solving suitable for clinical study. Informal procedures must be used.

1. *Analysis of Oral Responses*. Select or prepare a group of problems of average difficulty for the pupil's level of ability. Then proceed as follows with each problem and observe closely the responses made by the pupil to the steps given below. Ask supplementary questions such as those given below as may be necessary to get at underlying difficulties and the pupil's methods of thinking and computing:

a. Please read the first problem aloud for me. (Observe methods of reading and make a note of any evidence of reading difficulties. Check with results of reading tests.)

b. Are there any words in the problem that you do not understand? (Check on range of vocabulary.)

c. What is the question the problem asks you to answer? Read it. Now state the problem and the question in your own words. (Testing ability to analyze the problem and to remember its elements. The pupil's responses will show whether or not the problem is within his experience.)

d. What facts are given in the problem that will help you to answer the question? Are there any other facts that you need to know? Where can you find them? (Problems in modern textbooks are often based on tables and charts, or on information given in preceding problems. Look for difficulties in locating information in such sources. Knowledge of measures given in the appendix is also needed in changing given measures to larger or lower units, requiring the use of the appendix when necessary.)

e. How will you find the answer to the problem? Tell me what computations you must make. Is there a rule (or formula) that you can use to find the answer? (In the lower grades, pupils often make random guesses as to methods to be used in solutions, indicating complete lack of comprehension of the meaning of the problems or of the processes, or both. See if the pupil has had experiences related to the problem situation. Have the pupil also explain the reasons why he thinks that the process he mentions is the one to be used, so as to get at the nature of the pupil's thought processes. Have the pupil do his thinking aloud.)

f. Now make a guess (or estimate) as to what the answer to the problem is. Tell me how you arrived at your answer. (Testing ability to estimate answers.)

g. Now find the answer by writing out the work. (Observe the pupil's computational procedures and his methods of work. Note errors made.)

The information secured by the analysis of pupil responses to the above questions for a selected group of problems will give the teacher valuable data to be used in planning an improvement program.

A pupil may simply be asked to work some selected problem, stating his thinking aloud, so that the observer can study his responses, their clarity, effectiveness, and general quality. This procedure can be supplemented by questions which may probe more deeply into his thought processes as may seem to be advisable. The teacher should check for degree of insight into the situation presented in each problem, the quality of the thought processes used in solving the problems, and evidence of understanding of the mathematical relationships.

Similar questions to these given above for problems may be based on a table, graph, diagram, geometric figure, or picture to help the teacher to evaluate the ability of the pupil to read and interpret these kinds of materials and to plan a remedial program. Special exercises can also be prepared to test concepts and relationships expressed in formulas, such as perimeter, area, volume, and interest, and in such a series as the cost-price-number of items and time-rate-distance relationships.

2. *Analysis of Written Work.* Considerable valuable information can be secured through an analysis of the written work of pupils on daily papers or on tests. Such points as the following should be borne in mind in making the analysis:

a. The extent to which the correct methods of solution were used to find the answers.

b. The nature and extent of computational errors, since it is known that a very large proportion of incorrect answers to problems are usually due to incorrect work although the correct method of solution is applied. Look for evidence that the answer was checked in some way.

c. Evidence of lack of understanding of the situation on which the problem was based, suggesting lack of experience. Answers are often meaningless in the situation presented owing to a random choice of method so as to find some answer.

d. Evidence of lack of knowledge of measures, facts, rules, formulas, and relationships, or of inability to apply them.

e. Orderliness and neatness of arrangement of work.

f. Evidence of the misreading or careless copying of numbers and data in the problem.

The difficulties listed above also should be analyzed by having the pupils solve easy sets of problems involving simple computational skills, such as are found in textbooks for lower grade levels, in order to determine the level at which the pupil can solve problems with a fair degree of success. This procedure is similar to that used to determine the level of reading ability, described in Chapter 7. Many children are confused by large numbers in problems but can solve problems that contain small numbers and apply operations which they understand, showing that they understand the meaning of the operations but become confused when large numbers or difficult computations are involved.

3. *Observation of Pupil Behavior.* Such items as the following can be studied through direct observation of actions of the pupil in the classroom:

a. Attitudes toward arithmetic.
b. Effectiveness of methods of work.
c. Evidences of dawdling; indifference.
d. Use of roundabout computational procedures.
e. Group relations.
f. Method of attacking solutions of problems.

4. *Interviews.* The case-study procedures described under 1 above are essentially interviews with the learner. These methods of diagnosing difficulties in solving verbal problems can be extended by asking questions to reveal the learner's interests in arithmetic, to determine factors not revealed by other means that may be interfering with progress, such as his health, uses of leisure time, opportunities for studying home, and the like.

An Illustrative Case Study

The following description of the results of a case study in problem-solving shows some of the kinds of information that can be secured through a systematic diagnostic analysis, including observation of the pupil at work in a test situation.

Pupil G lacked persistence. When it was evident that she had not comprehended the problem she would say she was "stuck." She was unable to formulate any questions which would throw light on the difficulty. Rather than be questioned too much by the investigator, she would set to work, usually with the wrong process. She was desperately lacking in ability to do quantitative thinking. She was willing to try to do the problems but her inability destroyed any self-confidence she might have had and led her to take the line of least resistance when possible. All computation was very laborious for her.

Her work habits were poor. She erased incessantly, partly because of changing her mind about the process and partly because of lack of mastery of the fundamentals. She counted on her fingers, chewed her pencil, sighed, raised her eyebrows, and was easily distracted by shouts of children on the playground some distance away. She guessed the correct answer to the estimation problem but said she did not know how to estimate. It took her longer than the average amount of time required by the group as a whole. She looked up three words but did not comprehend their meaning as was evidenced by her incorrect solutions! [13]

SUGGESTED ACTIVITIES

1. Outline a program for appraising pupil growth in relation to the objectives of instruction in arithmetic. Include in your plan standard tests as well as descriptions of evaluation procedures.
2. Examine a modern arithmetic textbook to determine the kinds of tests that it contains, including inventory tests, readiness tests, diagnostic tests, and progress tests. Evaluate these tests according to criteria suggested in this chapter.

[13] This description is an adaptation of the report of a case study by Myrtle Scripture, graduate student, Univ. of Minnesota.

3. Discuss with several teachers the diagnostic procedures they apply as a part of the regular instructional program. Suggest possible improvements in line with suggestions made in this chapter.

4. What procedures can be used that will assist the pupil to appraise his achievements and to locate his strengths and weak spots? Why is it desirable to administer screening tests at the beginning of the school year? Construct a screening test.

5. Administer tests of the number facts in some process to one or more pupils, according to the plans discussed on page 215. Analyze the results. Which method of testing do you think is most satisfactory?

6. Construct and administer an analytical diagnostic test as described on page 217, or administer one of the analytical tests that is given in this chapter. Analyze the test papers and comment on the types of difficulties identified.

7. Make a careful individual diagnostic study of the work of some pupil who is seriously deficient in one or more phases of arithmetic. Utilize the case study methods that are discussed in this chapter. In connection with Chapter 9 you will have the opportunity to plan a remedial program.

8. How can you account for the incorrect, involved, roundabout mental processes that children use in working examples? Suggest some things the teacher might do to prevent the incidence of these faulty procedures.

9. Discuss methods of organizing the work in the class period so that the teacher would find time for diagnosis.

10. Why might continued practice by a pupil on examples he does not understand fail to produce an improvement? Why is understanding necessary? How can you test for understanding?

SELECTED BIBLIOGRAPHY

BROWNELL, W. A., "The Place of Meaning in the Teaching of Arithmetic," *Elementary School Journal,* Vol. 47 (January, 1947), pp. 256-265.

————, "When Is Arithmetic Meaningful?" *Journal of Educational Research,* Vol. 30 (March, 1937), pp. 481-498.

————, "The Effect of Premature Drill on Third Grade Arithmetic," *Journal of Educational Research,* Vol. 29 (September, 1935), pp. 17-29.

BRUECKNER, L. J., *Diagnostic and Remedial Teaching of Arithmetic,* pp. 17-29 (Philadelphia, J. C. Winston, 1930).

————, and GROSSNICKLE, F. E., *Making Arithmetic Meaningful* (Philadelphia, J. C. Winston, 1953), Chs. 11, 12, 13.

CHASE, W. L., "Subject Preferences of Fifth Grade Children," *Elementary School Journal,* Vol. 50 (December, 1949), pp. 208-211.

Child Development and the Curriculum, Thirty-eighth Yearbook, Part I, National Society for the Study of Education (Chicago, Univ. of Chicago Press, 1939), Chs. 15 and 16.

DAHLE, C. O., "The Verbal Thought and Overt Behavior of Children During Their Learning of Long Division," *Journal of Experimental Education,* Vol. 9 (September, 1940), pp. 1-9.

Educational Diagnosis, Thirty-fourth Yearbook, National Society for the Study of Education (Chicago, Univ. of Chicago Press, 1935), Ch. 14.

FERNALD, Grace, *Remedial Techniques in the Basic Skill Subjects* (New York, McGraw, 1943), Ch. 14.

Hansen, Carl, "Factors Associated with Successful Achievement in Problem Solving in Sixth Grade Arithmetic," *Journal of Educational Research,* Vol. 38 (October, 1944), pp. 111-119.

Johnson, H. C., "The Effect of Instruction in Mathematical Vocabulary Upon Problem Solving in Arithmetic," *Journal of Educational Research,* Vol. 38 (October, 1944), pp. 97-110.

Koenker, R. A., "Certain Characteristic Differences of Good and Poor Achievers in Long Division," *Journal of Educational Research,* Vol. 35 (April, 1942), pp. 578-587.

Measurement of Understanding, Forty-fifth Yearbook, Part I, National Society for the Study of Education (Chicago, Univ. of Chicago Press, 1946), Chs. 7 and 8.

Sueltz, B. A.,"Measuring the Newer Aspects of Functional Arithmetic," *Elementary School Journal,* Vol. 47 (February, 1947), pp. 323-330.

Spencer, P. L., and Brydegaard, Marguerite, *Building Mathematical Concepts in the Elementary School* (New York, Holt, 1952), Ch. 10.

The Teaching of Arithmetic, Fiftieth Yearbook, Part II, National Society for the Study of Education (Chicago, Univ. of Chicago Press, 1951), Ch. 9.

Treacy, J. P., "The Relationship of Reading Skills to the Ability to Solve Problems," *Journal of Educational Research,* Vol. 38 (October, 1944), pp. 89-97.

Wheat, H. G., *How to Teach Arithmetic* (Evanston, Ill., Row, 1951).

9 TREATMENT OF LEARNING DIFFICULTIES IN ARITHMETIC

THERE ARE many kinds of faulty learnings and deficiencies in arithmetic, any one of which may contribute to a specific or general disability. Since these deficiencies will vary from child to child, it is not to be expected that there can be a uniform approach to the correction of learning difficulties in arithmetic for all children in a given class or grade. The corrective program must be adapted to the needs of each child from the standpoint of his characteristics and the nature of his disability.

In this chapter it is not possible because of lack of space to discuss fully methods of dealing with all of the specific faulty learnings in arithmetic that were presented in the preceding chapter. Instead we shall consider the methods of treatment to be applied to the more prevalent and crucial categories of arithmetic difficulties in number operations and problem-solving.

In this chapter we shall discuss the following topics:

1. Factors underlying difficulties in arithmetic.
2. Principles of remedial teaching with specific reference to arithmetic.
3. Treatment of difficulties in number operations.
4. Improving problem-solving ability.

We shall assume that when reading difficulties are an apparent cause of poor achievement in arithmetic they will be dealt with according to the procedures discussed in Chapter 7. The reader should also review the discussion of general principles of remedial teaching given in Chapter 5.

FACTORS UNDERLYING DIFFICULTIES IN ARITHMETIC

Conditions That Contribute to Arithmetic Disability

When a major difficulty in arithmetic has been identified and its nature determined, the possible causes should be considered to complete the diagnostic process and to plan corrective measures. It is generally recognized that the causes of unsatisfactory growth are to be found in some element of the educational program as such, or in the characteristics of the learner.

For example, the content of the curriculum may be too difficult, not well graded, or too narrow in scope to develop interest in the work. Similarly, teaching procedures may be unskillful or stress mechanistic procedures and repetitive drill to the exclusion of social applications of arithmetic, or fail to recognize individual differences. There may be very little done by the teacher to diagnose and treat learning difficulties. The instructional equipment may be inadequate, highly abstract, not clear in its development of topics, and lacking in provisions for applying and maintaining skills. The teacher may make little use of manipulative materials, visual aids, and community resources as aids to learning. Conditions in the home and community also may affect the learners of arithmetic unfavorably.

Obviously, factors inherent in the child himself may be involved, such as his constitutional, intellectual, social, and emotional characteristics. Because of the important role of reading in arithmetic, those traits of the individual that interfere with success in reading—poor health, physical defects, loss of hearing, or vision, low intelligence level, emotional and social maladjustment, and limited experiential background—should be considered in making a diagnosis of disability in arithmetic and in planning corrective measures. The reader should review Chapter 3 in connection with this discussion.

Complexity of Factors Contributing to Arithmetic Disability

The fact is that the causes of a particular pupil's disability in arithmetic are usually multiple in nature, a complex that must be considered in planning remedial measures. Sometimes the causes are deep-seated and difficult to determine. In many cases the teacher can quickly determine the nature of a difficulty or deficiency and should attack it directly without attempting to establish the actual cause of the shortcoming. These causes may in some cases be quite remote, for example, inefficient teaching in some preceding grade or excessive pupil absence at some time due to illness. When after a time it appears that the steps being taken to correct the deficiency are not proving to be effective, the teacher obviously must take steps to discover the underlying causes, such as low intelligence level, physical handicaps, lack of interest, deficiencies in component skills, poor study habits, emotional blocking, and unfavorable home conditions, and then make necessary adjustments in the improvement program. In cases when serious deficiencies are apparently due to a complexity of causes the advice of specialists should be secured, such as the members of the staff of a child guidance clinic.

PRINCIPLES OF REMEDIAL TEACHING

Basic Principles Underlying Remedial Teaching

When the nature of a disability in arithmetic has been determined and its probable causes tentatively established, steps should then be taken to correct the condition. Minor difficulties and incorrect procedures that are discovered from time to time in the usual daily work can be eliminated quickly by direct teaching; in some cases medical care will alleviate underlying causes of learning difficulty; other factors, such as an unfavorable attitude toward arithmetic, are much more difficult to correct. In some cases radical adjustments of curriculum, instruction, and home conditions may be necessary to bring about desired changes.

Basic principles underlying remedial work, in addition to those that are fundamental to all good teaching of arithmetic, may be briefly stated as follows:

1. Because needs vary from pupil to pupil, corrective measures must be planned on an individual basis and adapted to the particular needs of each learner.

2. Every effort should be made to secure the interest and co-operation of the individual. He must be dealt with sympathetically and understood as a personality. He must have confidence in the therapist.

3. Treatment should begin with a direct attack on specific difficulties on the level at which success in the initial stages of treatment is assured, thus providing for an enjoyable and profitable learning experience.

4. A self-directed attack by the learner on the solution of his own learning problems and the establishment of goals to be achieved is highly desirable. The needs as well as the stage of development and rate of growth of the learner should be considered in setting up goals.

5. Continuing diagnosis is essential so that incorrect and inefficient methods of thinking and work can be promptly detected and corrected. Continuous guidance is necessary.

6. The sequence of learning activities should proceed step by step in a carefully graded sequence, introducing only one new element or difficulty at a time.

7. When there is evidence of growth, it can be assumed that the measures being taken are proving to be effective. When there is little evidence of growth, a new attack should be made on the problem. Awareness of progress by the learner is an important stimulus to efforts to improve.

8. The classroom teacher should ordinarily assume responsibility for the diagnosis and treatment of learning difficulties, except in cases involving specific disabilities or complex disabilities, when treatment should be guided by specialists and clinical workers.

Principles Underlying the Treatment of Disability Cases

The methods that are used in all good teaching of arithmetic should be used in the treatment of deficiencies. In many cases minor difficulties will be detected and corrected in the course of regular instruction. This will happen with normal pupils or cases of simple retardation. The teacher will be called on to make a careful diagnosis in specific disability cases and to plan a corrective program adjusted to the needs of the learner. In cases of complex disability, the teacher should feel free to call on specialists for assist ance in making the diagnosis and planning the remedial program.

When serious learning difficulties are identified, the steps to be taken in treatment are substantially as follows:

1. Utilize diagnostic procedures to determine as definitely as possible what the nature of the difficulty is and what the factors are that underlie it. Consider possible adjustments that should be made in curriculum, goals, instruction, materials, and social relations as a part of the corrective program. Give special consideration to the pupil's physical characteristics, his attitudes, and his social background.

2. Make a special effort to secure the interested participation of the individual in the steps needed to bring about an improvement. This can be done by bringing to his attention when possible the ways in which what he is learning functions in his everyday social experiences.

3. Begin the improvement program by remedying any discovered lack of knowledge of the basic number facts. Have the pupil learn to use manipulative and representative materials, as will be described shortly, to discover number groupings and to find answers to number facts he finds difficult. Help him to discover generalizations among groups of related facts, since these will structure his learning and facilitate memory work.

4. Use manipulative and representative materials (described in the following pages) to make the number operations and the steps within operations meaningful. Begin corrective work at a level just below the point in the developmental sequence where an inventory or diagnostic test indicates that the skill tends to break down. Then proceed gradually step by step to rebuild the complete process in such a way that the pupil may be aware of his success in overcoming his deficiencies. An awareness of success is a vital element in learning.

5. Gradually raise the level of thinking required by the use of manipulative and representative materials by introducing methods of visualizing the steps in number operations through diagrams, charts, and other kinds of visual representation so as to make them increasingly meaningful. Finally, reteach the actual algorism itself that is causing difficulty.

6. Help the learner to see the relationships among the various operations so that he will come to sense the way in which the number system functions in them and gain insight into the efficiency of the systematic procedures that have been invented by the human race to deal with quantitative aspects of the affairs of daily life.

7. When the pupil understands the step and has learned the method of solution, he should be assigned practice to develop control and proficiency.

Applying This Approach to Remedial Teaching

To make the application of this approach to remedial teaching concrete, let us consider the steps that were taken by a diagnostic worker to correct the specific difficulty a pupil had in working examples in subtraction of whole numbers in which regrouping in the minuend is required, as in the example below at the left.

It was found that the pupil knew most of the subtraction facts and could subtract in examples such as $47 - 23$ in which regrouping in the minuend was not necessary. It was also discovered that he had invented a method of counting by ones in similar examples requiring regrouping in ones' and tens' places, for instance, counting by ones from 38 to 52 to find the answer, an inaccurate, roundabout method not easy to use in working examples with large remainders. He was eager to secure help, since he was very unhappy about the number of incorrect subtraction examples in his daily papers. His teacher evidently had not discovered the cause of his incorrect work, namely, inability to proceed efficiently when regrouping was necessary. Apparently this process had been taught during a period of the child's absence from school because of illness.

$$\begin{array}{r} 52 \\ -38 \\ \hline \end{array}$$

The steps taken to teach the pupil the correct subtraction procedure were as follows:

1. First the pupil and examiner discussed the written example and identified the step in the example that presented difficulty, namely, that 8 ones cannot be subtracted from 2 ones.

(a)   (b)

(c)

2. Next the meaning of the number 52 was shown by the examiner by means of a place-value chart and tickets, namely, 5 bundles of ten tickets each and 2 single tickets, as pictured in chart (a). The pupil readily saw that the problem was to get more ones in the ones' pocket, so that 8 ones could be taken out.

3. To get more ones the pupil soon discovered a method, namely, by taking a tens' bundle from the 5 bundles in tens' pocket and opening it up as 10 ones so that there were then 12 ones in ones' pocket, as shown in B. It was then a simple matter to take 8 ones out of the ones' pocket and 3 tens' bundles out of the tens' pocket, shown crossed out in C.

$$\begin{array}{r} 4 \;\; 12 \\ \cancel{5} \;\; \cancel{2} \\ -3 \;\; 8 \\ \hline 1 \;\; 4 \end{array}$$

4. The examiner then wrote out with figures the work shown by manipulative aids above, in the complete written form given at the left, explaining each step in the written solution by reference to the steps in using the place-value charts. The written-out work in the solution visualized for the learner the series of mental steps involved in regrouping, namely, first taking 1 of the 5 tens, leaving 4 tens, and then getting 12 ones by regrouping the 1 ten and 2 ones.

$$\begin{array}{r} 52 \\ -38 \\ \hline 14 \end{array}$$

5. After the pupil had worked out several similar examples with the assistance of the place-value chart as described above and had written out the solutions in full form as also shown above, it was evident that he understood the step and could proceed with other examples without writing out all of the work, using the mature form shown at the left.

6. Then the pupil was given a group of similar examples to work, which he did quickly and correctly to his obvious satisfaction.

Notice the steps taken in the correction of this difficulty. They should be applied in the treatment of all learning difficulties. The corrective treatment grew out of a need of which the pupil was aware. The difficulty involved was clearly identified. First, the manipulation of representative materials through the use of the place-value pockets and tickets demonstrated the steps to be taken in solving the example. The steps in the solution were then written out so as to visualize the thinking involved. Both manipulation and visualization were thus used at the start to make the steps in the process meaningful to the pupil. By working out several examples himself in this way, the pupil gained insight into the procedures involved and then was able to use more mature thought processes when practicing the new step with similar examples.

This illustration of the method of diagnosing and correcting a specific difficulty in subtraction may appear to be obvious and very simple, a method that any effective teacher surely would apply. However, it is unfortunately true that many teachers do not use diagnostic procedures nor do they use manipulative materials and visualization to make operations meaningful. Overburdened by large classes and unfamiliar with diagnostic procedures, they fail to identify the learning difficulties of their pupils and often blindly assign more "drill" on processes in which weaknesses are apparent, trusting that the drill will overcome the difficulty. The fact is that under such conditions repetitive practice may actually establish faults and fixate inefficient methods of work that it will become increasingly difficult to correct. Diagnosis must precede treatment. Treatment must be based on a diagnosis.

TREATMENT OF DIFFICULTIES IN NUMBER OPERATIONS

We shall now discuss methods of treating the three most prevalent and crucial sources of difficulties in the learning of number operations, namely:

1. Lack of understanding of numbers and the number system.
2. Lack of knowledge of the basic number facts.
3. Faulty procedures in performing number operations.

A. LACK OF UNDERSTANDING OF NUMBERS AND THE NUMBER SYSTEM

1. METHODS OF DIAGNOSIS

a. Meaning of Place Value in Whole Numbers, Including Regrouping

A simple test to determine how well the pupil understands the meaning of numbers and ways in which the number system functions is given below. The test should be administered to an individual pupil; the teacher should read aloud the items, observe the answers given, and make any necessary records of pupil reactions.

HOW WELL DO YOU UNDERSTAND WHOLE NUMBERS?

$$\begin{array}{r} 408 \\ +365 \\ \hline \end{array}$$

1. Please read the numbers in the example for me. (Correct reading of easy numbers, including 0.)
2. Which is the larger number? How can you tell? (Knowledge of sizes of numbers.)
3. What is the name of the place in which the 6 is written? the 8? the 4? the 0? (Place value.)
4. Now find the sum of the two numbers. (Observe the order of the steps taken by the pupil and his methods of work, his use of crutches, and evidences of difficulty.)
5. After the sum has been found, ask: "How did you get the 3 in the answer? What number did you carry? What is the value of the 1 you carried?" (If the child answers, "1 ten," he evidently understands the regrouping done to change the 13 ones to 1 ten and 3 ones, which is the essential relationship in applying the number system in working this example.)
6. How did you get the 7 in the answer? (Test of concept of adding numbers having the same base and also of the carrying process.)

Similar questions can be asked about solutions of other examples, such as these:

$$\begin{array}{r} 305 \\ -247 \\ \hline \end{array} \qquad \begin{array}{r} 4080 \\ \times 6 \\ \hline \end{array} \qquad \begin{array}{r} \$3.50 \\ \times 8 \\ \hline \end{array} \qquad 2/\overline{8164}$$

In each case the purpose of the interview should be to see how well the pupil understands the number relations involved in carrying and regrouping and the role of zero as a place holder, rather than to discover deficiencies in the methods of computing in processes as such. The methods of diagnosis in operations as such are discussed in the next section.

b. Meaning of Fractions

In a similar manner, a pupil's understanding of fractions can be evaluated by the short test below:

HOW WELL DO YOU UNDERSTAND THE MEANING OF FRACTIONS?

1. Tell what part of each circle is shaded:

2. Read these numbers for me:

   $\frac{1}{2}$ $\frac{3}{4}$ $\frac{7}{5}$ $\frac{1}{3}$ $\frac{4}{4}$ $\frac{5}{12}$ $\frac{6}{8}$

3. Which fraction has 5 as the numerator? 3? (Terms)
4. In which fraction is 8 the numerator? 4 the denominator?
5. Which of the fractions above has the smallest value? the largest value? How can you tell?
6. Which two fractions have the same value? How can you tell?
7. Which of the fractions has the value of 1? How can you tell? What do we call that kind of fraction?
8. Which of the fractions has a value greater than 1? How can you tell? Write it as a mixed number.

c. Meaning of Place Value in Decimals

As has been indicated, decimals represent an extension of the number system by using the places to the right of ones' place. The following questions are a simple test of insight into the meaning of decimals.

HOW WELL DO YOU UNDERSTAND THE MEANING OF DECIMALS?

1. Read these numbers for me:

   a. .24   b. .4   c. .034   d. .105

2. Which of the numbers has the greatest value? the least value? (Relation of place value to size)
3. In which number is the 4 in hundredths' place? (Place value)
4. In what place is 0 written in c? in d?
5. How many places to the right of ones' place is the 5 in d written?
6. Write a number in which 6 is written in tens' place and also in tenths' place.
7. Write as a common fraction: .4; .34; .002.

2. TEACHING THE MEANING OF NUMBERS

Every good textbook contains a more or less adequate treatment of the abstract aspects of the number system. Slow learners, however, find it difficult to grasp many of the underlying concepts because so often the development is largely if not wholly verbal, and little is done to make the system meaningful by the use of manipulative materials and visual aids that have been found to be so helpful. In the following discussion, we shall emphasize the use of concrete representative aids and visualizations to make whole numbers, fractions, and decimals meaningful to children who do not understand the number system. The level at which the teacher will begin treatment will depend on the needs of the case at hand.

a. Teaching the Meaning of Numbers to 29

Secure a supply of toothpicks, disks, one-inch circles, or similar small objects to be used to represent quantities. First have the pupil show the numbers 1 to 9 with the objects, then successively the numbers 10 to 20 with no attempt at grouping. Next show that a group of ten of the objects can be placed together to make a pile which is called "1 ten," because it is "ten of a kind." Then show that eleven (11) means 11 ones or 1 ten and 1 one, that 12 means 12 ones or 1 ten and 2 ones, and so on. Show that 20 is the same as 20 ones or 2 tens. Show also at this time that in the number 10, the 1 means 1 ten and the 0 shows that there are no extra ones in 10.

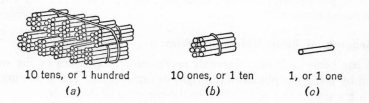

| 10 tens, or 1 hundred | 10 ones, or 1 ten | 1, or 1 one |
| (a) | (b) | (c) |

Now explain that the 1 in 10 is written in tens' place and the 0 in ones' place. Show also that 20 means 2 tens and no ones. Have the pupil then show with objects the meaning of such numbers as 15, 18, 21, 24, and so on, in terms of place value. Also lay down groups of tens and ones and have the pupil tell the numbers they represent as tens and ones, and then have him write the whole numbers shown. To make the work more abstract, draw pictures of tens and ones to represent small numbers and have the pupil tell what the numbers are. Also use drawings in available workbooks or textbooks to extend the practice.

When it is apparent that the meanings of numbers to 29 are clear, the meaning of numbers up to 100 can be taught without using objects unless this proves to be advisable for slow children. By reference to a hundred-square, such as the one on page 266, the meaning of any number

a.   32
-14 to 100 can be made clear. For example, 40 means 4 rows of ten, or 4 tens and no extra ones; 53 means 5 rows of ten or 5 tens, and 3 ones in the next row, in all 53 ones. Similarly 24 means 2 tens and 4 ones, or 24 ones in all; likewise 32 ones means 3 tens and 2 ones, or 2 tens and 12 ones; the latter form is the transformation used

b.   24
$+38$ in regrouping in subtraction, as in example *a.* Similarly 12 ones are the same as 1 ten and 2 ones; which is the transformation made in carrying 1 ten in addition, as in example *b.* These transformations can be extended to larger groupings.

b. Using Place-Value Charts to Show Meanings of Numbers

Place-value charts have been found to be an excellent means for teaching the meaning of place value in larger numbers by using manipulative and visual methods. First, it is necessary to prepare three pocket charts such as those shown below. This can be done by folding sheets of heavy wrapping paper 15 inches wide so as to form pleats in the paper 1 inch deep held in place by stapling the edges or with scotch tape. These pleats serve as pockets to hold small tickets that are used to represent numbers; there should be four pleats in each chart so that the steps in number operations can be demonstrated, as will be explained in the following section. To represent numbers up to 200, cut 1 x 3 cards from ordinary art paper, using a paper cutter. A single ticket represents 1 one, a bundle of 10 tickets 1 ten, and a large bundle of 10 tens 1 hundred, which is also equal to 100 ones. Use small rubber bands or paper clips to form bundles of tens and hundreds (see illustrations).

Begin with the single tickets. Place a row of 10 tickets in a ones' pocket. Explain that as soon as there are 10 tickets in ones' pocket the ten tickets must go as 1 ten to tens' pocket. Fasten the 10 tickets into a bundle and place (carry) it in tens' pocket. Then insert single tickets one at a time, telling what each number shown is (11, 12, 13, etc.) until there is another ten which is also carried to the tens' pocket to show 2 tens or 20. Continue in this way until the number 99 is reached. Then show that by adding 1 one another ten is made which with the 9 tens makes 10 tens, a bundle which is then attached to the hundreds' pocket as 1 hundred. The series of three charts below pictures the meaning of the number 108 as 1 hundred, no tens, and 8 ones.

Hundreds	Tens	Ones
▭░░		▯▯▯▯▯▯▯▯
1	0	8

The role of zero as a place holder in 108 is shown by the charts. Since there are no tens' bundles in the number shown, it serves as a place holder to keep the 1 in hundreds' place in the written number.

Under guidance the pupils should then use the tickets and charts to show numbers such as the following:

| 10 | 20 | 40 | 80 | 32 | 63 | 79 | 94 |
| 112 | 130 | 106 | 143 | 150 | 102 | 200 | 127 |

Larger numbers such as 397, 569, and others can be shown with tickets in the same way. However, it is possible to use in the proper pockets 1 red ticket to represent 1 hundred, 1 blue ticket to represent 1 ten, and white tickets to represent ones. Thus 317 would be shown with 3 red tickets, a blue ticket, and 7 white tickets. Other colors can be used to mean thousands, ten thousands, and so on, to show larger numbers if additional place-value pockets having the proper place designations are provided. In this way, any number can be shown with charts when desirable for teaching meanings.

In the absence of place-value charts, numbers also can be shown by placing tickets in spaces properly labeled at the top of a desk, as shown below.

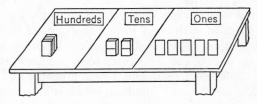

Another excellent device for teaching the meaning of numbers is the hundred-square shown below. It is divided into 100 half-inch squares, 10 small squares to a row. When cut into strips of 10 squares and into single squares it is easy to represent any number with them, for instance 135 as shown below. With ten hundred-squares, ten strips of 10 squares, and ten ones any number to 1000 can be shown.

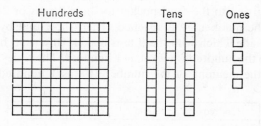

The abacus shown on page 251 is another excellent device for teaching the meaning of numbers. Each rod represents a place in a number. The number shown in the picture is 1079. Children quickly see the role of 0 in a number and enjoy showing numbers on the abacus.

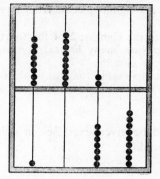

c. Teaching the Meanings of Fractions

The meanings of fractions can very easily be developed by means of manipulative materials and visual aids.

The simplest and most meaningful aid in the teaching of fractions is cutouts of circles and parts of circles. Each pupil should have a "fraction kit" for which a large envelope and 14 circles are needed: 5 whole circles, 3 cut into halves, 3 cut into fourths, and 3 cut into eighths. Four-inch circles cut from stiff paper (about the size of the bottom of a size 2½ can, which may serve as a pattern) are of a good size. Different colors can be used for the different-sized parts. The parts are easily made by folding the circles carefully and cutting along the creases. These parts can also be used to find answers to examples in the four operations as will be explained later. Fractional parts, shown with pie plates, apples, and so forth, are also useful.

Any pupil having difficulty with fractions should first be given the opportunity to play with the various fractional parts and then be led to discover equivalent fractions, such as ½ = ²⁄₄, ⁴⁄₈ = ½, and the like. He may be asked to write the pairs of fractions he shows.

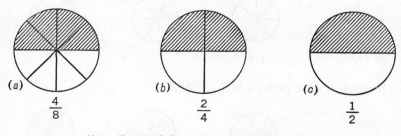

Using Fractional Cutouts to Discover Equivalents

Later, more systematic exercises with cutouts can be used:

1. Use your cutouts to show ½; ¼; ⅜; ¾; ⅝; ⅞; 1.
2. Use your cutouts to show one-half in three ways.
3. Show one-fourth in two ways; three-fourths.

4. Place together 4 of the eighths pieces. What larger piece will cover them exactly?

5. Do the same for 2 of the eighths; 2 of the fourths.

6. In 1 whole there are how many halves? how many fourths? how many eighths? Show this with your cutouts.

7. Change 1 ½ circles to halves; to fourths; to eighths.

8. Use your cutouts to show that 1 ½ = 1 ²⁄₄; that 1 ½ = 1 ⁴⁄₈; that 1 ²⁄₈ = 1 ¼; that 1 ²⁄₄ = 1 ½.

Then the pupil should be given exercises in coloring circles drawn on paper or given in workbooks:

1. Color half of circle *a;* ¾ of circle *b;* ⅝ of circle *c;* and ⁷⁄₁₂ of circle *d.* Draw four squares and color the same fractional parts.

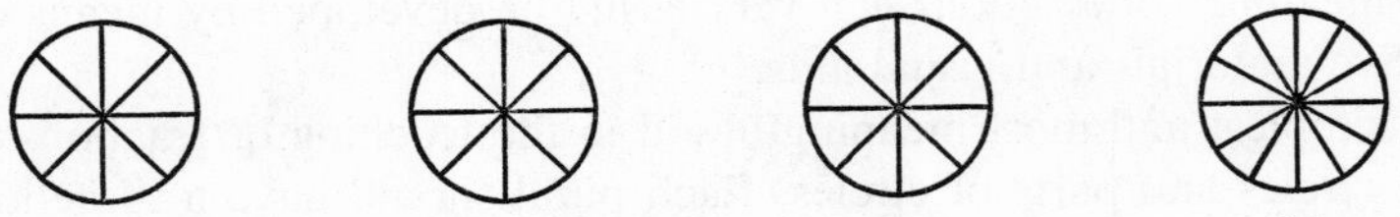

(a) (b) (c) (d)

2. Color ¼ of each circle below.

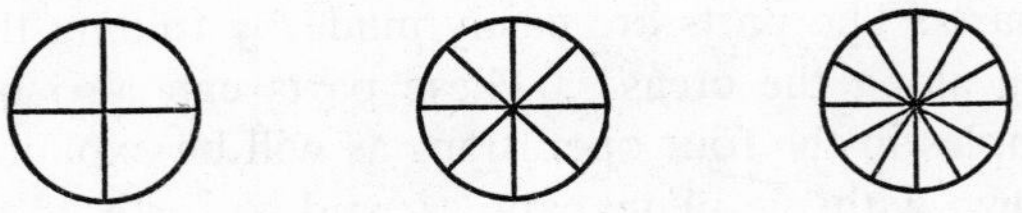

(a) (b) (c)

3. In which of these circles is ¼ shaded? ⅓? ⅙? Prove your answer.

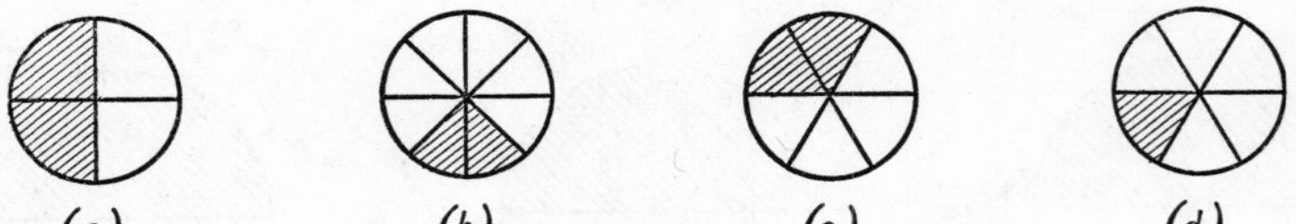

(a) (b) (c) (d)

4. In which of these circles is ¾ shaded? ⅔? ⅚?

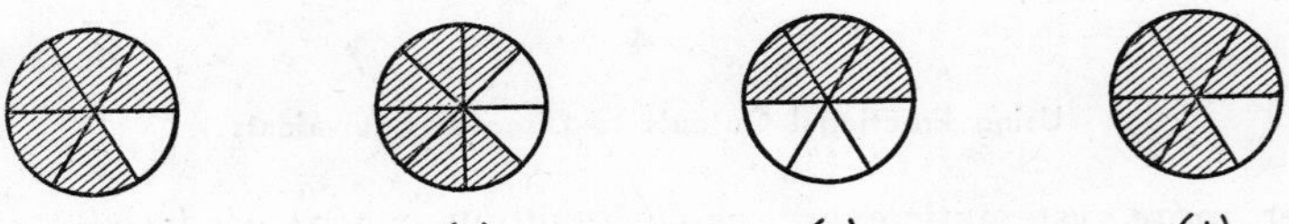

(a) (b) (c) (d)

5. Draw 3 circles; shade ¼ of the first one, ¾ of the second one, and ⅝ of the third one.

6. Use your ruler to find the missing numbers below:

a. 1 in. = 4 in. = 8 in. = 16 in.   d. ⅛ in. = 4 in.
b. ½ in. = 4 in. = 8 in. = 16 in.   e. ½ in. = ___ in.
c. 1 ¼ in. = 4 in. = 8 in.   f. ¾ in. = ___ in.

The chart below can either be made with a drawing or with separate sectional parts of plywood or cardboard. The pupil can be given the problem of using the chart to make a list of as many groups of equivalent fractions as he can discover. This exercise is excellent for use in reduction of fractions or in changing fractions to higher terms. When used together with the circle

1															
$\frac{1}{2}$								$\frac{1}{2}$							
$\frac{1}{3}$					$\frac{1}{3}$					$\frac{1}{3}$					
$\frac{1}{4}$				$\frac{1}{4}$				$\frac{1}{4}$				$\frac{1}{4}$			
$\frac{1}{6}$			$\frac{1}{6}$			$\frac{1}{6}$			$\frac{1}{6}$			$\frac{1}{6}$			$\frac{1}{6}$
$\frac{1}{8}$		$\frac{1}{8}$		$\frac{1}{8}$		$\frac{1}{8}$		$\frac{1}{8}$		$\frac{1}{8}$		$\frac{1}{8}$		$\frac{1}{8}$	
$\frac{1}{12}$	$\frac{1}{12}$	$\frac{1}{12}$	$\frac{1}{12}$	$\frac{1}{12}$	$\frac{1}{12}$	$\frac{1}{12}$	$\frac{1}{12}$	$\frac{1}{12}$	$\frac{1}{12}$	$\frac{1}{12}$	$\frac{1}{12}$				
$\frac{1}{16}$	$\frac{1}{16}$	$\frac{1}{16}$	$\frac{1}{16}$	$\frac{1}{16}$	$\frac{1}{16}$	$\frac{1}{16}$	$\frac{1}{16}$	$\frac{1}{16}$	$\frac{1}{16}$	$\frac{1}{16}$	$\frac{1}{16}$	$\frac{1}{16}$	$\frac{1}{16}$	$\frac{1}{16}$	$\frac{1}{16}$

cutouts, the learner will quickly discover and learn a great many fractional relationships that will make it easy for him to change unlike fractions to like fractions when adding or subtracting them. The greater the frequency and variety of experiences of this kind and the more interesting they are, the more insight there will be into processes with fractions and their interrelationships.

d. Teaching the Meanings of Decimals

The meaning of tenths can be demonstrated by such manipulative and objective materials as a ruler divided into tenths, a speedometer or odometer, or a clinical thermometer. The series of charts below is excellent for showing the relationships of ones, tenths, and hundredths.

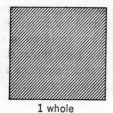

1 whole

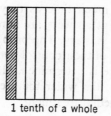

1 tenth of a whole

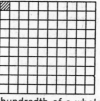

1 hundredth of a whole

Similar charts drawn on the blackboard or on wallboard can be used to have the pupil show the meaning of such numbers as .2; 1.5; .03; .35; .002; 1.024; .349. The shaded parts in the charts above picture the number 1.11. The teacher also can shade parts of charts and have the pupil identify the numbers shown. The pupil can also shade equivalent parts.

Extra place-value pockets, such as those described above for whole numbers, placed to the right of ones' pocket, also can be used to represent tenths, hundredths, and so on. Gray tickets should be used to represent values of less than 1; thus 1 gray in tenths' pocket has the value of 10 grays in hundredths' pocket, and so on.

Squares cut from the hundred-square (page 250) can also be used to show decimal fractions. Thus the smallest square can be identified with 1 hundredth or .01. A strip of 10 hundredths is the same as .10 or .1.

B. LACK OF KNOWLEDGE OF THE BASIC NUMBER FACTS

1. DIAGNOSTIC PROCEDURES

Diagnostic procedures in this area should include not only actual tests of knowledge of number facts but also tests of knowledge of generalizations and relationships among the facts which facilitate their mastery.

a. Testing Knowledge of Basic Number Facts

The usual plan of having the pupils write the answers to a group of number facts given on a sheet of paper with no set time limits is wholly inadequate for securing dependable information about the pupil's actual mastery of the facts, since under such circumstances he may actually count to find answers or use other inefficient, roundabout procedures which indicate lack of mastery. In most instances, the pupil will know the easier facts in an operation while groups of the more difficult facts present the greatest amount of trouble; for example, facts with sums greater than 10, with minuends of 11 or more, with products of more than 36, especially 42, 54, 56, 63, and 72, and division facts which have quotients of 6, 7, 8, and 9, and with dividends of more than 36 related to the multiplication facts just mentioned. The uneven division facts present unusual difficulty to many children.

Children tend to guess at the answers of difficult facts, especially when under time pressure, which almost invariably results in incorrect responses. When pupils are given as much time as they need, counting, and roundabout methods of arriving at answers are sure to be used by some of the pupils; these reveal lack of mastery. The problem is to test children in such a way that the effectiveness of their control over the basic facts under different degrees of time pressure is determined. Slow, incorrect responses are a sure symptom of difficulty; the wider the area of incorrect responses, the greater the urgency of remedial treatment.

SAMPLING TESTS OF THE 30 MOST DIFFICULT NUMBER FACTS IN EACH PROCESS

1. ADDITION

a.	8	9	7	6	8	6	9	7	7	0
	3	5	7	9	6	0	9	5	9	8

b.	8	6	7	9	5	9	7	8	8	6
	7	6	4	7	9	4	6	4	9	5

c.	9	6	8	7	6	8	9	6	9	9
	8	3	5	8	7	8	3	8	6	2

2. SUBTRACTION

a.	14	13	15	12	12	13	16	14	17	13
	9	4	9	4	7	8	8	8	9	5

b.	13	16	14	11	18	15	12	14	13	15
	7	9	7	7	9	6	9	5	9	8

c.	17	12	15	12	13	14	11	16	12	12
	8	6	7	3	6	6	8	7	5	8

3. MULTIPLICATION

a.	9	6	4	8	7	6	9	7	8	5
	9	5	9	8	9	8	4	5	9	9

b.	7	0	8	6	9	6	4	7	0	9
	6	7	7	6	8	7	8	8	9	7

c.	8	9	5	7	6	3	8	9	4	5
	5	6	7	7	9	8	6	5	7	8

4. DIVISION

a.	9/45	6/36	7/63	8/48	5/45	9/63	4/28	8/56	9/54	7/28

b.	6/42	9/72	5/35	7/49	8/64	4/32	9/27	7/35	6/48	8/32

c.	8/40	4/36	7/42	9/81	6/54	7/56	5/40	8/72	3/27	9/36

Any of the following testing procedures are sure to give both teacher and pupil a clear notion of how well the number facts actually are known, of the facts that are not known, and of the extent to which there is random guessing.

1. Give each pupil a blank sheet of squared paper, having 10 one-inch squares to a row. Prepare a similar test sheet containing the facts to be tested, a fact in each square. Test 25 to 30 facts at a time. (See sets above.) As you dictate the facts one at a time, have the pupils write the answers

only in the proper squares. Read the first fact; then silently count "one-two-three" before dictating the second fact, and so on. Instruct the pupils to omit any answer that they cannot write within the time interval and skip the square. Have the pupils exchange test papers, then dictate the answers, and have the pupils mark the answers as follows: *C*—correct, *X*—incorrect, and *O*—omitted. Have each pupil find the total for each kind of mark on the paper he is checking. A large number of *X*'s indicates much guessing and also lack of knowledge of facts; a large number of *O*'s indicates an awareness on the part of the pupil that he does not know the facts or that he is not able to respond quickly enough to write the answers within the time limits and that he refuses to guess or to write random numbers. Pass out sheets containing the facts tested and have each pupil check the facts he did not answer correctly.

2. Some teachers prefer the plan of giving the pupils papers containing sets of facts to be tested, which the teacher then reads one at a time at a set rate of 3 seconds between facts as described above, and requiring the pupils to write the answers at the rate at which the facts are read. The scoring is the same as in plan 1, except that the test paper itself is the pupil's record of facts not answered correctly.

3. To facilitate self-diagnosis by pupils, a highly valuable learning activity, the teacher may direct the pupils to proceed with the test as follows: "Write the answers to the facts on the test rapidly and carefully. If you find that you cannot write the answer to a fact promptly but must count or use some other way to work out the answer, mark that fact with a check or encircle it, showing that you will want to do special work on that fact later on."

4. Simply have the pupils write the answers to facts included on a test paper containing all basic facts in one process, arranged in random order. To get a measure of each pupil's rate of work, write on the blackboard consecutively beginning with 1, 2, and so on, the number of 10-second intervals that elapse until all pupils have completed the work. Have each pupil write the last number written on the blackboard when he finishes his paper and then lay the paper on his desk face downward. When all have completed the test, have the pupils exchange papers and mark them as described in plan 1. The results of plan 4 give a measure of both rate and accuracy of work. The papers of individual pupils with many errors can be analyzed as the teacher may deem necessary.

5. In dealing with cases of serious disability, some teachers find it advisable to test the individual child with flash cards, one for each fact, which are placed into four piles as follows as the test proceeds: (1) facts for which correct answers are given promptly, indicating mastery; (2) facts for which incorrect answers are given, indicating guessing or mislearning; (3) facts for which correct answers are given rather slowly, evidently because they were worked out in some way, such as counting, that slowed up

the work; and (4) refusal. Ordinary practice is probably sufficient on facts in group 3, whereas special work must be done on the facts in groups 2 and 4, as described in the following pages.

When testing knowledge of the number facts by dictation, state them in the following form or in some similar form with which the children are familiar:

Addition—say "2 and 3"
Subtraction—say "10 take away 3"
Multiplication—say "3 fours," for 3 × 4
Division—say "2's in 12," for 2/12
Uneven division say, "2's in 13," for 2/13

Thiele [1] has suggested the following standards for average pupils in grades 4 to 8 for the facts in the various processes:

NUMBER OF CORRECT RESPONSES PER MINUTE

Grade	Addition	Subtraction	Multiplication	Division
4	20	20	20	15
5	25	25	25	20
6	30	30	25	25
7-8	35	35	35	30

The rate for uneven division facts is about half that for even division facts.

b. Testing Knowledge of Generalizations and Relationships Among Number Facts

When the number facts are taught as isolated, unrelated bits of knowledge, as is done when traditional drill is used in teaching, the learning of the children is unstructured and little use is made of basic generalizations and relationships within the various processes and the number system itself to speed up learning and to assist the pupils to master the facts. When the teacher makes no effort to develop generalizations and relationships, the more able children will often discover a few of them independently; unfortunately, slow learners lack the capacity to generalize to any extent and consequently have a difficult time learning the facts which must appear to them as a mass of unorganized information to be learned by rote methods, just as the memorization of the tables in multiplication and division.

An informal test such as the following will quickly give an indication of the extent to which children can generalize about number facts:

1. When you subtract a number from itself, what is the answer?
2. Have you discovered a quick way to find the answer when you add 9 to a number?

[1] File No. 5499, p. 4, Exact Science Department, Detroit, Michigan.

3. When you multiply an odd number by 5, what is the last figure in the product?

4. Is the product of two even numbers ever an odd number? Prove your answer.

5. Write the numbers between 30 and 90 for which there is a remainder of 6 when you divide them by 9.

6. What two multiplication facts can you see in this group of numbers?

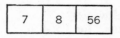

| 7 | 8 | 56 |

7. What two division facts and two multiplication facts can you discover in this group of three related numbers?

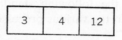

| 3 | 4 | 12 |

8. What two addition facts and two subtraction facts can you see in this group of three numbers?

| 8 | 4 | 12 |

The number of generalizations within each process similar to those in the first five items can be greatly extended, as will be shown in the corrective work described below. Similarly, the kinds of relationships between processes illustrated in the last three items can also be broadened in many ways as will also be shown. The more readily a pupil discovers and applies generalizations and senses the relationships among the number facts of related processes, the keener and broader are his insights and the more easily he will learn the facts. Slow learners lack the power to generalize independently and must be helped by the teacher through direct instruction to discover underlying generalizations and relationships.

2. REMEDIAL TEACHING OF NUMBER FACTS

The steps to be taken to remedy deficiencies in knowledge of number facts will depend on the results of tests of these facts described in the preceding pages. When answers are given or written rapidly and correctly, the performance can be adjudged to be satisfactory. In some cases only a few facts that have been mastered require study. When responses are slow but correct, steps should be taken to increase the rate of response, but not at the sacrifice of accuracy. When responses are either rapid and inaccurate, or slow and inaccurate, or there are many omissions of answers, the remedial measures must be adjusted to the needs of the pupil. The first pupil should be taught not to guess at answers but to proceed more slowly and to work for increased accuracy; the second and third pupils both have such serious deficiencies that special adjustments of instruction are necessary, such as are described below. These plans largely represent extensions of procedures that apply the principles underlying all good teaching, discussed briefly in the preceding chapter, especially the use of manipulative and visual aids to make the facts meaningful to the learner, and methods of helping him to discover generalizations and relationships which will aid in memorizing the combinations by structuring his learning.

a. Discovering Smaller Groupings Within a Larger Group

Have the pupil discover the various groupings that can be made with a group of small objects, such as disks, beads, buttons, pennies, and the like. For instance, begin with a group of 7 one-inch disks. First take a sheet of drawing paper 9 by 12 inches and fold it in the middle as shown at the left. Then have the pupil place a single disk in the upper half of the slip and group the remaining 6 disks in a systematic pattern as shown in the lower half of the slip. All groupings should be systematic in form. The disks show that $7 = 1$ and 6, which can be written as the addition fact 1. By sliding the paper around he will get 6.

$$\begin{array}{r} +6 \\ \hline 7 \end{array} \qquad\qquad \begin{array}{r} +1 \\ \hline 7 \end{array}$$

In a similar way, the pupil should discover the other groupings of 7 by using the 7 disks, namely, $\begin{array}{r} 2 \\ +5 \\ \hline \end{array}$ $\begin{array}{r} 3 \\ +4 \\ \hline \end{array}$ $\begin{array}{r} 4 \\ +3 \\ \hline \end{array}$ $\begin{array}{r} 5 \\ +2 \\ \hline \end{array}$ and $\begin{array}{r} 6 \\ +1 \\ \hline \end{array}$. In this work the pupil knows what the sum is and does not have to add or count to find it. In a similar manner, the pupil can use up to 18 disks to discover all addition groupings. He should write out all groupings discovered for any number of disks, as shown above for 7. In the course of these activities many valuable generalizations will be learned, especially if the teacher helps the pupil to discover them by carefully directed explorations and questioning.

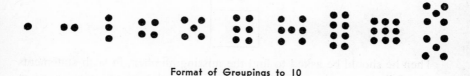

Format of Groupings to 10

Teaching the Groupings of Numbers to 10. When it appears that a child does not have a clear understanding of the meaning of a number, such as 5, he should be given the opportunity to use blocks, disks, or similar objects to "learn all about the number."

First he should lay 5 disks or squares in group, as in *a,* below. Then he should be led by the teacher to work out the groupings shown in the drawings below, using halves of a folded paper for the groups:

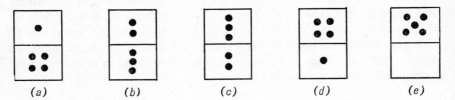

(a)   (b)   (c)   (d)   (e)

Each time he should write the grouping shown, thus:

$$\frac{1}{4}\ \ 5 \qquad \frac{2}{3}\ \ 5 \qquad \frac{3}{2}\ \ 5 \qquad \frac{4}{1}\ \ 5 \qquad \frac{5}{0}\ \ 5$$

He should be asked to state the fact he writes thus: 1 and 4 are 5. Then he should be asked to use pictures such as those shown above, or objects, to find the missing numbers in exercises such as these:

$$1 + \_\_ = 5 \qquad 4 + \_\_ = 5 \qquad 5 + \_\_ = 5$$
$$\_\_ + 4 = 5 \qquad 2 + \_\_ = 5 \qquad \_\_ + 2 = 5$$
$$3 + \_\_ = 5 \qquad \_\_ + 3 = 5 \qquad \_\_ + 5 = 5$$

Finally, he should give the missing numbers without using objects or pictures with the groupings given in the usual vertical form.

In a similar way, he should work out the subtraction facts for 5. First he should lay a row of 5 objects on his table. Then he should remove 1 object, then 2 objects, and so on to 5 objects. Each time he should state the fact that he has worked out and also write it. Then he should be asked to cover dots in a drawing like the one below, instead of working with objects, each time stating the fact discovered and writing the fact.

Then he should be asked to find the missing numbers in such statements as the following, using objects or covering circles in the picture when necessary.

$$5 - 1 = \qquad 5 - 3 = \qquad 5 - 4 =$$
$$5 - 5 = \qquad 5 - 2 = \qquad 5 - 0 =$$

Finally, he should be able to give the missing numbers without using objects or pictures, and to give answers to facts written in vertical form.

A similar procedure should be used for all groupings of 10 or less when the pupil seems to lack concepts of numbers.

The sequence of steps should be:

1. Manipulation of objective materials leading to discovery.
2. Visualization, using drawings, pictures, diagrams.
3. Abstractions, using numbers as such to express ideas.

b. Finding and Learning Answers to Number Facts

(1) *Addition Facts.* Have the pupil make a list of the addition facts that the diagnostic test shows he has not mastered. Then have him discover the answer by placing groups of disks on the folded slip of paper to show each number fact. Then have him find the total number of disks on the card by grouping, counting, or in some meaningful way. Next have him make a study-practice card (2 x 3 inches) such as the one shown below,

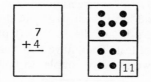

showing the fact on the front side, and the disk picture of the fact with the sum on the reverse side of the card. The front side may be regarded as the test side and the back as the study side. After a group of cards for ten difficult facts has been prepared, the pupil can test himself by giving the answers using the test side and checking his answers by turning to the reverse side. Systematic practice of this kind will produce remarkable gains when the learner attacks the problem purposefully. The teacher should encourage the pupil to use his disks repeatedly to find answers to facts that he continues to find difficult. From time to time the teacher should use the cards to test the pupil's knowledge of the facts, and also provide written practice.

The memorization of the addition facts is greatly facilitated by helping the learner to discover such generalizations [2] as the following which help him to structurize his knowledge, a valuable aid to learning:

1. When we add 1 to a number or a number to 1, the sum is the next higher number.
2. When we add 2 to a number, skip up a number.
3. The sums of two reverse addition facts are the same.
4. Because $+4$, $+4$ must be 9, because 5 is one more than 4. This is using

            4   5

            ‾8

---

[2] C. L. Thiele, *The Contribution of Generalization to the Learning of the Addition Facts*, Contributions to Education No. 762 (New York, Bureau of Publications, Teachers College, Columbia Univ., 1938).

the doubles to find sums of near doubles. Similarly, $+\underline{5}^{6}$ must be 11 because 5 and 5 are 10 and 6 is 1 more than 5.

5. Adding 9 to a number is the same as adding 10 to the number and then taking away 1.

6. When we add 0 to a number, or add a number to 0, the sum is the same as the number.

(2) *Subtraction Facts.* By using groups of small objects, described for addition, have the pupil first discover the various subtraction facts. Thus, have the pupil lay a group of chips on his table, for instance, 7, and then remove groups of them varying from 0 to 7 to discover the 8 subtraction facts given below:

$$\begin{array}{cccccccc} 7 & 7 & 7 & 7 & 7 & 7 & 7 & 7 \\ -1 & -2 & -3 & -4 & -5 & -6 & -7 & -0 \end{array}$$

In a similar manner, have all subtraction groupings discovered, especially by the slower children, and have them write out the facts discovered.

Have each pupil make a list of the facts that proved to be difficult for him on the subtraction fact test. Then have him manipulate disks to picture them and to find the answers. For example, to find the answer to 12 — 5,

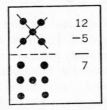

he should lay 12 disks on his table, next take away 5 of the disks, and then count to find the remainder. Finally the pupil should make a test-study card for each difficult fact, using groupings of circles as shown on addition cards and crossing out circles as at the right to show the number subtracted from the total number. He should also write the answer as shown. This visualization enables the learner to check the answer by counting or by addition if he wishes to do so. There is no limit to the amount of practice that these cards make possible. Written practice under time pressure should be included in the program.

The discovery under teacher guidance of such generalizations as the following is a valuable aid to learning the subtraction facts:

1. When we subtract a number from itself, the remainder is zero.
2. When we subtract 1 from a number, the answer is the next smaller number.
3. To subtract 2 from a number, skip down a number.
4. When we subtract 0 from a number, the number is not changed.
5. The remainder is 1 when we take away the next smaller number.
6. When we subtract 9 from a number, the answer is 10 less than the number, plus 1.

The recognition of relationships between the addition and subtraction facts is also a valuable aid to learning. Thus, when the pupil learns the two related addition facts $\begin{array}{r}7\\+4\\\hline 11\end{array}$ and $\begin{array}{r}4\\+7\\\hline 11\end{array}$, he should at the same time learn the two related subtraction facts $\begin{array}{r}\\-4\\\hline\end{array}$ and $\begin{array}{r}\\-7\\\hline\end{array}$. The card showing $7 + 4 = 11$ can

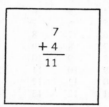

be used to show all of the relations. The pupils should learn to tell the whole story of the card by giving the four facts.

He should learn also to identify the four related facts growing out of the horizontal arrangement below, an excellent experience in perceiving rela-

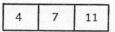

tionships which later will be extended to multiplication and division. Knowledge of one fact unlocks the remaining related facts.

The following sets of three numbers each include all addition and subtraction relationships with sums above 10 and minuends above 10. Each set should be placed on a rectangular card and for practice the children should tell or write the whole story for each card:

5—6—11	3—9—12	8—7—15
4—7—11	6—7—13	6—9—15
3—8—11	5—8—13	8—8—16
2—9—11	4—9—13	7—9—16
6—6—12	7—7—14	8—9—17
5—7—12	6—8—14	9—9—18
4—8—12	5—9—14	

"New views" of the number facts, such as the following, also provide valuable and interesting practice on them:

1. Write all facts whose sum is 8; 12; or any other given number.
2. Write all facts in which the remainder is 5; 9; 0; 1; or any other given number.
3. Write all of the doubles for addition. Write the related subtraction facts.
4. Write the near doubles for any given double; for example, for $7 + 7 = 14$, the near doubles are $8 + 7$ and $7 + 8$.
5. Write four facts based on 3—5—8.

The construction by the pupil of a table of the addition and subtraction facts such as the following is a valuable learning aid. It structures the facts and facilitates the discovery of many relationships.

	0	1	2	3	4	5	6	7	8	9
0	0	1	2	3	4	5	6	7	8	9
1	1	2	3	4	5	6	7	8	9	10
2	2	3	4	5	6	7	8	9	10	11
3	3	4	5	6	7	8	9	10	11	12
4	4	5	6	7	8	9	10	11	12	13
5	5	6	7	8	9	10	11	12	13	14
6	6	7	8	9	10	11	12	13	14	15
7	7	8	9	10	11	12	13	14	15	16
8	8	9	10	11	12	13	14	15	16	17
9	9	10	11	12	13	14	15	16	17	18

There are many number games that can be used to add interest to the practice required to establish mastery.

(3) *Multiplication Facts.* It is essential that the pupil understand the relationship between addition and multiplication, since this idea provides him with a method of finding any product that he cannot recall, either by addition as such or by adding to products that he already knows. For example, 4×5 is the same as $5 + 5 + 5 + 5$, or 20. He can see that 4×5 also is the same as 3×5, or 15, plus 5, or 20; also that since $5 \times 5 = 25$, so $4 \times 5 = 25 - 5$, or 20.

The pupil who has a general weakness in multiplication can learn much by developing under teacher guidance a group of related easy multiplication facts in the form of a table. Thus, he can complete the

$1 \times 3 = 3$
$2 \times 3 = 6$
$3 \times 3 = 9$
$4 \times 3 = 12$
$5 \times 3 =$
$6 \times 3 =$
$7 \times 3 =$
$8 \times 3 =$
$9 \times 3 =$

table of 3's as at the left by adding designated groups of 3's to find the missing products, or by adding 3 to each of the successive products in turn, or by using either method to check the other. He can also write out the reverse table. In a similar manner, the pupil can develop each of the other groups of related facts in tabular form, an activity that will clarify for him the general concept of multiplication as related to addition. His tables can be used for reference.

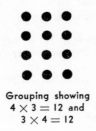

Grouping showing
$4 \times 3 = 12$ and
$3 \times 4 = 12$

The pupil should next list the various multiplication groupings that were shown on the fact test to be difficult for him and then work out the product for each grouping by addition or by using his tables. When facts prove to be very difficult, they can be worked out with manipulative materials as was done for addition and subtraction. Then the pupil should make similar study-test cards for all difficult facts and do special practice with them. The amount of practice will be determined by the needs of the learner.

Numerous generalizations can be developed to facilitate memorization of the basic multiplication facts:

1. When the figures in a multiplication fact are reversed, the product is the same.
2. The products of whole numbers multiplied by 5 end in 5 or 0. When do we end in 5? When in 0?
3. When we multiply a number by 1, or 1 by a number, the product is the same as the other number.
4. When we multiply 0 by a number, the product is 0.
5. The sums of the two figures in the products of the nines are always 9. Other interesting relationships for the 3's, 6's, and 9's are readily discovered.
6. If the product of $4 \times 8 = 32$, the product of 5×8 must be 8 more than 32, or 40. This approach supplies the key for finding any product when some other related product is known.
7. The products of 2, 4, 6, and 8 are all even numbers.

The pupil should learn to identify at a glance the relationships in such groups of numbers as those given below, namely, $4 \times 7 = 28$, and $7 \times 4 = 28$.

The related division facts can also be identified at the same time, as will be shown shortly.

(4) *Even Division Facts.* The relationship between the grouping of a number of objects and division is fundamental; division also may be regarded as a quick way of finding how many groups of a given size can be "taken out of" any given number, a process that is essentially subtracting.

When the learner apparently does not understand the meaning of division, its nature should first be developed by using manipulative materials. For example, to find how many 2's there are in 16, that is, $2/\overline{16}$, he should first lay out 16 disks in a row on the table, and then by grouping them by 2's find how many groups of 2 he can make with the 16 disks. A fact-finder containing 18 buttons can also be used, as shown on page 266. In the same way, he can find how many groups of 4 or 8 he can make with the 16 blocks. Each time he should write the division fact he discovers. In the same way, the learner should discover even division groupings that can be made with other numbers of blocks, such as 4, 6, 8, 9, 10, 14, 15, 18, 20, 21, 24, 25, 27, 28, and 30. For dividends larger than 30 it should not be necessary to use

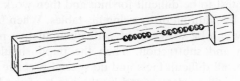

Fact-finder Showing 6 + 8

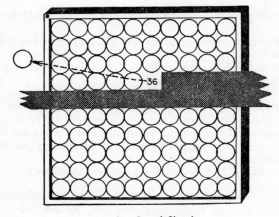

Number Board Showing
36

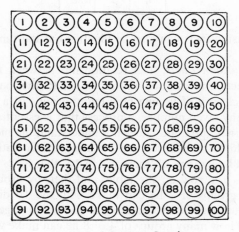

① ② ③ ④ ⑤ ⑥ ⑦ ⑧ ⑨ ⑩
⑪ ⑫ ⑬ ⑭ ⑮ ⑯ ⑰ ⑱ ⑲ ⑳
㉑ ㉒ ㉓ ㉔ ㉕ ㉖ ㉗ ㉘ ㉙ ㉚
㉛ ㉜ ㉝ ㉞ ㉟ ㊱ ㊲ ㊳ ㊴ ㊵

Hundred Counting Board

manipulative procedures except in extreme cases, since the concept of division should have become clear by this time.

The pupils should also develop the division facts for 2, 3, 4, and other divisions systematically in the form of tables as for multiplication. The tables for 2's, 3's, and 4's should be developed through manipulative methods which can be discarded for the other tables in favor of more mature methods, such as the use of relationships with the multiplication facts. For instance, when the pupil has learned to perceive the multiplication relationships with simpler groups of numbers such as 5 —7 —35, he will readily see that the same numbers have division relationships expressed by the two division facts $35 \div 7 = 5$ and $35 \div 5 = 7$. Thus, this group of numbers represents four basic facts, two for multiplication and two for division.

Each pupil should work out answers with manipulative materials and then prepare test-study cards for each division fact shown by the fact test to present difficulty, following the plan used for the other processes. For the 2's and 3's the groupings can be shown with rows of circles.

The pupil should also be led to discover generalizations among the division facts which will facilitate their memorization:

1. When we divide a number by itself, the quotient is 1.
2. When zero is divided by a number, the answer is zero.
3. We can use what we know about multiplication facts to find answers of division facts.
4. We can use what we know about division facts to find answers to multiplication facts.
5. Any number less than 50 that ends in 0 or 5 can be divided by 5.
6. All even numbers can be divided by 2.
7. The sum of the figures in numbers less than 90 that can be divided evenly by 9 is 9.
8. Similar generalizations can be made for the divisors 3, 4, and 6.
9. If $3/\overline{12}$ is 4, then $4/\overline{12}$ is 3; a useful generalization about reverse facts.

Groupings of real objects or pictures of groupings also can be used to help children to discover related facts for multiplication and division in meaningful ways:

By using rows *a* and *b* the pupil can quickly find the answers to the following facts:

$$\begin{array}{cccc} 2 & 5 & 2/\overline{10} & 5/\overline{10} \\ \times 5 & \times 2 & & \end{array}$$

Similarly he can use rows *a, b,* and *c* to find four facts related to 3 — 5 — 15. In the same way he can work out all facts shown by the groupings above. Similar arrangements can be made for 3's, 4's, and 6's. When these facts have been worked out, only a few facts involving 7's, 8's and 9's remain. They probably should not be worked out by use of groupings of objects except in rare cases.

The following sets of three numbers each include all multiplication and division relationships for products and dividends above 30. Each set should be placed on a card and for practice the children should be required to "tell or write the whole story" for the card:

4—8—32	6—7—42	7—8—56
5—7—35	5—9—45	7—9—63
4—9—36	6—8—48	8—8—64
6—6—36	7—7—49	8—9—72
5—8—40	6—9—54	9—9—81

"New views" of these number facts provide a variety of valuable and interesting practice:

1. Write all facts whose products are 12, 15, 24, 36, or any other given number.
2. Write all of the multiplication facts for the 3's, 4's, etc.
3. Write all facts whose quotients are 4, 7, or any other given number.
4. Write all of the even division facts in which you divide 9, by 7, etc.
5. Write all numbers less than 90 that never are products for multiplication facts.
6. Write all numbers less than 90 that never are the number divided in the even division facts.
7. Write the four number facts based on any given grouping, such as 7—8—56.
8. How many groupings can you write for any double?

(5) *The Uneven Division Facts.* There are 360 uneven division groupings, such as $3\overline{/7}$ and $2\overline{/19}$, in which there is a one-figure quotient and there also is a remainder. Just as is done in even division, the learner should discover these groupings by using manipulative materials such as fact-finders, disks, and the like. Begin with a group of, say, 7 disks. The pupil should first discover how many groups of 2 disks each can be made with the 7 disks. As shown below,

he will quickly discover that $2\overline{/7} = 3$ and that there then is a remainder of 1. In a similar way he can discover the answers for other facts, such as $3\overline{/7}$, $4\overline{/7}$, $5\overline{/7}$, and $6\overline{/7}$. After proceeding in a similar manner with 8, 9, 10, and any other group of disks, he will come to understand the meaning of uneven division. Drawings of rows of circles or crosses can also be used to discover the uneven facts by encircling groups of given sizes.

Next the pupil should build several tables for uneven division similar to the one for the 3's shown below. The numbers at the foot of the table include the even division facts, while those above are the "in-between numbers" included in uneven division facts for 3's.

2	5	8	11	14	17	20	23	26	29
1	4	7	10	13	16	19	22	25	28
0	3	6	9	12	15	18	21	24	27

Finally he should be required to write out the solutions.

The thinking to be taught for use in writing out uneven division facts is illustrated by the following statement:

$$\begin{array}{r} 4 \\ 3\overline{)14} \\ 12 \\ \hline 2 \end{array}$$

Think: What is the next smaller number than 14 that can be divided by 3? 12 is right. Write 12 under the 14. *Think:* $3\overline{)12} = 4$. Write 4 as the quotient figure. Check the quotient by finding 4×3. This is 12. So 4 is correct. Subtract: $14 - 12 = 2$. Since 2 is less than the divisor 3, 4 is the correct quotient figure.

The above procedure of first writing the 12 and then dividing the 12 by 3 will tend to reduce random guessing of quotient figures. Writing out the work in this way also greatly simplifies the division, since the difficult step of mental subtraction used in short division is thereby eliminated. Slow learners should always write out the work in uneven division. They should not be expected to master the difficult mental steps used in short division.

Such exercises as these are helpful in making uneven division facts meaningful:

1. Write the uneven division facts in which there is a remainder of 1 when you divide by 2; by 3; by 4; etc.
2. Write the uneven division facts in which there is a quotient of 7 and a remainder of 1; of 2; of 3; of 5; of 6.
3. Use the example at the right to find the answers to the following examples:

a. $\begin{array}{r} 7 \\ \times 8 \\ \hline \end{array}$ *b.* $8\overline{)56}$ *c.* $7\overline{)56}$ *d.* $\begin{array}{r} 56 \\ +5 \\ \hline \end{array}$ *e.* $\begin{array}{r} 61 \\ -56 \\ \hline \end{array}$ $\begin{array}{r} 7 \\ 8\overline{)61} \\ 56 \\ \hline 5 \end{array}$

Aids to Recall

Various forms of imagery are related to recall. In the teaching of number facts to young children, sensory experiences involving kinesthetic, visual, and auditory perceptions should be introduced. Thus the manipulation of objects to discover groupings and answers, the analysis of pictures, drawings, diagrams, and other visual representations of number facts and processes, talking about them, and writing them lead to the formations of imagery that aid recall. An image is the mental reproduction of a past perception in whole or in part in the absence of the original stimulus or experience. Sensory perceptions should be closely associated with aggressive efforts to recall. The type and amount of imagery that learners should utilize undoubtedly varies from pupil to pupil, but all types are sure to contribute in some measure to recall.

Sheer intellectual aids to recall should also be stressed, such as the formation of associations and the application of generalizations and relationships discovered in the course of learning. Thus when a pupil recalls the product of $7 \times 8 = 56$ by using the series 5-6-7-8, or the sum of $9 + 7$ by recalling $10 + 6$, he is using the kinds of associations that all of us use as aids to recall. Similarly, recalling that 36 can be divided by 9 because $3 + 6 = 9$, a basic relationship, aids in learning this and other division facts. It is the teacher's problem to assist the pupils to organize, systematize, and classify their learnings by utilizing relationships among facts and processes and to form associations that will aid recall. The wastefulness and futility of learning "isolated" facts and unrelated processes is generally recognized.

The Place of Practice

When the learner has grasped underlying meanings of facts and operations and understands the processes involved, practice is necessary to assure retention and to refine and establish skills. Various forms of practice should be provided, including recurring use of what has been learned in a variety of situations, guided practice to establish initial learnings, and repetitive "drill" in which meaningful elements similar in nature are practiced repeatedly to develop skill and proficiency. Initial practice should be carefully guided so that the child uses correct methods of thinking and working. To assure retention, distributed "drills" systematically spread over a period of time should be arranged, especially for arithmetic operations that are not used often in the lives of the learners.

Helpful Practice Exercises on Number Facts

Modern textbooks and workbooks provide a wide variety of developmental practice exercises on number facts which should be freely used in corrective work. It is advisable to use materials prepared for lower grade levels in some cases when very detailed reteaching is necessary. The following kinds of practice, in addition to frequent opportunity to use number facts in social situations, are sure to be useful with slow learners:

1. Have the slow children feel free to work out with concrete manipulative aids any difficult number facts they cannot recall.
2. Have them make pictures or drawings showing selected number facts to make them meaningful.
3. Use a number scale, fact-finders, etc., to show number groupings.
4. Have the children dramatize various facts.
5. Have pairs of children work together on the study of groups of number facts.

6. Have children work in pairs, testing each other on their sets of test-study cards.
7. Use a variety of interesting games, spelldowns, and contests to motivate practice.
8. Have pupils keep charts showing their progress on several weekly written tests of the same sets of number facts, or on their own sets of test-study cards.
9. Encourage children to use known generalizations and relationships and to discover others in learning the number facts.
10. Encourage the children to drop immature, roundabout methods of finding answers in favor of more mature procedures.
11. For younger children some sort of award such as a badge indicating success is very satisfying and is eagerly sought.
12. Emphasize that accuracy on the facts is necessary to mastery of any of the processes. Delay the presentation of interesting new steps until the basic number facts are fairly well under control.

A very valuable device for group testing or practice on facts is the "Show Me" game. Each child should have a pocket made of a piece of art paper 4 inches wide and 6 inches long, folded to make a 1-inch pocket with the two sides of the pocket stapled, and also a set of 11 cards: a card for each of the ten digits 0 to 9 and an extra (1) card needed to show 11. As the teacher dictates a given fact, such as 3 fours, or 8 and 4, each pupil selects the cards from the row placed before him on his table or desk to represent

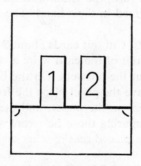

Pocket Showing 12

the answer, in this case the 1 and 2 cards, places them properly in his pocket, as shown above, and then at the signal of the teacher holds up his answer so that the teacher can see it. The teacher can quickly tell at a glance which of the pupils in a classroom have incorrect answers. None of the children can see the answers of the others, so that each one's knowledge actually is tested. Each child should make a record of the facts he missed. When working with small groups or individuals, the teacher can keep a record of facts now known by each child and the rate at which he finds the answers to secure information of diagnostic value. Slow pupils and also those who are quick but inaccurate are quickly spotted in the "Show Me" game.

Self-Testing Practice Materials

In order to assist individual children to practice to correct their own weak spots, self-testing exercises of various kinds can be used.

1. *Facts with Answers.* Prepare mimeographed sets of facts, giving the answers also. Teach the pupil to place a slip of paper over the answers to a row of examples, write the answers to the row on the slip, and then slide down the slip to check his work. Have him make a list of the facts he misses and do special work on them as described in preceding pages. To speed up his practice, he can place a small card over the answers of several facts, state the answer to the first fact, and then slide the card to the right to uncover the answer given on the paper, and thus see if the answer he gave is correct. A second pupil can also give the facts on the paper orally and the other pupil can check the answers given.

2. *Matching Groupings and Answers.* A simple game in which answers are matched with groupings is very interesting to many children. Select 25 facts in some process. Cut out 50 cards of equal size; a good size to use is 2 x 3 inches. Write a grouping on one card, and the answer on another card. Shuffle the cards. The game consists in matching groupings and the answers. A game can be played in which several children can participate as follows: Pass out seven cards to each player and place the remainder of the pack in the center of the table. In turn, the children draw from the pack and place on the table any pairs formed in their hand. The others check the pairs to see that they are correct.

3. *Self-Checking Cards.* Cut out cards about 3 inches wide and 8 inches long. At the foot of the front of the card write a row of number facts, ordinarily ten of them, without the answers. On the back of the card write the answers at the bottom. Have the pupil place the front of the card on a sheet of paper, write the answers on the paper, and then turn over the card and check his answers by comparing those he wrote with the answers given. A second row of facts can be placed on the other end of the card.

FAULTY PROCEDURES IN NUMBER OPERATIONS

1. METHODS OF DIAGNOSIS

a. Testing Ability to Use Number Operations in Finding Answers to Easy Verbal Problems

To test the ability of the pupil to select the correct number operations in solving a variety of simple problems requiring very easy computations, use the set of problems given on page 273 in this fashion:

1. Have the pupil read the problems aloud one at a time and note evidences of reading difficulty or ineffective reading habits.
2. Have the pupil find the answer to the problem mentally and state it.
3. Then have the pupil tell the method he used to find the answer.

Question him closely to see if he used a simple, direct method of computation or if he possibly used some ingenious or unusual procedure. The examiner will be amazed by the strange methods that are often used by children in lieu of simple, direct computational procedures.

Our purpose here is to determine whether or not the pupil understands the meanings of computational methods well enough to apply them correctly in simple situations, not to test his computational ability. This test is also of value in studying the pupil's general ability to solve problems, as will be shown later.

HOW WELL CAN YOU USE THE NUMBER OPERATIONS? (ORAL; INDIVIDUAL)

NAME _____ GRADE _____ SCHOOL _____

Read the problems one at a time. Tell what the answer is without using a pencil.

Answers

1. Bob has 24 cents. Mary has 30 cents. How much money do the two children have? 1 _____
2. Alice had 35 cents. She spent 10 cents for a cone. How much money did she then have? 2 _____
3. At 40 cents a yard how much do 2 yards of lace cost? 3 _____
4. Marvin paid 42 cents for 2 loaves of bread. How much did one loaf cost? 4 _____
5. How many feet are there in 6 yards? 5 _____
6. Arthur has 20 cents. He wants to buy a 45 cent toy. How much more money does he need? 6 _____
7. Three boys earned 75 cents raking a lawn. If they shared the money equally how much was each boy's share? 7 _____
8. At 5 cents each how many post cards can you buy for 30 cents? 8 _____
9. Tom is 64 inches tall. Alice is 59 inches tall. How much shorter than Tom is Alice? 9 _____
10. At 2 for 5 cents how much do 6 sticks of gum cost? 10 _____
11. How much does ¼ yard of ribbon cost at 80 cents a yard? 11 _____
12. There are 40 children in a certain class. There are 18 girls. How many boys are there in the class? 12 _____

A variation of the above test is to have the pupil give original problems based on examples such as the following:

$$\begin{array}{cccc} 37 & 247 & 64 & 3\overline{)\$2.85} \\ 25 & -128 & \times 5 & \\ +18 & & & \end{array}$$

b. Locating Operational Difficulties with Whole Numbers

In addition to knowledge of the basic number facts, the pupil must know certain basic operational procedures, primarily transformations used in carrying in addition and multiplication, and regrouping used in subtraction and division, in order to do correct work. As has been shown above, a great many errors are due to incorrect performance of these basic operational steps. The following analysis indicates the ways in which the skills appear in key types of examples in each process. The sets of examples can be used for diagnostic purposes to see if the operational steps indicated are used correctly, disregarding errors in the number facts.

KEY TYPES IN ADDITION

a.	24 43	50 2	47 300	No carrying
b.	27 35	16 4	58 139	Carrying from ones' place
c.	142 293	57 352	490 90	Carrying from tens' place
d	273 258	316 89	4806 2998	Carrying from consecutive places
e.	2582 3908	87060 38479		Carrying in alternate places

These types can be extended to longer columns of numbers in which the basic process of carrying is used but in which difficulties arise because of adding numbers in columns. The longer the column, the greater the possibility of errors. Slow learners should not be required to add more than three numbers in examples.

KEY TYPES IN SUBTRACTION

a.	47 −26	89 −40	302 −102	No regrouping necessary
b.	48 −19	72 −6	470 −129	Regrouping in tens' and ones' places
c.	473 −183	500 −70	7863 −7793	Regrouping in hundreds' and tens' places
d.	526 −378	800 −73	9012 −8236	Regrouping in consecutive places
e.	4238 −3919	60402 −15192		Regrouping in alternate places

KEY TYPES IN MULTIPLICATION

a.	42 ×2	21 ×6	30 ×3	No carrying; a zero difficulty
b.	46 ×2	58 ×3	209 ×4	Carrying from ones' to tens' place

c.	150 ×5	371 ×7	3051 ×9	Carrying from tens' to hundreds' place
d.	195 ×7	286 ×9	4857 ×8	Carrying in consecutive places
e.	2519 ×3	6807 ×3		Carrying in alternate places
f.	43 ×10	267 50	487 ×600	Multiplying by numbers ending in 0
g.	25 ×12	358 ×347	469 ×408	Multiplying by two- and three-place numbers

KEY TYPES IN DIVISION

1. One-place divisors

a.	3/96	2/180	4/2408	Even division
b.	4/72	3/174	5/3925	Uneven division—no remainders
c.	5/57	4/163	7/6934	Uneven division—remainders

2. Two-place divisors

See pages 283-285 for types of difficulties in estimations of quotients Division types, including zeros in quotients:

a.	25/575	43/519	34/714	Easy types
b.	92/3423	45/2393	56/8456	Complex types
c.	37/15928	26/2376	18/13410	Estimation difficulties
d.	43/1720	97/4859	85/680439	Zeros in quotients

The key types above range from the simplest possible type to very complex examples. The sequence of examples given above enables the teacher to locate the steps at which difficulties begin to emerge, thus establishing a basis for knowing where to begin corrective work in each process. Case-study procedures, described on pages 219-222, should be applied to determine the efficiency of the thought processes used in working examples. As has been shown previously, incorrect work in such a process as multiplication may be due in part to incorrect addition, while in division errors may be due to incorrect work in one or more of the four processes that are involved, as was shown on page 216.

c. Locating Operational Difficulties in Fractions

The screening test on fractions on page 276 is useful for locating major processes in which deficiencies exist. The sets of examples that follow aid the teacher to locate in a more definite way the specific points of difficulty in each process. They can be used for diagnostic purposes. The teacher should be guided by a knowledge of the lists of most common faults in fraction processes given on page 230. For a more detailed diagnosis, the Brueckner Diagnostic Tests in Fractions may be used.

SCREENING TESTS IN ARITHMETIC—FRACTIONS

1. Addition

a.	b.	c.	d.	e.
$2\frac{1}{4}$	$4\frac{1}{2}$	$7\frac{3}{8}$	$6\frac{2}{3}$	$7\frac{5}{6}$
$+4\frac{1}{4}$	$+2\frac{1}{2}$	$+\frac{1}{2}$	$+4\frac{1}{2}$	$+6\frac{7}{8}$

2. Subtraction

$3\frac{3}{4}$	$8\frac{1}{2}$	6	$3\frac{1}{4}$	$9\frac{1}{2}$
$-1\frac{1}{4}$	$-2\frac{1}{2}$	$-4\frac{2}{3}$	$-1\frac{3}{4}$	$-2\frac{7}{8}$

3. Multiplication

$$\frac{1}{2} \times 7 = \qquad \frac{1}{2} \times \frac{2}{5} = \qquad 2\frac{1}{4} \times \frac{2}{3} = \qquad \frac{1}{2} \times 2\frac{2}{3} = \qquad \begin{array}{r} 8\frac{1}{4} \\ \times 6 \end{array}$$

4. Division

$$3 \div \frac{2}{3} = \qquad 7 \div 1\frac{1}{2} = \qquad \frac{3}{4} \div \frac{5}{6} = \qquad 2\frac{1}{4} \div \frac{5}{8} = \qquad 1\frac{1}{2} \div 6 =$$

ADDITION OF FRACTIONS

a.	$\frac{1}{3}$	$2\frac{2}{5}$	$5\frac{2}{3}$	Like fractions—no reduction
	$\frac{1}{3}$	$3\frac{2}{5}$	$1\frac{2}{3}$	
b.	$\frac{1}{4}$	$3\frac{1}{8}$	$5\frac{1}{2}$	Like fractions—reduction
	$\frac{1}{4}$	$2\frac{3}{8}$	$\frac{1}{2}$	
c.	$\frac{1}{2}$	$2\frac{3}{8}$	$5\frac{3}{4}$	
	$\frac{1}{4}$	$3\frac{1}{2}$	$6\frac{1}{2}$	Easy unlike fraction types
d.	$4\frac{2}{3}$	$6\frac{1}{8}$	$4\frac{3}{4}$	Other unlike fractions
	$3\frac{1}{4}$	$2\frac{5}{6}$	$7\frac{5}{6}$	

SUBTRACTION OF FRACTIONS

a.	$\frac{3}{4}$	$2\frac{5}{6}$	$6\frac{2}{3}$	Like fractions—no regrouping
	$-\frac{1}{4}$	$-1\frac{1}{6}$	$-5\frac{2}{3}$	
b.	2	$1\frac{1}{4}$	$5\frac{1}{3}$	Like fractions—regrouping
	$-1\frac{1}{4}$	$-\frac{3}{4}$	$-2\frac{2}{3}$	
c.	$6\frac{1}{2}$	$1\frac{1}{4}$	$5\frac{1}{6}$	Easy unlike fraction types
	$-2\frac{1}{4}$	$-\frac{1}{2}$	$-2\frac{2}{3}$	
d.	$\frac{3}{4}$	$5\frac{3}{4}$	$4\frac{3}{4}$	Other unlike fractions
	$-\frac{2}{3}$	$-1\frac{4}{5}$	$-2\frac{5}{6}$	

MULTIPLICATION OF FRACTIONS

a. $\frac{1}{2} \times 5 =$ $3 \times \frac{1}{4} =$ $4 \times \frac{7}{8} =$ Fractions and whole numbers

b. $\begin{array}{r} 5\frac{1}{2} \\ \times 4 \\ \hline \end{array}$ $7\frac{1}{2} \times 5 =$ $\begin{array}{r} 8 \\ \times 4\frac{2}{3} \\ \hline \end{array}$ Mixed numbers and whole numbers

c. $\frac{1}{2} \times \frac{2}{3} =$ $6\frac{1}{4} \times \frac{2}{5} =$ Fractions and mixed numbers
  $5\frac{1}{4} \times 3\frac{1}{3} =$

DIVISION OF FRACTIONS

a. $2 \div \frac{1}{2} =$ $3 \div \frac{5}{6} =$ $3 \div 1\frac{3}{4} =$ Whole numbers by fractions

b. $3\frac{1}{2} \div \frac{1}{4} =$ $4\frac{1}{2} \div 1\frac{1}{2} =$ $\frac{5}{6} \div 1\frac{1}{3} =$ Fractions and mixed numbers

c. $\frac{1}{2} \div 2 =$ $3\frac{1}{2} \div 4 =$ $1\frac{5}{6} \div 4 =$ Division by whole numbers

It should be pointed out again that much incorrect work with fractions is due not only to lack of knowledge of how to proceed with fractions or failure to understand them but also to purely computational errors such as we find in operations with whole numbers.

d. Locating Difficulties with Decimals

The screening test for decimals shown below is ample in most instances for diagnostic work with decimals. There of course are numerous other subtypes of examples that are minor variations of those included in the screening test. The lists of the most common faults in each process given on page 231 will assist the teacher to locate the weak spots and to identify faults in the work of pupils having difficulty with decimals. Since most difficulty is closely related to lack of understanding of the meaning of decimals, diagnosis of difficulty with processes should be closely associated with the improvement of meaning of decimal fractions, by methods described in preceding sections.

SCREENING TESTS IN ARITHMETIC—DECIMALS

1. Addition

a. $\begin{array}{r} 7.4 \\ 2.6 \\ +3.1 \\ \hline \end{array}$ b. $\begin{array}{r} 2.75 \\ 81.62 \\ + \ .08 \\ \hline \end{array}$ c. $\begin{array}{r} 9.643 \\ .02 \\ +12.7 \\ \hline \end{array}$

d. Copy and add: $3.85 + 31.18 + 127.39 =$

2. Subtraction

a. $\begin{array}{r} 38.4 \\ -27.2 \\ \hline \end{array}$ b. $\begin{array}{r} 97.68 \\ - \ 25.59 \\ \hline \end{array}$ c. $\begin{array}{r} 7.642 \\ -1.47 \\ \hline \end{array}$

d. Copy and subtract: $38.672 - 5.795 =$

3. Multiplication

a. 28.6   b. 79.6   c. 4.35   d. 38   e. 7.86
   ×5   × .04   × .8   × .6   ×10

Put the decimal points in the products below:

f. 3.7   g. 1.25   h. 246   i. .275   j. .28
   ×5   × .3   × .07   100   × .02
   ‾‾‾   ‾‾‾   ‾‾‾‾   ‾‾‾‾‾   ‾‾‾
   185   375   1772   27500   56

4. Division

a. $3\overline{)8.4}$ b. $.6\overline{)7.74}$ c. $.4\overline{)48}$ d. $5\overline{)12.4}$ e. $8\overline{)1.1}$

e. Locating Difficulties with Per Cents

The use of the screening test for per cents given below will enable the teacher to determine quickly weak spots in all aspects of percentage except for difficult, involved types of examples that are rarely encountered in the affairs of daily life.

SCREENING TEST IN PERCENTAGE

1. Express as per cents:

   a. 0.6_____   b. .15_____   c. .2_____   d. 1.3_____   e. .125_____

2. Express in decimal form:

   a. 3%_____   b. 30%_____   c. 37½%_____   d. 28%_____   e. 115%_____

3. Find the values:

   a. 5% of 420 =   c. 100% of 327 =   e. 12½% of 576 =
   b. 20% of 240 =   d. 28% of 480 =   f. 106% of 356 =

4. Find the missing per cents:

   a. 8 = _____% of 200   c. 48 = _____% of 60   e. 6 = _____% of 16
   b. 60 = _____% of 80   d. 160 = _____% of 120   f. 75 = _____% of 60

5. Find the missing numbers:

   a. 6 = 4% of _____   c. 75 = 15% of _____   e. 49 = 87½% of _____
   b. 36 = 30% of _____   d. 90 = 150% of _____   f. 153.9 = 114% of _____

2. REMEDYING UNDERLYING DIFFICULTIES IN PROCESSES

a. Making Processes Meaningful

As has been indicated earlier in this chapter, there is sure to be marked improvement in all computation if special work is done at the start on the basic number facts to increase both rate and accuracy of responses. The teacher also must make every effort to see to it that the pupils not only understand the steps in working examples but also use efficient procedures. It is often necessary to eliminate slow, roundabout, inefficient methods of work, often meaningless, that are used by the pupils, many of them devised by the learners and complicated by use of counting procedures because they lack knowledge of the number facts.

b. Inadequacies of Methods of Teaching Number Operations

The same types of instructional aids used to make the different kinds of numbers meaningful should also be used to give meaning to number operations and to the procedures involved in working the different types of examples. The limitations of traditional methods of teaching number operations and the superiority of more modern methods can be made clear by an analysis of the four different methods used in teaching children how to think in the regrouping step in subtraction. Method I is highly abstract. A trick is taught which is sure to have so little meaning that it will not be understood and hence soon forgotten. In Method IV, on the other hand, an effort is made to make the operation itself and the thought processes involved completely meaningful through the use of manipulative aids and visualizations of steps before the algorism itself is taught.

LEVELS OF METHOD USED IN TEACHING OPERATIONS

$$\begin{array}{r} 52 \\ -36 \\ \hline \end{array}$$

Method I. The teacher simply says: So that we can subtract in the example, we take 1 from the 5, join the 1 to the 2 making 12. Then we subtract: $12 - 6 = 6$; $4 - 3 = 1$. (Suppose the child thinks: I thought 1 and 2 are 3." What then? The method as stated is mathematically meaningless.)

$$\begin{array}{r} 52 \\ -36 \\ \hline \end{array}$$

Method II. Here the thought process is as follows: We take 1 ten from the 5 tens, making in all 12 ones. Then we subtract the ones: $12 - 6 = 6$. Then we subtract the tens, $4 - 3 = 1$. (Note that some attention is given to place value to show how we get the 12, but the method is wholly abstract. For most children it may be meaningless. It is wholly verbal.)

$$\begin{array}{r} 4\ 12 \\ \not5\ \not2 \\ -3\ \ 6 \\ \hline \end{array}$$

Method III. The teacher says: We take 1 ten from the 5 tens, leaving 4 tens, as written out in the example. Then we change the 1 ten to 10 ones, join the 10 ones and the 2 ones, and we have 12 ones. The teacher writes out the work as shown in the example. Then we subtract first the ones, then the tens. $12 - 6 = 6$; $4 - 3 = 1$. (The procedure is wholly abstract, but the thought process is shown by writing out the transformations as they are made in working the example.)

Method IV. Here the teacher closely follows the steps described in the remedial work in subtraction as presented on page 244. First the number 52 is displayed with tickets in the place-value charts, as shown on page 244. The pupil sees that there are not enough ones in the ones' pocket to take out 6 ones. To get more ones the pupil takes 1 ten from the 5 tens in ten's pocket, opens up the 1 ten to get 10 ones, making in all 12 ones. Then 6 ones' cards and 3 tens' bundles are taken out of the respective pockets, showing the subtraction of 36. The presentation is completed by writing out the solution as shown above in Method III. (Notice the use of manipulative materials and visualization to make the operation meaningful before the actual algorism itself was presented. Check with the discussion on page 244.)

There can be no question that brief explanations such as those in Methods I and II are too abstract to be meaningful to many children, especially those slow in learning arithmetic. The step is presented as a "trick" that gets the answer and is usually mathematically meaningless. On the other hand, Method IV uses all available means that are known to be of value in making any number operation meaningful to children, namely, manipulation of representative materials, then the use of visualization and visual aids, and finally the presentation of the abstract form of solution to be mastered which then has been made fully meaningful.

The gradual development in Method IV emphasizes that learning is a growth process beginning with objective aids, then proceeding to visual aids, and ending with the abstract procedure. Each of the basic subtraction types on page 275 should be demonstrated by Method IV, using tickets and place-value pockets. Because of limitations of space, the procedures cannot be presented here; however, the basic approach is the same as that described for regrouping in tens' and ones' place in the example given above.

For illustrative purposes we give below visualizations of methods of demonstrating basic types in the other operations with tickets and place-value charts.

ADDITION: 36 + 27—carrying to tens' place.

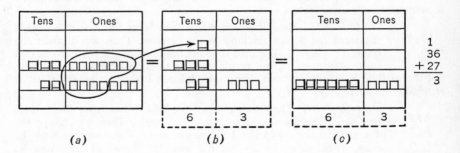

(a)　　　　(b)　　　　(c)

MULTIPLICATION: Carrying to tens' place in 2 × 37.

Note that carrying in multiplication is shown to be similar to carrying in addition. This relationship should be emphasized.

DIVISION: Uneven division in 2/34

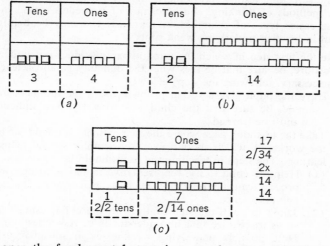

(c)

When once the fundamental steps in a number operation shown in the above diagrams are understood, the meaning of transformations in two or more places or in alternate places is easily and quickly learned by most children, except the slower learners for whom the steps should be demonstrated with representative materials as shown above.

c. Steps in Rebuilding Basic Skills

In rebuilding a general skill, such as addition, the development should be by carefully graded steps, paralleling the types listed in the preceding sections, and beginning with the simplest type. Well-constructed practice exercises, such as are found in modern textbooks and workbooks, usually are satisfactory for this purpose. However, before a slow pupil is assigned practice on a new step, it should be carefully retaught and the thought processes used by the learner and his understanding of the process should be rechecked to make certain that he will practice simple, direct thinking. As new steps are added, mixed practice exercises should be prepared to maintain the skills previously taught. The rate of progress should be so adjusted that the learner will work comfortably, successfully, and with a minimum of tension.

The sequence of rebuilding skills for slow learners should be first addition, then subtraction, then multiplication, and finally division. The difficulty of examples should be limited to the types that have social utility. Long, difficult examples containing large numbers confuse the slow learner and discourage him.

When difficulties persist and the need of individualized work is evident, the teacher should proceed more slowly and reteach carefully by using even simpler concrete materials and methods as described below.

1. Begin corrective teaching at some point below the step in which the diagnostic screening testing shows that difficulty exists. Check on understanding, methods of thinking, and efficiency of procedures used in working these easier types of examples. A readiness test may be helpful at this point in locating underlying weak spots

2. Take the first step in which the pupil apparently does not understand the procedure, be sure that he sees what the difficulty is, and reteach as may be necessary, following the steps below:

   a. Have the pupil give a verbal problem using the numbers in the type example. Be sure that the child sees what the new difficulty is and what must be learned

   b. Take the textbook page where the step actually is taught, or better still, the workbook which should give even simpler special helps for slow learners. The steps in teaching the page should be:

      (1) Help the child to use representative materials to demonstrate the process causing difficulty, such as place-value charts, fraction cutouts, etc.

      (2) Think through the step orally with the child, using visualization so as to be sure that he understands it. Ask questions to check. Note possible underlying weaknesses in subsidiary skills, *e.g.,* subtraction in division.

      (3) Write out with figures the thought processes shown with representative materials and visual aids in (*a*) and (*b*). This is not to be regarded as teaching "crutches" but as the visualization of the steps to be taken.

      (4) Have the pupil work out several similar examples in the same way to be sure that he understands and has learned the step. Reteach with simpler means as may be necessary. Check on faults in underlying skills in other processes.

      (5) Then provide "bunched" practice on the step. Check to see how successful the pupil is and for any difficulties.

      (6) Finally, provide mixed practice in which the step is imbedded among other types of processes previously studied ("distributed" practice for maintenance of skill). Check frequently and reteach as may be necessary.

3. Continue in a similar way with the more complex steps that follow in the same operation.

d. Correcting Special Difficulties in Column Addition

It was observed that in a certain fourth-grade classroom many children at work on a practice exercise of adding columns of seven digits seemed to
count to find sums or to skip around in the columns apparently
trying to find combinations that were easy for them; others would
add five or six of the digits in sequence, stop, and then begin adding
again from the top or bottom of the example. The cause of the first
type of response apparently was unfamiliarity with certain number
facts or lack of ability to add by endings with certain number facts
or lack of ability to add by endings with thought of numbers or to
bridge the tens (see page 283). A pupil may know the basic number

7
9
8
4
5
6
7
—

facts perfectly, yet not be able to apply them in column addition without counting. Practice exercises on adding by endings similar to the following are helpful in this connection. They may also be used for diagnostic purposes and can be extended as may be necessary.

Adding by endings—no bridging

1. $15 + 2 =$ Sixteen $+ 3$ Add to twenty-two: 4, then 3, etc.
2. $17 + 1 =$ Seventeen $+ 2$ Add to thirty: 5, then 4, etc.

Adding by endings—bridging the tens

1. $16 + 5 =$ fifteen $+ 7$ Add to eighteen: 5, then 7, etc.
2. $18 + 9 =$ twenty-six $+ 9$ Add to twenty-four: 7, then 9, etc.
3. $17 + 6 =$ thirty-eight $+ 6$ Add to thirty-six: 4, then 8, etc.

The second type of difficulty described above, namely, starting the example again before completing it, was undoubtedly due to the break in attention which occurs sometimes after adding five or six figures. This often happens under the strain of adding a column of digits, especially when the addition facts are difficult. Pupils should be instructed about the nature of this break and be told that when it occurs they should repeat the sum to the point reached two or three times until the lapse is over and then complete the example.

There are no new carrying difficulties in column addition. "Thought of" numbers must be added after the first addition. Young children become discouraged when given long columns of numbers to add which actually have no real social value for them. The number of numbers to add in columns should begin with two in grade 3 and increase one number a year until five or six numbers with not more than three digits each can be added with a fairly high degree of speed and accuracy.

e. Special Help in Division by Two-Place Numbers

Slow learners should be taught to use the apparent method to find quotient figures in dividing by two-place numbers. First, the pupil should master division by even tens, such as 20 or 50, since the steps involved are very similar to division by one-place numbers. Thus $40/\overline{160}$ is essentially the same as $4/\overline{16}$, insofar as estimating the quotient figure in division is concerned. The tens' digit is used as the "guide" figure. In both examples the step involved is to find $4/\overline{16}$, a step that is characteristic of the apparent method. Next the steps with other kinds of two-place divisors should be taught. Here again the solution of such examples as $21/\overline{85}$, $21/\overline{97}$, $42/\overline{129}$, and $42/\overline{158}$ requires the pupil to find $2/\overline{8}$, $2/\overline{9}$, $4/\overline{12}$, and $4/\overline{15}$. The tens' digit is again used as the guide figure. In each case the quotient in these types of examples should be the true quotient of the example.

To this point the work should be restricted to finding one-figure quotients only so the learning will not be complicated by the additional difficulties encountered with examples having two or more quotient figures, including zeros in the quotients, with and without remainders. Pupils with mental ages of 11-12 years can readily master these easy steps, but they are sure to encounter serious difficulty in dividing when the estimated quotient found by the apparent method is too large and must be made smaller until the true quotient is found, as in the examples below:

a. $23\overline{/81}$ $2/8$ is 4. The estimated quotient 4 is too large since $23 \times 4 = 92$, which is greater than 81. So try the next smaller quotient figure, 3. Because $23 \times 3 = 69$, the true quotient is 3. One correction is needed.

b. $27\overline{/191}$ $2/19 = 9$. But $27 \times 9 = 236$, so try 8. But $27 \times 8 = 196$, so try 7. Since $27 \times 7 = 189$, the true quotient is 7. Two corrections are necessary.

c. $28\overline{/188}$ $2/\overline{18} = 9$. But $28 \times 9 = 252$, so try 8. Since $28 \times 8 = 216$, try 7. Since $28 \times 7 = 196$, try 6. Since $28 \times 6 = 168$, then 6 is the correct quotient figure. Three corrections are necessary.

When the apparent method is used, the quotient figure either is correct or the estimated quotient figure is too large, in which case it is always made smaller until the true quotient is found. When the "increase by one" method is used with divisors ending in 6, 7, 8, or 9, for instance, 36, 29, and so on, the pupil must use the apparent method when dividing by the other divisors. When the increase by one method is used, in some cases the estimated quotient is correct, as in $26/\overline{80}$; frequently it is too large, as in $26/\overline{235}$ where the estimated quotient is 7 ($3/\overline{23}$), but the true quotient is 9, that is, the estimated quotient is increased by 2. A slow learner would be confused by the opposite changes in the corrections required in finding the true quotients below:

    $24/\overline{191}$—the true quotient is 2 less than the estimated quotient.

    $26/\overline{234}$—the true quotient is 2 more than the estimated quotient.

It is not easy for children of below-average mental ability to learn to find quotients when corrections are necessary. Because of its greater consistency in the direction of corrections, use the apparent method with slow learners.

Slow children who have difficulty in mastering such hard spots in division as division by the teens are often helped by working out tables of products to be used to find quotient figures. The procedure is illustrated below:

1. Complete the table for 18's at the right.
2. Use the table to find 3×18.
3. If $3 \times 18 = 54$, how much is $18\overline{)54}$?
4. Use the table to find:
   $18\overline{)72}$ $18\overline{)108}$ $18\overline{)36}$ $18\overline{)144}$
5. Since $18\overline{)36}$ is 2, then $18\overline{)39}$ is 2 and a remainder
   of ____.
   How much is $18\overline{)79}$? $18\overline{)96}$? $18\overline{)129}$?
6. How much is $18\overline{)86}$? Think: I see by the table that 86
   is between 4×18 and 5×18. So $18\overline{)86}$ must be 4 and
   a remainder. Work the example.
7. Use the table in the same way to find the quotients of the following:
   $18\overline{)30}$ $18\overline{)62}$ $18\overline{)140}$ $18\overline{)104}$ $18\overline{)175}$

$1 \times 18 = 18$
$2 \times 18 = 36$
$3 \times 18 = 54$
$4 \times 18 = 72$
$5 \times 18 = 90$
$6 \times 18 = 108$
$7 \times 18 = 126$
$8 \times 18 =$
$9 \times 18 =$

This exercise should be extended in a similar way to include divisors of 13, 14, 15, 16, 17, and 19. Gradually the children will gain insight into this difficult step and be able to proceed without use of the tables.

The exercises below give excellent practice in the multiplication and subtraction used in division. Isolated practice on these skills in the usual form is not as helpful.

SPECIAL PRACTICE IN DIVISION

Multiply and then subtract. The quotient figures that are given are correct:

a	b	c	d	e
4	7	6	9	8
$23\overline{)104}$	$36\overline{)262}$	$58\overline{)370}$	$75\overline{)712}$	$69\overline{)591}$

An analysis of the pupil's work will show quickly if there are deficiencies in these two operations.

f. Corrective Work with Fraction Processes

When children have acquired an adequate understanding of the nature and meaning of fractions through the kinds of experiences with representative materials and visualizations, discussed on page 197, they usually have little difficulty in overcoming deficiencies in number operations with fractions. Ordinarily, a major cause of learning difficulty is the tendency of the teacher to present the operations with fractions by highly abstract verbal methods that actually have little meaning for children, just as was true of the methods of teaching whole-number processes described in the lower levels of the scale on teaching regrouping in subtraction (page 279).

It is entirely possible completely to visualize solutions of examples with fractions and to make the processes meaningful by drawings and diagrams. The solutions, however, can also be demonstrated with manipulative materials, such as the cutouts used to make fractions themselves meaningful (pages 251-252). The ideal method is to combine manipulation and visualization. The sequence of methods of presenting algorisms now in use varies from those that are wholly abstract to others that use concrete and visual methods. This is illustrated by the following descriptions of methods used to teach the procedure in solving the example, 2¼ − ¾.

$$
\begin{array}{r}
2\frac{1}{4} = 1\frac{5}{4} \\
-\ \frac{3}{4} = \ \frac{3}{4} \\
\hline
\end{array}
$$

Method I. To subtract, first take 1 from the 2 and change the 1 to ¼, making ⁵⁄₄ in all. Then subtract 1 ⁵⁄₄ − ¾. (This procedure is wholly verbal and abstract. Usually the transformation is not written out as shown but must be made mentally by the learner.)

Method II. Here the solution is visualized by the drawing. The transformation of 2 ¼ to 1 ⁵⁄₄ is shown. The three dropped out parts in the diagram in *b* represent the ¾ subtracted. (Visualization is used.)

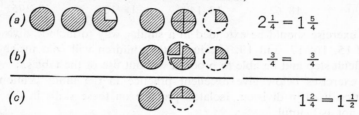

Method III. Prior to presenting the drawing in II, which may appear in the textbook or be drawn on the blackboard, the teacher has the pupil use the fractional cutouts in his fraction kit (see page 197) to work out the solution with representative materials. First, 2 ¼ circles are placed on the table. To take away ¾ we must get more fourths. So take 1 of the 2 circles and change it to 4 quarter-circles, making in all 5 quarter-circles. Now take away ¾ circle. How many circles remain? Next the drawing in the textbook is discussed with the pupils, showing its meaning with the cutouts. Then the steps in the solution are explained by reference to the drawing, or when necessary by means of the cutouts.

Illustrations of methods of using cutouts to visualize solutions of examples in all processes are shown by the diagrams below. The sequence of steps in presenting any new step should be those used in Method III above, namely:

1. Use of cutouts to discover the answers.
2. Discussion of the diagrams given so as to clarify the steps in the solution.
3. Presentation of the algorism, using manipulative materials and visualization as may be necessary to make it meaningful.

ADDITION

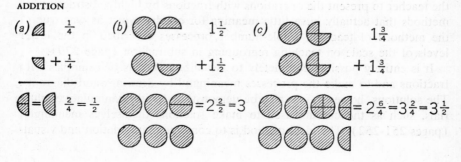

SUBTRACTION

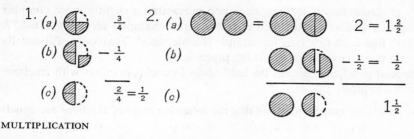

MULTIPLICATION

(a) $2 \times \frac{1}{4} =$ □ + □ = □ = □

(b) $2 \times 1\frac{1}{2} =$ ○ ○ + ○ ○ = ○ ○ ○ = ○ ○ ○

(c) $\frac{1}{2}$ of $\frac{1}{2} =$ ○

Note that in 1 and 2, solutions by cutouts require addition to find answers. Multiplication in these cases is a quick way to find sums.

DIVISION

1. Use cutouts to show how many times you can take ¼ out of 1.
2. Use cutouts to find out how many times you can take ⅛ out of ½.
3. Use cutouts to find how much ¾ divided into two equal parts is.
4. How many times can you take 1 ¼ circles out of 2 ½ circles? 2 ½ ÷ 1 ¼ =

The first three sets of solutions visualize the algorisms to be learned. The pupils should be taught to apply these methods in finding answers to many simple examples until it is clear that they understand the solutions.

○ = ⊕

$1 \div \frac{1}{4} = 4$

The four solutions for division given above show the pupil how to discover answers to selected examples and they make the answers sensible and meaningful to him. However, he must then learn the algorism requiring the inversion of the divisor as a method that will always find the answer, even when the solution cannot be discovered through the use of manipulative materials, for instance, with examples like ½ ÷ ⅘, 1 ⅓ ÷ ¼, or 3 ⁷⁄₁₀ ÷ 5. The method of inversion itself cannot be visualized. Slow learners in any case will find division of fractions very difficult, and little effort should be made by the teacher to make the

$\frac{1}{2} \div \frac{1}{8} = 4$

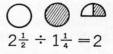

$\frac{3}{4} \div 2 = \frac{3}{8}$

○ ⊘ ⬤

$2\frac{1}{2} \div 1\frac{1}{4} = 2$

algorism completely meaningful. Finding answers for easy examples by manipulation methods is all that can be expected of them.

To rebuild skills in any process with fractions, follow the steps of a carefully graded series of lessons, each one presenting a slightly more complex group of skills, as is illustrated in the series of examples on pages 276-277. Be sure that each new type of example is understood. Textbooks will usually contain the necessary materials for practice.

Special practice exercises on hard spots in each operation with fractions also are helpful:

1. Use your cutouts to prove that the following pairs of fractions are equal:

   $\frac{2}{4} = \frac{1}{2}$ $\qquad$ $\frac{2}{8} = \frac{1}{4}$ $\qquad$ $\frac{4}{8} = \frac{1}{2}$ $\qquad$ $\frac{6}{8} = \frac{3}{4}$

2. Use your cutouts or a ruler to find the missing numbers:

   $\frac{3}{4} = \frac{?}{8}$ $\qquad$ $\frac{1}{2} = \frac{?}{4}$ $\qquad$ $\frac{2}{4} = \frac{?}{8}$ $\qquad$ $1\frac{1}{2} = \frac{?}{4}$

3. Use your cutouts to show that the following pairs of numbers are equal:

   $2 = 1\frac{2}{2}$ $\qquad$ $3 = 2\frac{4}{4}$ $\qquad$ $2 = 1\frac{8}{8}$ $\qquad$ $1\frac{1}{4} = \frac{?}{4}$

4. Use your cutouts or a ruler to find the missing numbers:

   $1\frac{1}{2} = \frac{?}{2}$ $\qquad$ $1\frac{3}{4} = \frac{?}{4}$ $\qquad$ $2\frac{5}{8} = 1\frac{?}{8}$ $\qquad$ $2\frac{3}{4} = 1\frac{?}{4}$

5. Use your cutouts to change these numbers to improper fractions:

   $1\frac{1}{4} = \frac{?}{4}$ $\qquad$ $2\frac{3}{4} = \frac{?}{4}$ $\qquad$ $2\frac{7}{8} = \frac{?}{8}$ $\qquad$ $2\frac{1}{2} = \frac{?}{2}$

6. Express each of these answers in simplest form:

   $2\frac{2}{2} =$ $\qquad$ $3\frac{4}{8} =$ $\qquad$ $1\frac{4}{4} =$ $\qquad$ $1\frac{10}{8} =$

From time to time, pupils should be given short exercises consisting of correct solutions with typical errors embedded in them, preferably those that they make themselves. The purpose of these exercises is to focus the learner's attention upon his own errors so that he will learn to recognize them, hence will be less likely to make them in his daily work.

A valuable series of generalizations about answers to division examples can be derived from the group of examples at the right:

Tell which of the examples prove that the following statements are true:

1. When we divide a number by a smaller number, the quotient is greater than 1.
2. When we divide a number by itself, the quotient is equal to 1.
3. When we divide a number by a larger number, the quotient is less than 1.

$a.$ $3\frac{1}{2} \div 2 = 1\frac{3}{4}$

$b.$ $1\frac{1}{2} \div 1\frac{1}{2} = 1$

$c.$ $1 \div \frac{1}{2} = 2$

$d.$ $1\frac{1}{2} \div 3 = \frac{1}{2}$

$e.$ $\frac{1}{4} \div \frac{1}{2} = \frac{1}{2}$

$f.$ $\frac{3}{8} \div \frac{3}{8} = 1$

Now have the pupils give examples of their own with whole numbers, or fractions, or decimals to illustrate each statement. Have the pupils also apply the set of principles to their work in a mixed drill exercise in division of fractions to see if their answers are sensible.

Similar exercises can be developed for generalizations for each of the operations with fractions, whole numbers, and decimals.

g. Decimals

Because of their similarity to adding and subtracting dollars and cents, the operations of addition and subtraction of decimals usually are not difficult for pupils above the fifth grade. The screening test on page 277 will indicate weak spots. The steps in addition and subtraction can easily be taught by using the place-value pockets to visualize them, much as is described for whole numbers.

Multiplication and division of decimals by whole numbers are rather easy, but multiplication and division of decimals by decimals are exceedingly difficult for many pupils in grades 7 and 8, especially the slower ones of less than average mental ability. It probably would be a wise policy not to attempt to teach these skills to these children to the point of mastery, but only for informational purposes so that they can see that solutions are possible.

Aside from inaccuracies found in any computation, the chief source of difficulty in multiplication and division of decimals is the placement of the decimal point in the answers. It is strongly recommended that all pupils be taught to use the method of approximation described below to determine what a sensible answer to the example would be rather than to try to apply the rules so often taught which have little meaning for children.

CHECKING ANSWERS BY APPROXIMATION

$$\begin{array}{r} 4.67 \\ \times 7 \\ \hline 32.69 \end{array}$$
Because 7×4 is 28, the only sensible answer would be 32.69, for 3.269 would be too small and 326.9 too large.

$$\begin{array}{r} 7.3 \\ \times 1.2 \\ \hline 146 \\ 730 \\ \hline 8.76 \end{array}$$
Because 1×7 is 7, the answer cannot be 876, or 87.6. It must be 8.76.

$$\begin{array}{r} 6.92 \\ 3\overline{)20.76} \end{array}$$
Because $3\overline{)20}$ is 6, the answer cannot be .692, 69.2, or 692. It must be 6.92.

$$\begin{array}{r} 3.2 \\ 1.2\overline{)3.72} \end{array}$$
Because $1\overline{)3}$ is 3, the answer cannot be as small as .32 or as large as 32. It must be 3.2.

With a little practice on similar examples, the pupils learn to apply the methods of approximation very effectively. Checking quotients by multiplication is also helpful. Checking answers by using common fractions also is often very useful.

IMPROVING PROBLEM-SOLVING ABILITY

Changing Conceptions of Problem-Solving

In recent years there has been a considerable shift from the concept of problem-solving as the solution of traditional verbal problems formulated largely to illustrate the applications of number operations, but actually a form of "disguised drill" in arithmetic computations. Instead, it is recognized today that quantitative thinking in realistic social situations, in analyzing described situations, in discovering and using number relationships, and in using study skills in analyzing and interpreting graphs, tables, charts, diagrams, and the like, is a broad, even more valuable area of ability to develop. Consequently, modern courses of study and textbooks provide a wide variety of activities and interesting vital materials to give pupils experiences with arithmetic in all curriculum areas that will improve the ability to think quantitatively in the broad sense of the term *problem-solving* described above.

Reading Ability as a Factor in Problem-Solving

It is obvious that children must actually have experiences in which they apply quantitative thinking if this important ability is to be developed. If the work in arithmetic is largely limited to repetitive drill with routine computations, not only is the ability to think quantitatively in all areas of the curriculum and in life situations certain to be neglected, but there also is serious danger that the thinking that should be done in performing meaningful number operations intelligently will not be stressed.

The ability to read also plays an important role in quantitative thinking, for there are special kinds of reading skills required in problem-solving as defined above in addition to the ability to read and comprehend explanations of algorisms that are included in textbooks and workbooks.

Research has shown that pupils who excel in problem-solving are significantly superior to those who are poor in problem-solving in the following fields:

1. Computational ability.
2. Ability to apply the sequence of steps involved in problem-solving.
3. Ability to estimate answers to verbal problems.
4. Range of information about social uses of arithmetic.
5. Ability to read graphs, charts, tables.
6. Ability to see relations in number series.
7. General and nonverbal reasoning ability.
8. General reading level.
9. Level of mental ability.

The good and poor problem-solvers are not significantly different in the general reading skills used in literary reading, such as those included in the Gates Tests in General Reading, but they do differ significantly in the special reading skills required in arithmetic, namely, ability to follow the steps in problem-solving. It evidently is necessary to give special attention to teaching pupils inferior in problem-solving the special reading skills peculiar to arithmetic.

Well-constructed arithmetic textbooks and workbooks often provide excellent reading exercises which develop the reading skills required in problem-solving and extend the vocabulary. Teachers should not hesitate to use suitable reading exercises in arithmetic textbooks and workbooks, beginning with those that are somewhat below the level of problems which the pupil can solve reasonably well and gradually progressing to exercises of greater difficulty found in textbooks for the higher grades. Some of the more valuable kinds of helps in problem-solving are described below.

The following outline shows the skills in reading that must be established in a well-rounded arithmetic program:

1. Knowledge of the vocabulary of arithmetic.
   a. Meaning of technical mathematical terms, such as *digit, add,* and *numerator.*
   b. Meaning of units of measure (also abbreviations and symbols of these units).
   c. Meaning of the quantitative vocabulary related to social applications of arithmetic, such as *stamp, price, taxation, density of population, area.*
   d. Use of dictionary, glossary, etc., to get definitions.

2. Basic skills involved in reading and solving verbal textbook problems.
   a. Comprehension of the meaning of the items and statements contained in a problem and the ability to visualize the situation presented.
   b. The reading necessary in carrying out the steps usually followed in problem-solving, which are:
      (1) What question does the problem ask me to answer?
      (2) What facts are given in the problem? Is other information needed?
      (3) What steps must be taken to solve the problem? (It is necessary to see the relations among the facts in a problem to determine the steps to be taken to find the answer.)
      (4) Is my answer sensible?
   c. Locating information not stated in a problem but necessary for its solution:
      (1) In accompanying tables, graphs, charts, pictures, etc.
      (2) In preceding problems and discussions.
      (3) In reference books, catalogs, and other printed sources.
      (4) In the appendix of the textbook.
      (5) In schedules, forms, plans, maps, etc.
   d. Reading with understanding various formulas, equation, rules.

3. The reading and interpretation of various kinds of statistical tables, such as are found in textbooks, reference books, and other printed sources.
   a. Reading standard tables, such as interest tables and tables of products of numbers.
   b. Reading tables presenting factual information of a social nature.
      (1) Identifying the contents of the table.

(2) Understanding the structural elements and arrangement of the scale.

(3) Selecting detailed information included in the table.

(4) Interpretation of information included.

(5) Summarizing information secured.

(6) Evaluating the information included.

(7) Making generalizations and comparisons based on the data.

(8) Predicting future happenings on the basis of the information given in the table.

(9) Remembering information.

4. The reading and interpretation of graphs wherever found.

   a. The comprehension of graphs of various kinds, such as bar graphs, circle graphs, histograms, etc.

   b. Reading skills similar to those listed under 3b above are involved in the reading of graphs.

5. The reading and interpretation of quantitative elements included in diagrams, charts, schedules, maps, plans, and pictures.

   a. Interpretation of quantitative symbols on charts, maps, etc.

   b. Reading of scales, and scale drawings.

   c. Longitude and latitude readings.

   d. Time tables, class schedules.

   e. Use of guide lines to locate information, places, etc.

   f. Comprehending quantitative concepts included in advertisements, business forms, pictures, etc.

6. Reading skills involved in securing information in printed sources about assignments in the study of social applications of arithmetic, such as:

   a. Locating information in various printed sources.

   b. Comprehending what is read.

   c. Organizing what is read, as, making an outline of contents, a graph, or table.

   d. Evaluating what is read.

   e. Summarizing what is read.

   f. Making generalizations.

   g. Remembering what is read.

General Principles Basic to the Development of Ability to Solve Verbal Problems

The following principles [3] are of demonstrated value in improving problem-solving:

1. Having the pupils solve many interesting, well-graded problems during the arithmetic period will yield large returns. More problems of this sort are needed than now are found in some arithmetic textbooks. The teacher should take advantage of the many opportunities that arise in the work of the class in their other subjects to bring out the uses of number processes and to give concrete experience in the use of number in practical situations.

2. Superior pupils apparently can devise efficient techniques of problem-solv-

[3] Leo J. Brueckner in *Educational Diagnosis,* Thirty-fourth Yearbook, National Society for the Study of Education (Chicago, Univ. of Chicago Press, 1935), pp. 299-300.

ing, and they should not be taught a single, set technique. All pupils should be encouraged to suggest solutions when new types of work are presented; that is sounder pedagogically than to assume that solutions must be presented initially by the teacher.

3. Increasing the accuracy of computation in problems by systematically organized practice exercises on number processes and insisting that all computations be checked will increase scores on problem tests by eliminating the errors arising in computation.

4. Exercises in careful reading, of the kind included in many reading and arithmetic textbooks and in supplementary worktype reading materials and arithmetic workbooks, are very helpful. The value of re-reading problems should be emphasized. Requiring pupils to restate problems in their own words is a valuable check on their comprehension of the problem's situation.

5. Vocabulary exercises on important arithmetic terms and number concepts are essential. Buswell has shown clearly the need for this type of work, since many of the technical terms used in arithmetic do not appear in the materials in reading textbooks.

6. Original problems prepared by pupils and concrete applications growing out of local situations and experience are valuable means of developing in the pupil the ability to "sense" number relations and to generalize his number concepts. The teacher must make certain that essential relations are educed in such a way that the pupils see the relations in the solution of novel problems.

7. In work on various original problems that require independent study by the pupils, such specific reading skills as use of the index and table of contents and an ability to summarize often are involved. These reading skills should be taught as part of the instruction in arithmetic.

8. Neatness of work and orderly arrangement of solutions should be emphasized.

9. Standardized progress tests and other methods of showing the pupil his improvement in solving arithmetic problems, applied at regular intervals through the year, are an essential element in a well-rounded arithmetic program.

Sources of Difficulty in Problem-Solving

The deficiencies in problem-solving fall into the following major categories:

1. Meaning of number operations and perception of relations among them.
2. Ability to compute with numbers.
3. Ability to sense quantitative relations involved in verbal problems.
4. Control of special types of reading skills required in problem-solving.
5. Knowledge of vocabulary of a quantitative nature.
6. Knowledge of essential information, facts, rules, and formulas.
7. Breadth of knowledge about uses of arithmetic as applied in social situations.
8. Amount of practice in solving verbal problems.

These limitations arise from such causes as a low level of mental capacity of the pupil, a limited social and experiential background, inferior reading ability, and the limited scope and ineffectiveness of the instructional program and methods of teaching arithmetic.

Specific Procedures for Improving Problem-Solving

a. Making Number Operations Meaningful. Underlying all effective quantitative thinking is an understanding of the nature and meaning of number operations and an awareness of the ways in which numbers function in a wide variety of social situations both in and out of school. Number operations must be made mathematically meaningful by methods of teaching suitable to a learning laboratory, methods that demonstrate their meaning by the manipulation of representative materials, the visualization of procedures by drawings, diagrams, and charts, and finally by the teaching of the abstract algorisms the learner is expected to utilize in computations.

b. Experience in Using Operations in Social Situations. Number operations must also be made socially significant by applying them in a wide variety of activities in which their meaning is brought into focus. In well-planned instruction, the teacher has pupils work out in concrete, meaningful ways solutions of problems as they arise in the course of learning. The wider the variety of experiences in which real problems are solved, the richer the background of the pupil to draw upon when facing new problems or the kinds of verbal problems found in textbooks and standard tests.

c. Using Objects to Show the Meaning of Processes Used in Solving Problems. Objects such as chairs, books, disks, and squares can be used to good advantage to help children gain insight into the meaning of number operations as they are used in problem-solving. This use is of great value in teaching pupils who have difficulty in reading and solving simple verbal problems. Oral tests administered to young children show that without writing out the solution they easily solve problems involving simple addition groupings, that easy subtraction problems are more difficult, multiplication problems still more difficult, whereas division problems are most difficult of all.

Addition problems. To teach the child to solve addition problems, first state simple problems orally, have the pupil present the objects which correspond to each fact, then have him "join" the objects to see how many there are in all. Then have him read the problem, show the solution with objects, then write the numbers as an addition example. Repeat this process on several days until it appears he understands the meaning of addition. Use easy facts with sums of less than 10 at first; gradually increase the difficulty of the problems. Finally use problems including larger numbers. Have the pupil in all cases show that he is "joining" two or more numbers to find how many in all, so that he develops a meaningful concept of what addition is.

Subtraction problems. Subtraction is used in four different ways, as illustrated by the following type problems:

a. Finding how many are left, or the remainder.

Type: Harry has 5 pennies. He spent 1 penny. How many pennies did he then have?

Solution: Lay down 5 objects as in (1) to represent the pennies. Take away one object representing the 1 penny spent, as in (2). Then 4 objects remain, which represent 4 pennies.

Type (a)

b. Finding how many more are needed.

Type: Ann has 2 cents. She wants to buy a 5-cent postcard. How many cents more does she need?

Solution: Draw 2 small circles to represent the 2 cents, as shown in drawing (1). Encircle them as shown. Then draw additional circles as in (2) until there are 5 circles in all. Count the other circles. Objects can also be used.

Type (b)

c. Comparing two numbers. (Difference)

Type: John has 5 cents. Mary has 2 cents. How many cents have John more than Mary?

Solution: Draw 5 circles to show John's money. Below them draw 2 circles to show Mary's money. Now cross off 1 circle in each row, then another circle, as shown in the drawing. The 3 circles not marked off are the answer to the problem. Objects can also be used.

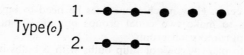

Type (c)

d. Finding a component part. (Missing number)

Type: Kate has 5 coins. Two of the coins are nickels, the others are pennies. How many pennies has she?

Solution: Draw 5 circles as in (1). Encircle two of them as nickels as in (2), or label them. Those not encircled represent the pennies.

Type (d)

Multiplication problems. Pupils should be led to discover that the following problems can be solved by both addition and multiplication, and that multiplication is the shorter process. The solution should first be shown using groups of objects of equal size.

1. How many plants are there in 3 rows if there are 5 plants in each row?
2. Find the cost of 3 loaves of bread at 19 cents a loaf.

Division problems. There are two key types of division problems. In Type 1 we find how many times a group of a given size can be taken out of a larger group, essentially a subtraction process, easily demonstrated by the "taking away" procedure.

> Type 1. How many rows of 3 chairs each can we make with 12 chairs? If 1 cake costs 5 cents, how many cakes can I buy for 20 cents?

In Type 2 problems we are called on to divide a group into a number of parts, a partition or "sorting process," or to find the size of a given part of a group. In this case, the size of the group is not known.

> Type 2. Tom wants to make two equal groups of marbles. He has 18 marbles. How many should he place in each group?

The solution can be shown with objects by sorting the 18 objects one at a time into two groups. This concept of division is quite different from the first type.

When children grasp the meanings of these different kinds of uses of the four operations through demonstrations and experiences with representative materials, their ability to solve verbal problems is sure to be improved.

   d. Using Manipulative Materials to Work Out Solutions of Problems. Children who are low in problem-solving ability should be taught how to join or separate groups of manipulative materials such as disks, pennies, and toothpicks to find the answers to written problems such as the following:

1. Tom has 4 cents. How much more does he need to buy a 10-cent cone?
2. Mary wants to make two equal groups out of 12 stamps. How many should she put into each group?
3. Bob wants to plant 4 rows of tulip bulbs with 6 bulbs in each row. How many bulbs does he need?
4. Alice has 9 books and Ann has 4 books. How many more books has Alice than Ann?

   e. Visualizing Solutions of Problems. Pupils weak in problem-solving are helped considerably by making drawings with circles, crosses, and tally marks to picture the solutions of verbal problems like those given above.

   It is especially desirable for pupils to learn to make drawings that visualize situations, such as those included in the problems below, to prevent the giving of answers that are incomplete or meaningless:

1. What is the distance around a flower bed that is 12 feet long and 8 feet wide?
2. How many degrees colder is it at 4° below zero than at 14° above zero?
3. How many pieces of cloth ½ yard long can be cut from a piece 2½ yards long?
4. How many trees are there in each row in an orchard having 20 trees if there are 4 rows of trees?

Diagrams may also be used to help the pupil to grasp the meaning of the relationships among the numbers in problems, as illustrated below:

1. If ¼ pound of tea costs 20 cents, how much does 1 pound cost? Use the drawing below to find the answer.

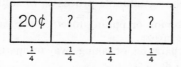

2. If ¾ yard of ribbon costs 36 cents, how much does ¼ yard cost? How much does 1 yard cost? Use the drawing below to find the answers. Hint: ¼ yard costs ⅓ of 36¢, or ? 1 yd. or 4/4 yard costs . . . .

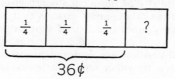

3. Use the drawing below to find how 4 children could share 3 cakes. $3 \div 4 =$?

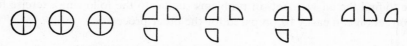

4. Make a drawing of this problem: If ½ pound of butter costs 40¢, how much do 2 pounds cost?

e. Improving the Quality of Verbal Problems. The problem content of various textbooks differs greatly in both merit and difficulty. In some textbooks, groups of uninteresting, unrelated problems with little appeal to children, obviously intended to provide practice in difficult computations, constitute the greater portion of the problem content. Sometimes the problems are of a puzzle type and are unrelated to the experiences of children, and hence they are very difficult for children of below-average mental or reading ability. In other textbooks, problems are grouped around the activities of children, applications of arithmetic in other curriculum areas, and topics whose contents are of genuine social value. They arouse the interest of the pupils. In the diagnosis and treatment of weakness in solving verbal problems, the teacher should select groups of interesting, simply stated problems grouped about some experience or topic related to child life, and involving computations that are not above moderate difficulty for the children. After all, the optimum function of problem-solving should be to develop important types of quantitative thinking in functional situations, not to give practice in making complicated computations.

f. Developing Relationships Among Number Processes. The modern teacher also will make an effort to bring out underlying meanings of number operations and relationships among the various processes. Such generalizations as the following, which pupils will discover under careful guidance in the course of activities requiring the solving of many simple problems, are of great value in assisting pupils to analyze more difficult problems and thereby help them to choose suitable processes of solution.

1. Addition means joining or putting together two or more numbers. They may be alike or different in size.

2. Subtraction is a separating, or taking away or apart, process. The numbers may be alike or different in size.

3. Addition and subtraction are opposite processes, one meaning putting together and the other taking apart.

4. Multiplication is a quick way, faster than addition, of putting together or finding the total number in two or more equal-sized groups.

5. Division is a short-cut taking-apart process that is faster than subtraction by which to find how many times equal-sized subgroups can be separated from a number.

6. Multiplication and division are opposite processes, one meaning putting together equal-sized groups, the other separating equal-sized groups.

g. Explaining Reasons for Using Processes. Pupils should learn to explain how they can tell from the contents of a problem what process to use to find the answer. Sets of problems similar to the following exercise for subtraction can easily be prepared for the other processes.

WHY DO WE SUBTRACT TO FIND THE ANSWERS?

What is there in the problem which tells us that we subtract to solve each of the four problems below?

1. Tom has 48 cents. He wants to buy a ball that costs $2.50. How much more money does he need?

2. Bob has 75 marbles and Arthur has 56 marbles. How many more marbles has Bob than Arthur has?

3. Mary had 32 Christmas postcards. She mailed 26 of the postcards. How many postcards did she have left?

4. In a school there are in all 412 children. There are 207 boys. How many girls are there?

5. Make four problems of your own that are like those given above.

h. Identifying Processes to Use. In order to determine whether or not a pupil can select the correct procedure for solving problems without computing the answers, exercises containing such problems as the following can be used. The level of difficulty can be adapted to the pupil's ability and stage of development.

HOW WELL CAN YOU TELL HOW TO FIND THE ANSWER?

Under each problem, mark the method you would use to find the answer.

1. Tommy has 18 cents. Bobby has 3 cents more than Tommy. How many cents has Bobby?

_____*a.* Add 18¢ and 3¢   _____*c.* Multiply 18¢ by 3

_____*b.* Subtract 3¢ from 18¢   _____*d.* Divide 18 by 3

2. What is the perimeter of a garden that is 40 feet long and 20 feet wide?

____*a.* Add 40 ft. and 20 ft.   ____*c.* Divide 40 by 20
____*b.* Multiply 40 by 20   ____*d.* Find 2 times 40 ft. + 20 ft.

i. Problems Without Numbers. Another helpful exercise is to have the pupil state the method of solving a problem without numbers:

1. How do you find the average weight of 3 boys?
2. If you know the cost of a number of baseballs, how can you find the cost of one baseball?
3. If you know how many rows of seats there are in a classroom and the number of seats in each row, how can you find the total number of seats in the classroom?

j. Learning to Sense Relationships in Equations. Good problem-solvers are significantly more able to detect relationships among numbers. Exercises in quantitative thinking which require finding missing numbers or signs are very valuable in assisting children to perceive relationships among groups of numbers when they are expressed in simple equation form:

1. $3 \ ? \ 9 = 27$	5. $34 + \ ? \ = 70$
2. $18 \ ? \ 18 = 0$	6. $? \div 6 = 47$
3. $12 \ ? \ 16 = 28$	7. $263 - \ ? \ = 4$
4. $4 \ ? \ 3 = 2 \ ? \ 10$	8. $4 \times \ ? \ = 100$

The pupils should work out the relationships between pint-quart-gallon by actual physical experimentation. Relationships between other units of measure can be worked out experimentally in the same way and arranged in the form of tables of measure. In the case of area, squares can be used to represent square units of the different sizes.

The relationships involved in changing larger units to smaller units by multiplication, e.g., 4 ft. = _____ in., and changing smaller units to larger units by division, e.g., 8 qt. = _____ gal., should also be worked out experimentally with measuring devices to make both procedures meaningful to the pupils.

k. Making the Vocabulary of Problems Meaningful. Many kinds of vocabulary-building exercises similar to those used in reading can be used to broaden and sharpen the meanings of words used in problems:

1. Matching words with pictures, drawings, objects.
2. Completion exercises in which missing words are to be inserted.
3. Classifying groups of words under proper headings.
4. Using the dictionary to find meanings of words.
5. Restating problems and questions in one's own words.
6. Writing the words for given abbreviations.
7. Naming parts of drawings, pictures, figures, designs.
8. Dramatizing the meaning of some action word.
9. Listing words that suggest joining groups or separating groups.
10. Writing lists of expressions associated with such words as *fraction, circle, distance, time, area, money,* and so on.

11. Cancelling words that do not belong in a group.
12. Making a list of measuring devices used in the home, at school, on the farm, in a grocery store, and so on.
13. Writing the names of parts of examples in the various operations.
14. Writing original problems.
15. Writing synonyms, homonyms, and opposites.

l. General Program for Improving Problem-Solving. Special exercises such as the following, adapted to the needs of the learner, should be used to remedy weaknesses revealed by diagnosis.

1. Discuss uses of number in social situations that arise, or in pictures and illustrations in textbooks to develop vocabulary and background experiences.
2. Give the pupil many opportunities to solve verbal problems that may arise in real social situations. Have pupil tell how he finds the answers and explain or give reasons for method of solution used.
3. Give the pupil abundant experience in reading and solving easy, meaningful verbal problems in textbooks and workbooks, beginning at or slightly below his level of development. Keep the numbers small at the start. Gradually increase the difficulty of the vocabulary, computations, and situations.
4. Be sure to help the learner to understand the meaning of each number process by manipulative experience and by exercises which embody the various types of situations or meanings each process implies. Textbooks often provide suitable exercises which visualize the meanings of the various processes. Have pupil give original problems.
5. Have pupils use manipulative materials to demonstrate and work out solutions of simple problems so as to help them to visualize the situations and the relations involved. Have them tell orally about the procedures they use.
6. Plan reading experiences which will develop the special reading skills in problem-solving listed in the outline on diagnosis on page 290. Take one skill at a time on the sequence listed. This is very important. See workbooks for special helps.
7. Emphasize vocabulary development by suitable exercises similar to those used in reading.
8. Do special work on measures and their use in social situations. Help pupils to develop and then use tables of measure. Demonstrate or visualize the processes of conversion from "large to small," and "small to large," a basic element of difficulty in problem-solving.
9. Develop basic rules, formulas, and procedures through real situations, involving manipulation of representative materials, drawings, visualization and thinking through the relations involved; for example, perimeter, area, costs, interest, percentage, etc.
10. Use problems without numbers to help the pupil learn to state in his own words how to find answers.
11. Emphasize the need of accuracy in all computations. Teach pupils to go over their work to check it.
12. Teach pupils above fifth grade procedures for approximating and estimating answers to see if their answers are sensible.

SUGGESTED ACTIVITIES

1. Following a diagnostic case study of deficiencies in number operations in connection with the preceding chapter, describe what in your opinion would be a suitable remedial program. Select from the specific remedial procedures given in this chapter the corrective measures that you think would be helpful. Locate sources of such exercises in arithmetic textbooks and workbooks. If possible try to apply these procedures to the case at hand. Measure the effectiveness of your plan.

2. Develop a similar program for problem-solving.

3. As a special activity, try the methods of testing a pupil's knowledge of number facts in some process described in this chapter and to do corrective work to improve his knowledge of these facts. Try to devise methods of teaching him how to discover generalizations and relationships among related number facts as described in this chapter. Examine textbooks for grades 3 and 4 for help along this line.

4. Discuss methods of grouping children for remedial instruction in operations and in problem-solving. Differentiate between methods of dealing with children of high and low mental ability who have learning problems in arithmetic. Why may there be complex disability cases in arithmetic?

5. What help, if any, do reading textbooks give in the development of reading skills in arithmetic, such as those listed on pages 291-292. What are the implications for arithmetic instruction?

6. Examine the comprehensive series of diagnostic tests and self-helps published by the California Test Bureau. Discuss their usefulness.

7. Discuss with local teachers instructional procedures they have found helpful in the correction of certain specific kinds of difficulties in arithmetic.

8. Examine basic textbooks in arithmetic to find what is done to make number and number operations meaningful to children.

9. Evaluate the contents of arithmetic workbooks as to their value for remedial work.

SELECTED BIBLIOGRAPHY

See bibliography at end of Chapter 8.

10 DIAGNOSIS AND TREATMENT OF LANGUAGE DIFFICULTIES

IN THIS CHAPTER we deal with methods that may be used in the diagnosis and treatment of learning difficulties in oral and written expression. Problems specifically related to spelling and handwriting are treated in Chapters 11 and 12. The following topics are discussed in this chapter:

1. The fundamentals of an effective program in oral and written expression.
2. Foundations of diagnosis.
3. General diagnosis in oral and written expression.
4. Analytical diagnosis in oral and written expression.
5. Case-study procedures.
6. The treatment of learning difficulties.

THE FUNDAMENTALS OF AN EFFECTIVE PROGRAM IN ORAL AND WRITTEN EXPRESSION

The Objectives of Instruction in Oral and Written Expression

Training children in the use of oral and written language, including listening, is one of the most fundamental tasks of the school. Speech is a form of behavior that has been evolved as a means of setting up relations among human beings. Oral and written expression make it possible for individuals to communicate and exchange ideas and experiences, to convey feelings and emotions, and to create new values, as poetry, plays, and creative writing.

The general objectives of the language arts program in the modern school were recently stated as follows in the report [1] of an important commission:

1. Wholesome personal development.
2. Dynamic and worth-while allegiances through heightened moral perception and a personal sense of values.
3. Growing intellectual curiosity and capacity for critical thinking.
4. Effective use of language in the daily affairs of life.
5. Habitual and intelligent use of the mass modes of communication.

[1] The Commission on the English Curriculum of the National Council of Teachers of English, *The English Language Arts* (New York, Appleton-Century-Crofts, 1952), Ch. 3.

6. Growing personal interests and increasingly mature standards of enjoyment.
7. Effective habits of work.
8. Competent use of language and reading for vocational purposes.
9. Social sensitivity and effective participation in the group life.
10. Faith in and allegiance to the basic values of a democratic society.

This statement of objectives is very broad in its scope. It includes not only outcomes of general education to which all education contributes, including personal and social development and traits necessary for effective group living in a democratic society, but also the special goals of direct instruction in the language arts curriculum. McKee has suggested that the language arts program should provide definite instruction and practice in each of the ten major types of speaking and writing activities listed below.[2] The purpose of instruction should be to develop in the learner an appreciation of the social significance of each kind of activity and a desire to acquire the ability to participate in each of them with growing effectiveness.

1. Taking part in conversation and general discussion.
2. Using the telephone.
3. Taking part in meetings, as chairman, recorder of minutes, and active participant or listener.
4. Preparing and giving oral or written reports, talks, and speeches.
5. Telling and writing stories, jokes, anecdotes.
6. Giving oral or written reviews of books, programs, plays.
7. Giving directions and explanations, oral or written.
8. Making announcements of events and preparing written notices.
9. Giving descriptions of objects, places, events, or persons, oral or written.
10. Writing friendly letters of various kinds, also business letters.

In order to participate effectively in these kinds of language activities the learner must acquire certain competencies, including the ability to select ideas to be expressed, the ability to speak and write simply, clearly, and precisely so that others will understand what is meant, knowledge of the social amenities and good taste that should accompany communication with others, and the ability to speak and write correctly as judged by standards of good usage commonly accepted by cultured persons. Diagnosis is concerned with the evaluation and improvement of all of these forms of oral and written communication.

Principles Underlying the Teaching of Oral and Written Expression

In planning the instructional program in oral and written expression, with special reference to the diagnosis and treatment of learning difficulties, the teacher should bear in mind the following principles:

[2] Adapted from discussion by Paul McKee on pages 12 and 13 in *Teaching Language in the Elementary School.* Forty-third Yearbook, Part II, National Society for the Study of Education (Chicago, Univ. of Chicago Press, 1944).

1. The teacher should create a free, informal learning environment that is favorable to language development by arranging functional situations in which natural oral and written expression are essential. Language should be regarded as an integral element of all learning experiences.

2. The development of language power is an integral part of the child's growth pattern. Growth patterns differ from child to child. Hence it is necessary to adjust goals to the rate at which the individual is progressing. The attempt of some schools to set a given level of achievement and mastery of prescribed content as goals for all learners within a given class does violence to all the known facts about individual differences in growth.

3. The teacher should continuously study the growth of each individual in the class with a view to determining his stage of development and his strengths and weaknesses in oral and written expression. This can be done by studying the results of standard tests and scales, by the use of informal tests prepared by the teacher, and by observational data collected in daily contacts.

4. The pupils should be grouped according to their language needs. Language experiences adjusted to the difficulties and deficiencies of each learner should be planned, both group activities and individualized instruction, that are stimulating and satisfying to the individual.

5. In co-operation with the pupils, the teacher should develop means of individual and group evaluation which will make the pupils aware of the physical, intellectual, social, and emotional factors that influence their learning and lead them to desire improvement.

6. Special provision should be made for developmental and remedial instruction directed at specific learning difficulties of individual pupils. The basic understandings, skills, and abilities of language expression must be taught as systematically and definitely as similar items in arithmetic. Incidental teaching is not adequate for this purpose.

The reader should consult such books as the following, in addition to those referred to above, for an extended discussion of the application of these principles:

Paul McKee, *Language in the Elementary School* (Boston, Houghton, 1939).

R. C. Pooley, *Teaching English Usage* (New York, Appleton-Century-Crofts, 1946).

Teaching Language in the Elementary School, Forty-third Yearbook, Part II, National Society for the Study of Education (Chicago, Univ. of Chicago Press, 1944).

W. F. Tidyman and Marguerite Butterfield, *Teaching the Language Arts* (New York, McGraw, 1951).

FOUNDATIONS OF DIAGNOSIS IN ORAL AND WRITTEN EXPRESSION

Factors Underlying Oral and Written Expression

The aim of instruction in oral and written expression should be to provide a series of educative experiences which will develop in the learners the desire as well as the ability to express their ideas or to relate experiences in a clear, direct, interesting and forceful manner. At the same time, special consideration must be given to the correctness and suitability of the forms of expression used.

Language ability is very complex. It is made up of many component elements. Its development is affected by the social milieu. Three areas that are of special concern in diagnosis are (1) technical factors, (2) grammatical factors, and (3) rhetorical factors.

1. *Technical factors.* By technical factors are meant such items as fluency, pronunciation, enunciation, use of abbreviations, punctuation, capitalization, spelling, and handwriting.

2. *Grammatical factors.* By grammatical factors are meant such items as usage, forms of expression, and sentence structure.

3. *Rhetorical factors.* By rhetorical factors are meant such items as the choice of words, the richness and vividness of the vocabulary, the quality and suitability of the materials, the format used in writing materials, and the organization and logic of the discussion.

These three factors are involved in both oral and written speech. The essentials of oral and written expression are almost identical. Any statement, oral or written, should be made up of words that say clearly and precisely what is meant, should be grammatical, and should be well constructed. Since for most people oral language is the chief means of verbal expression, it should be given far greater emphasis than it receives at present.

In most schools, language instruction also includes the teaching of outlining, letter writing, use of the dictionary, bibliographical format, creative writing, appreciation of literature, and dramatics. Emphasis should be placed not on knowledge as such in all of these areas, but on the development of the ability of the pupils to use the procedures involved effectively in functional situations both in and out of school. Spoken English is used in a functional way in such activities as conversation, group meetings, practical discussions in everyday social situations, telling anecdotes and stories, and the like. Written language is used in a functional way in such activities as writing letters, preparing notices, writing reports of various kinds, taking notes, filling out forms, creative writing of various kinds, and the like. In the modern school every effort is made to provide pupil experiences in which oral and written expression are used in a functional way. Under such conditions there is likely to be genuine interest in improving the quality of expression and in mastering correct forms of expression.

The functions of diagnosis in oral and written expression are the appraisal of its effectiveness in life situations, the systematic analysis of weaknesses and deficiencies in all language areas, and the identification of factors that underlie them. On the basis of these findings, corrective measures can be undertaken.

GENERAL DIAGNOSIS IN ORAL AND WRITTEN EXPRESSION

Appraisal of the General Merit of Compositions

Appraisal in composition is almost wholly confined to written expression. Four methods of appraisal can be identified:

1. Composition scales for measuring general merit.
2. Scales for different kinds of discourse.
3. Standard tests of elements of written compositions.
4. Informal evaluative procedures.

Scales for Measuring General Merit of Compositions

Composition scales consist of a series of specimens of increasing merit. Each specimen is assigned a fixed value established by appropriate statistical procedures. To rate a composition, the rater compares its characteristics with those of specimens in the scale and gives it a value equal to that of the specimen which in the judgment of the rater its general merit most closely resembles.

The Hillegas and the Hudelson scales are the best-known scales of this kind. They are used to measure the general merit of compositions, not to analyze in detail the characteristics or the specific defects of the written work.

Two specimens of the Hillegas Scale [3] are given below. The first has a value of 3.6, which according to Hillegas is the standard for grade 4; the second has a rating of 5.9, which approximates the standard for grade 9. Thus the growth in composition ability between grades 4 and 9 is equal to the difference between these two specimens.

SPECIMENS FROM THE HILLEGAS SCALE
Sample 94

Value 3.6. Written by a boy in the second year of the high school, age 14 years.

When Sulla came back from his conquest Marius had put himself consul so sulla with the army he had with him in his conquest seized the government from

---

[3] Bureau of Publications, Teachers College, Columbia Univ., New York City.

Marius and put himself in consul and had a list of his enemys printy and the men whoes names were on this list we beheaded.

Sample 534

Value 5.9. Written by a boy in the fourth year of the high school, aged 16 years.

Fluellen

The passages given show the following characteristic of Fluellen: his inclination to brag, his professed knowledge of History, his complaining character, his great patriotism, pride of his leader, admired honesty, revengeful, love of fun and punishment of those who deserve it.

The following three specimens represent three levels of general merit on the Hudelson Scale:[4]

Value 1.0

A smow roll Fight om slatters hill

the boys wen up there am they had about a 150 smowballs arn Jack Harris hit Mat ames right in the stomict and they had smow balls goming fron side to side am about sunset the boy wer I happy am ome with his eye all with a rag aroung it the Gernorl what find soldiers I got they went doun the Hhill playing Yonce doe dolle dod

Value 4.0

A Snowball Fight on Slatter's Hill

The boys that lived in the south end of the town built a snow fort and had three hundred snowballs ready for their attack against their enemies, the boys from the North end of town. As their enemies passed they hit the leaden the very first one and then started on the rest. Not more than a dozen reached the fort and they were taken prisoners. After that when any fight was talked about the boys would always mention the Fight on Slatter's Hill.

Value 6.0

A Snowball Fight on Slatter's Hill

"Slatter's Hill was a rise of ground covering prhaps an acre and quarter of ground, generally termed "No Man's Land.""

"One Night the North Enders under command of Jack Harris quietly took charge of the hill and erected a strong snow fort. Fancy the chagrin of the South Enders next morning when they saw the North Enders in posassion of the stronghold. News traveled rapidly and soon it was learned that the South Enders under command of Mat Ames would attack the following Saturday.

"Saturday came and there was about thirty of we North Enders in the fort and a pile of about three-hundred snowballs. About 2 P.M. the South Enders made their attack, fifty strong and charged the fort. A well directed snowball from the hand of General J. Harris took General M. Ames in the pit of the stomach and the fight was on. The fight waged fiercely and thrise we were almost driven from the fort. But the boys fough gamely and we defeated the South Enders who marched away whistling "Yankee Doode," and we jeered them as they wnet."

[4] From Hudelson's *English Composition Scales* (Yonkers, N. Y., World Book).

"After the fight General Harris paying no attention to his black I said "Men I'm proud of you"

After that when any deed of bravery or pluck was mentioned the boys would say, "Golly you ought to have been at Slatter's Hill"

Detailed standard directions for securing and scoring compositions to be rated by these scales are given in the teachers' manuals that accompany them. The scales are not intended for the rating of the written materials prepared in connection with regular lessons. Hence their usefulness is limited.

Scales for Different Kinds of Discourse

Several scales have been published which can be used to evaluate different kinds of written composition.

1. *Harvard-Newton Composition Scales.* In 1914 Ballou produced separate scales for measuring four forms of discourse—narration, description, exposition, and argument. For each of the six specimens in each scale there is a brief summary of its merit and specific defects, and a discussion of the reasons for its rank in the scale.

2. *Willing Scales for Measuring English Composition.*[5] Willing devised a scale for measuring the story value and the form value of compositions. The scale consists of eight compositions, arranged in order of merit, each assigned a value in multiples of 10 ranging from 20 to 90. Each specimen is given a story value in terms of general merit. Each specimen is also assigned a form value based on the number of mechanical errors it contains. Each specimen in the scale is followed by a note indicating the number of errors per 100 written words in spelling, punctuation, and syntax. Thus a rating on this scale provides a general index of story value and form value. No provision is made for the detailed analysis of the three aspects of form or for any other factors.

The following specimen taken from the Willing Scale, value 40, shows the nature of the scale.

My antie had her barn trown down last week and had all her chickens killed from the storm. Whitch happened at twelve oclock at night. She had 30 chickens and one horse the horse was saved he ran over to our house and claped on the dor whit his feet. When we saw him my father took him in the barn where he slepped the night with our horse. When our antie told us about the accident we were very sory the next night all my anties things were frozen. The storm blew terrible the next morning and I could not go to school so I had to stay home the whole week.

Number of mistakes in spelling, punctuation, and syntax per hundred words, 17.

[5] Public School Publishing Co., Bloomington, Ill.

3. *Lewis English Composition Scales for Measuring Business and Social Correspondence.*[6] These scales consist of specimens written by school children in grades 3 to 11 under standard schoolroom conditions. The scales measure the general quality of order letters, letters of application, narrative social letters, expository social letters, and simple narration.

4. *Van Wagenen English Composition Scales.*[7] These are separate scales for judging expository, narrative, and descriptive writing. Each specimen on the scales is assigned separate values for structure, for content, and for mechanics, each term being defined to assist the rater. Each composition is assigned a threefold rating based on the values on the scale. It is possible to give a composition a final composite general rating according to directions accompanying the scales. To train raters, a series of sample specimens with standard ratings is provided. There is no specific analysis of elements of written compositions to facilitate diagnosis of deficiencies.

The following specimen taken from the narration scale illustrates the nature of the Van Wagenen Scales.

Structure 62   Mechanics 55   Thought Content 54

When Mother was Away

It was late in the spring when my mother went to the cities. It was so hot the most of the boys did not like to go to school in the afternoon so as no body was home to write my excuses I did not have to bring one and could stay out when ever I want to.

There was a bunch of us boys who were build a spring board and was staying out ever onc in while so we could get it done. Thise went one for about a week and the teacher found that we were staying out for our own good. And so she made us make up our time which was not so much fun as it was very hot and had to stay till six o'clock and then got a poor report card.

Informal Scales for Rating General Merit of Compositions

To assist teachers and children to rate written work in the course of day-to-day teaching, schools construct from time to time informal scales for rating various kinds of written work. Sometimes informal scales consist of specimens of written composition of varying degrees of merit based on daily work. The characteristics of the various samples are analyzed to bring out their values and limitations. These scales can thus be thoroughly functional in their use. An illustrative informal scale for rating friendly letters was developed in the Minneapolis schools. There are four models for each grade that serve as standards for rating letters. The following scale for grade 5 illustrates the nature of the scales for each grade.

[6] World Book Co., Yonkers, N. Y.
[7] *Ibid.*

MINNEAPOLIS LETTER RATING SCALE [8]

Fifth Grade

Poor

603 Tenth Avenue South,
Minneapolis, Minn.
May 28, 1924

Dear Friend:

Oh, say Vincent would you like to come to Minneapolis on your summer vacation? I know you would like to come up here. We can have a good time together. We could go swimming, fishing, hiking. We would visit Longfellows Gardens. We would go to the court house and see the statue of Father of Waters and we would hear the new chimes. Minneapolis is a very interesting city. It has many large buildings. I have a good time in Minneapolis here well good by come as soon as you can

From your loving friend,

The ejaculation in the opening sentence, the faulty sentence structure, monotonous repetition, poor organization, and errors in punctuation and capitalization classify this letter as poor. In content, it is better than the poor for fourth grade, because there is an effort on the part of the writer to interest his friend.

Fair

2450 First Ave. S.E.
Minneapolis, Minn.
May 28, 1924

Dear Max:

Will you come and visit me? I will be very happy if you do. All my friends have gone away. I will let you play with Blackie and our kittens. We will play with my bat and ball, and my football. I will take you to parks, and we will go for hikes.

We will go swimming and rowing with my boat. If you do not know how to swim, I will show you. It is very easy.

Your loving friend,

This letter is not good because of the meager vocabulary, immature sentence structure, and needless repetition. The form and mechanics are correct.

Good

2738 Bryant Avenue,
Minneapolis, Minn.
May 26, 1924

My dear Friend:

Mother and I would like very much to have you come to Minneapolis and spend the summer with us. I am sure you would have a delightful time for you could see the wonderful flour mills for which Minneapolis is noted. Also you could see the wonderful lakes. There are also sports that you would enjoy, such as horsebackriding, golfing, fishing, and swimming.

Kindly let us know as quickly as possible so we can make the necessary arrangements.

Your loving chum,

This letter is good because it is a sincere, earnest invitation, correct in form and mechanics. It is not excellent because the tone is formal and the personal note is lacking. It is also weakened by the repetition of "wonderful" and "also."

[8] Unpublished

Excellent   909 Oliver Ave. N.
                                                                        Minneapolis, Minn.
                                                                        May 26, 1924

Dear Lois:

Mother says I may have any guest I wish to spend the summer with me. I choose you from a large group of dear friends and cousins. At our summer home near Minneapolis we have a beautiful lawn which extends to the lake. On the south side of the house there is a garden, bordered by many trees, not orange or fig trees as you have in California, but trees which bear nice juicy, red apples which I'm sure you would like. Please, Lois, write at once telling me when you are coming.

                                        Your loving cousin,

The personal touch in this letter, the good descriptive words, and the skillful use made of comparison mark it as excellent. It is also correct as to form and mechanics.

Standardized Survey Tests of Elements of Written English

Standard batteries of achievement tests in almost every instance include tests in the field of language. For example, one section of the Stanford Achievement Test,[9] intermediate battery, is called "language." The test contains seventy selected items, some of them testing knowledge of capitalization and punctuation, others sentence structure, others language usage. The language score is based on the composite results for these three kinds of knowledge. The test is intended for survey purposes; the items are merely representative of the knowledges tested and are not comprehensive enough for diagnosis of the ability of individual pupils. Similarly the California Achievement Tests, intermediate form, contain 65 items: 15 in capitalization, 10 in punctuation, 20 in words and sentences, and 20 in parts of speech. For each part and for the composite data, grade scores are derivable which are suitable for survey purposes. However, the tests are not suitable for diagnosis of individual needs. This same limitation applies to the language tests in other batteries of tests.

There are also standard tests of various aspects of English composition which are suitable for general survey purposes but not for analytical diagnosis. Illustrations are the Briggs English Form Test [10] and the Wilson Language Error Test.[11]

There are no standard scales for rating oral composition or speech.

The Limitations of Scales and Tests

The chief limitation of composition scales and most of the available language tests is that they remove language from the social setting in which it normally occurs and in which the learner's most serious difficulties emerge.

---

[9] World Book Co., Yonkers, N. Y.
[10] Bureau of Publications, Teachers College, Columbia Univ.
[11] World Book Co., Yonkers, N. Y.

Hence standardized tests should be supplemented by informal techniques of evaluation, including anecdotal records, free and directed observation of the behavior and work habits of children in social situations both in and out of school, recordings of oral speech, collections of the written work of pupils that can be examined for evidences of growth, interest inventories, check-lists, and similar procedures that are discussed in Chapter 2.

Another limitation of scales and tests is that they have stressed the rhetorical, grammatical, and mechanical elements of expression and have neglected such vital factors as the organization of ideas, the originality, freshness, and inventiveness of thought, and the vividness of language for which teachers are always striving. Furthermore, a pupil's ability to use a particular mark of punctuation or word usage in a test is no assurance that he will use it properly in ordinary writing. Nor does the recognition of incorrect forms of expression insure the use of the correct form in conversation. In testing language abilities, every effort must be made to devise methods of appraisal that require the learners to respond in functional situations [12] which approximate closely those in daily life.

The lack of reliability in the ratings of compositions by both trained and untrained scorers also makes it difficult to compare measurements made by different persons. When reliable ratings of general merit are desired, the average of the ratings of three scorers should be used.

Perhaps the most serious limitation in the use of quality scales is the "over-all" character of the ratings. A composition may be rated low on a scale, yet the pupil gets no information as to the reasons for the low rating. Such ratings do not clarify goals for the learner, do not direct his learning, and do not supply the teacher with information useful in planning the instructional program.

Informal Evaluative Procedures

Many appraisal procedures less formal than the scales and standard survey tests described above can be used by teachers in studying pupil progress in language. These are similar to the general evaluative procedures discussed in Chapter 2 and should be regarded as essentials of the instructional program. Pupil participation in the evaluation of their progress will help them discover their needs and interests. The following analysis summarizes the evaluative procedures that can be applied in the course of regular instruction:

1. Objective test found in textbooks and workbooks, or prepared by the teacher as the need arises.
2. The application of criteria and standards prepared co-operatively by teacher and pupils to evaluate any oral or written composition or performance.

[12] Dora V. Smith, "Recent Procedures in the Evaluation of Programs of English," *Journal of Educational Research,* Vol. 38 (December, 1944), pp. 262-275.

3. Product or behavior rating scales.
4. Questionnaires: of interests, of extent of participation in language activities in life outside the school.
5. Informal interviews with learners and associates about aspects of language work.
6. Anecdotal records of significant behavior, creative power, speech difficulties.
7. Sound recordings kept for closer examination.
8. Use of check-lists to study responses of pupils.
9. Keeping lists of language errors in oral speech in classroom and elsewhere; also of speech defects and difficulties.
10. Evidence of extent of creative writing by pupils, and participation in language experiences connected with the school activity program.

ANALYTICAL DIAGNOSIS IN ORAL AND WRITTEN EXPRESSION

Analytical Diagnostic Tests

Ratings of compositions based on scales and the results of survey tests of language abilities provide general information about the level of a pupil's language development, but more complete diagnosis is needed to determine the nature of shortcomings and deficiencies which may require corrective treatment or further development. There are available a number of carefully constructed diagnostic tests that provide separate measures of specific language abilities. Typical tests are the following:

1. *Iowa Elementary Language Tests.* These tests measure word meaning, language usage, grammatical form recognition, sentence sense, sentence structure, capitalization and punctuation, and paragraph organization. The profile of test results reveals at a glance areas of weakness. An item analysis will reveal specific deficiencies in the items included for the class as a whole or for individuals. However, the sampling of items is too limited for detailed diagnosis.

2. *Iowa Every Pupil Tests of Basic Skills, Test C, Language Skills.* The elementary form of this test contains five parts: punctuation, capitalization, usage, spelling, and sentence sense.

3. *Metropolitan Achievement Test—English Test.* This eleven-page test covers language usage, punctuation, capitalization, grammar, literature, and spelling.

4. *Pribble-McCrory Diagnostic Elementary Language Tests, Forms A, B, and C.* Four tests are included: language usage, capitalization, pronunciation, and punctuation.

None of the survey tests or analytical diagnostic tests now available provides for a comprehensive diagnosis of specific deficiencies in language. For example, tests of punctuation, such as that of Briggs, contain only a small sampling of the uses of the various marks of punctuation from which a general measure of ability is derived. Tests are needed which include examples of all of the socially useful applications of the various marks. The same is true of tests of capitalization, sentence structure, and usage. Procedures for constructing analytical diagnostic tests will be described in a later section of this chapter.

Analytical Diagnosis of Technical Aspects of Composition

By technical aspects of composition we mean the format of various forms of writing, such as letters and outlines, punctuation, capitalization, spelling, and handwriting. No available analytical diagnostic tests in either punctuation or capitalization are comprehensive enough for adequate diagnosis of specific deficiencies. Most of the available tests contain only small samplings. A detailed discussion on diagnosis of deficiencies in spelling and handwriting is given in Chapters 11 and 12.

Diagnosis of Format. In most language textbooks and workbooks there are standard forms for letters of various kinds and outlines with which the pupil can compare the format of his own written work. Departures from acceptable forms can thus be quickly discovered by the pupil himself.

Diagnosis in Punctuation. The most direct method of analyzing punctuation difficulties is through scrutiny of the pupil's written work. The teacher can prepare a check-list of the various marks of punctuation and on it tally the number of times each is incorrectly used or omitted in the composition. As a general index of ability, the teacher may count the total number of errors made by the pupil. A total of at least 1200 written words should be examined to get a fairly dependable measure of the pupil's ability to punctuate. A smaller sampling is inadequate. This procedure is time-consuming and rather difficult but very useful, especially in studying the work of pupils whose scores on standard or informal tests were low.

The diagnostic analysis of errors in the pupils' free written work has a number of limitations. It is quite probable that the need for some of the important uses of various marks does not arise in his composition, hence his knowledge of these and his ability to use them will not be tested. It is also difficult to analyze the errors made in compositions since they occur in a random, disorganized way, not as they would appear in a set sequence in a systematically constructed test. It should be recognized that written composition is a functional test of ability to use punctuation marks correctly. However, to test actual knowledge of a wide variety of important marks a systematic printed or dictated test is more fruitful.

The Construction of Proofreading Tests

A simple diagnostic technique is the administration of a proofreading exercise so constructed that the pupils' knowledge of the various important uses of each punctuation mark is tested in a functional way. There are no standard tests of this kind available, but competent research has developed effective diagnostic test procedures suitable for classroom use. The work of Lines [13] will be used to illustrate the steps to be taken in the preparation of a proofreading test in punctuation. The test appears on pages 317-319.

The first step is to make a detailed analysis of the usages of punctuation marks to be tested. Then short sentences should be prepared, each involving one example of a specific usage, such as the period after initials in proper names. Lines found that to insure reliability of diagnosis at least three illustrations of each usage should be included in the test. This is necessary because of significant variations in the specific usage under differing conditions. In the test itself, the mark being tested is omitted and is to be inserted by the pupil. The three sentences testing each use should be placed together in a group to facilitate diagnosis.

In Lines's diagnostic test in punctuation 32 specific uses of seven different marks are tested. The complete list of uses is given below with illustrations and also the numbers of the three sentences in the Lines test on pages 317-318 that deal with each usage of a given mark.

PUNCTUATION USAGE ILLUSTRATED IN THE LINES DIAGNOSTIC TEST

PART I—THE PERIOD

Use	Illustration	Sentences
1. At the end of a sentence:	"The books are on the desk."	1-2-3
2. After an abbreviation in titles of persons and things:	"Dr. Jones"	4-5-6
3. After an abbreviation of parts of an address:	"The Baker Co."	7-8-9
4. After initials in proper names:	"H. A. Brown"	10-11-12

PART II—THE COMMA

Use	Illustration	Sentences
5. Between the parts of a compound sentence joined by a short conjunction:	"Mr. Anderson took Everett, and Lowell went in Mrs. Frank's car."	13-14-15
6. In nouns of address:	"Friends, I am here!"	16-17-18
7. After words or phrases of introduction:	"Yes, we expect to be home."	19-20-21
8. After clauses of introduction:	"While we were eating, the fire siren sounded."	22-23-24
9. After words in a series:	"John, George, Fred, and Grace are cousins."	25-26-27
10. Before and after appositives:	"The governor, Stanley B. Franklin, addressed the crowd."	28-29-30

[13] Clifton Lines, *Diagnostic Testing in the Field of English.* Unpublished Masters dissertation, Univ. of Minnesota, 1936.

Use	Illustration	Sentences
11. Before and after a non-restrictive clause:	"This man, who has a very large house, is well to do."	31-32-33
12. Before and after parenthetical expressions:	"You told your mother, I suppose, about the accident."	34-35-36
13. To set off short direct quotations:	"We are ready to leave," called the boys.	37-38-39
14. To separate the parts of a date—the day from year:	"May 26, 1936"	40-41-42
15. To set off the name of city from state or country:	"Duluth, Minnesota"	43-44-45
16. After such expressions as "hello":	"Hello, Jack."	46-47-48

PART III—THE SEMICOLON

17. Between co-ordinate clauses which are not joined by a conjunction:	"William's dog is a fox terrier; mine is a spaniel."	49-50-51
18. Between co-ordinate clauses which contain internal punctuation:	"If you find the pin, please let me know; but don't bother to look for it."	52-53-54

PART IV—THE COLON

19. To separate figures indicating hours and minutes:	"Our train leaves at 2:30 A.M."	55-56-57
20. Before long or formal enumerations:	"Mother asked us to buy the following groceries: apples, sugar, salt, and cocoa."	58-59-60

PART V—QUOTATION MARKS TO ENCLOSE DIRECT ADDRESS

21. In unbroken quotation, with the descriptive element preceding the quotation:	He wired, "Meet me tonight at six."	61-62-63
22. In an unbroken quotation, with the descriptive element following the quotation:	"This is the road," shouted Harry.	64-65-66
23. In a broken quotation:	"All right," said he, "I'll do it."	67-68-69

PART VI—THE APOSTROPHE

24. In a singular possessive:	"My father's car."	70-71-72
25. In a plural possessive:	"Girls' school."	73-74-75
26. In a proper noun ending in *s*:	"Dickens' best novels."	76-77-78
27. In a contraction:	"Doesn't."	79-80-81

Use	Illustration	Sentences
28. In a plural possessive that is a proper name:	"Norwegians' annual celebration."	82-83-84
29. In the possessive of children (and similar words)	"Children's hour."	85-86-87
30. In the plurals of letters of the alphabet and numbers:	"Have you learned your A, B, C's?"	88-89-90

PART VII—THE QUESTION MARK

31. At the end of a direct question:	"Is this your bill?"	91-92-93
32. After a direct question but within the sentence:	"Will you be ready?" the man asked.	

An Illustrative Diagnostic Test in Punctuation

The diagnostic test in punctuation devised by Lines is given below. It is divided into seven parts, one for each mark of punctuation. The ability of the pupil to insert the missing mark correctly is regarded as a measure of his knowledge of its use.

LINES DIAGNOSTIC TEST IN PUNCTUATION

NAME_____ AGE_____ GRADE_____ SCHOOL_____ DATE_____ SCORE_____

Directions: There are exercises in seven (7) kinds of punctuation marks: the period, comma, semicolon, colon, quotation marks, apostrophe, and question mark. Each sentence illustrates one usage, so read carefully each exercise. Be sure to get the meaning; then to make it clear, insert the proper mark or marks.

PART I:

1. The new books are on the desk
2. I have just finished reading a book called "Hitty"
3. Sister said, "I hoped we might have chicken"
4. Dr Jones came to see me.
5. We heard a speech by Mr Nelson.
6. We often write Jan for January.
7. Ia is the shorter form for Iowa.
8. The Baker Co sells dry goods and groceries.
9. He lives at No 18 Grant Street.
10. J B Hagen is chairman of the meeting.
11. Do you know H A Brown?
12. The Y M C A is in charge of the contest.

PART II:

13. I didn't like their plan but there seemed no better proposition.
14. Mother had cleaned the house for she expected company that day.
15. Mr. Anderson took Everett and Lowell went in Mrs. Frank's car.
16. Where are you going Allen?
17. Friends I am here!
18. My book John is in the desk.

19. Yes we expect to be home.
20. By the way I have your book.
21. Well what shall we do about it?
22. While we were eating the fire siren sounded.
23. As the boys approached the battle began.
24. Before the exercises began the boy scouts marched on to the platform.
25. We shall elect a president a secretary and a treasurer.
26. John George Fred and Grace are cousins.
27. Our cook put up sandwiches pickles milk and cake for our lunch.
28. The governor Stanley B. Franklin addressed the immense gathering.
29. It is Mary my sister who has been very ill.
30. Willow Beach a summer resort is in northern Minnesota.
31. This man who has a very large house is well to do.
32. Los Angeles where I spent the summer is the pride of southern California.
33. Charles Lindbergh who flew the Atlantic was born in Minnesota.
34. You told your mother I suppose about the accident.
35. There was as I have often said no question about his being guilty.
36. The result will depend of course on how hard you work.
37. "We are ready to leave" called the boys.
38. Bob said "Don't forget to bring your lunch."
39. "Oh dear" sighed Dora "What next!"
40. May we expect you June 10 1936?
41. We shall arrive in Minneapolis, May 26, 1936.
42. Stories of July 4 1776 shall ring again in picturesque style.
43. They plan to visit in Duluth Minnesota this summer.
44. London England is an interesting city.
45. The oldest store in Helena Montana was rocked by an earthquake.
46. "Hello Jack, you're just in time!" shouted his roommate.
47. We heard her say, "Hello Mr. Johnson."
48. Well, hello Elsie. How are you today?

PART III:

49. William's dog is a fox terrier mine is a spaniel.
50. Some houses are small others are large.
51. Robert intends to study medicine he will enter the university in September.
52. If you find the pin, please let me know but don't bother to look for it.
53. No, Merrill, you may not go swimming today you're going to stay home and help me with the garden.
54. We invited Madge, Esther, and Evelyn but, it seems, they could not come.

PART IV:

55. Our train leaves at 2 3 0 A.M.
56. Hurry, it is past 2 0 0 o'clock now!
57. It is 1 0 3 0, and all is well.
58. Mother asked us to buy the following groceries apples, sugar, salt, and cocoa.
59. Our teacher has taught us to draw four things, a house, a tree, a flower, and a rabbit.
60. Tell me the author of this quotation "Friends, Romans, Countrymen, lend me your ears. I come to bury Caesar, not to praise him."

PART V:

61. The passing tourist yelled, What town is this?
62. He wired, Meet me tonight at six.
63. He waited patiently until mother called, Dinner is served.
64. This is the road, shouted Harry.
65. Where is my cap? he asked.
66. It's on fire! she shrieked.
67. All right, said he, I'll do it.
68. It is impossible, declared Dick, to work all of the problems.
69. I'm not going, Dad, said Jack, but brother Bill is.

PART VI:

70. My fathers car is here.
71. He hurt Bills dog.
72. He is a wolf in sheeps clothing.
73. Womens hats are so unusual.
74. Ethel is attending a girls school.
75. Several pupils books are badly worn.
76. One of Dickens best novels is "David Copperfield."
77. Mr. Jones house is that big white one on the left.
78. Charles promise to his mother was kept.
79. Doesnt the driver realize the danger?
80. I am not so sure that well be home early.
81. John isnt here yet, so we shall wait.
82. The many Indians tepees were made of birch bark.
83. The teacher pictured clearly the early Vikings boats.
84. Minneapolis is the center of the Norwegians annual celebration.
85. You may play after the childrens story hour.
86. The childs book is very beautiful.
87. "The Childrens Hour" was written by Longfellow.
88. Have you learned your A, B, Cs?
89. Don't forget to dot your is and cross your ts.
90. You need practice on your figure 8s.

PART VII:

91. Do you think he will permit us to attend
92. Where are you going
93. Is this your ball
94. "Will you be ready" the men asked
95. "Do you expect her today" questioned father.
96. "My dear, what is disturbing you" asked Jerry. "I'll wager it is your friend, Alice"

The Scoring of Proofreading Tests

Scoring a proofreading test is quite simple. First the items should be checked on the test paper as right or wrong. Insertions of unnecessary marks can be noted but need not be tabulated at this time. Then the number of items correct on each part of the test should be found. To get a composite score, the teacher should find the total number correct on all parts of the test. A comparison of the total scores for individual pupils provides a basis for evaluating their work. For more detailed diagnosis, the number of times each item was not answered correctly should be found for the class as a whole. It is even better to find the number of correct answers for each group of three sentences testing the same idea. On this basis, a dependable diagnosis can be made of the weak spots for the class as a whole and also of the specific needs of each pupil in the class. A tally of the specific items missed by each pupil can be made for detailed diagnosis on a blank such as the one below.

Test Items on Part I

Pupil	1	2	3	4	5	6	7	8	9	10	11	12
John	x	x	x				x			x	x	

The Relative Difficulty of Marks of Punctuation

A summary of the results of the administration of the Lines test to 200 pupils in each of grades 5, 7, 9, and 11 is given in the table below. Data are given for each of the seven parts of the test, including the average number of errors and the percentage of error on each part of the test for each grade, and also for the total test.

SUMMARY OF ERRORS FOR TEST PARTS; AVERAGE NUMBER
OF ERRORS AND PERCENTAGE OF ERRORS

TEST PART *	GRADE 5		GRADE 7		GRADE 9		GRADE 11	
	Avg. No. Errors	*% of Error*	*Avg. No. Errors*	*% of Error*	*Avg. No. Errors*	*% of Error*	*Avg. No. Errors*	*% of Error*
I ..	1.8	15	0.5	4	0.3	2	0.2	1
II ..	17.8	50	9.7	27	3.8	11	2.8	9
III ..	4.2	70	2.5	41	1.5	25	1.0	16
IV ..	3.0	50	1.2	20	0.6	10	0.3	6
V ..	4.5	50	1.3	14	0.5	5	0.2	3
VI ..	13.7	65	7.6	36	4.3	20	3.2	15
VII ..	2.1	35	0.9	15	0.3	5	0.3	5
Total	47.1	49	23.7	25	11.3	12	8.0	8

* The seven parts of the test follow in this order: period, comma, semicolon, colon, quotation marks, apostrophe, and question mark.

The data reveal in an interesting way growth in the ability of children to use the various punctuation marks measured by this test. The stage of most rapid growth on all parts of the test is from grade 5 to grade 7. By grade 11 the percentages of error are quite small, except for Parts III and VI. In grade 5 the percentages of error are greatest for Part III—Uses of semicolon, and Part VI—Uses of Apostrophe. In grade 5 the percentages of error are smallest, but they are substantial, on Part I—Period, and Part VII —Question mark. The reader should carefully scrutinize the data for other parts of the test and for the other grades. The teacher who administers the Lines test or a similar home-made test will secure valuable information about the specific deficiencies of the class as a whole, and also of individual pupils, to be used as a basis for planning an improvement program.

Analytical Diagnosis in Capitalization

According to Dawson,[14] the following common uses of capitalization, not arranged in teaching sequence, should be included in the language program. The list can be used to analyze errors in capitalization made in regular written work as described for punctuation above. It can also be the basis of a proofreading test in capitalization which can be constructed and scored according to the plan described above for punctuation. Both methods should be used, one to check the other. In diagnosis, special consideration should be given to incorrect uses of capitalization which occur most frequently.

CAPITALIZATION

1. Capitalization of first words of:
    a. Sentence.
    b. Line of poetry.
    c. Direct quotation.
    d. Title.

2. Capitalization of names and titles of particular:
    a. Places: schools, streets, cities, states, nations, and important geographic localities.
    b. Days of week, months, special days.
    c. Persons, pets.
    d. Initials, abbreviations of proper names.
    e. Organizations with which children have contacts.
    f. Races, nationalities, school subjects named for nationalities.
    g. Company or firm.
    h. Brand or special product.

3. Capitalization of the following miscellaneous items:
    a. The pronoun "I."
    b. Topics in an outline.
    c. The first and each important word in titles of books, pictures, magazine articles, etc.

Acceptable Formats for Objective Tests

Teachers are frequently called on to prepare objective test items to evaluate various aspects of composition. The following formats are recommended:

[14] Mildred A. Dawson and Frieda H. Dingee, *Directing Learning in the Language Arts* (Minneapolis, Burgess Publishing Co., 1948), p. 169.

1. CAPITALIZATION:

    a. Mark any word in the sentences below that should be capitalized. Be careful not to mark any word which should not be capitalized.

    Sample: Where was Washington born?

    b. Read the sentences below carefully. See the words with numbers under them. In the spaces at the right put *X* under "capital" if the word should be capitalized and under "small" if it should be written with a small letter.

    Sample: Did tom hear the bell?   Capital   Small
              1   2   1 (*X*)   ( )
                                          2 ( )   (*X*)

2. PUNCTUATION:

    a. Draw a line under the word that is written correctly.

    Sample: (Isnt) (Isn't) (Is'nt) Tom here?

    b. Draw a line under the correct mark in the sentence.

    Sample: Is John going with us (:) (?) (.)

3. USAGE

    a. Mark with a cross the word below that is correctly used in the sentence.

    Sample: (There, their) are twelve things in a dozen.

    b. Two deer $\begin{smallmatrix}\text{was}\\\text{were}\end{smallmatrix}$ seen in the field.

The Usefulness of Dictation Exercises for Test Purposes

To test specific kinds of knowledge in written composition the teacher can at times prepare short, simple sentences in which the items to be tested are embedded, for instance, marks of punctuation, capitalization, or usage. The teacher can then dictate the sentences and the children write them as a test of their knowledge. This procedure is functional in nature, since the conditions approximate those of normal writing. An analysis of the written work by the teacher quickly reveals the weak spots in the items tested. Care must be taken not to use words in the test sentences which the children do not know or may find difficult to spell. Proofreading tests are preferable to dictated test exercises, but both forms should be used, one to check the other.

Evaluating Oral Composition

There are no standard tests for measuring the quality of oral composition. Preliminary work along this line has been done by Netzer,[15] who secured recordings of oral reports and compositions, had them transcribed, and then attempted to derive scale values. In a number of schools, tape recordings have been made for similar purposes, and in some instances informal scales

[15] Royal F. Netzer, *The Evaluation of a Technique for Measuring Improvement in Oral Expression*. Unpublished Ph.D. thesis, Univ. of Iowa, 1937.

have been developed. However, little progress has been made in the construction of dependable scales or procedures for measuring the quality of oral composition.

A discussion of the diagnosis of speech problems as such is included in a later section of this chapter.

Diagnosis in Spelling and Handwriting

A general measure of accuracy of spelling in written composition can be secured by finding the coefficient of misspelling. Briefly, this amounts to finding the percentage of all words written that were misspelled in the composition. The details of the method of finding the coefficient of misspelling are given on page 351.

The quality of handwriting can be measured by scales described in Chapter 12. More detailed analysis of handwriting deficiencies is possible by applying diagnostic procedures also described in the same chapter.

Diagnosis of Errors in Pronunciation and Articulation

According to Abney,[16] the most frequent errors of pronunciation easily detected in oral speech are:

1. Incorrect vowel quality, as in *get, catch, just.*
2. Incorrect consonant quality, as in *what, immediately, walking.*
3. Misplaced accent, as in *research, discharge.*
4. Omission of requisite sounds, as in *recognize, really, February.*
5. Sounding silent letters, as in *often, toward, corps.*
6. The addition of superfluous sounds, as in *athlete, once, elm.*
7. The utterance of sounds in improper order, as *children, hundred.*

According to McKee,[17] some of the most common difficulties in articulation are the *s* lisp; *t* for *k; d* for *g, th, r, l; w* for *wh;* and *n* for *ing.*

Analytical Diagnosis of Grammatical Factors

Basic problems in grammar involve sentence structure, agreement of subject and verb, relations of nouns and pronouns, verb forms and auxiliaries, usage of various forms of adjectives and adverbs, and the use of modification and subordinate clauses. Deficiencies in most of these knowledges are revealed by several of the analytical diagnostic tests described on page 313. Errors also manifest themselves in all types of oral and written expression and are easily identified and recorded.

Analysis of Grammatical Errors in Oral Speech. Analysis of errors in oral speech is greatly facilitated if the teacher uses a check-list of the most fre-

[16] *Teaching Language in the Elementary School,* Forty-third Yearbook, Part II, National Society for the Study of Education (Chicago, Univ. of Chicago Press, 1944), p. 186.

[17] Paul McKee, *Language in the Elementary School* (Boston, Houghton, 1939), p. 318.

quent types of errors that are known to be present in oral speech. An excellent illustration is the check-list used by teachers in Minneapolis on which were given the most common errors in verbs, pronouns, prepositions, adjectives, adverbs, negative forms, and syntactical redundancy. Each type was illustrated. Teachers were instructed to observe the oral speech of their pupils for a period of a week and to record in the proper space on the blank the types of errors they made. Space was provided for recording additional errors not listed.

The observation of children's responses during free activity periods, civic league meetings, and similar occasions when there was uninhibited expression proved to be the most productive way of securing data on language errors in oral speech. Apparently few errors are made in ordinary lessons when pupil responses are often limited to single words, such as *yes* and *no,* and so on, and brief statements.

The outline of the Minneapolis check-list is given below. An analysis of it will show the kinds of errors that are peculiar to oral speech. They reflect the speech habits of the community and as such appear less frequently in written speech.

CHECK-LIST FOR ANALYSIS OF ERRORS IN ORAL SPEECH

1. Verbs
   a. Wrong verbs, as *learn* for *teach, set* for *sit.*
   b. Impossible tense forms, as *seen* for *saw, drawed.*
   c. Perfect participle for past tense and reverse, as *done, have came.*
   d. Wrong tense-present for past, as *come* for *came, says* for *said.*
   e. Use of verb for noun, as *that doesn't hurt* for *that doesn't make any difference.*
   f. Incorrect use of mood, as *if it was not* for *were not.*
   g. Failure of verb to agree with subject in number, as *he don't.*

2. Pronouns
   a. First personal pronoun standing first in series, as *I and my brother.*
   b. Accusative pronoun for subject, as *Frank and me.*
   c. Pronoun for demonstrative adjective, as *them* for *these.*
   d. Predicate nominative not in nominative case, as *it was me, it's us.*
   e. Wrong pronoun, as *that, which,* for *who, whose.*
   f. Object of verb or preposition not in objective case, as *I know who he saw, with George and I.*
   g. Failure of pronoun to agree with antecedent in number, as *each of them took their guns.*
   h. Pronoun for adverb, *They are two pens lying,* etc.
   i. Wrong form of pronoun, as *hisself, hisn.*

3. Prepositions
   a. Confusion of preposition and conjunction, as *He does it like she does.*
   b. Wrong preposition, as *by my aunt's; would of, had a* for *would have had to; stays to home, different to.*

4. Adjectives and Adverbs
   a. Confusion of adjective and adverb, as *that there, awful* for *very, good* for *well*.
   b. Wrong article, as *a* for *an*.
   c. Misuse of adjective, as *funny, lots*, etc. for *queer, many*.
   d. Double comparison, as *more stronger, worser* for *stronger, worse*.
   e. Wrong comparison, as *gooder*.
   f. Superlative for comparative, as *largest*.
   g. Misuse of adverb, as *awfully* for *very, dreadfully*.

5. Negatives
   a. *Haven't no* for *haven't any; never gave*.

6. Ambiguous Expressions
   a. *A hand and an arm with a sword in it*.

7. Words Mispronounced, as *somepin* for *something; readin', nothin'*, etc.; *onct; youse; viaduck* for *viaduct; half* for *have*.

8. Syntactical Redundancy, as *got* (in *ain't got, haven't got*); *my mother, she; all two, all both; he says, says he*.

Classroom teachers should prepare similar check-lists and use them to survey the oral speech of their children. A special study may be made of the oral speech characteristics of particular individuals whose responses indicate many faults and marked deficiencies. The direct use of this form of analysis is more time-consuming than ordinary paper-and-pencil tests of knowledge of correct forms of written speech, but it illustrates the possibility of testing the oral speech characteristics of children in normal, natural social situations.

Diagnosis of Grammatical Errors in Written Speech. The teacher can use the Minneapolis check-list of errors in oral speech to analyze many kinds of grammatical errors in written speech.

Another list based on studies of errors in written speech other than punctuation and capitalization is an error guide developed by Willing. It stresses more technical aspects of grammar than are encompassed in the Minneapolis check-list. He used it to make a systematic analysis and summary of errors in grammar that appeared in written compositions. To arrive at a dependable diagnosis of deficiencies in grammar for individual pupils, he found it necessary to secure a series of compositions containing approximately 1200 words. Because of the time-consuming nature of this procedure, Willing recommended the use of proofreading exercises similar to those described above for capitalization. They test actual knowledge under test conditions. Tests are easily scored and the results quickly summarized, but they do not actually indicate the errors the pupil will make in free written work.

A portion of Willing's error guide, the sections for grammar and sentence structure, is given below.[18] Teachers can adapt it as they may wish in making an analysis of faults in written speech.

A. GRAMMAR

1. Agreement of Verbs and Subjects:
    a. Compound subject with single parts.
    b. Intervening expressions.
    c. Expletive *there* constructions.
    d. *Don't* usages.
    e. Subjects such as *each, everyone.*
    f. Attraction of predicate nouns.
    g. Other cases, verbs following subject.
    m. Miscellaneous.

2. Agreement of Pronouns and Antecedents:
    a. In number, where antecedents are such as *each, everyone.*
    b. In number, miscellaneous.
    c. In gender.

3. Agreements, Miscellaneous:
    a. Subjects and predicate nouns.
    b. Adjective pronouns.
    m. Miscellaneous.

4. Pronoun Cases:
    a. As object of preposition.
    b. As object of verbal.
    c. As complement of verbal.
    d. As object of transitive verb.
    e. As predicate pronoun.
    f. As subject of a verb.
    g. In elliptical clauses.
    h. As an appositive.
    i. With gerunds requiring possessive.
    j. As subject of infinitive.

5. Verbs—Tense and Tense Forms:
    a. Present for past or vice versa.
    b. Past for past perfect.
    c. Complementary infinitive.
    d. Sequence.
    g. Participle for past and vice versa.
    h. Wrong participle form.
    i. Omitted tense endings, participles.
    j. *Shall* and *will* in future.
    k. *Should* and *would* in future.
        (Note: Confusion of verbs—e.g., *lie* and *lay; sit* and *set*—are under word usage. *Of* for *have* also.)

[18] M. H. Willing, *Valid Diagnosis in High School Composition,* Contributions to Education No. 230 (New York, Bureau of Publications, Teachers College, Columbia Univ., 1926).

6. Verbs—Miscellaneous Errors:
   a. Subjunctive in contrary-to-fact conditions.
   b. Other subjunctive mode errors.
   d. Errors with modal auxiliaries (*may* and *can* in word usage).

7. Nouns—Miscellaneous Errors:
   a. Form of possessive (not apostrophe)
   b. Possessive with gerunds.
   c. Confusion with adjectives.
   d. Wrong number forms.
   e. Plural endings carelessly omitted.
   f. Wrong number.
   m. Miscellaneous.

8. Adjectives and Adverbs:
   a. Confusion of the two.
   b. Wrong comparative or superlative forms.
   c. Superlative for comparative.
   d. Comparative for superlative.
   m. Miscellaneous.

9. Conjunctions and Prepositions:
   a. Confusion of the two.
   b. Error in matching correlatives.
      (Note: Various types of similar errors are under sentence structure and word usage.)

B. SENTENCE STRUCTURE (S)

1. Incompleteness:
   a. Nouns, alone or with modifiers, for sentences.
   b. Participial phrases for sentences.
   c. Prepositional phrases for sentences.
   d. Infinitive phrase for sentences.
   e. Dependent clauses for sentences.
   f. Missing subjects.
   i. Missing verb.
   j. Missing complement.
   s. Sentences too short.
   m. Miscellaneous.

2. Overloadedness and Disjointedness:
   a. Sentence with vague *so* clause.
   c. Sentence with unrelated or vaguely related clauses strung together with or without conjunctions ("comma blunder" type not here).
   d. Sentences separated by comma instead of by period (or semi-colon).
   e. The "and" sentence (At least two *and's* joining clauses).
   f. The "but" sentence (At least two *but's* joining clauses).
   g. The "so" sentence.
   h. The "then" sentence.
   i. Other rambling sentences.
   m. Miscellaneous.

3. Reference of Pronouns and Modifiers:
    a. Weak, broad, or divided reference of pronouns.
    b. Dangling participles.
    c. Dangling gerund phrases.
    d. Dangling elliptical phrases.
    e. Indefinite *thus* or *so*.
    f. Reference of participle or adjective to a possessive.
    m. Miscellaneous.

4. Arrangement of Parts:
    a. Misplaced words, modifiers chiefly.
    b. Misplaced phrases.
    c. Misplaced clauses.
    d. Split constructions.
    m. Miscellaneous.

5. Parallel Structure:
    a. Different parts of speech in series.
    b. Verbals not balanced.
    d. Phrases over against clauses.
    e. Words over against phrases and clauses.
    f. Clauses not balanced.
    g. Verbs not balanced as to voice.
    m. Miscellaneous.

6. Point of View or Consistency:
    a. Uncalled-for shift of subject.
    b. Uncalled-for shift in mode, modal aspect, or kind of conjugation.
    c. Uncalled-for time shift.
    d. Mixed construction.
    e. Confusion.
    m. Miscellaneous.

7. Co-ordination and Subordination:
    a. *And* versus *but*.
    b. Other confusions of co-ordinate conjunctions.
    c. Wrong subordinating conjunctions.
    d. Co-ordinate versus subordinate conjunctions.
    e. *And* between non-co-ordinates.
    m. Miscellaneous.

8. Omissions:
    a. *That* and *as if*.
    b. Prepositions.
    c. Articles.
    d. Conjunctions in comparisons.
    e. *Other* after *any* in comparisons.
    f. Miscellaneous omissions in comparisons.
    g. Omitted *and* or *but* between words.
    h. Careless omissions.
    m. Miscellaneous.

9. Repetitions—Wordiness:
   a. Unnecessary repetition of same conjunction in sentence.
   b. Unnecessary repetition of relatives.
   c. Unnecessary repetition in general.
   d. Careless repetitions.
   e. Careless leaving of superfluous words after correction.
   f. Nouns repeated instead of using pronouns.
   g. Double prepositions.
   h. Other redundancies.
   i. General tautologies.
   m. Miscellaneous.

10. Errors of Logic:
    a. *Is where* and *is when* clauses for predicate nouns.
    b. Discrepancies between subjects and predicate nouns or adjectives.
    c. Contradictions.
    d. Wrong word of *saying.*
    e. Impossibilities of fact.
    f. Undeveloped thoughts.
    g. Chronological order violated.
    m. Miscellaneous.

An Abbreviated Check-List

The twelve most frequent errors reported by Charters,[19] after a comprehensive study of written compositions by children of Kansas City, were the following:

1. Use of wrong part of speech due to similarity of sound.
2. Failure of verb to agree with subject in number and person.
3. Wrong form of noun or pronoun.
4. Omission of subject or predicate.
5. Confusion of past and present tenses.
6. Syntactical redundancy.
7. Wrong verb.
8. Confusion of adjectives and adverbs.
9. Misplaced modifier.
10. Wrong tense forms.
11. Confusion of past tense and past participle.
12. Disagreement of noun and pronoun in number, person, and gender.

The teacher may prefer to use this abbreviated list of faults as a basis for analyzing errors in the oral or written work of the pupils.

Analytical Diagnosis of Rhetorical Factors

It is very difficult to diagnose specific faults in written or oral speech that are related to rhetorical factors such as vividness and richness of expression, clarity of style, and organization of the content, although differences among compositions in such elements are quite apparent.

[19] W. W. Charters and Edith Miller in *A Course of Study in Grammar Based on Language Errors of Children of Kansas City, Missouri* (out of print).

One approach that can be made to the problem is to make an analysis of various types of faults or errors in sentence structure. For instance, Pressey [20] reported the frequency with which the faults in sentence structure shown in the table below appeared in written composition.

FREQUENCY OF FAULTS IN SENTENCE STRUCTURE
(ADAPTED FROM PRESSEY)

Fault or Error	*Per Cent*
Stringy sentences	33
Fragments used as sentences	11
Pronoun with no antecedent	11
Pronoun not near antecedent	7
Change in tense	7
Lack of parallel construction	5
Redundancy and repetition	5
Omitted word or phrase	5
General incoherent sentence	5
Choppy sentences	4
Miscellaneous	7

The data in the table show that errors in sentence structure are due to a few frequently recurring errors or faults, including stringy sentences, the use of "fragments as sentences," and incorrect relationship of pronouns and antecedent. These three faults constitute 55 per cent of all errors reported by Pressey. However, each of the other types of faulty structure occurs frequently enough to be of concern to the teacher.

The evaluation of such characteristics of composition as structure and thought content must be based on the personal judgment of the rater. It is not possible to prescribe specific techniques of analysis such as can be used to determine faults in spelling and punctuation. However, the dependability of the analysis can be increased by considering various criteria in evaluating written expression. For example, Van Wagenen listed the following guides for the person who evaluated the thought content and structure of the compositions used in deriving his scales:

In grading for thought content, take into consideration:

For exposition:
Adherence to subject.
Interest of the treatment.
Continuity of thought.
Clearness of perception.
Discrimination in selection of words.

For description:
Maintenance of point of view (both physical and mental).
Vividness of picture.

[20] S. L. Pressey, "A Statistical Study of Children's Errors in Sentence Structure," *The English Journal*, Vol. 14 (September, 1925), pp. 520-535.

Emotional reaction.
Vigor and originality of diction.

For narration:
Sufficient explanation of the situation.
Naturalness and appropriateness of dialogue (if used).
Clear progress of narrative to a definite conclusion.
Use of suspense or surprise.
Descriptive touches.
Adequacy and variety of diction.

In grading for sentence and paragraph structure, take into consideration:
Unity.
Coherence.
Emphasis.
Variety and complexity of sentences.

The writer who uses many complex sentences shows a greater maturity of mind than the one who uses very simple or unnecessarily compounded sentences, even though from the very fact of the greater complexity, he may make more actual mistakes in structure.

Van Wagenen's basis of analysis should be helpful for teachers who are concerned with improving the quality of written expression.

The Diagnosis of Speech Defects

About 5 per cent of the school population have speech defects of sufficient severity to warrant diagnostic study and remedial attention. The percentage of children with articulatory speech defects decreases gradually from the lower to the higher grades, whereas the percentage of stutterers remains practically constant from grade to grade. In grade 1 about 10 per cent of the children have difficulties in articulation; in grade 8 about 4 per cent. About 1 per cent of school children regardless of age stutter. Speech defects of all kinds are more prevalent in children of preschool age than in any other age group.

The goal in speech education is not only to identify and diagnose speech defects but also to develop in all children the ability to speak effectively and interestingly. The alleviation of speech difficulties in most cases requires the services of a trained speech correctionist to assist the teacher in diagnosing the deficiency and in planning a developmental remedial program. The classroom teacher should be sufficiently familiar with speech problems to recognize pupils who need special help. These cases should then be referred to the specialist for diagnosis. The teacher should make every effort to cooperate with the speech specialist in carrying out the corrective program by creating a classroom environment that is without tensions and strains.

Diagnosis of severe speech problems should be on an individual basis. Techniques will be discussed in the section of the chapter which deals with case-study procedures.

CASE-STUDY DIAGNOSTIC PROCEDURES

The analytical diagnostic procedures described in preceding pages enable the teacher to evaluate the oral and written work of pupils, and to locate and identify limitations in its quality and forms of expression as well as specific deficiencies in technical aspects of language. In the chapters on spelling and handwriting, detailed descriptions of diagnostic procedures in these areas are described. They will not be presented in this chapter. We shall limit the discussion to the types of diagnostic procedures that can be used in the study of the behavior and responses of pupils with serious language problems. As will be seen, they are similar to methods of diagnosis in other fields of learning.

The important point to bear in mind is that the available analytical tests usually test *knowledge* of technical aspects of written expression, such as capitalization, punctuation, grammar, and language usage, but not the actual use of this knowledge in functional situations. Hence it is necessary to supplement data derived from tests by continuing scrutiny of all of the pupils' oral and written work in their various activities both in and out of school. It is unfortunately true that in many classrooms undue stress is placed on these technical aspects of language with the result that creative expression is neglected.

Administration of Standardized Diagnostic Tests in Oral and Written Expression, Including Speech

At the present time there are no standardized diagnostic tests that are intended for the study of individual ability in oral and written expression such as there are for reading, arithmetic, and spelling. Hence in diagnosis, informal procedures must be used that are similar to those described in the section on analytical diagnosis, as will be shown below.

To illustrate the possibilities of case-study procedures in language diagnosis, the main steps necessary in a systematic diagnosis of speech problems are given below. The list demonstrates vividly the technical approach used by specialists [21] in speech correction when dealing with disability cases.

1. Diagnosis should begin with a detailed study of the speech defects exhibited.
2. It should include inspection of the specific structures of the speech mechanism for evidences of malformation, injury, disease, and habitual nonuse.
3. It should note any evidences of improper functioning of the central nervous system, particularly as to the sensory and motor control of the structures involved in speech and the higher associative faculties.

[21] C. E. Kantner, "The Role of Diagnosis in a Speech Re-education Program," in *The Role of Speech in the Elementary School,* Department of Elementary School Principals (Washington, National Education Association, 1946), pp. 50-54.

4. It should look for more general bodily conditions and diseases which might be causally related to defective speech and evaluate the degree of general physical maturation.

5. It should attempt to evaluate the individual's native ability and the degree of his present mental maturation and educational achievement.

6. It should summarize his personality traits as evidenced by his attitudes toward himself and his defect and his adjustment to others at home and at school.

7. It should include consideration of his home environment and family background as well as of heredity factors that might influence his speech defect.

8. It should include a routine check on the possibility of a hearing loss.

9. It should proceed with an attempt to ascribe the speech defects exhibited to some cause or causes to which they can be proved to be directly related on a cause and effect basis or, if this is not possible, on a highly logical basis.

10. It should end with the formulation of a program of treatment and/or speech training as indicated by the findings.

Similar specific diagnosis is possible in other areas of language, but the necessary procedures have not been devised.

A detailed discussion of the procedures used in the diagnosis and correction of speech defects is too large a problem to consider in this volume. The following publications should be consulted by teachers who wish to inform themselves about this area of instruction:

Educational Diagnosis, Thirty-fourth Yearbook, National Society for the Study of Education (Chicago, Univ. of Chicago Press, 1935), Ch. 19.

James S. Green, *Cause and Cure of Speech Disorders* (New York, Macmillan, 1927).

Wendell Johnson, ed., *Speech Problems of Children* (New York, Grune & Stratton, 1950).

S. M. Stanchfield and E. H. Young, *Children with Delayed or Defective Speech* (Stanford, Calif., Stanford Univ. Press, 1938).

L. E. Travis, *Speech Pathology* (New York, Appleton, 1931).

Charles Van Riper, *Speech Correction: Principles and Methods* (New York, Prentice Hall, 1954).

————, *Teaching Your Child to Talk* (New York, Harper, 1950).

Informal Uses of Other Diagnostic Procedures

Because of the nature of language expression, it is essential that diagnosis be approached on an individual basis. Diagnosis of specific faults of individuals in oral expression is difficult because there are so many possible errors and they are affected by the social situation in which the learner reacts. Thus in the classroom the errors are not likely to appear that characterize his oral speech on the playground and in the home. The data gathered by applying the analytical procedures described in preceding pages can be made the basis of a systematic study of the oral and written language habits of individual pupils whose performance reveals serious limitations in language development. The following outline lists some of the useful informal diagnostic procedures:

1. ANALYSIS OF WRITTEN WORK

   a. Detailed analysis of errors in the sections of analytical tests of knowledge that deal with technical aspects of written expression.
   b. Analysis of compositions and other written work with the aid of check-lists to determine specific technical errors and omissions.
   c. Analysis of teacher-prepared objective tests of usage, etc.
   d. Evidence of lack of knowledge of rules of grammar and conventions.
   e. Analysis of format of letters, outlines, etc.
   f. Detailed application of criteria for evaluating structure, etc., such as Van Wagenen's.
   g. Finding coefficient of misspelling in written work.
   h. Extent of participation in creative writing experiences.
   i. Vividness and range of vocabulary.

2. ANALYSIS OF ORAL RESPONSES

   a. Keeping record of errors and incorrect usage in oral speech in classroom and in free activities both in and out of school (Minneapolis Check-list).
   b. Pronunciation, articulation, colloquialisms.
   c. Fluency, sentence structure.
   d. Mannerisms, speech defects, quality of tone.
   e. Extent of participation in discussions.
   f. Evidences of creative oral expression.

3. INTERVIEWS WITH PUPILS AND ASSOCIATES

   a. Asking pupil to explain reasons for incorrect usages.
   b. Questioning him about rules of punctuation, grammar, etc.
   c. Discussing interests in language; uses of oral and written language in daily activities outside of school; extent of reading; televiewing, etc.
   d. Studying methods of work used by pupil.

4. OBSERVATION OF BEHAVIOR IN COURSE OF DAILY WORK

   a. Attitudes toward written work and oral expression.
   b. Social acceptability in group.
   c. Evidences of emotional maladjustment.
   d. Evidences of physical handicaps and defects.
   e. Evidence of ability to evaluate his own work and the work of others by setting up and applying criteria.
   f. Study habits and methods of work.
   g. Reactions to errors pointed out in his work.

5. CONTROLLED OBSERVATION OF WORK ON SET TASKS

   a. Closer observation of reactions on specific assignment of a special kind of written work.
   b. Specific analysis of performance on a test set up for testing a definite area of knowledge.
   c. Test of knowledge of rules and ability to apply them and to explain them.
   d. Analysis of tape recordings, stenographic records, etc.
   e. Photographs of performance or product for detailed analysis.

6. ANALYSIS OF AVAILABLE RECORDS
   a. Examination of scores on reading, spelling, and handwriting scores of preceding years and current data.
   b. School history and marks.
   c. Health data and physical examination results.
   d. Intelligence test results.
   e. Sociological data about home, associates, environment.
   f. Anecdotal records on file.

The data secured by these and other methods about the oral and written expression of a particular pupil, when considered together with the data secured by group analytical procedures, should give the teacher a very clear picture of the problems and suggest the basis of a corrective program.

THE TREATMENT OF LEARNING DIFFICULTIES IN LANGUAGE

Factors Associated with Language Deficiencies

It is not an easy matter to determine the causes of deficiencies in language expression. The development of communication by oral and written language is a product of the learner's inherited capacities and his entire social milieu. The ideas he wishes to communicate gradually increase in difficulty and complexity. Sentence structure becomes more involved, and the learner encounters grammatical forms and technical ways of writing that make it increasingly difficult to express his ideas.

The commonly recognized causes of deficiencies may be grouped under (1) personal and social factors, and (2) instructional factors, somewhat as follows:

1. PERSONAL-SOCIAL FACTORS
   a. Physical development—immaturity, defects.
   b. Low mental level and intellectual immaturity.
   c. Slow vocabulary and speech development; limited writing vocabulary, lack of facility in language.
   d. Emotional status, poise, tension, attitudes toward language expression.
   e. Speech defects; poor breath control; inability to express ideas logically and forcefully.
   f. Lack of knowledge about specifics of written or oral expression; failure to understand them; low spelling ability.
   g. Limited background of social experiences, including reading.
   h. Failure to appreciate social standards of expression.
   i. Unfavorable environmental influences contributing to the use of incorrect forms of speed.

2. INSTRUCTIONAL FACTORS
   a. Curriculum does not include social situations that motivate the learning of language expression; contents too difficult and not well arranged.
   b. Undue emphasis is placed on formal aspects of expression; uses obsolete procedures, materials, content.

    c. Teacher uses method of incidental teaching.

    d. Instruction fails to deal with specifics that may be the source of difficulty.

    e. Diagnosis is not provided for and mass methods of teaching are used.

    f. Teaching may be unskillful and ineffective.

    g. Instructional materials may be inadequate.

    h. Goals not adjusted to capacity of learners.

In general, failure or inability of the teacher to apply the principles of good teaching in language given at the beginning of this chapter is the source of many learning difficulties in language expression.

The Treatment of Language Disability

The treatment of language disability is a complex problem because of the many possible approaches. Because of space limitations, we shall limit the discussion in this chapter to major elements of a general program of remedial treatment which the teacher should adapt to the needs of particular individuals. In the chapters on spelling and handwriting the reader will find detailed consideration of techniques of diagnosis and treatment in these areas.

The authors take the position that the best way to improve language development is to set up an instructional program on a learning laboratory basis which is in line with modern principles of teaching, especially insofar as diagnosis is concerned. Time should be set aside for concerted attention to the mastery of specific skills and techniques. The best modern instructional materials include many suitable practice exercises.

An excellent statement of principles which should guide a developmental program in oral and written communication was recently published by an important western city. It states clearly and concisely the point of view of the authors and is given in full below:

  I. Words are symbols of understandings and language is the expression of ideas. Growth in language, therefore, is inextricably interwoven with a child's experience. Language and thought are parts of the same whole. Experiences should be promoted which provide balanced development in the many aspects of oral and written expression.

    A. Language should be considered a part of every school activity; it should be developed in a free and informal atmosphere.

    B. Considerable emphasis should be placed upon vocabulary development; words should not be presented in isolation from experience.

    C. All language should be functional; it should grow out of situations that promote speech and writing.

    D. Instead of having children memorize rules and principles which have little meaning to them, effective expression should be developed through actual experience and inferences made from them.

    E. Concrete experiences should serve as a basis for much of the written language work.

    F. Audio-visual materials as vicarious experiences should be used to stimulate expression in both oral and written language.

G. Letter writing probably should receive a major emphasis in the teaching of written composition in the primary grades.

H. In addition to utilizing purposeful situations occurring in natural school activities, time should be set aside for concerted attention on the mastery of specific techniques.

I. Language programs should place emphasis on meaning first and on form next.

II. Language and a child's adjustment to his world and all that is in it are interdependent.

A. Good mental health should be recognized as being fundamental to the growth of speech.

B. The performance of social amenities should be considered an essential part of the language program.

C. The personality of each child should be respected by his contemporaries and teacher so that the child will experience joy in expression because he knows that his contribution will be received courteously.

D. The influence of the language of the home on the child's expression should be taken into consideration by the teacher.

III. The teacher should manage the learning experiences in the school in a way that will encourage free expression in a child's daily living, but special time should be provided for specifically planned developmental and correctional instruction.

A. Conversation should be pre-eminent in language in the primary grades; the amount of time spent in oral language should exceed that given to written language; oral expression should be considered basic to written expression.

B. In dramatizations, joy in the activity, provisions for group co-operation, clear expression and the development of desirable personalities, should be considered more important than a finished product.

C. Choral speaking should be used as a means of developing desirable speech habits and of enabling all children to participate in an activity.

D. Oral language should be utilized in all situations; it should not be entirely relegated to any one period of the day; however, certain periods should be set aside in the intermediate and upper grades for a definite attack upon specific language skills.

E. Opportunities should be provided for the group, under the guidance of the teacher, to plan and evaluate its work.

F. Remedial work in usage should be based upon the individual child's spontaneous speech in natural situations.

G. From the very first, when children dictate stories and letters to the teacher, correct form should be used.

H. In the primary grades, close supervision should be given to the children's writing, and help should be provided as needed to prevent the establishment of wrong habits.

I. The understanding of what a sentence is, and the use of capital letters, periods, and question marks, should not be confined to a given grade on the primary level but should be taught when the need arises and stressed in all the elementary grades.

J. Creative writing that is done for pleasure, as well as that which is done for utilitarian purposes, should be given a place in the curriculum of the elementary school.

K. In the intermediate and upper grades, drill should be carried on in close connection with significant speech and writing. Because corrective language is an individual matter, drill work should be based upon the child's own usage errors.

L. Group and individual evaluation of work, under teacher guidance, should be considered of prime importance.

M. The development of techniques of expression in the intermediate and upper grades should be considered a gradual process; special grade hurdles should not be definitely established and tenaciously stressed.[22]

The Construction of Remedial Practice Materials

There is ample evidence that the approach to the correction of errors in language should be an attack on specific difficulties rather than on a broad, general basis. It has been shown that most errors can be corrected when individuals or small groups of individuals with a common difficulty work together rather than by classes as a whole. Practice exercises should sample the area of difficulty fully and specifically, much as is done by the Lines tests in punctuation. These exercises should provide numerous opportunities to practice in a variety of real situations and in well-motivated drill as nearly functional and natural as can be arranged. The teacher should continually emphasize the applications of the items being corrected as the need for using them arises in regular written work. Self-diagnosis by the learner should have a prominent place in the developmental and remedial program. The learner should be aware, both of his faults and also of the success of his efforts to improve his use of language. (See typical exercise of this kind on page 343 from *Learning English*.)

Specific Instructional Procedures Useful in Remedial Teaching in Language

In an important yearbook,[23] Dora V. Smith summarized instructional practices whose validity for remedial teaching in language has been established through competent research. The eight following practices were included in this statement:

1. Since sound plays so large a role in errors in usage, *oral* drill should constantly supplement the written exercise.

2. The more methods of attack the teacher can use, the better are the results.

3. The more initiative the pupils take in the overcoming of their own errors and in the planning of their own remedial programs, the quicker the elimination of error.

4. Drill upon specific points of error is the greatest single factor in producing results.

5. Motivation of the problem through charting of errors, urging improvement, and keeping of progress scores may, however, reduce the drill necessary by one-half.

[22] San Diego County Schools, California, *Trends in Elementary Education—A Teacher's Guide*, 1954, pp. 53-54.

[23] *Educational Diagnosis,* Thirty-fourth Yearbook, National Society for the Study of Education (Chicago, Univ. of Chicago Press, 1935), Ch. 13.

6. Language games, in at least one experiment in the sixth grade, proved the least effective of six methods of attacking errors. Their value appears to be in direct proportion to the frequency of repetition of the usage in question and the naturalness of the language situation involved.

7. Mere repetition of correct forms, unaccompanied by consciousness of the wrong form to be avoided, has been proved ineffective when compared with methods placing right and wrong in juxtaposition.

8. Individualized drill upon errors made is notably more effective than putting all pupils through the paces required by the course of study, whether they are in need of drill on every point or not.

Illustrative Corrective Procedures

The teacher should base remedial instruction on observation of the child's spontaneous use of language and his speech habits in natural situations where he is more concerned with what he is saying than with how he is saying it; for instance, in an absorbing discussion of some interesting personal or group experience which is marked by considerable give-and-take. Ordinarily the speech of children is full of errors under such circumstances, and the teacher can gain valuable information about the natural forms of speech used by them, a real measure of the needs of the children. The teacher can compile a list of faults and errors and attack them on an individual basis. In a similar way, the teacher should base remedial instruction in written expression on an analysis of what the child writes freely in natural situations where he has an urge to express his ideas in written form.

Five of the most common sources of faulty oral and written expression are these:

1. Inability to organize and present ideas in an interesting, coherent, logical manner.
2. Limitations of vocabulary.
3. Incorrect language usage and forms.
4. Incorrect punctuation and capitalization.
5. Spelling deficiencies and poor quality of handwriting.

The basic problem in language instruction is to help the child develop his ability to express ideas clearly, effectively, and in good form in oral and written expression. As power to express ideas in writing grows, the teacher should help the child to learn the social conventions of usage, format, punctuation, and capitalization that common courtesy requires him to use. He should learn that they assist the reader to understand what has been written. However, the teacher should at all times place the emphasis on helping the child to have something worth while to say or write rather than stress the correction of errors through drill exercises. The learning of language should not be what has been so well described as "the bloody highway to English," which requires the correction of errors in written work checked by the teacher. To facilitate remedial work, the teacher should work with the class on only one or two points at a time.

1. *Improving the Ability to Organize and Present Ideas*. The child at all levels of the school should be given every opportunity to express his ideas in social situations that are meaningful and of significance to him. In the lower grades the children may tell about some experience they have had, such as an excursion, field trip, a visit to a store, an event, and so on. They can formulate simple letters of invitation to parents or letters of inquiry or thanks.

In later grades the children can be given systematic guidance in learning how to prepare reports, write stories or letters, make outlines of talks to be given, and in similar uses of language. For instance, the following procedure provides excellent guidance for a class in the writing of a simple story:

a. The class selects a subject about which to write.

b. After the pupils discuss briefly what might be written, a list of the possible topics that might be included in the story is written on the blackboard.

c. Using this list, the teacher then helps the children to formulate an outline of the composition, giving the possible headings of paragraphs to be written.

d. The class then organizes as groups, each of which is to compose a paragraph on one of the topics in the outline. A pupil in each group serves as secretary of the group.

e. These paragraphs are next written one at a time on the blackboard. Then they are discussed by the class as a whole, improved, revised, and extended as the class believes desirable. Here the opportunity is given the teacher to bring to the attention of the children questions of vocabulary, format, style, sentence structure, usage, punctuation, and capitalization.

f. The original group then assumes the responsibility of revising the paragraph in the light of these suggestions. The group of paragraphs can then be assembled and reproduced for the members of the class.

g. The class can develop standards to be considered in improving their language usage.

In connection with this work, the general as well as specific needs of the class as a whole and also of individual pupils will become evident to the teacher and thus afford a basis for planning the improvement program. Pupils can be grouped according to apparent shortcomings and disabilities and the necessary remedial work provided.

Incidentally, the teacher can at the same time by tactful guidance and correction help the pupils to improve poor enunciation and pronunciation, breath and voice control, and similar speech defects.

2. *Vocabulary Development*. The vocabulary of many children is exceedingly limited and hence they are unable to express their ideas and convey their feelings or emotions in a clear, precise, vivid way. The following kinds of vocabulary exercises will be found to be helpful in vocabulary development:

a. Expanding the vocabulary

(1) Listing words that can be used to convey ideas in a composition about some topic, to add interest and color to the language.

(2) Selecting interesting, colorful, important, or new words in what they read in books, stories, etc.

(3) Discovering and listing synonyms of words, such as for *large, beautiful,* etc.

(4) Having the children discover words built on root words; for example, *care, careful, careless; credible, incredible, creed,* etc.

(5) Discussing the meanings of important prefixes and suffixes, such as *un, dis, mal, mis, ful, ology.*

b. Improving precision of vocabulary

(1) Discussing shades of meanings in synonyms, such as *big, immense; tasty, luscious.*

(2) Classifying words according to categories, such as names of fruit, animals, etc.

(3) Arranging given words on some basis, such as the size implied, for example, *gallon, pint, quart, cup, barrel.*

(4) Discussing appropriateness of words used to convey ideas.

(5) Selecting from among several words the most suitable or appropriate expression; as, home—*large* or *immense.*

c. Enriching vocabulary

(1) Discussing different possible meanings of words; for example, *cold, picture, plant, check, way.*

(2) Gathering lists of words that are particularly interesting, colorful, vital, pleasant, etc.

(3) Trying to restate ideas in different and improved ways.

(4) Learning about the sources of vocabulary.

(5) Giving synonyms and opposites of words.

(6) Encouraging creative writing.

d. Helping children to make effective use of the dictionary.

e. Dramatizations.

3. *Improvement of Usage.* The development of language power is a process of gradual growth. No set standards of mastery to be achieved can be imposed on all children at any given age or grade level. Knowledge of the child's language development and the conditions under which he lives sets the direction of growth to be expected and the conditions which are likely to best foster it.

The elimination of errors of usage is an individual matter. Growth is achieved by means of a motivated attack by the learner himself upon the errors which he makes and upon improving the quality of his language expression. He should participate in such activities as those listed early in this chapter, in which he recognizes that the use of correct and vivid English is of importance.

The extent of incorrect usage varies from child to child. Some children come from homes in which they hear only correctly spoken English, and at an early age they achieve a high degree of mastery of correct forms of expression. The problem of correction is infinitely complicated and difficult when children come from homes where they have been exposed to faulty habits of usage and slovenly speech from infancy. The influence of these and other social pressures is very difficult to overcome.

There are two methods of attack on language errors that are known to produce better results than any others. One is to give the learner oral practice in using correct forms of expression so that they will come to sound right to him. When this occurs; he will use them habitually in oral and written expression. Having children fill in blanks in written exercises ignores the use of sound, which is the most potent factor in improving usage. Hearing the right form frequently at school is the most effective antidote for hearing the wrong form frequently at home and on the playground. Another method involves placing right and wrong forms before the learner in such a way that he is required to make a conscious choice of the right form by referring to some guiding principle or example which he should be led to discover. This experience presents a problem to the learner for solution.

Example: 1. Jane and me
                     are going to school.
             Jane and I

         2. What are you doing (? , .)

4. *Improvement of Punctuation and Capitalization.* The learner should be led to realize that correct punctuation and capitalization help to make clear to the reader the meaning the writer wishes to convey. Problems in these areas arise as the child grows in the sensing of relationships among ideas, in capacity for modifying and enriching thought, and in the use of formal forms of writing, such as letters and compositions. Appreciation of the period, comma, question mark, and exclamation point first comes when the learner becomes conscious of how these marks affect his voice when he reads. Gradually he comes to understand the purpose of punctuation and also its meaning.

In a similar way, children become familiar with the use of the apostrophe in contractions and possessive forms, the period after abbreviations, and the various situations in which capital letters are used. Correct usage follows understanding of their meaning and function. Practice on specific uses of marks of punctuation and on uses of capitalization should be regarded as an integral part of all written work. Special practice exercise on specific usages, understandings, and applications should not be assigned until the teacher is sure that the child understands what is to be practiced and it is meaningful to him.

To help pupils to correct faulty formats in letter writing, outlining, and the like, they should be taught to compare their written work with standard forms. These are usually found in language textbooks and workbooks. Then the children can correct any incorrect form they discover in their own work. They should be taught that any time they feel the need for help, they should

Diagnostic Test
USE OF CAPITAL LETTERS

This diagnostic test is to be taken before the remedial lessons are begun.

This test will reveal to you whether or not you need to study the rules governing the use of capital letters.

If you make errors in this test, you will find remedial lessons indicated. These have been planned to help you overcome your difficulties. You will be studying, therefore, only those rules which are troubling you. It will not be necessary for you to spend time on the work you already have mastered.

Directions: 1. *Underline the words which you think should have been capitalized.*

2. *When you have completed the test, correct your work as indicated in the sample.*

	Error?	Drill	O. K.
Sample: He went to church on sunday. (Sunday is the word which should have been underlined. The error is indicated by writing *yes* in the first column and encircling the number of the page for remedial help. When the page was worked, L. J. corrected it. He signed his initials because the lesson was worked perfectly.)	yes	Page 41 Lesson 5	L. J.
1. the chief feature of all insects is that all of them have six legs. their bodies are always divided up into segments or rings.	*no*	Page 37 Lesson 1	
2. Abraham Lincoln once said, "All i am or hope to be i owe to my sainted mother."	*no*	Page 38 Lesson 2	
3. The teacher said, "anyone who does his work with skill may be called an artist."	*Yes*	Page 39 Lesson 3	*K.m.*
4. "the poems of Longfellow were written almost a hundred years ago", the librarian said.	*yes* *no*	Page 39 Lesson 3	*K.m.*
5. "true worth is in being, not seeming; in doing, each day that goes by, some little good; not in dreaming of great things to do by-and-by." Alice Cary	*no*	Page 40 Lesson 4	
6. Thanksgiving Day is celebrated on a thursday in November.	*no*	Page 41 Lesson 5	
7. Washington's soldiers suffered many hardships at Valley Forge in december, 1777.	*no*	Page 41 Lesson 5	
8. He told us that memorial day is a legal holiday.	*no*	Page 41 Lesson 5	
9. Among the greatest of American inventors is thomas a. edison.	*no*	Page 42 Lesson 6	

feel free to refer to these models. Self-evaluation and self-criticism should at all times be encouraged.

Practical Application of Diagnostic Tests in Classroom Instruction

The portion of a diagnostic test given on page 343 is an excellent illustration of a practical procedure for use in remedial work in classroom instruction. The complete test includes 23 items dealing with specific uses of capitalization at the fifth-grade level.[24] The directions call on the pupil to underline the words in each item that he thinks should be capitalized. Under the direction of the teacher, each item is checked "Yes" if it is correct and "No" if it is incorrect. Each is keyed to a specific page on which appears a remedial lesson dealing with that difficulty. When the pupil works the exercises on that page correctly, the teacher initials it. The workbooks, *Learning English,* contain similar tests keyed to practice exercises for word study, parts of speech, sentence sense, use of marks of punctuation, word usage, and the writing of friendly letters. Language textbooks, teachers' manuals, and workbooks often contain exercises on specific points that provide valuable corrective materials. The teacher should examine these materials for suitable corrective exercises and prepare a card file listing them for later use.

SUGGESTED ACTIVITIES

1. Secure a specimen composition and evaluate it, using one of the standard scales described in this chapter.
2. Devise an informal scale of letter writing for use in a classroom situation.
3. Administer the Lines Diagnostic Test in Punctuation, or some portion of the test, to a class and analyze the results.
4. Construct a similar diagnostic test in capitalization. If possible administer it to a class and analyze the results.
5. Check errors in capitalization and punctuation in some pupil compositions. Comment on the efficiency and adequacy of this diagnostic procedure.
6. Observe the oral speech of children for a period of time and make an analysis of errors in oral speech. Use as a guide the Minneapolis list given on pages 324-325. Comment on the results. Can you list conditions in the community that may be causes of poor language development?
7. Try to apply Van Wagenen's techniques to the evaluation of structural and grammatical aspects of a group of compositions. Comment on your experience.
8. Attempt to analyze grammatical errors by applying Willing's check-list of errors.
9. Examine language textbooks and workbooks to determine the types of test and diagnostic procedures they contain.
10. Discuss with teachers the types of remedial procedures they have found

---

[24] The series of language workbooks, *Learning English,* grades 3 to 9, is published by Benton Review Publishing Co., Fowler, Ind.

most effective in correcting faulty work in technical phases of language expression.

11. What provisions are made for the diagnosis and correction of speech problems in local schools?

12. What is the place of grammar in the language program?

13. Why should corrective work in language be individualized? How can this be done?

14. What can be done to improve oral speech?

SELECTED BIBLIOGRAPHY

BRUECKNER, L. J., and MELBY, E. O., *Diagnostic and Remedial Teaching* (Boston, Houghton, 1931), Ch. 9.

COOK, W. W., "Evaluation in the Language Arts Program," in *Teaching Language in the Elementary School,* Forty-third Yearbook, Part II, National Society for the Study of Education (Chicago, Univ. of Chicago Press, 1944), pp. 196-214.

Educational Diagnosis, Thirty-fourth Yearbook, National Society for the Study of Education (Chicago, Univ. of Chicago Press, 1935), Ch. 13 and 19.

FITZGERALD, J. A., and KNAPHLE, L. C., "Crucial Language Difficulties in Letter Writing," *Elementary English Review,* Vol. 21 (January, 1944), pp. 14-19.

GREENE, H. A., "English-Language, Grammar, and Composition," in *Encyclopedia of Educational Research* (New York, Macmillan, 1950). Excellent summary of research.

Language Arts for Today's Children, Commission on the English Curriculum of the National Council of Teachers of English. (New York, Appleton-Century-Crofts, 1954). Especially Part IV.

LEE, J. M., and LEE, Dorris, *The Child and His Curriculum,* 2nd ed. (New York, Appleton-Century-Crofts, 1950), pp. 656-686.

LYMAN, R. L., *Summary of Investigations Related to Grammar, Language, and Composition,* Supplementary Educational Monograph No. 36 (Chicago, Univ. of Chicago Press, 1929).

POWELL, R. L., *Valid Testing and Diagnosis in the Mechanics of Ninth Grade English Composition,* University of Iowa Studies in Education, Vol. IX (1934), No. 1, pp. 97-128. (Research on error count, error quotient, and proof reading tests.)

TRAVERS, Robert M. W., "A Review of Procedures for the Evaluation of the Outcomes of the Teaching of English," *Journal of Experimental Education,* Vol. 17 (December, 1948), pp. 325-333.

WILLING, M. H., "Individual Diagnosis in Written Composition," *Journal of Educational Research,* Vol. 13 (February, 1926), pp. 77-89.

Test manuals should be consulted for suggestions on diagnostic procedures and correction measures.

11 DIAGNOSIS AND TREATMENT OF SPELLING DIFFICULTIES

IN THIS CHAPTER we discuss in detail problems associated with the diagnosis and treatment of learning difficulties in spelling under the following headings:

1. The fundamentals of an effective spelling program.
2. Foundations of diagnosis in spelling.
3. General diagnosis in spelling.
4. Analytical diagnosis in spelling.
5. Case-study diagnostic procedures.
6. The treatment of spelling difficulties.

THE FUNDAMENTALS OF AN EFFECTIVE SPELLING PROGRAM

The Objectives of Instruction in Spelling

The ability to spell is often thought of as the ability to reproduce in written or oral form the correct letter arrangement of words. However, it is quite apparent that successful spelling is a complex form of response influenced by certain physiological traits of the individual, such as vision and hearing, various intellectual factors, attitudes toward spelling, methods of studying spelling, speech habits, and a variety of related reading and handwriting skills—to mention some of the most important items to consider in the diagnosis and treatment of the most common learning difficulties in spelling.

The major objectives of instruction in spelling are:

1. To teach children how to spell selected words of undoubted social utility in their own affairs and in the affairs of life outside the school.
2. To help children to develop effective methods of studying new words.
3. To assist children to make efficient use of the dictionary in word study.
4. To develop in children a "spelling conscience," a desire always to use correct forms in spelling and to check spelling in all of their written work.
5. To assist children to extend and enrich their personal writing vocabularies.

Principles Underlying the Teaching of Spelling

The basic principles underlying an effective developmental program that is most likely to assure spelling power and prevent disability in spelling may be summarized as follows:

1. There should be provided a rich functional program in all aspects of the language arts that necessitates the expression of ideas in written form, so that a genuine desire to spell correctly in all written expression will be aroused. The need for written expression arises in all curriculum areas and in many social situations both in and out of school.

2. Learning to spell is a growth process which requires expert guidance. Pupils do not all learn at the same rate and in the same way. Adjustments of curriculum content and methods of instruction should be made to the learner's level of development. The relationships of spelling to basic skills in reading, speech, and handwriting should be fully taken into account in planning the instructional program in spelling.

3. Emphasis should be placed on helping each pupil to discover methods of learning how to spell words that he finds are effective. These may vary from pupil to pupil but should be of demonstrated value as judged by the growing success of the individual in learning to spell. Awareness of success motivates learning.

4. Diagnosis of spelling needs should be continuous and should be participated in by both teacher and pupil whenever spelling problems arise. The learner should become conscious of his own spelling problems and be guided in solving them.

5. Remedial procedures should be adapted to the needs of individuals and should deal with the treatment of specific deficiencies and factors related to them.

6. Frequent, well-distributed practice is necessary to insure retention. Overlearning beyond the point of immediate recall is essential.

FOUNDATIONS OF DIAGNOSIS IN SPELLING

Relation of Spelling to the Language Arts

The relationship between the ability to spell and other phases of the language arts has been the subject of a number of investigations whose results are of undoubted significance in the diagnosis and treatment of spelling difficulties. For example, in a recent study Hughes [1] reported the following correlations between spelling and selected language abilities for a group of 332 fifth-grade pupils, IQ's from 90-110:

[1] Vergil H. Hughes, "A Study of the Relationships Among Selected Language Abilities," *Journal of Educational Research*, Vol. 47 (October, 1953), pp. 97-106.

Word meaning	.69
Reading	.53
Sentence sense	.46
Language usage	.45
Capitalization	.42
Punctuation	.42

The implications are that these language abilities are differentiated from each other, but that there exist areas of overlap which relate one area to another. For example, the relatively high relationship between word meanings and spelling indicates the need of emphasizing the meanings of words in teaching children to spell them. The correlation between reading and spelling indicates that spelling and reading are, to a considerable degree, discrete. A person can be an able reader and still be a very poor speller or the reverse. The correlation is high enough, however, to indicate that reading and spelling may have some skills in common. There is evidence to show that these are in the areas of word knowledge and methods of word study.[2] It is reasonable to assume that basic reading skills contribute heavily to spelling, for example, pronunciation of words, knowledge of phonics, skill in word analysis, syllabication, and the like. It should be recognized that children learn to spell many words through reading and through incidental contact with words in social situations.

The present tendency also is to teach as a part of the spelling program certain conventions, such as capitalization, contractions and abbreviations of words, plurals, possessive forms, and the like, errors in which are regarded by many as incorrect spellings.

Incidentally, it may be pointed out that in general the correlation between spelling and vocabulary has been shown by a survey of other studies [3] to be approximately +.60. The correlation between spelling and intelligence has similarly been shown to be only +.45. Evidently knowledge of vocabulary is a more significant determinant of spelling success than intelligence, particularly in the lower grades. It also is clear that at all levels of intelligence we may find good and poor spellers, a fact that has been repeatedly reported, although poor spellers on the average have a lower level of intelligence than good spellers. These data must be interpreted with care, since group intelligence tests are essentially reading tests. As has been shown, poor spellers tend to be poor readers. Hence incorrect measures of intelligence are likely in their cases because of the effects of poor reading. This would have a tendency to make the observed correlations between spelling and intelligence higher than is the true relationship. The contamination of read-

[2] Aronson's unpublished Ph.D. thesis, Univ. of Minnesota, 1954.

[3] George D. Spache, "Spelling Disability Correlates I—Factors Probably Causal in Spelling Disability," *Journal of Educational Research*, Vol. 34 (April, 1941), pp. 561-586.

ing in the relationship between spelling and intelligence makes the observed correlation spuriously high.

Special Aspects of Diagnosis in Spelling

Many methods of analyzing and classifying errors as such have been reported. However, it is clear that a much broader approach to the problem of diagnosis of spelling difficulties is necessary. Frequently much additional information can be obtained by means of diagnostic reading tests in word recognition and word pronunciation. If these tests are sufficiently broad and analytical, they will reveal the nature of the pupil's error tendencies in word recognition, his knowledge and skill in phonics and word analysis including syllabication, the possible influence of disorders in articulation and pronunciation, the effects of dialect on pronunciation and enunciation, and the use of slovenly speech habits.

The pupil poor in spelling should be asked to read orally the words in spelling tests, especially those misspelled, and to define them. Analyses of his responses similar to those described above for word pronunciation should be made as the pupil reads the spelling words. Obviously, much valuable information about speech habits also can be obtained through observation of responses during class discussions, interviews, and informal school activities.

In interpreting the results of this analysis, the teacher should not consider the different types of errors as discrete, separate entities but should try to identify possible relationships among the different kinds of responses, for example, between misspellings and mispronunciations, articulatory errors, and phonic skills.

It is apparent that the spelling of words presents many difficulties because of the nonphonetic qualities of our language. Many misspellings actually represent an intelligent effort to apply reasoning by analogy to spelling. Thus pupils tend to make phonetic substitutions by using interchangeable vowels or consonant variants, to omit silent or doubled letters, and to insert letters. Often words are misspelled because they are not familiar, or because they are not pronounced correctly. In many cases faulty generalizations are applied. Often the pupil lacks knowledge of the formal spelling rules and social conventions that determine correctness of spelling.

There is a sharp contrast between the kinds of errors made by good and poor spellers. Good spellers tend to make relatively more errors of a phonetic type than are made by poor spellers; on the other hand, poor spellers tend to make more nonphonetic errors, many of them unintelligent and meaningless. Often random groups of letters are used by poor spellers in place of intelligent substitutions. It is a fact that one of the most certain ways to identify a pupil who is a spelling disability case is to note the prevalence of meaningless, "unique" misspellings in his written work. A large proportion of nonphonetic errors is a symptom of serious deficiency in spelling.

Pupils who are eager to express their ideas in writing often feel impelled to use words about whose spelling they are uncertain. Hence they write them as they sound phonetically and therefore usually incorrectly. This procedure should not be discouraged. However, the pupils should be led to see the desirability of identifying by some symbol any words that they want to write whose spelling they wish to check afterwards. If this is done, the flow of thought is not interrupted and the pupil is less likely to substitute simpler, less colorful words for those he wishes to write. Pupils should be encouraged to compile in a card file or in spelling notebooks special words they wish to add to their own personal writing vocabularies.

Every word that the child misspells is not a suitable word for the spelling lesson. In the regular spelling program, the teacher should stress particularly the words carefully selected for their social value as a result of the research of Horn, Gates, Rinsland, McKee, Fitzgerald, Dolch, and others. For a critical discussion of the principles of selecting and gradation of the spelling curriculum, the reader is referred to the article by Horn on "Spelling" in the *Encyclopedia of Educational Research*.[4]

GENERAL DIAGNOSIS IN SPELLING

The methods used to evaluate the growth of a pupil's general ability to spell should include the following:

1. A test of general spelling ability.
2. A measurement of progress in the ability to spell the words he uses in social situations and in regular classwork.
3. An estimate of the pupil's success in learning to spell new words.
4. Evidence of "spelling conscience."

Tests of General Spelling Ability

All modern achievement test batteries such as the Stanford, Coordinated Scales, and Iowa Every Pupil Tests include standard tests to measure spelling ability. Scores are ordinarily expressed as a spelling age or spelling grade. They give the pupil's level of ability but they do not reveal the extent, nature, and mastery of underlying knowledges and skills comprising spelling. Diagnostic tests are necessary for these purposes.

The form of survey tests varies considerably. In some cases the test words are dictated in list form; in others they are embedded in sentences that are dictated; in others the pupil is asked to select the correct form of spelling from among a group of given forms. Recall tests are superior to recognition types, and also more difficult.

---

4 New York, Macmillan, 1950.

The results of these survey tests show wide variations in the ability of pupils to spell. It is customary to regard any pupil whose score is more than one year below his grade level as a possible disability case, making due allowance for his level of intelligence.

Certain textbooks contain standard tests based on their contents. It is often assumed that a test of the words being studied is a more satisfactory method of evaluating spelling ability than some test which is not based on the words contained in the course of study. Under such conditions, rote memory learning of words is encouraged and insufficient weight is given to the development of certain skills and abilities in spelling which make it possible to learn words outside the lists.

Certain spelling diagnostic tests include suitable spelling scales for use in measuring spelling ability, as will be shown.

Measurement of Spelling in Social Situations and in Regular Classwork

Undoubtedly the best test of the pupil's ability to spell is the writing he does in social situations, such as letter writing, and the written work he does in all classes. Courtis devised the coefficient of misspelling to measure misspelling in pupil compositions and other informal written work. The steps in findings the coefficient of misspelling are these:

1. Secure one or more specimens of a pupil's written work, such as a composition or some theme, a report, a letter, or some similar written work. The specimens should contain approximately 200 words.
2. Count the total number of words written.
3. Check the words misspelled in the specimens and then find the total number of words misspelled, including lapses and slips such as *the* for *they,* or failure to cross *t* or to dot *i.*
4. Divide the number of words misspelled by the number of words written. Carry the division to three places, or thousandths.
5. Drop the decimal point. The resulting figure gives the number of misspellings per thousand running words.

Example: Composition—220 words
　　　　　Misspellings—11 words
　　　　　$11 \div 220 = .05$
　　　　　Coefficient is 50, the number of misspellings per 1000 words

To assist in the interpreting of coefficients of misspelling at various grade levels, the following results reported by Courtis [5] some years ago are given. By "lapses" are meant errors due to lapses or slips such as failure to dot *i* or to cross *t;* under "total" are given data for all actual misspellings.

The median for grade 4 was 74 words per 1000 words, or 7.4 per cent of the total number. Note the gradual reduction in size of the coefficients from grade to grade until grade 12 where it is 9, or .9 per cent of the words

[5] S. A. Courtis, *Measurement of Classroom Products,* Survey of Gary Schools, Vol. 8 (New York, General Education Board, 1919), p. 93.

written. The writers have found coefficients of as high as 500 in the lower grades. In the upper grades they rarely exceed 100.

It is advisable to score several pieces of written work in this way to secure a reliable and broader measurement of the extent of the errors made. If desirable, the spelling errors made also can be classified as to type by methods described later in this chapter. It should be pointed out that coefficients of misspelling secured in this fashion may in some cases misrepresent the actual spelling ability of creative writers who sometimes tend to extract from their speaking or reading vocabulary colorful and unusual words that they are not able to spell at the time rather than to substitute simpler words that they know how to spell. Hence it is advisable to use discrimination in interpreting the coefficients of misspelling.

SPELLING COEFFICIENTS FOR COMPOSITION TESTS

Grade	Lapses	Misspellings	Total
4	17	57	74
5	13	53	66
6	11	43	54
7	8	24	32
8	6	14	20
9	3	14	17
10	3	10	13
11	3	9	10
12	3	6	9

Testing Pupil Ability to Learn to Spell New Words

In most spelling classes, words are taught in weekly units. A series of five daily lessons on a group of words includes basically the following steps:

1. A presentation and pretest of the new words for the week.
2. Each pupil studies the words he misspelled in the pretest.
3. A retest of the list to see if and where improvement has been made.
4. Further study of especially difficult words by pupils under guidance.
5. Final test on the list.

The teacher should informally survey the nature of errors made by the pupils and note the scores of individual pupils from day to day, especially the progress of those whose pretest contained a considerable number of misspellings. If relatively little progress is made in the course of the week, the need for a diagnostic study of the pupil's spelling is indicated and the discovery of possible underlying factors that may be contributory to failure to improve.

Securing Evidence of "Spelling Conscience" and Attitude Toward Spelling

Evidence of "spelling conscience" and general attitude can be most readily secured by observation of the pupil's behavior and by the quality of spelling in his regular written work. Such behavior as the following is very revealing:

1. Avoidance of writing or reluctance in writing.
2. No apparent effort to check spelling of new words.
3. Extent of use of dictionary to look up spellings about which the pupil is uncertain.
4. Experimenting by writing words on scratch paper.
5. Requests of a pupil for help on spelling of difficult words.
6. Proofreading to detect slips, lapses, and misspellings.
7. Resentment of criticism of spelling in other written work.
8. Eagerness and promptness with which the study of new words is begun.
9. Satisfaction with evidence of improvement in spelling.
10. Evidence of dislike for spelling.
11. Statements such as "My father says he was a poor speller. So am I."

It is an unfortunate fact that children who find spelling difficult and whose writing contains many misspellings often develop negative attitudes toward spelling and are indifferent to spelling errors in their written work. The teacher's red ink, showing the many misspellings on written compositions, often is the source of faulty attitudes of pupils toward spelling in general which leads to unwillingness, even fear, to express ideas in written form. These children represent *complex disability* cases in spelling.

ANALYTICAL DIAGNOSIS IN SPELLING

A more detailed analysis of difficulties of pupils low in spelling ability utilizes the following diagnostic procedures:

1. Measuring the effectiveness of the pupil's study habits.
2. Classifying spelling errors according to categories.
3. Determining knowledge of certain important spelling rules and conventions.
4. Measuring range of vocabulary and knowledge of meanings of words.

Measuring the Effectiveness of Study Habits

Investigations have shown that the study habits of good and poor spellers differ considerably and also vary widely from pupil to pupil. This is true in spite of the fact that authors of textbooks usually present a systematic plan for studying words that pupils are expected to master. Good spellers usually have systematic methods of study which, however, differ from pupil to pupil, whereas poor spellers apparently use methods of study that are unsystematic, variable, and often unintelligent. The teacher should have a quick, dependable, objective way of measuring the relative effectiveness of study habits.

It may be assumed that the effectiveness of study habits in spelling can be measured by growth in the ability of pupils to spell a selected group of words in a given period of time. The Courtis Learning Test in Spelling is based on this principle. The general procedure used in administering this test is as follows:

1. Select the one of the four lists of words given below that is judged to be of average difficulty for the class. Usually list *A* is satisfactory for grades 3 and 4, list *B* for grades 4 and 5, list *C* for grades 5 and 6, list *D* for grades above 6.

2. Dictate the list to the pupils to secure a measure of their ability to spell the words before studying them. Collect these test papers.

COURTIS STANDARD LEARNING TESTS

Test A

do	cat	not	girl	some
it	cow	old	give	tell
me	day	run	good	them
my	eat	sat	hand	this
us	for	see	home	time
we	get	ball	like	tree
all	has	come	look	want
bad	his	dear	make	will
big	let	door	play	wind
can	man	find	ring	little

Test B

easy	noise	leaves	bottom	careful
wait	music	leader	raised	soldier
hurry	penny	record	August	sitting
rainy	watch	safety	return	forward
score	brown	passed	loving	pleased
speak	color	invite	follow	railroad
visit	ready	helped	anybody	fourteen
reach	dozen	office	mistake	building
learn	liked	lesson	cleaned	branches
study	person	change	enjoyed	grandfather

Test C

brief	finally	ordinary	furniture	invitation
usual	similar	familiar	extremely	attractive
error	extreme	terrible	necessary	profession
article	possess	received	difficult	attendance
attempt	special	announce	certainly	collection
arrival	exhibit	glorious	generally	examination
anxious	sincere	accident	practical	electricity
disease	planned	material	literature	announcement
expense	journal	practice	completely	accomplished
foreign	suggest	definite	successful	disappointed

Test D

immense	judgment	unusually	continuous	fundamental
possess	immediate	physician	especially	acquaintance
license	authority	committee	sufficient	occasionally
leisure	sincerely	apparatus	attendance	confirmation
analysis	permanent	essential	regretting	accompanying
thorough	associate	definitely	arrangement	conveniently
enormous	community	originally	possibility	professional
physical	ambitious	scientific	consequence	recommendation
familiar	privilege	exhibition	unnecessary	correspondence
annually	executive	enthusiasm	accommodate	representative

3. Then distribute mimeographed copies of the same list of words just dictated. Tell the pupils, "You are now to study for 10 minutes the words that I just dictated to you. You may study them in any way you wish. After you have studied the words, I shall repeat the test to see how much your score on the test has improved. Begin." Be sure to allow exactly 10 minutes.

4. Collect the study papers.

5. Then repeat the same test given in step *a*. Collect the test papers.

6. Match the two papers for each pupil. Score the two tests. Multiply the number of words spelled correctly on each test by 2 to express the scores as percentages. These are the indices of maturity.

7. List the names of the pupils and their scores on the pretest and on the retest. Then use the table given on page 356 to find each pupil's learning index. The method is described in the table.

To give the reader some notion of the scores that are made on the learning test, data for 397 pupils in grades 4A-5B and 6A-7B from a study by Atkin [6] are given below.

DISTRIBUTION OF LEARNING INDICES OF 397 PUPILS

Learning Index	4A-5B	6A-7B
160-179	2	
140-159		3
120-139	4	4
100-119	5	4
80-99	8	11
60-79	16	17
40-59	21	42
20-39	41	82
0-19	36	82
Loss	4	15
Total	137	260
Median	34.5	27.5
Median I. Q.	108.0	108.0

Note the wide range in learning indices in both groups. They vary from actual losses to very high indices. The losses indicate that after the 10-minute period of study, some pupils actually made lower scores on the test than before studying the words. Evidently they had very poor study habits.

The results of this test enable the teacher to identify pupils whose study habits are relatively inefficient, as measured by the growth made. Their inadequacies can be determined by individual diagnostic procedures described in a following section of this chapter.

The teacher will find it a revealing experience to observe the study methods used by various children during the study period. Ordinarily they will vary from pupil to pupil, especially when the children feel free to choose any method they may prefer. However, the primary purpose of the teacher

[6] S. Atkin, *Learning Indices and Study Methods in Spelling*. Unpublished Master's dissertation, Univ. of Minnesota.

INDICES OF LEARNING

Percentage Scores in Final Test

%	1	5	10	15	20	25	30	35	40	45	50	55	60	65	70	75	80	85	90	95	99	%
95																				0	71	95
90																			0	31	102	90
85																		0	19	50	121	85
80																	0	14	33	64	135	80
75																0	11	25	44	75	146	75
70															0	9	20	34	53	84	155	70
65														0	8	18	29	42	61	92	163	65
60													0	7	16	25	36	50	68	99	171	60
55												0	7	14	22	32	43	56	75	106	177	55
50											0	6	13	21	29	38	49	63	82	113	184	50
45										0	6	12	19	27	35	44	55	69	88	119	190	45
40									0	6	12	19	25	33	41	50	61	75	94	125	196	40
35								0	6	12	18	24	31	38	47	56	67	81	100	131	202	35
30							0	6	12	18	24	30	37	45	53	62	73	87	107	138	208	30
25						0	6	12	18	24	30	37	44	51	59	68	79	93	112	143	214	25
20					0	6	12	18	24	30	36	43	50	57	65	75	86	100	118	149	220	20
15				0	7	14	20	26	32	38	44	50	57	64	73	82	93	107	126	157	227	15
10			0	8	16	22	28	34	40	46	52	58	65	73	81	90	101	115	134	165	236	10
5		0	11	20	27	34	40	46	51	57	64	70	77	84	92	102	113	127	145	176	247	5
1	0	19	30	38	46	52	58	64	70	76	82	89	96	103	111	129	132	148	164	195	266	1

Percentage Scores in Initial Test

Instructions: Express scores as percentages of maturity. Then at the left of the table, locate row for percentage in the initial test, and at the top the column for percentage in the final test. The number at the intersection of the two is the Index of Learning.

For percentages not given in the table, find the index for the nearest lower percentages and estimate the amount to be added. Change score in "words right" to percentage scores by the formula

Percentage of maturity (for a given test) = (100 × words right) ÷ number of words in test

Illustration: At the beginning and end of a semester, a teacher gave a 30-word test in spelling. One pupil had 2 words right in the initial test and 25 in the final. That is, he had percentage of maturity scores of 7% and 83% respectively. The next lower percentages are 5% and 80%. In the table the index for these scores is 113. The index for 10% and 85%, the next higher scores, is 115. Therefore, the index for 7% and 83% is estimated to be 114. Actual value, 115.

at this point should be to secure a measure of the effectiveness of their study habits. Poor spellers usually have poor study habits.

Clinical workers will find that the application of the Courtis test to individuals will provide an excellent opportunity to observe closely how the pupil studies, information that will be valuable in further detailed diagnostic study.

Classifying Spelling Errors According to Type

Methods of classifying spelling errors have been devised by many investigators, including among others Book and Harter, Cornman, Mendenhall, Watson, Russell, and Spache. A rapid classification of errors will reveal a pupil's error tendencies and enable the teacher to detect excessive or infrequent types of errors. Knowledge as to the types of errors a pupil makes in excessive degree provides a point of departure in the diagnosis and treatment of particular kinds of spelling deficiencies. The classification of errors also furthers the teacher's understanding of the nature of a pupil's difficulties. The classification of errors also enables the teacher to determine the relationships between misspellings and phonic skills, mispronunciation, and speech difficulties. Spelling errors made on tests, daily spelling exercises, and other written work can be classified if the teacher or examiner wishes to do so.

Spache [7] has devised a "Spelling Errors" test which reveals not only the particular types of errors that are characteristic of the pupil, but confirms impressions growing out of informal observations of limitations in his knowledge of phonics, skills in word analysis, and other basic abilities that enter into spelling performance. The possible influence of the pupil's speech habits and limitations in his reading skills such as pronunciation, phonics, and syllabication can be investigated by having the pupil read aloud the words he misspelled on the tests.

The table following presents a scheme for analyzing spelling errors developed by Spache that is recommended by the authors. The table makes possible a comparison of characteristic errors of groups of good and poor spellers in grades 3 and 4. The table gives the mean percentage that each of the errors was of the total number of errors made by individual good and poor spellers [8] on a 100 word test from the 50 per cent level of the Buckingham-Ayres Scale. The critical ratio is also given for each type of error. Teachers who do not wish to make as detailed an analysis of errors as is suggested by the complete list can use the major headings given in the outline as the basis of their groupings.

---

[7] George Spache, "Validity and Reliability of the Proposed Classification of Spelling Errors," *Journal of Educational Psychology,* Vol. 31 (March, 1940), pp. 111-134.

[8] George Spache, "Characteristic Errors of Good and Poor Spellers," *Journal of Educational Research,* Vol. 34 (November, 1940), pp. 182-189.

MEAN PERCENTAGES OF ERRORS BY POOR AND AVERAGE SPELLERS
(ADAPTED FROM SPACHE)

| | MEANS | | |
ERROR	*Poor Spellers*	*Average Spellers*	C.R.
1. Omissions	30.8	32.1	.41
a. Single letter			
(1) Silent	12.0	13.5	1.18
(2) Sounded	12.7	9.5	2.05
(3) Doubled	5.7	7.4	1.78
b. Syllable	3.4	1.7	2.17
2. Additions	14.0	18.0	2.81
a. Single letter			
(1) Doubling	3.0	3.3	.46
(2) Phonetic	2.1	5.5	5.03
(3) Nonphonetic	9.5	9.2	.25
b. Syllable	.8	1.1	1.27
3. Transpositions	4.7	5.2	.52
a. Phonetic	1.5	1.5	.00
b. Nonphonetic	3.2	3.7	.78
4. Phonetic substitutions	36.2	40.1	1.76
a. Vowel	17.0	19.8	1.53
b. Consonant	9.3	10.0	.53
c. Diphthong	2.6	2.6	.00
d. Syllable	3.5	6.0	3.64
e. Entire word	2.8	1.7	1.55
5. Nonphonetic substitutions	11.3	7.6	2.48
a. Vowel	3.2	1.6	1.85
b. Consonant	4.3	3.0	1.64
c. Diphthong	.7	.7	.00
d. Syllable	2.0	1.4	1.40
e. Entire word	1.1	.9	.90
6. Homonyms	1.4	1.7	.85
7. Incomplete	4.5	2.1	2.35
8. Unrecognizable	3.8	1.8	2.2

Phonetic substitutions constituted the major proportion of error for both poor and average spellers; omissions were the next most important source of error for both groups; then in order additions, nonphonetic substitutions, transpositions, incomplete words, unrecognizable words, and finally homonyms. It should be recalled that the figures for each kind of error in the table are mean percentages of the total number of errors made by individual pupils in each group. Poor spellers, of course, made a much larger total number of errors than good spellers.

In his article Spache summarizes the implications of the table as follows:

1. When errors are classified as phonetic and non-phonetic, there appears a definite tendency for the average spellers to make a greater number and per cent

of phonetic errors than do the poor spellers. Conversely, there is an equally definite tendency for the poor spellers to make a greater number and per cent of non-phonetic errors than do average spellers.

2. Specific error types in which average spellers may exceed in number or per cent to a significant extent are phonetic addition of single letters and phonetic substitution for a syllable.

3. Errors in which poor spellers may exceed average spellers to a significant extent are non-phonetic substitutions for a syllable, incomplete and unrecognizable spellings.

4. Although not wholly reliable differences were found in the present study, there appears to be a strong tendency for average spellers to exceed the poor in number and per cent of total additions. Similarly, there is a strong tendency for poor spellers to exceed in number and per cent of omission of sounded letters, omission of a syllable and total non-phonetic substitutions.

Spache Test of Error Tendencies in Spelling. The analysis of spelling errors in a pupil's regular written work is a rather painstaking, laborious process but an exceedingly revealing method of studying a pupil's error tendencies, especially of pupils who misspell many words. However, because of the informal nature of this procedure, it is not possible to evaluate the results of the analysis by comparison with norms.

Spache's [9] "spelling errors" test is constructed in such a way that the pupil's tendencies to make errors of the twelve most common types can be determined. Other types occur relatively infrequently. The words in the tests were selected from Gates's study, "A List of Spelling Difficulties in 3876 Words." [10] Only those words were used in the tests in which according to Gates's data a single type of spelling error was made by more than 50 per cent of the pupils tested. Thus words were used in the test in which the pupil was likely to make a given type of error. There are three tests of 120 words each: one for grades 2-4, one for grades 5 and 6, and one for Grades 7 and 8. Spache's test for Grades II-IV appears on page 360.

The types of errors checked by Spache's test and suggested norms for each type include the following:

		Norms
1.	Omission of a silent letter (*bite-bit*)	9-17
2.	Omission of a sounded letter (*and-an*)	5-17
3.	Omission of a doubled letter (*arrow-arow*)	3-10
4.	Addition by doubling (*almost-allmost*)	1-5
5.	Addition of a single letter (*dark-darck*)	7-19
6.	Transpositions or reversals (*ankle-ankel*)	2-7
7.	Phonetic substitutions for a vowel (*enjoy-injoy*)	11-25
8.	Phonetic substitution for a consonant (*prison-prizon*)	5-14
9.	Phonetic substitution for a syllable (*neighborhood-naborhood*)	2-8
10.	Phonetic substitution for a word (*obey-obay*)	0-5

---

[9] Distributed by George D. Spache, University of Florida, Gainesville, Fla.
[10] New York, Bureau of Publications, Teachers College, Columbia Univ.

SPELLING ERRORS TEST—II-IV

George D. Spache, Ph.D.
Reading Laboratory and Clinic
University College, University of Florida

1. bite—bit	41. rent—reant	81. though—thow
2. and—an	42. giant—gaint	82. bake—back
3. arrow—arow	43. caught—cought	83. hoe—how
4. almost—allmost	44. fishing—fiching	84. lamp—lanp
5. dark—darck	45. laughing—lafing	85. alone—alon
6. ankle—ankel	46. buy—by	86. starve—stave
7. bead—beed	47. flew—flow	87. hammer—hamer
8. bush—buch	48. am—an	88. lily—lilly
9. flies—flys	49. comes—coms	89. hop—hope
10. bare—bear	50. bound—bond	90. nickel—nickle
11. bags—bogs	51. broom—brom	91. obey—obay
12. bottom—botton	52. melon—mellon	92. pony—pone
13. boxes—boxs	53. so—sow	93. babies—babys
14. bridge—brige	54. drum-durm	94. meat—meet
15. asleep—aslep	55. dollars—dollers	95. hot—hat
16. also—allso	56. lace—lase	96. room—roon
17. negro—negrow	57. looked—lookt	97. awhile—awile
18. ate—aet	58. deer—dear	98. street—steet
19. creep—creap	59. he—hi	99. begged—beged
20. buzz—buss	60. jumping—junping	100. hoped—hopped
21. bull—bool	61. cookies—cookes	101. an—and
22. four—for	62. march—mach	102. patch—pacth
23. pail—pale	63. dropped—droped	103. cellar—celler
24. bump—bunp	64. until—untill	104. recite—resite
25. fasten—fasen	65. books—bookes	105. parties—partys
26. farther—father	66. girl—gril	106. rake—rack
27. bigger—biger	67. hall—holl	107. let—lat
28. later—latter	68. mice—mise	108. seem—seen
29. plank—planck	69. paw—por	109. cracker—craker
30. born—bron	70. eight—ate	110. studying—studing
31. cotton—cotten	71. her—har	111. bonnet—bonet
32. cave—kave	72. rich—rick	112. already—allready
33. gain—gane	73. match—mach	113. grab—grabe
34. here—hear	74. crack—crak	114. piece—peice
35. did—ded	75. glass—glas	115. heap—heep
36. him—hin	76. welcome—wellcome	116. slice—slise
37. breast—brest	77. coming—comeing	117. aim—ame
38. hatch—hach	78. field—feild	118. pear—pair
39. cutting—cuting	79. ton—tun	119. red—rad
40. lose—loose	80. often—offen	120. bedroom—bedroon

11. Nonphonetic substitution for a vowel (*struck-strick*)		1-4
12. Nonphonetic substitution for a consonant (*watching-washing*)		2-5
13. Unrecognizable or incomplete (*cano for cotton*)		0-13

TYPICAL SPELLING ERRORS ON TEST

Word Given	Child's Spelling	Word Given	Child's Spelling
1. can	can	21. struck	struce
2. ten	ten	22. personal	prsnly
3. old	old	23. address	adddroes
4. six	sixre	24. several	sevrl
5. ice	ice	25. known	kone
6. child	ciled	26. their	there
7. his	his	27. perhaps	prappe
8. that	that	28. popular	popler
9. far	far	29. against	agnst
10. form	forn	30. treasure	trersher
11. glad	glaed	31. investigate	envstgaet
12. same	sane	32. certain	sretine
13. night	niethe	33. really	rely
14. cent	cent	34. conference	conferase
15. within	within	35. business	bisnens
16. point	pont	36. citizen	cityzine
17. money	nonye	37. elaborate	elprer
18. picture	picher	38. association	ashoeasa
19. change	chage	39. evidence	eventdes
20. number	number	40. secretary	seirty

Any pupil who makes more errors on the test than the norms, which represent the range for average pupils, is in the poorest 16 per cent of the population in making this type of error.

For quick analysis of misspellings in regular written work, the types of errors included by Spache can be conveniently grouped under the six headings:

1. Omissions.
2. Additions or repetitions.
3. Transpositions or reversals.
4. Phonetic substitutions.
5. Nonphonetic substitutions.
6. Unrecognizable or incomplete words.

Spelling difficulties often lie in certain sections of words, seldom in the beginnings, more often in the center of words and to the right of center. The number of errors in the third syllable is double the number in the first syllable. Special help in word study should be given, to aid the child in seeing the whole word, in getting syllables clearly in mind, and in exercising care in pronunciation.

Russell [11] has shown that poor spellers are reliably inferior to good spellers in such phonic skills as giving letters for letter sounds, blending

[11] David H. Russell, *Characteristics of Good and Poor Spellers,* Contributions to Education No. 727 (New York, Bureau of Publications, Teachers College, Columbia Univ., 1937). One of the most exhaustive studies of the problem that is available.

letters to form syllables and words, and in spelling one- and two-syllable nonsense words. Poor spellers lack necessary knowledge of phonics and therefore tend to make fewer phonetic additions or substitutions. These deficiencies are all closely related to the kinds of errors made most frequently by poor spellers.

By way of practice, the reader should use Spache's classification of errors to analyze a pupil's spellings of the test words given on page 361.

Testing Knowledge of Spelling Rules and Conventions

It is known that lack of knowledge of certain important spelling rules and of conventions of written English, such as capitalization, form of writing possessives, use of hyphens in numbers and words, contractions, and abbreviations, contributes significantly to what are sometimes regarded as spelling errors. Methods for measuring knowledge of the conventions of capitalization were dealt with in Chapter 10. Here we shall discuss methods of testing knowledge of some important rules directly involved in spelling.

Horn [12] has suggested that only such spelling rules be taught as apply to a large number of words and have few exceptions. He lists the following rules:

a. Words ending in silent *e* usually drop the final *e* before the addition of suffixes beginning with a vowel, but they keep the final *e* before the addition of suffixes beginning with a consonant.

b. When a word ends in a consonant and *y,* change the *y* to *i* before adding all suffixes except those beginning with *i.* Do not change *y* to *i* in adding suffixes to words ending in a vowel and *y,* or when adding a suffix beginning with *i.*

c. Words of one syllable or words of more than one syllable accented on the last, ending in a single consonant preceded by a single vowel, double the final consonant when adding a suffix beginning with a vowel.

d. The letter *q* is always followed by *u* in common English words.

e. Proper nouns and most adjectives formed from proper nouns should always begin with capital letters.

The rules for the use of periods in writing abbreviations and for the correct use of the apostrophe to show possession or the omission of letters in contractions also meet the above requirements.

ILLUSTRATIONS OF EACH RULE

Rule *a.*	like, liking, likely
Rule *b.*	baby, babied, babying
	play, played, playing
Rule *c.*	run, running
	forget, forgetting
Rule *d.*	quick, queen, quiet
Rule *e.*	America, American

[12] Article on "Spelling" in *Encyclopedia of Educational Research* (New York, Macmillan, 1950), p. 1257.

Informal tests can quite easily be prepared for these and similar rules. The following test, consisting largely of second-grade words, illustrates the procedure:

DIAGNOSTIC TEST ON SPELLING DIFFICULTIES

1. *ie* and *ei* difficulties
   piece, receive, ceiling, field, weigh

2. *y* to *i* when suffix is added
   (*happy*), *happiness*; (*pretty*), *prettily*; (*fly*) *flying*

3. *y* to *i* in plurals and tenses
   (*fly*), *flies*; (*story*), *stories*; (*try*), *tries*

4. *os* and *oes*
   (*radio*), *radios*; (*hero*), *heroes*

5. Dropping final *e* when suffix is added
   (*hope*), *hoping*; (*come*), *coming*

6. Keeping final *e*
   (*late*) *lately*; (*safe*) *safely*

7. Effect of final *e*
   (*hat*), *hate*; (*not*), *note*

8. Doubling final consonant
   (*plan*), *planning*; (*stop*), *stopped*

9. *u* follows *q*
   quick, quiet

10. Possessive forms
    children's, boys' (plural), *dog's* (singular)

11. Contractions
    don't, 2's, I'm

12. *ful* as an ending
    helpful; careful

Key words in parentheses should be dictated first, followed by related words not in parenthesis. A systematic scrutiny of the written work of the pupils will reveal difficult spots and evidences of confusion.

Determining Specific Difficulties in Writing Phonetic Elements

To determine specific deficiencies in writing phonetic elements, a simple procedure may be used which is illustrated in the chart on page 364. First, the teacher prepared a list of sixteen easy words including 16 vowel sounds and 16 phonograms that occur most frequently in the Kindergarten Union Word List. The list of words was next dictated to a group of 24 second-grade children and the children wrote the words. Then the teacher tabulated the number of times each word was misspelled and each phonetic element was not handled correctly. In all, there were 282 misspellings of the individual words or 73 per cent of all words written. An examination of the data for specific phonetic elements given at the right in the table shows that the number of times each one was not handled correctly by this class varied from *r*, which was not incorrectly handled by any child, to the grouping *ed*, which was not handled correctly by any of the children.

HOW ONE TEACHER DIAGNOSED HER CLASS *

by Mrs. Dorothy Erickson, Grade 2, Poulsbo, Wash.

Words	Times Missed												
1. Stick	19	st - i - ck		s - o - ng		b - a - t			t - e - nt				
2. Song	23	5	13	17	1	19	23	1	7	9	2	20	11
3. Bat	9											Total...128	
4. Tent	19												
5. Cans	6	c - a - ns		p - o - t		st - ar - s			b - ar				
6. Pot	14	3	3	6	3	14	5	11	19	14	1	18	
7. Stars	19											Total... 97	
8. Bar	18												
9. Cakes	19	c - a - k - es		p - a - d		n - u - ts							
10. Pad	13	1	4	16	18	5	4	11	9	22	13		
11. Nuts	22											Total...103	
12. Rushed	24	r - u - sh - ed		st - i - ll		r - ea - ch							
13. Still	17	0	17	22	24	15	9	9	2	20	20		
14. Reach	24											Total...138	
15. Send	20	s - e - nd		w - e - t									
16. Wet	16	1	18	16	2	14	8						
												Total... 59	
Total	282											525	

* Data reported in University of Washington *Remedial News Letter*, Vol. X (December-January, 1948-1949), p. 4.

A detailed analysis may be also made of the specific errors by a particular pupil, including the position in which they occurred—initial, medial, or final. In the analysis shown above it can be seen that in many cases the final elements were the ones most frequently incorrect. Corrective and remedial work can be planned in terms of the data revealed by the analysis.

Range of Vocabulary and Knowledge of Meanings of Words

To measure range of vocabulary and knowledge of the meanings of words, standard vocabulary tests in reading can be used, such as are described in Chapter 6. The teacher should have the pupil read aloud the words in the spelling test, especially those misspelled, to see if there is a relationship between spelling errors and pronunciation. It should be recalled that there is a close relationship between knowledge of meanings and spelling.

CASE-STUDY DIAGNOSTIC PROCEDURES

The analytical diagnostic procedures described in preceding pages will enable the teacher to locate and identify specific areas of deficiencies in spelling, but more penetrating methods must be used to determine the exact nature of the weaknesses and, if possible, the causes of the unsatisfactory performance so that the proper kind of corrective treatment can be applied. For this purpose, when dealing with cases of serious spelling disability, procedures that are essentially clinical in nature must be utilized. They range from the use of systematic, standardized techniques to the application of informal observational analytical procedures.

The Administration of Standardized Spelling Diagnostic Tests

Standardized methods of studying spelling disabilities are utilized in certain diagnostic tests. The Gates-Russell Spelling Diagnostic Tests [13] are the best-known standardized diagnostic tests available. They include the following series of nine tests:

1. Spelling words orally (power test).
2. Word pronunciation (reading and speech).
3. Giving letters for sounds (oral).
4. Spelling two syllables (oral).
5. Spelling two syllables (oral).
6. Word reversals (oral).
7. Spelling attack (securing evidence as to usual methods of study).
8. Auditory discrimination (hearing).
9. Visual, auditory, kinesthetic, and combined study methods (comparison of effectiveness).

The nature of the contents of the first eight tests is identified by the titles. Standardized materials and procedures are provided in each case. Test 9 of the Gates-Russell Spelling Diagnostic Test series applies a simple procedure for measuring the effectiveness of four different methods of studying words: the visual, the auditory, the kinesthetic, and a combined plan. The pupil studies four groups of three words of equal difficulty, one group by each method as carefully described by the teacher. The relative effectiveness of the four methods is determined by comparing the results of studying words by the four different methods. The visual method emphasizes "looking" at the word and studying it; the auditory method involves "hearing" the word and "spelling it letter by letter as the teacher spells it"; the kinesthetic method "writing" the word, getting the "feel" of it, writing it with eyes closed; the combined method involves elements of the visual, auditory, and kinesthetic methods. As the pupil studies the words, the teacher should note such factors as intelligence of approach, number of trials, effort made, hesitations, reading difficulties, attitude toward each method, and evidences of success in using the method. With the help of the teacher, the pupil in the remedial program should make subsequent use of these data to master an effective method of study.

Russell has shown that poor spellers are unable to make a varied or

[13] Distributed by Bureau of Publications, Teachers College, Columbia Univ., New York.

analytic approach to new words. Their methods are characterized by (1) incorrect syllabication and unsystematic division into word units, (2) spelling letter by letter, (3) spelling by small phonic elements, and (4) lack of syllabic analysis or syllabication. All of these deficiencies can be corrected by systematic instruction.

Performance on each of the nine diagnostic tests is evaluated in terms of grade scores and by recording brief descriptions of pupil reactions and responses. Details of scoring are given in the manual for the test.

The above data are supplemented by scores on standard tests of intelligence, spelling, silent and oral reading, vocabulary, memory of numbers and words, handwriting, vision, hearing loss, handedness, eyedness, and speech, as may be deemed necessary by the examiner. On page 367 there is an illustrative summary of the Gates-Russell test results.

The synthesis of the comprehensive information compiled by this many-sided testing program leads to the diagnosis of the nature of the spelling disability and to the identification of the causes most likely to be at the root of the difficulty. A remedial program can then be planned and undertaken.

An Illustrative Diagnosis in Spelling

A summary of test results for a third-grade boy appears on page 367. His grade scores on both written and oral spelling were more than a year below his actual grade level, 3.7. His reading scores, both silent and oral, were approximately one year below normal. According to test 6, he had serious deficiencies indicated by reversals and numerous spelling errors. His intelligence quotient of 119 indicated that he should be doing superior work.

He rated high on test 3, giving letters for letter sounds, and on test 8, auditory discrimination. An examination of his written work showed that most of his misspellings were approximately correct phonetically. Evidently auditory abilities were not at the root of his spelling difficulties.

On the Betts telebinocular test he failed on six of the subtests and was rated doubtful on three others. He failed on both near-point and far-point fusion tests and on tests of refraction including nearsightedness and astigmatism for both eyes at 80 inches and at infinite distance; and was rated doubtful on lateral imbalance (tendency for eyes to deviate inward and outward from their normal position) and other ametropia tests. Clearly, this boy had definite visual difficulties that likely were causally related to his spelling problems and also his reading disability.

The first step in an improvement program in this case should be a medical examination and a fitting of glasses. Subsequent steps in improvement should be planned in light of the corrections of vision that prove to be possible and in light of his spelling needs as indicated by the spelling diagnosis. The mere correction of his visual difficulties will in no way correct the faulty

GATES–RUSSELL SPELLING DIAGNOSIS TESTS

Name _____ Age _10_ I.Q. _119_ Grade _9.7_

Examiner _____ School _____ Date _____

Language parents speak   (a) to one another _English_ (b) to children _English_

To the Examiner:
This booklet contains tests fully described in Gates and Russell, *Diagnostic and Remedial Spelling Manual* (Bureau of Publications, Teachers College). The subject and the examiner must both be provided with booklets. They should exchange them for certain tests so that the written records of both subject and examiner may be contained in one booklet.

TEST	RAW SCORE	GRADE SCORE
1. Spelling Words Orally	7	2.4
2. Word Pronunciation	36	2.8
3. Giving Letters for Letter Sounds	9.7	5.5
4. Spelling One Syllable	6	3.0
5. Spelling Two Syllables	2	2.1
6. Word Reversals	17 errors	2.5
7. Spelling Attack		Poor
8. Auditory Discrimination		Excellent
9. Visual, Auditory, Kinaesthetic and Combined Study Methods		Poor

SUPPLEMENTARY DIAGNOSIS
Grade Score

1. Standard Test—Written Spelling   2.2
2. Standard Test—Silent Reading   2.8
3. Standard Test—Oral Reading   2.7
4. Vocabulary Test   4.8
5. Memory for Numbers   E+
6. Memory for Words   E+
7. Handwriting—Speed _70_ letters per minute.
8. Handwriting—Quality 40-50
9. Vision Test Comments: *Betts Tests:* Failed on 6 tests; doubtful on 3; passed 6. Nearsighted; poor fusion; lateral imbalance

10. Hearing Loss. Left _None_ %, Right _None_ %.
11. Handedness. Comments: *Right*
12. Eyedness. Comments: *Right*
13. Speech. Comments: *Good*
14. Forming of Derivatives. Comments: —
15. Use of Homonyms. Comments: —

BUREAU OF PUBLICATIONS, TEACHERS COLLEGE
COLUMBIA UNIVERSITY, NEW YORK
Copyright, 1937, by Teachers College
4M-L-7-45
Printed in U. S. A.

approaches to spelling which he has established. The correction in vision will make success in improving his spelling more likely.

A Suggested Informal Diagnostic Approach

A less formal diagnostic program than the Gates-Russell tests was developed by Watson.[14] It can be utilized in diagnostic study by any interested teacher. The essential elements of Watson's procedure are as follows:

1. Select a list of 30 to 50 words of average difficulty on some such basis as the frequency with which they are misspelled in written work, the kinds of errors usually made in spelling or pronouncing them, or the spelling rules that are applied in spelling them. The informal test on page 363 illustrates the approach.

2. Administer the words as a list test to the class.

3. Score the test papers. Select the four or five poorest papers for further analysis. Begin with the pupil whose score was lowest.

4. Have the pupil define the words he misspelled. Discard all words he cannot define, indicating that he does not know their meaning.

5. Then have the pupil spell the remaining words orally one at a time. Keep an exact written record of the spelling. Observe also spelling rhythm, syllabication, and phonic quality of every syllable.

6. Compare the original spelling with the oral spelling to see if the errors made are the same or if there are specific new or unique spellings.

7. Have the pupil pronounce the words in the test. Note difficulties in speech, phonics, syllabication, etc.

8. Make a quick analysis of the spelling errors made, classifying them according to major categories such as those given in the table on page 358, or according to the point of view from which the list of words was prepared; for instance, according to rules not known, or confusions of phonetic sounds. Note also lapses and slips.

9. Draw conclusions as to the nature of the pupil's spelling difficulties. If possible, estimate the quality of his method of attack in studying new words in daily lessons.

On the basis of this and other available related information, steps to be taken to improve the pupil's spelling can be planned.

Informal Uses of Other Diagnostic Procedures by Teachers

The teacher should not hesitate to apply informally, in the course of regular instruction, analytical diagnostic procedures similar to those applied systematically in the Gates-Russell Test.

Below are given illustrative uses of the various methods of case study and individual diagnosis, described in Chapter 4, which the teacher can use to good advantage in the diagnosis of spelling difficulties.

[14] Alice E. Watson, *Experimental Studies in the Psychology and Pedagogy of Spelling,* Contributions to Education No. 638 (New York, Bureau of Publications, Teachers College, Columbia Univ., 1935), pp. 47-53.

A. ANALYSIS OF WRITTEN WORK, INCLUDING TEST PAPERS

1. Legibility of handwriting.
2. Defects in letter forms, spacing, alignment, size.
3. Classification of errors in written work, letters, tests, etc.
4. Range of vocabulary used.
5. Evidence of lack of knowledge of conventions and rules.

B. ANALYSIS OF ORAL RESPONSES

1. Comparison of errors in oral and written spelling.
2. Pronunciation of words spelled incorrectly.
3. Articulation and enunciation.
4. Slovenliness of speech.
5. Dialect and colloquial forms of speech.
6. Way of spelling words orally.
   a. Spells words as units.
   b. Spells letter by letter.
   c. Spells by digraphs.
   d. Spells by syllables.
7. Rhythmic pattern in oral spelling.
8. Blending ability.
9. Giving letters for sounds or sounds for letters.
10. Technics of word analysis used.
11. Quality and errors made in oral reading.
12. Oral responses on tests of word analysis.
13. Analysis of pupil comments as he states orally his thought processes while studying new words.

C. INTERVIEW WITH PUPIL AND OTHERS

1. Questioning pupil about methods of study.
2. Questioning pupil about spelling rules.
3. Questioning pupil about errors in conventions.
4. Securing evidence as to attitude toward spelling.

D. QUESTIONNAIRE

1. Applying check-list of methods of study.
2. Having pupil rank spelling according to interest.
3. Surveying use of written language.

E. FREE OBSERVATION IN COURSE OF DAILY WORK

1. Securing evidence as to attitudes toward spelling.
2. Evidence of improvement in the study of new words.
3. Observing extent of use of dictionary.
4. Extent of error in regular written work.
5. Study habits and methods of work.
6. Social acceptability of learner.
7. Evidences of emotional and social maladjustment.
8. Evidences of possible physical handicaps.

F. CONTROLLED OBSERVATION OF WORK ON SET TASKS

1. Looking up the meanings of given words in dictionary.
2. Giving pronunciation of words in dictionary.

370 The Diagnosis and Treatment of Learning Difficulties

3. Writing plural forms and derivatives of given words.
4. Observing responses on informal tests.
5. Observing methods of studying selected words.
6. Estimating pupil success when using a variety of methods of studying selected words.

G. ANALYSIS OF AVAILABLE RECORDS

1. Records of scores on tests in reading, spelling, language, handwriting.
2. School history.
3. Health data; physiological deficiencies and defects, especially vision, loss of hearing, and motor co-ordination.
4. Sociological data.
5. Anecdotal records.

The brief descriptions below, based on informal observations of study habits used by six fifth-grade children when studying a list of 50 words, show how they varied and how unintelligent some of the learning procedures were:

Pupil 1. Copied the first word in the list and then rewrote it five times; then he did the same for the second word; and so on. He completed less than half of the words in the test during the study period. (Poor method.)

Pupil 2. Looked at the first word, closed his eyes and whispered the letters, and checked his spelling by looking at the word; then proceeded to the next word. (Fairly good method.)

Pupil 3. Looked at the first word, looked up, whispered the letters, and traced them in the air using large sweeping arm movements; then he wrote the word on his paper; he did this for all words studied. (Good method.)

Pupil 4. Dreams, looked at whole list in a random way; no whispering; no writing; no evidence that he had a systematic study procedure of any kind. (A poor speller and a typical complex disability case.)

Pupil 5. First skimmed the list of words, checking those about which she was uncertain; studied the words checked by using the "look, study, spell orally, check, write, check" method, a systematic study procedure. (Excellent speller.)

Pupil 6. Copied a word letter by letter, then with his pencil traced slowly the word he had written five or six times, whispering the letters as he traced them; no syllabication; he did the same for six other words he copied. (A low learning index.)

It obviously is necessary to attempt to appraise the effectiveness of the methods of study used by poor spellers and also to teach poor spellers how to study words. The teacher should first observe the pupil's methods of studying words either during the usual spelling lesson, or preferably under closer observation when he is studying a selected group of misspelled words. To evaluate the effectiveness of his study methods, the teacher then should test to see how many of the words he has learned to spell. On the basis of the observations and test results, the steps to bring about an improvement should then be planned.

THE TREATMENT OF SPELLING DIFFICULTIES

Factors Associated with Low Spelling Accomplishment

The major factors associated with low spelling accomplishment, which have been alluded to frequently in the preceding pages, may be summarized as follows:

1. Poor study habits. Many pupils do not acquire effective methods of learning to spell, perhaps in large part due to inadequacies of instruction in spelling and written composition.
2. Lack of interest and the presence of undesirable attitudes.
3. Weakness in essential techniques, such as phonics, word analysis, and syllabication.
4. Faulty speech habits, particularly in pronunciation.
5. Slow, illegible handwriting.
6. Visual defects and limitations.
7. Inferior auditory discrimination.
8. Low level of intelligence.

Some of these factors, vision, for example, can be corrected to a considerable extent. A skillful teacher can alleviate all of them by adapting the instructional program and methods of teaching to the needs and requirements of individual pupils. Usually a combination of several of these factors is contributory in a particular case. The approach to corrective treatment should therefore be multiple as well as directed to the correction of special disabilities.

The following references contain comprehensive discussions of factors associated with spelling disability. They should be consulted for details by anyone interested:

James A. Fitzgerald, *The Teaching of Spelling* (Milwaukee, Bruce Publishing Co., 1951).

A. I. Gates, *The Psychology of Reading and Spelling with Special Reference to Disability,* Contributions to Education No. 129 (New York, Bureau of Publications, Teachers College, Columbia Univ., 1922).

David H. Russell, *Characteristics of Good and Poor Spellers.* Contributions to Education No. 727 (New York, Bureau of Publications, Teachers College, Columbia Univ., 1937).

George Spache, "Spelling Disability Correlates I—Factors Probably Causal in Spelling Disability," *Journal of Educational Research,* Vol. 34 (April, 1941), pp. 561-587.

George Spache, "Spelling Disability Correlates II—Factors That May Be Related to Spelling Disability," *Journal of Educational Research,* Vol. 35 (October, 1941), pp. 119-137.

Alice E. Watson, *Experimental Studies in the Psychology and Pedagogy of Spelling,* Contributions to Education No. 638 (New York, Bureau of Publications, Teachers College, Columbia Univ., 1935).

The Gates-Russell Diagnostic and Remedial Spelling Manual contains a helpful discussion of the causes of spelling disability, case studies, and specific suggestions for remedial work in spelling.

In this section we shall deal primarily with general procedures for improving spelling rather than with specifics applied to special problems.

Factors Related to the Efficiency of Methods of Study

Evidence revealed by research about the methods that contribute to learning to spell may be summarized as follows:

1. A pretest should reveal to the pupil the words he does not know how to spell.
2. The pupil should focus his attention on the words or parts of words that he is unable to spell.
3. In presenting words, visualization should be the predominant procedure. Correct pronunciation and syllabication of words should be emphasized. The writing of the word in all cases should be included in word study.
4. Pupils should be encouraged to use any form or combination of types of imagery that will assist them to learn to spell, including visual, auditory, and kinesthetic imagery. It is very doubtful if there are dominant specific imagery types which can be the basis for deciding on methods of learning for all individuals.
5. Sensory impression should be accompanied by attempts to recall the spelling of words as an aid to temporary retention at the time of initial learning. Overlearning also is desirable.
6. Subsequently, distributed practice is necessary to insure retention of words learned, particularly in the case of slow learners. The amount and distribution of review needed will vary from learner to learner.
7. Tests by which the pupil can measure his progress are essential, since awareness of improvement is a valuable method of motivation.

There is no evidence as to which of a variety of particular study procedures is the most effective. Undoubtedly, because of individual differences among learners, no one plan will be equally effective for them all. A general approach to learning to spell such as the following, suitable for grades above the primary level, incorporates to a considerable extent the essentials of the seven principles listed above:

STUDY GUIDE TO SPELLING (GRADES 4-8)

1. Look up in the dictionary the meaning, pronunciation, and syllabication of each unfamiliar word to be studied.
2. Say the word as directed by the dictionary, first as a whole, then slowly several times syllable by syllable.
3. Spell the word orally without looking at it; then check your oral spelling by referring to the printed word.
4. Write the word, saying the syllables as you write. Do not say the letters. Check the written word.
5. Repeat step 4 about three times for each new word.
6. When reviewing difficult words, apply steps 1 to 4 as may be necessary.

With disability cases, the approach to the problem of improving study habits should be individual. In the early stages, close supervision of the pupil's work is necessary. The basis of the steps in the guide to study outlined above should be carefully explained to the learner. They should be demonstrated to him by the teacher. Under sympathetic guidance he should then try to apply them to the study of words he is learning to spell. The teacher should make every effort to secure the wholehearted co-operation of the individual. Evidence of success in applying the steps in the guide to learning is sure to arouse his interest and motivate his efforts to improve his spelling. It should not be expected that all learners will eventually use the same pattern of study habits. Intelligent adaptation within the general framework of the above principles should be permitted. Fernald [15] has stressed the value of kinesthetic imagery in the treatment of spelling disability.

The Teaching of Spelling Rules

The teaching of a few important spelling rules should be done inductively, following a series of steps somewhat as follows:

1. Select a particular rule to be taught. Teach a single rule at a time.
2. Secure a list of words exemplifying the rule. Develop the rule through the study of words that it covers.
3. Lead the pupils to discover the underlying generalization by discussing with them the characteristics of the words in the list. If possible, the pupils actually should formulate the rule. Help them to sharpen and clarify it.
4. Have the pupils use and apply the rule immediately.
5. If necessary, show how the rule in some cases does not apply, but stress its positive values.
6. Review the rule systematically on succeeding days. Emphasize its use, and do not require the pupils to memorize a formalized statement.

The rules of capitalization, the writing of possessives and contractions, and other conventions should also be taught inductively in a similar manner.

Lack of Interest and the Presence of Unfavorable Attitudes

These undesirable types of behavior patterns are undoubtedly due in large part to an instructional program that is highly formal and that fails to take into consideration the interests and needs of the learners. Instruction in spelling in such cases is focused on the spelling of lists of words rather than on helping children to spell the words they need to use in their experiences. The words being studied also may be too difficult for the learner. Lacking success in spelling because of poor study habits, pupils

[15] Grace E. Fernald, *Remedial Techniques in Basic Skill Subjects* (New York, McGraw, 1943), Ch. 13.

often become discouraged and fail to make the effort necessary to learn to spell.

Three essential steps to bring about an improvement are:

1. Provide a rich, vital series of learning experiences in which social pressure will make the learner increasingly aware of the necessity of being able to spell correctly.

2. Make a study of the characteristics of individual learners to determine the possible factors that may have caused them to develop a bad attitude toward spelling.

3. Make every effort to adjust the work of the pupil to his needs, requirements, and level of development. Especially try to help him to acquire efficient ways of learning to spell.

The reader should consult the many excellent books on the teaching of spelling for details as to curriculum and instruction.

Overcoming Weaknesses in Word Analysis Including Phonics and Syllabication

The procedures for improving knowledge, skills, and abilities in word analysis should be based on those that are used in reading, with the added stipulation that writing must be an integral part of the learning activity.

In some spelling cases, weakness in word analysis may be due to lack of knowledge of letter sounds, inability to blend sounds, and other faults revealed by reading diagnosis. Treatment should begin with procedures for overcoming these reading deficiencies, and then be carried over into the field of oral and written spelling. (See pages 375-376.)

In other spelling cases, weakness in using word elements may not be associated with reading but more specifically with inability to recall what the word looks like, how it is pronounced, and how the elements are spelled. There is a vast difference between recognizing the elements within a written word in reading and recalling those elements for spelling. In such cases, a direct attack on the spelling difficulty, as shown by the diagnosis, is indicated.

For poor spellers, emphasis should be placed on the spelling of word elements rather than practice in reading them. First, the learner should learn to associate sounds of single letters and their written symbols, and then proceed to the study and writing of combinations of letters and phonograms. Each lesson should include the correction of the pupil's written work and a discussion of phonetic variants. Similar lessons should next deal with the spelling of common stems, prefixes, and suffixes. The learner thus gradually will become familiar with the spelling of a large number of useful word elements. Next he should study their use in selected groups of common words containing certain letters, phonograms, or other word elements, and practice writing the words. Every effort should be made to aid recall by using visual, auditory, and kinesthetic imagery to strengthen sensory impressions.

Games and devices similar to those commonly used to create interest in remedial reading should be freely used in remedial work in spelling. Stress should be placed on correct spelling, not on reading correctly.

SPELLING GAMES

1. Anagrams. Pupils rearrange a disarranged group of letters as a word.
2. Naming the words. The teacher says, "What is one word in the lesson?" A pupil names one, spells it, then pronounces another word. The next pupil spells it and so on until all of the words have been given and spelled.
3. "Spelling and guessing." A pupil writes a word from the spelling lesson, for instance, *apple,* on a slip of paper and places it on the teacher's desk. Then he calls on some pupil to spell it. This child says, "Is it h-o-r-s-e?" "No, it is not horse." The next child called on says, "Is it a-p-p-l-e?" "Yes, it is apple." Then that child becomes "it," and the game continues.
4. "Naming letters." Teacher writes a word from the spelling lesson on the blackboard. The children notice the order of the letters in the word carefully. Then they shut their eyes. The teacher passes about the room and touches children, who spell the word aloud with eyes closed.
5. "Rhyming game." Children give and spell a word that rhymes with a word pronounced by the teacher or some pupil.
6. "Picture game." Children spell names of objects in a picture.
7. "Relays." Two teams are selected. A word family is chosen, such as *ate.* The children one by one from each team hurry to the blackboard and write a word in the family. The side with the most words and the fewest spelling errors wins.

Exercises such as the following, similar to some of those given for reading described in Chapter 7 and functional in nature, are especially useful in teaching word-analysis techniques required in spelling.

SPECIAL EXERCISES IN WORD ANALYSIS

1. Word study involving initial letter sounds
   a. Write lists of words that begin with the same initial letter sounds, such as *boy, bird, big; cat, come, cow; hat, horse, house.*

2. Word study involving vowel sounds
   a. Writing words that contain long vowel sounds, such as long $\bar{a}$ in *late, came, fail, plane.*
   b. Similar exercise for the long sounds of *e, i, o, u.*
   c. Writing words that contain the short sound of *a,* as in *cat, cap, nap, camel, plan.*
   d. Similar exercise for the short sounds of *e, i, o, u.*

3. Word study involving initial blends and phonograms
   a. Writing words that start like *blue; stop; play; street; thread, etc.*
   b. Writing words that start with the initial sounds of the words chosen: *this; shed, what, etc.*

4. Word study involving word endings

    a. Writing other words rhyming with words ending with longer-sound elements, such as *day, skate, peck, like,* etc.

    b. Writing words with their variant endings, such as

	ed	ing	s
walk	_____	_____	_____
plan	_____	_____	_____
like	_____	_____	_____
suffer	_____	_____	_____

    c. Writing comparative forms of words, such as:

	er	est
small	_____	_____
fast	_____	_____
big	_____	_____
large	_____	_____

    d. Special exercises on the spelling of plurals, contractions, and possessive forms of words.

5. Word study involving structural analysis

    a. Writing compound words made from two lists of words:

A	B	Compound word
sand	road	_____
under	man	_____
rail	thing	_____
some	stand	_____

    b. Locating and writing root words:

        (1) When suffixes are present:

wonderful	_____	workable	_____
likeness	_____	bigger	_____

        (2) When prefixes are present:

unkind	_____	indoor	_____
relive	_____	improve	_____

        (3) When affixed elements are present:

unlikely	_____	important	_____
reworked	_____	unwrapping	_____

    c. Drawing lines between syllables heard in a word:

below	_____	decide	_____	natural	_____
danger	_____	ornament	_____	declaration	_____

Alleviating Faulty Speech Habits, Particularly Incorrect Pronunciation

It is obvious that misspelling often is due to the mispronunciation of words. In some sections of the country, dialects and local ways of speaking may lead to misspelling. In the same way, slovenly speech often leads to misspelling.

It is necessary that special attention be given to both the meaning and the correct pronunciation of all spelling words being studied, as described in the guide for studying words given on page 372. Language instruction must pay particular attention to pronunciation, syllabication, and word analysis. In cases of serious speech difficulty or defective speech, the corrective speech teacher can make a valuable contribution to the improvement of spelling.

Speech faults are closely associated in spelling with an excessive proportion of errors of omissions of sounded letters and syllables, additions of syllables, and nonphonetic additions and substitutions. These errors can be identified by tests of oral reading, mispronunciation tests, and by having the pupil pronounce the words misspelled in written spelling tests. Correction of speech faults will gradually reduce the proportion of these spelling errors.

Improving Slow, Illegible Handwriting

Russell [16] reported a small but significant difference in the quality of handwriting of good and poor spellers. Procedures for improving slow, illegible handwriting are discussed in Chapter 12. Information about illegibilities and malformation of letters, the rate and quality of usual writing, and the analysis of defects in slant, spacing, and alignment, are especially valuable in the diagnosis and treatment of low spelling performance. The letters that contribute most frequently to illegibility are *a, d, e, u, r,* and *t.* Writing inaccuracies such as failure to close and complete such letters as *a, d, q,* and *g,* and failure to dot the letter *i* or to cross the letter *t* often cause pupils to write words incorrectly. Calling the pupil's attention directly to such specific eccentricities and their effects on the correctness and legibility of written speech usually will suffice for correction with older pupils. For younger children, direct handwriting practice to correct deficiencies may be required. See Chapter 12 for details on improving handwriting. It must be recognized that poor spellers frequently write poorly in order to cover up spelling inadequacies. For example, in writing the word, *receive,* the poor speller may make the *e* and *i* look alike, since he isn't sure which one comes first.

Manuscript writing may be substituted for cursive writing in an effort to overcome handwriting difficulties in cases where they are due to motor inco-ordination or lack of training. Manuscript writing is of particular value in dealing with spelling cases where disability is due to poor handwriting, inferior motor control, or marked loss of vision.

Consideration of Visual Defects and Limitations

Russell reports that there was no significant difference on the whole in visual acuity, vertical and lateral imbalance, and ametropia for good and poor spellers. However, he emphasized the importance of checking the

[16] D. H. Russell. *loc cit.*

vision of poor spellers because faulty visual imagery may be an important factor in specific cases.

Whenever it appears evident that a pupil may not be learning to spell or read because of visual defects and limitations, corrective measures should be taken under competent medical guidance. The teacher can also make such adjustments as seating the pupil with poor vision nearer the blackboard, using books with enlarged type, emphasizing auditory imagery, and the like.

As was indicated above, the substitution of manuscript writing for cursive script is regarded as desirable in spelling cases due to marked deterioration of vision.

Eye movements of good spellers have fewer regressions, shorter time of fixation, and more regular fixations than those of poor spellers. These points should be borne in mind when teaching poor spellers how to "look at" words when studying them, as required in the suggested guide for study.

Inferior Auditory Discrimination

Russell [17] found that there is a significant difference in auditory discrimination between good and poor spellers. Inferior auditory discrimination may be due either to loss of hearing, which can be alleviated by hearing aids, or to lack of training in sound perception. Inability to give sounds for letters or letters for sounds, failure to discriminate letter sounds, blending difficulties, and weakness in phonics are symptoms of this deficiency.

A simple test of auditory discrimination of sounds of letters is the following:

1. Give the pupil a paper on which are given the pairs of words shown below:
2. Have the pupil mark the word (starred) in each pair that you pronounce. Speak in a normal tone. The pupil should be seated with his back to the examiner at a distance of 6 to 10 feet.

TEST OF AUDITORY DISCRIMINATION OF SOUNDS

war was*	far fair*	sad sand*	noon*none
night*sight	mind find*	think*thank	these there*
say*hay	chip*ship	black*block	better butter*

This test would not be suitable for a poor speller who is also poor in reading. A better one for him would be to say a list of word pairs, such as *which* and *witch; bin* and *bin; pig* and *big;* and so on, and have him tell which pairs are the same and which are different.

When inferior auditory discrimination is owing to lack of ear training, exercises similar to those used in reading should be used to train pupils to discriminate sounds, to identify sounds, and to give sounds. These exercises should be closely integrated with phonic training, pronunciation, and improvement of speech. See Chapter 4 for details.

[17] *Loc. cit.*

Level of Intelligence

As indicated earlier in this chapter, there is a positive but rather low correlation between intelligence and spelling. It is known that pupils of low intelligence are very likely to be inferior in spelling. However, a high level of intelligence does not guarantee a high level of spelling ability. In planning remedial work in spelling, adaptations should be made in all cases to the pupil's level of intelligence and language development, including adjustments of the number of words to be studied, instructional procedures used, and the rate of progress to be expected. Individual progress goals should be set up by which each learner can measure the progress he is making.

SUGGESTED ACTIVITIES

1. Outline basic methods that you think teachers should use to appraise the spelling ability of their pupils. Go beyond the spelling lesson. Prepare a timed dictation test and administer it to a class. (See Chapter 12 for method.)

2. Secure a pupil's written composition. Mark the spelling errors it contains and find the coefficient of misspelling. Students enrolled in a course will find the scoring of the papers of a whole class of children an interesting and revealing experience.

3. Find the spelling learning index of one or more pupils, using the plan described on pages 354-355. Observe closely the methods of study of some pupil whose scores on survey tests or in daily spelling lessons are at a low level. Write a description of his behavior and be ready to discuss it. Compare the methods of study used by good and poor spellers.

4. Secure compositions for some pupil containing about 1200 written words, and analyze the spelling errors according to the plan given in the table on page 358. Find also the coefficients of misspelling on each composition, and a composite figure for all of the compositions.

5. Find the learning indices for the five pupils below whose scores on the learning test on page 356 were as follows:

	Initial Test	*Retest*
A.P.	40	70
R.C.	10	25
C.B.	20	80
P.T.	70	98
C.F.	18	21

6. Analyze the kinds of errors made on the list of words according to a plan that you regard as acceptable and helpful.

7. Administer the Spache Spelling Errors Test on page 360, and analyze the results according to the plan described.

8. Administer the diagnostic test on spelling difficulties given on page 363. Analyze the results.

9. A teacher of a primary grade may be interested in diagnosing specific phonetic difficulties by applying the method described on page 364.

10. Select a pupil who has serious spelling problems. Either administer the the Gates-Russell test, or apply the informal case-study procedures described in

this chapter, pages 369-370. Formulate a statement describing this pupil's spelling problems and listing the factors that appear to be the sources of his difficulty. Consult school records and other sources for information that may help you to understand the case. Outline remedial measures that you think would be helpful. Apply them over a period of time and determine their effectiveness.

11. Do you think that all pupils should be taught a particular method of studying spelling and be required to use it? Why? Why not? Compare study methods taught in several spelling textbooks. Evaluate them.

12. What remedial measures would you like to add to those given at the end of the chapter? Individual teachers often have discovered methods of teaching children that they find are successful. Can you give any illustrations?

SELECTED BIBLIOGRAPHY

BRUECKNER, L. J., and MELBY, E. O., *Diagnostic and Remedial Teaching* (Boston, Ginn, 1931), Ch. 10.

Child Development and the Curriculum, Thirty-eighth Yearbook, Part I, National Society for the Study of Education (Chicago, Univ. of Chicago Press, 1939), Ch. 12.

FERNALD, Grace M., *Remedial Techniques in Basic Skill Subjects* (New York, McGraw, 1943), Ch. 13.

GATES, A. I., and RUSSELL, D. H., *Diagnostic and Remedial Manual,* rev. ed. (New York, Bureau of Publications, Teachers College, Columbia Univ., 1940).

HILDRETH, Gertrude, *Learning the Three R's* (Minneapolis, Educational Publishers, Inc., 1947), Ch. 18.

KAY, Marjorie E., "Effect of Errors in Pronunciation in Spelling," *Elementary English Review,* Vol. 7 (March, 1930), pp. 64-66.

KING, Luella, *Learning and Applying Spelling Rules in Grades 3 to 8* (New York, Bureau of Publications, Teachers College, Columbia Univ., 1932).

RUSSELL, D. H., *Characteristics of Good and Poor Spellers* (New York, Bureau of Publications, Teachers College, Columbia Univ., 1937).

SPACHE, G., "Spelling Disability Correlates," *Journal of Educational Research,* Vol. 35 (October, 1941), pp. 119-138.

12

DIAGNOSIS AND TREATMENT OF HANDWRITING DIFFICULTIES

IN THIS CHAPTER we discuss in detail problems related to the diagnosis and treatment of learning difficulties and deficiencies in handwriting under the following headings:

1. The fundamentals of effective instruction in handwriting.
2. Foundations of diagnosis in handwriting.
3. General diagnosis in handwriting.
4. Analytical diagnosis in handwriting.
5. Case-study diagnostic procedures.
6. The treatment of handwriting difficulties.

THE FUNDAMENTALS OF EFFECTIVE INSTRUCTION IN HANDWRITING

The Objectives of Instruction in Handwriting

Handwriting is an essential tool for recording ideas and communicating them to others. Handwriting is basically a motor skill which develops gradually as the pupil progresses through school. The traditional concept of "penmanship" was that handwriting is essentially an art. This concept has been discarded by most schools in favor of the view that handwriting should be taught in a way that will assure its functional use in everyday life.

Handwriting should be taught in conjunction with the other language arts. In learning to read the child learns to recognize words that he later may wish to reproduce. The time normally comes when he wishes or needs to write. First he writes words, later sentences to communicate his ideas. This activity requires the correct use of capitalization and punctuation to set off thought units, which are basic elements of written composition. The ability to spell depends on the ability to form written letters and words correctly and to space them so the reader is carried along smoothly. It is thus apparent that handwriting is an integral part of the total communicative process.

The activities of the period devoted to handwriting instruction should be so conducted that they will contribute to the improvement of the handwriting required in all areas of the curriculum and in life outside the school. The pupil ordinarily readily senses at an early age the need for handwriting as a means of written expression. The teacher's goal should be to assist the learner to develop a fluent, easy style of writing that is so legible it can be read with little effort. The pupil should gradually become aware of and accept ordinary standards of rate, form, and quality. Thus he will develop a sense of consideration for others and a desire to attack directly aspects of his handwriting that contribute to its illegibility, as well as a feeling against eccentric individualization. He should learn what the causes of illegible or slow handwriting are, and learn to identify them in his own written work. Under the guidance of the teacher, he should undertake a systematic corrective program to improve his handwriting.

The ultimate outcome of handwriting instruction should be automatic control of the skills involved, so that the individual is free to devote his attention to the ideas he wishes to express. The contributions of instruction in written composition and spelling to this goal should be recognized in teaching handwriting.

Principles of Teaching Handwriting

The basic principles underlying the teaching of handwriting may be briefly stated as follows:

1. The teacher should take every opportunity to develop in children a desire to express ideas in written form by arranging a wide variety of interesting learning experiences in which handwriting functions directly.

2. The learning of handwriting is a growth process, proceeding gradually and by quite clearly defined stages from the scribbling and meaningless marks made on paper or blackboard by young children playing at writing to the mature form of writing used by adults. Direct instruction should not begin until the second year.

3. In the primary grades, manuscript or print-script writing should be used by the teacher and taught at the start. Gradually a shift should be made to cursive writing. In most schools, this shift takes place at about the third-grade level, although the rate at which different children can make the change varies considerably.

4. Children do not all progress at the same rate in gaining control over the motor skills involved in handwriting; hence individual guidance and close supervision in the early stages are necessary. At times, children in higher classes can be grouped according to their levels of development and common needs. Mass teaching should be avoided at all times.

5. There should be considerable emphasis on diagnosis in the teaching of handwriting, so that each pupil may become aware of the causes of illegibility in his written work and learn to identify them. Self-diagnosis by reference to specially prepared diagnostic charts is highly desirable.

6. The steps taken to improve rate and legibility of handwriting should be adapted to the needs of the individual. Specific difficulties, such as the forming of incorrect figures and letters or poor spacing, should be attacked directly. Goals that are possible of achievement should be co-operatively set up by the teacher and the pupil and they should be adjusted to the learner's potentialities and level of development. The children should be permitted considerable liberty in making handwriting adjustments in rate and movement, so that the positions of their bodies and the muscular efforts they make will be natural and comfortable. The requirement of a ritualistic adherence by all to some system induces fatigue, discouragement, and tension. It is not necessary to stress speed, since rate of work will increase as correct habits are formed and under the pressure resulting from increased demands for writing arising in the activities under way.

Why Manuscript and Cursive Writing?

Two forms of writing are taught in most schools. In manuscript writing, the letters are disconnected and are made in the form used by scribes before the printing press was invented. The writing may be slanting or vertical, but usually is vertical. Cursive writing was devised because of the demand for a fluent, easy style and is the ordinary form of writing used by adults.

Values that have been claimed for manuscript writing are its superior legibility and ease of learning and its contribution to the learning of other subjects, particularly reading and spelling. Experiments have shown that pupils in the primary grades learn manuscript writing more easily than cursive script and can write it slightly more rapidly. Children write more in the primary grades when manuscript writing is taught rather than cursive script. Children who use manuscript writing also learn to read more rapidly and are somewhat more accurate in their spelling. Cursive writing is more rapid for older children, but ordinarily less legible.

Freeman [1] reported in 1945 that in 84 per cent of 727 school systems surveyed, manuscript writing was taught in the primary grades, but that the general practice was to make a shift to cursive script at about the third grade. In some schools no change was made from manuscript to cursive writing at the third-grade level, whereas in others both forms are taught throughout the grades.

FOUNDATIONS OF DIAGNOSIS IN HANDWRITING

Stages in the Development of Ability in Handwriting

The procedures of diagnosis must be adjusted to the fact that the mastery of handwriting progresses through a number of stages until the skills mature.

[1] F. N. Freeman, "Survey of Manuscript Writing in Public Schools," *Elementary School Journal,* Vol. 46 (March, 1946), pp. 375-380.

At each stage, special problems arise that require careful consideration. These stages can be described as follows:

Stage 1. Readiness for Writing. As is true of reading and arithmetic, young children are not all equally ready for instruction in handwriting when they enter the first grade. During this first stage the children use crayons, chalk, and pencils to make drawings and scribblings that to them stand for something which they can explain or describe for others. As the child shares his experiences with others, he gradually begins to see that what he draws and scribbles must also be read or interpreted. Both he and others must be able to take out of the symbolic expression what he has put into it. When he becomes aware of this problem, mentally he is ready for handwriting. It is known that many young children have passed beyond this stage before they come to school, because of experiences with parents and others in the home, such as coloring pictures, making drawings, and similar things.

Stage 2. First Steps in Learning to Write in Grade 1. Many children know how to write their names when they come to school. Usually they have learned to print their names; this form of writing is much easier for young children to learn, since they can write single letters one at a time and do not have the problem of joining them as is required by cursive script.

During this stage the children learn to read manuscript writing that primary teachers use in guiding reading instruction, in recording stories told by children, or in writing accounts of experiences the class may have. The children may learn to write names of people, pets, and things they are reading about. When there is evidence of a desire to learn to write, the teacher takes them in small groups and gives them instruction in simple aspects of writing which include the development of word configurations, the contour, alignment, and spacing of words, the writing of letters, how to hold chalk, and so on. Words to be written are selected from those needed in various learning activities. The children are encouraged to write stories and diaries freely and independently as motor skills are developed. Spelling is not stressed.

At this stage, writing is limited to the use of crayon and chalk, which involve only the co-ordination of large movements.

Stage 3. Systematic Instruction Begins—Grade 2. Systematic instruction in handwriting is begun at this stage, usually limited to the pencil. The children learn to use the manuscript form in writing with pencils. Materials for practice to develop motor controls and knowledge of the correct letter forms are provided. Special attention is directed to the correct ways of writing letters. The length of what is written begins with short-span words such as *it, the, red,* and the like; then longer span words are copied and words with certain letter combinations; finally simple, short, familiar sentences are written.

The children plan independent writing activities. Special attention is given to reversals in writing numbers and letters.

Stage 4. Cursive Writing—Grade 3. At this stage a gradual shift is made from manuscript or print-script writing to cursive writing. Here children must learn a new way of writing words. Some learn cursive writing quickly, others find it difficult to learn. Because of difficulty of recalling letter forms and in forming them, spelling sometimes suffers. A great deal of practice is needed to master this form of writing. Because the needs of children are so different and because of differences in the rates at which they learn, it is necessary to group the children for instructional purposes. Considerable time must be devoted to the guidance of the work of some of the pupils. Special attention must be given to the writing of troublesome small letters, capital letters, and numbers. The size of the letters will be larger than in following stages.

Stage 5. Developmental Program in Grades 4, 5, and 6. At this stage, writing activities increase, children become aware of the need of improving their handwriting, and methods of self-help in diagnosing and correcting faults are taught. Speed and quality both tend to increase, the latter only slightly. Spot checks are made of all written work to emphasize the desirability of good writing at all times. Writing with a pen is taught at this stage. The size of the letters will gradually approach that normally used by adults.

Stage 6. Remedial Program. The systematic study of handwriting usually is completed by the close of the elementary school, and above that level the program is essentially remedial so as to attain and maintain desirable handwriting standards.

The methods to be used by the teacher and pupils at each of these six stages to evaluate progress in learning to write, and also the methods by which faults are diagnosed and remedied, must be adapted to the needs and levels of development of the various pupils. These methods will necessarily change as the child's control of the motor skills advances, and they should be adjusted to the rate of growth of each individual. It is essential that evaluations be based on the handwriting done in functional situations and in accordance with socially acceptable standards, adjusted to the individual's stage of development. Instructional programs and materials must take into consideration the range in the needs of the pupils and the variety of factors that may cause individual pupils to make unsatisfactory progress.

Movement in Handwriting

The sideward movement of the hand by rotating the forearm is perhaps the easiest and most rapid movement. When writing with the right hand, an easier movement results if the paper is tilted to the left so that the bottom of the sheet is perpendicular to the forearm. In left-handed writing, the paper should be tilted to the right in a similar way. In the former, the "pull" in writing is toward the body; whereas in the latter, the "pull" is toward the left elbow. Much of the awkward posture involving "hooks" and upside-down writing by children using left-handed writing would be eliminated if teachers insisted on the correct position of the paper and taught the proper "pull" or movement.

The composition of the movement has been the subject of considerable study. When left to themselves, children use the fingers chiefly to form letters and to carry the pen or pencil forward from letter to letter. In the past, supervisors and teachers attempted to have pupils use arm movement alone in forming letters. Freeman has shown, however, that both children and adults use a combined movement in which the fingers, hand, and arm work together in a rhythmic, co-ordinated manner. The important thing is that the individual learner should be led to discover a comfortable hand position, so that movement may proceed smoothly and easily from letter to letter and from one word to the next word. The production of correct form depends on varying the speed of the stroke to fit the part of the letter involved and the form which is to be produced.

Hand Preference in Handwriting

A rather large fraction of children prefer the left hand to the right hand in learning to write, as they do also in other activities. Some teachers insist that the right hand be used in all cases on the ground that the conditions of writing favor its use. However, there are many psychologists and speech specialists who warn that it actually is dangerous to compel the left-handed child to write with his right hand, on the grounds that poorer writing results and tensions may be produced which cause disorders of speech and reading. The evidence on this issue is conflicting.

If you are left handed

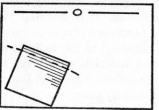

If you are right handed

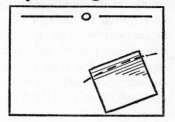

Strongly left-handed children should be allowed to learn to write with their left hands. It is generally agreed that when there is no marked preference in the case of young children, they should be encouraged to use the right hand. If the child prefers to write with his left hand, he should be taught to reverse the position of the paper as described above and to make the proper "pull" toward the left elbow. Otherwise he will learn to write in awkward positions and to use faulty types of movement. The teacher should permit the child to make any natural adaptations and adjustments that lead to comfortable, easy writing movements. Mirror writing is more prevalent among children who use the left hand in writing than among right-handed children. In such cases, the direction of the handwriting movement is reversed and also the form of letters and figures. Mirror writing is most frequently found in the primary grades, and this disability is usually eliminated or outgrown under careful instruction conducted on an individual basis. Reversals [2] in reading and spelling may be associated with factors that contribute to mirror writing.

GENERAL DIAGNOSIS IN HANDWRITING

The Basis of Appraisal

In the primary grades the teacher's evaluation of pupil progress in handwriting should be made individually. This is particularly necessary in the beginning years because of differences among pupils in readiness for handwriting, in motor control and co-ordination, in desire to write, and in ability to form and recall symbols. It is not desirable, for example, to set uniform standards for rate of writing that all children in a given age or grade group should be expected to achieve. A more satisfactory measure of a pupil's rate of writing would be to compare his present rate with that revealed by some preceding test.

In the higher grades it is possible to secure quite satisfactory measures of the quality and speed of handwriting by means of handwriting scales, free writing exercises, and timed dictation tests.

Handwriting Scales

Several kinds of scales for measuring the quality of handwriting have been devised. One of the earliest of them, still widely used, is the Ayres Handwriting Scale, Gettysburg edition. It consists of a series of eight specimens arranged in order of their legibility, as measured by the rate at which they can be read. The Thorndike Handwriting Scale consists of a series of specimens arranged in order of their general merit. The general merit of each specimen, including beauty, legibility, and character, was originally determined by the judgments of a large number of raters. Both of these scales consist chiefly of samples of the writing of pupils in the upper grades; hence they are difficult to apply in the lower grades.

To overcome this problem, several school systems have developed scales for different levels of the school, such as the Minneapolis scales for various

---

[2] B. G. Gilkey and F. W. Parr, "Analysis of the Reversal Tendencies of Fifty Selected Elementary School Pupils," *Journal of Educational Psychology,* Vol. 35 (May, 1944), pp. 284-292.

grade levels. The specimens in each scale consist of selections from the written work of pupils at each level. The samples change from one scale to the other in size of the writing and in other characteristics affected by the maturity of the pupils, such as evidence of motor control. Values can be assigned to the samples by comparison with the Ayres Scale. This plan makes it possible to measure progress in quality of handwriting from grade to grade. Even though ratings are based on different scales, each consisting of samples quite similar in general style and size of writing, the ratings for quality are directly comparable. Several commercial houses have prepared similar scales.

To measure the quality of handwriting of a given pupil, a specimen of his written work is matched with those in a scale and given the rating of the specimen in the scale which it most closely resembles.

Copying and Free Writing Exercises

Two simple ways in which to get a measure of the pupil's rate of writing are (1) copying, and (2) free writing exercises. In copying exercises the pupil is given some easy material to copy, and his rate is determined by the number of letters he can copy per minute over a short period of time. Ayres used this procedure in constructing his original scale. In free writing exercises, the pupil is asked to write from memory some sentence or some simple selection, such as a well-known poem. Freeman suggests use of the sentence, "A quick brown fox jumps over the lazy dog."

The following standards for rate and quality of handwriting are based on norms proposed by Ayres, Freeman, and others.[3]

HANDWRITING NORMS FOR RATE AND QUALITY OF FREE WRITING

	GRADES						
	2	*3*	*4*	*5*	*6*	*7*	*8*
Letters per minute	30	40	50	60	67	74	80
Seconds per letter	2.0	1.7	1.2	1.0	.9	.8	.7
Quality (Ayres Scale) ..	40	42	46	51	55	59	63

The application of these norms for speed and quality is as follows:

1. Suppose that a fifth-grade pupil writes at the rate of 67 letters a minute, and with a quality of 40 on the Ayres Scale. His rate is equivalent to that of the average pupil in the sixth grade, and his quality is below that of the average third-grade pupil.

2. Similarly, if a fourth-grade pupil writes a selection containing 60 letters in 54 seconds, he writes at the rate of the average sixth-grade pupil ($60 \times .9 = 54$).

[3] Taken from F. N. Freeman, "Teaching Handwriting," in Bulletin No. 4, *What Research Says to the Teacher,* Bulletin No. 4 (Washington, National Education Association, 1954), pp. 4-5.

Obviously, the directions given the pupils in securing the writing specimens affect his performance. Consider the possible relation of the following sets of directions to the kinds of handwriting resulting:

1. Write as well and neatly as you can.
2. Write as rapidly as you can.
3. Copy at your usual rate of writing.

Freeman recommends the use of the following directions: "Write as well as you can and as rapidly as you can."

On the basis of such test results, pupils can be grouped according to the general characteristics of their handwriting somewhat as follows:

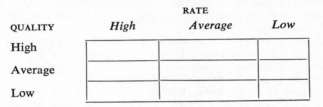

	RATE		
QUALITY	*High*	*Average*	*Low*
High			
Average			
Low			

Timed Dictation Exercises

Timed dictation exercises are used by the teacher to secure specimens of handwriting which result when the pupils write sentences at the standard rate for their grade. Similar timed dictation exercises are often used as spelling tests instead of list tests.

First, a series of short sentences is prepared, containing words that are of less than average spelling difficulty. Next the number of letters in each sentence is found. Then the number of seconds to allow for writing each sentence is determined by multiplying the number of letters in the sentence by the standard number of seconds per letter given in the table on page 388. To find the time to be allowed for dictation, divide the number of letters by 10.

The formula for finding the time for a sentence is $T = nt + \dfrac{n}{10}$. In the formula T is total time, n the number of letters, and t the time allowed per letter.

To find the time to allow for dictating and having pupils for grade 5 write the first sentence in the test given on page 390, proceed as follows:

$n = 21$ letters $\qquad\qquad\qquad\qquad$ $t = 1.0$ seconds per letter
Then $T = 21 \times 1.0 + \frac{21}{10} = 23.1$, or 23 seconds.
Round off to the nearest second.

How to Administer a Timed Dictation Exercise

The directions for giving a typical timed dictation test devised by the handwriting department of the Minneapolis Public Schools are given below:

HOW TO GIVE THE TEST

A practice test should be given two days preceding the actual test. After the heading is written and the children have *turned their papers* over, follow these steps in giving the test:

1. Say to the children, "We're going to write a paragraph to see how *fast* you write when you do your *very best writing.* Fifth graders should be able to write about *sixty-five* letters a minute. Let's see how well you write when you write that fast. I will dictate one sentence at a time. If you have not finished when I start a new sentence, just let it go, and start the new one with me.

   "But first I will read the whole paragraph to you so that you will know what it is about. If there are any words that you are not sure you can spell, let me know, and we'll write them on the chalkboard.

   "Be sure to begin your sentences with a capital, and end them with the right stop mark."
2. Then dictate the sentences, one at a time. If you have been unable to procure a watch with a second hand, stand near a good writer, and dictate to keep him writing continuously.
3. Collect the papers, sentence side up.
4. Place them in an envelope, labeled, and *file* for safe keeping until the *new* handwriting scales will be sent to you for scoring, including the new tabulation sheets for class scores.

THE TEST

The number in parenthesis indicates the position of the second hand at which you should dictate the sentence.

(Second hand) 60 __ __ __ __ __ __ __ __ 24 __ __ __ __ __ __ __ 45 __
Grade five is a good grade. You are now at the start. How
__ __ __ __ __ __ 11 __ __ __ __ __ __ __ __ 25 __ __ __
far can you go? You will have many helpers. The writing
__ __ __ __ __ __ 54 __ __ __ __ __ __ __ __ __ __ __
scale is one helper. The writing charts are other helpers.
25 __ __ __ __ __ __ __ __ __ __ __ 58 __ __ __ __ __ __ __
The writing records are helpers too. They will be fun to use.
18 __ __ __ __ __ __ __ 38 __ __ __ __ __ __ __ __ 5 __
Make this a happy year. Be a fine fifth grade writer. Stop.

ANALYTICAL DIAGNOSIS IN HANDWRITING

Analytical diagnosis in handwriting involves the use of such procedures as the following:

1. Testing knowledge of how to write letter forms and figures.
2. Discovering letter forms and figures illegibly or incorrectly written.
3. Determining qualities contributing to illegibility.
4. Testing knowledge of rules of capitalization and punctuation.

The purpose of these diagnostic procedures is to determine the lack of specific knowledges and skills essential in handwriting and the qualities in handwriting specimens that contribute to lack of legibility. These deficiencies can be attacked directly without further detailed diagnosis. However, in certain cases these analytical procedures must be supplemented by a more penetrating psychological study to get at underlying factors that may be involved. These special procedures will be discussed in the next section.

Testing Knowledge of How to Write Letter Forms and Figures

Some pupils do not know how to write the cursive forms of certain letters and confuse them with manuscript form. This lack can be measured informally by asking the pupil to write the series of letters in the alphabet, to copy certain printed materials, or to write letters as they are pronounced by the examiner. Simple timed dictation exercises can also be used.

Discovering Letter Forms and Figures Incorrectly Written

On the basis of eye-movement studies of the reading of handwritten materials, Quant [4] has shown that the most important factor in determining legibility is letter formation. Other factors of less significance are compactness in spacing and uniformity of moderate slant.

It is a relatively simple matter to analyze a pupil's written work to determine the letters and figures that are incorrectly written. The number of times incorrect forms are used can be tallied as the paper is read. For instance, reversals of letters and figures often appear in the written work of pupils in grades 3 and 4, especially at the point where the shift from print-script to cursive writing is being made. Confusions of forms also often appear at that time. Similarly, evidence of failure to join letters in cursive writing also can readily be noted. In most cases these faults respond quickly to treatment under careful guidance. The written work of left-handed children should be especially checked for incorrect letter forms and slant. Note any instances of mirror writing that may require further study.

It is probable that a direct attack on specific types of illegibility would contribute much to the improvement of handwriting.

The following table presents the results of an analysis by Newland [5] of letter malformations among 42,284 specific illegibilities made by 2381 individuals, ranging from first-grade children to adults. The data show the percentages contributed by twenty-six types of faults for elementary schools, high schools, adults, and the total for all groups combined. The facts in the table are self-explanatory and their implications for diagnosis are obvious.

Newland showed that illegibilities of only four letters (*a, e, r,* and *t*) contribute approximately half of the total number for each of the groups

[4] Leslie Quant, "Factors Affecting the Legibility of Handwriting," *Journal of Experimental Education,* Vol. 14 (June, 1946), pp. 297-316.

[5] T. E. Newland, "An Analytical Study of the Development of Illegibilties in Handwriting from the Lower Grades to Adulthood," *Journal of Educational Research,* Vol. 25 (December, 1932), pp. 3-12.

listed in the table. Writing the letter *e* like *i* resulted in 15 per cent of all illegibilities. The first four types of defects in the formation of letters given in the table caused over half of all the illegibilities. The gross frequency of the illegibilities tended to increase with age.

ANALYSIS OF LETTER MALFORMATIONS CAUSING ILLEGIBILITIES

TYPE	Percentages contributed			
	El.	H.S.	Ad.	Total
1. Failure to close letters (*a, b, f, g, j, k, o, p, q, s, y, z*)	24	20	16	18
2. Top loops closed (*l* like *t*, *e* like *i*)	13	14	20	18
3. Looping nonlooped strokes (*i* like *e*)	12	27	12	16
4. Using straight up-strokes rather than rounded strokes (*n* like *u*, *c* like *i*, *h* like *li*)	11	10	15	13
5. End stroke difficulty (not brought up, not brought down, not left horizontal)	11	6	9	9
6. Difficulty crossing *t*	5	5	9	7
7. Difficulty dotting *i*	3	5	5	5
8. Top short (*b, d, f, h, k, l, t*)	6	7	3	5
9. Letters too small	4	5	4	4
10. Closing *c, h, r, u, v, w, y*	4	3	3	3
11. Part of letter omitted	4	4	3	3
12. Up-stroke too long	2	3	1	2
13. Letters too large	2	1	—*	1
14. Beginning stroke off line	—	3	1	1
15. Bottom short (*f, g, j, q, y, z*)	2	1	—	1
16. Using rounded up-strokes instead of straight ones (*i* like *e*, *u* like *ee*)	—	1	2	1
17. Down-loop turned incorrectly	1	1	1	1
18. Excessive flourishes	—	1	1	1
19. Part added to letter	—	—	1	1
20. Down-stroke too long	1	1	—	—
21. Up-loop turned incorrectly	—	—	—	—
22. Down-loop closed	—	—	—	—
23. Printing	—	—	—	—
24. Palmer *r*	2	1	—	—
25. Unrecognizably recorded	2	1	3	3
26. Unclassified	10	9	9	9

* These dashes represent frequencies which accounted for less than one-half of 1 per cent of the total.

Newland points out that preventive and corrective work on illegibility in handwriting can be quite specific and can be focused on a relatively small number of aspects of the total problem. This recommendation has important implications.

Determining Qualities Contributing to Illegibility

As has been mentioned above in the discussion of Quant's study, there are certain characteristics of handwriting that affect its legibility, particularly form of letters, spacing, and slant.

Freeman has devised a scale which may be used to identify faulty characteristics of handwriting specimens. The scale consists of five sections, each containing a set of three specimens. Each section is intended for discovery of faults in one of the following characteristics:

1. Uniformity of slant.
2. Uniformity of alignment.
3. Equality of line.
4. Letter formation.
5. Spacing.

For each section of the scale there are specimens of three degrees of excellence, having ratings of 1, 3, and 5 respectively. Thus a pupil's written specimen is rated on each of the five characteristics according to the samples in each section which they most closely resemble. The information thus secured shows what the possible deficiencies are, but further study and observation are necessary to determine the specific factors contributing to them.

The Minneapolis Self-Corrective Handwriting Charts provide a more detailed analysis of defects in handwriting and a basis for getting at underlying causes. Their discussion is deferred to the next section.

Testing Knowledge of Rules of Capitalization and Punctuation

Because of their relationship to written expression, it is highly desirable to determine the extent to which lack of knowledge of rules of capitalization and punctuation may be a factor in poor writing. This deficiency may make the pupil feel insecure about how to express his ideas in written form. The inability to write possessive forms correctly is an illustration. Specific directions for testing capitalization and punctuation are given in Chapter 10.

CASE-STUDY DIAGNOSTIC PROCEDURES IN HANDWRITING

Comparatively few children are to be regarded as disability cases in handwriting. There are many whose handwriting reveals deficiencies that should be diagnosed and corrected. Many others have poor writing habits and are indifferent to social demands for fluent, legible writing. Many of these difficulties are due to regimented, undifferentiated instruction in the lower grades and failure to permit the child to make natural adaptations required by his physique, age, perceptual maturity, and readiness. These and other factors contributing to poor handwriting will be discussed later in this chapter.

The diagnostic study of the nature and seriousness of handwriting difficulties and deficiencies and of the underlying factors causing the condition can be approached in at least four ways:

1. Observation of the pupil at work.
2. Securing additional pertinent information.
3. Systematic diagnosis with standard devices.
4. Administration of special psychological and physiological tests.

Observation of the Pupil at Work

The rating given a specimen of handwriting and analysis of the faults it has gives the teacher or clinical worker no knowledge as to the posture the child assumed when writing, physiological handicaps he may have, how he formed the symbols, the letters with which he had difficulty, his rate of writing, how the pen or pencil was held, the position of the paper, visual deficiencies, perceptual shortcomings, motor control, his writing habits, and his attitude toward writing, any or all of which may contribute to poor handwriting. Information on all of these points can be secured by the teacher or clinical worker through careful observation of the pupil at work.

It is known that young children have few if any writing habits, whereas older children for a variety of reasons sometimes have firmly established incorrect habits that require prompt attention. The systematic observation of the pupil's traits, behavior, and work habits while engaged in writing, together with the analysis of his written work, are essential in diagnosing his needs and in planning an improvement program.

Special kinds of faults often exhibited in the writing habits of left-handed children, such as the faulty position or incorrect placement of the writing paper, and the use of the "hook" requiring "upside-down" writing, can be discovered by direct observation of the pupil as he writes.

Securing Additional Pertinent Information

The cumulative record usually contains information of value in a diagnostic study, including intelligence, school history, spelling and reading ability, state of health and physical condition, and possibly difficulties in learning to write in the primary grades. From the home, data can be secured about the child's developmental history, history of handedness, speech, illnesses, adjustment, nervousness, accidents, and interests along literary lines. His former teachers should also be interviewed about handwriting problems in preceding years and the steps taken to remedy them.

A Plan for Systematic Self-Diagnosis with Standard Devices

The Minneapolis Handwriting Charts provide the most practical device for self-diagnosis in handwriting with which the authors are familiar. The series of charts includes the following:

A. Your Handwriting Scale, for measuring general quality of writing.

B. Your Handwriting Record, which contains a record of the progress made by the pupil from test to test in overcoming specific faults of three fundamental types, defined as follows:

1. Alignment of letters.
   a. Correct top.
   b. Correct bottom.
   c. Uneven top.
   d. Uneven bottom.
   e. Under the line.
   f. Over the line.

2. Letter spacing.
   a. Correct.
   b. Too close.
   c. Too far apart.
   d. Uneven.

3. Word spacing.
   a. Correct.
   b. Too close.
   c. Too far apart.
   d. Uneven.

C. A series of diagnostic charts for diagnosing specific handwriting faults.

The charts listed below are included in the grade 4 kit for each child. The pupil diagnoses his own faults by comparing his handwriting with a series of charts consisting of samples which illustrate each kind of fault. A typical chart on letter spacing is shown on page 396. Below each specimen there is a short statement of the cause of the defect. Special corrective measures are given on each chart.

Chart 1. Your Alignment of Letters.
Chart 2. Hints and Tricks for Accurate Alignment (by both right and left-handed children).
Chart 3. Your Spacing of Letters.
Chart 4. Your Spacing of Words.
Chart 5. Your Alphabet and Numbers.
Chart 6. Alphabet Tricks (special guidance in writing small and capital letters).

By the use of these charts, the attention of the learner is focused on his own specific learning problems; instructional materials are provided which enable the teacher to adapt the work to his particular needs, thus individualizing instruction; evaluation becomes an integral element of the learning situation; provision is made for checking the pupil's regular written work; emphasis is placed at all times on the social value of easily-read handwriting. Instruction is so organized that pupils share responsibilities in diagnosing difficulties, rating specimens, setting goals, and in other ways that contribute to the socialization of the program.

SAMPLES OF LETTER SPACING

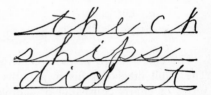

CORRECT LETTER SPACING.
The letters are evenly spaced, not too far apart, nor too close together. You can get these by **reaching forward naturally** for your letters, when your paper is in your arm track.

UNEVEN LETTER SPACING.
Why are these words hard to read? This is caused by **not reaching forward evenly** because you are **not holding your paper steady** in your arm track.

TOO-CLOSE-TOGETHER LETTER SPACING.
Why are these words hard to read? This is caused by **reaching sidewise** for your letters, usually because you are **slanting your paper above** the arm track.

TOO-FAR-APART LETTER SPACING.
Why are these words hard to read? This is caused by **reaching too straight forward** for your letters, usually because you are **holding your paper below** the arm track.

Nystrom, formerly supervisor of handwriting in Minneapolis, studied the frequencies with which various qualitative defects dealt with in her Self-Corrective Charts were found in five hundred specimens of the best, the median, and the poorest handwriting from grades 6 to 9. The findings appear in the table on page 397.

As can be seen, the largest number of defects were due to irregular and scattered word spacing. Irregular beginning and ending strokes, which are closely associated with faulty word spacing, were the next most frequent type of defects. Irregular letter spacing, irregular alignment, faulty slant, and defects due to size all contributed greatly to decreasing the legibility of the specimens.

The Minneapolis Self-Corrective Handwriting Charts provide excellent sets of exercises for correcting all of these qualitative defects. Problems of color, size, beginning and ending strokes, and many letter forms, to a considerable extent, are due to incorrect position of the pen. Problems in slant, letter spacing, and alignment are related to the posture of the pupil.

DEFECTS IN HANDWRITING AFFECTING ITS LEGIBILITY
(AFTER NYSTROM)

	Kind of Defect	Frequency of Occurrence	Total by Types
1. Color ....*a.*	Irregular *color*	177	177
2. Size ....*a.*	Irregular size	200	319
b.	Too large size	62	
c.	Too small size	57	
3. Slant ....*a.*	Irregular slant	240	326
b.	Too much slant	61	
c.	Lack of slant	25	
4. Letter spacing ...*a.*	Irregular letter spacing	267	331
b.	Crowded letter spacing	62	
c.	Scattered letter spacing	2	
5. Beginning and *a.*	Irregular beginning and ending strokes	270	381
ending strokes ...*b.*	Long beginning and ending strokes	63	
c.	Short beginning and ending strokes	48	
6. Word spacing ...*a.*	Irregular word spacing	171	415
b.	Scattered word spacing	177	
c.	Crowded word spacing	67	
7. Alignment ......*a.*	Irregular alignment	300	374
b.	Writing below the line	58	
c.	Writing above the line	16	

The Administration of Special Psychological and Physiological Tests

Whenever the situation seems to warrant it, special diagnostic tests of various kinds should be administered to secure necessary information. These include such tests as the following:

1. Tests of motor control and co-ordination.
2. Tests of perception of form and spatial relation.
3. Visual and auditory discrimination.
4. Visual and auditory accuity.
5. Visual and auditory memory.
6. Handedness.

Ordinarily, the administration of such tests should be left to the trained technician or clinical worker.

THE TREATMENT OF HANDWRITING DIFFICULTIES

Causes of Difficulties in Handwriting

Numerous factors that contribute to and are associated with handwriting deficiencies have been alluded to and in some cases discussed in the preceding pages. In general, they may be grouped under two headings: (1) those inherent in the pupil, and (2) those that involve some element of the instructional program.

1. *Factors Inherent in the Pupil.* The factors inherent in the pupil that contribute to handwriting problems vary in some respects from stage to stage in the pupil's development. The most significant of them are the following:

- *a.* Lack of readiness for learning to write.
- *b.* Visual defects causing faulty imagery.
- *c.* Immaturity in physical and motor development.
- *d.* Lack of perceptual acuity and other perceptual deficiencies.
- *e.* Lack of aptitude for learning motor skills.
- *f.* Emotional instability and social immaturity.
- *g.* Difficulty in retaining visual and motor images.
- *h.* Inability to hold the pen properly and the use of awkward incorrect posture.
- *i.* Inability to use proper movements in forming letters.
- *j.* Physical handicaps, brain injury, spastic conditions, lack of strength, etc.
- *k.* Conditions associated with handedness.
- *l.* Indifference to social demands for legibility of handwriting.

2. *Factors Associated with Instruction.* There can be no doubt that disability in handwriting often is due to inadequacies in the instructional program. To illustrate, the following may be mentioned:

- *a.* Regimented instruction and adherence to ritualistic, highly formalized systems of teaching handwriting requiring uniform, undifferentiated group drills.
- *b.* Failure to differentiate instruction according to needs of individual pupils and differences in their rates of growth.
- *c.* Failure to use diagnostic procedures so as to help learners to identify and correct their handwriting deficiencies.
- *d.* Too rapid and forced instruction in the beginning stages without consideration of differences of pupils in the degree of readiness for learning handwriting.
- *e.* Inadequate guidance in acquiring motor skills.
- *f.* Inadequate guidance when shift is made from manuscript to cursive script.
- *g.* Standards set are too high and are not adjusted to goals that are suitable and achievable for individual pupils.
- *h.* Undue stress on either speed or quality.
- *i.* Handwriting practice conducted as an isolated exercise unrelated to the use of handwriting in other learning activities.
- *j.* Unsuitable practice materials and poorly distributed practice.
- *k.* Failure to direct practice to the correction of specific faults of letter form, spacing, and the like.
- *l.* Failure to teach left-handed children to use proper position of paper and correct writing movement.

Diagnosis should take into consideration these and other causes of handwriting problems and necessary adjustments should be made as a part of the remedial instruction.

The Basis of Corrective Work in Handwriting

The nature of the corrective steps to be taken to assure the development of adequate skill in handwriting is implicit in the statement of principles underlying a well-planned instructional program, given on pages 382-383, and in the discussion of the nature and methods of diagnosing handwriting difficulties which followed that statement.

On the whole, it is true that the most effective way to correct deficiencies in handwriting is to utilize the same kinds of instructional procedures and materials that are applied in the effective teaching of handwriting in general. Their nature has been fully explained in the preceding sections of this chapter and they will not be reviewed here. This program requires (1) the effective motivation of learning; (2) the careful, systematic guidance of the growth process, especially in the early stages of its development; (3) the application of diagnostic procedures throughout the learning process so that steps can promptly be taken to correct deficiencies and to eliminate factors that are likely to interfere with the optimum growth of the learner; and (4) the adjustment of standards so that the goals will be achievable by the individuals concerned.

In some cases, special adjustments of methods and materials are necessary because of unusual conditions that may be contributory to a deficiency, for instance, to correct a tendency to use mirror writing, to eliminate reversals and wholly incorrect letter forms, or to adjust to a special physical limitation. It should be recognized that under guidance satisfactory results in handwriting as in other motor skills are achieved largely through the individual's own efforts and his desire to improve. At times it is necessary for the instructor to modify goals to be achieved, as in the case of a spastic child or a child with some other gross motor deficiency.

The Correction of Specific Handwriting Deficiencies

Nystrom has prepared what is perhaps the most systematic available analysis of the causes of the most common deficiencies in handwriting and of the steps that can be taken to correct them. Her suggestions are direct and explicit and should be of value to all concerned with these problems. Her statement in slightly abridged form follows: [1]

1. *Color.* Further study to determine the causes for these defects has resulted in a rather definite diagnosis. For instance, too light a line is caused by holding the pen too nearly vertical, too far from the point, or turned so that the eye is underneath. Shaded curves are caused by holding the pen so that the eye of the pen is toward the left or right. Heavy downstrokes are caused by pressing upon the pen with the forefinger. Very happy writing is caused by holding the pen so near the point that there is not room enough for the nails of the two little

---

[1] Quoted by permission of Ellen Nystrom, formerly supervisor of handwriting in the Minneapolis Public Schools.

fingers to carry the hand comfortably. This places the weight of the whole hand upon the pen. Correct color can be secured by bending the thumb so sharply that the tip of it lifts the pen in the hand, and by holding the pen far enough from the point to give the nails of the two little fingers room enough to carry the hand comfortably.

2. *Size.* Irregular size of writing is the result of an unsteady movement, usually caused by holding the pen with the thumb straight. Too large writing is the result of using only arm movement, usually caused by holding the pen too far from the point. Too small writing is the result of using only finger movement, usually caused by holding the pen too near the point. Correct size is the result of writing letters in the standard size for the grade by using the correct combination of finger and arm movement. This can be done by "digging" the thumb nail into the pen, a position of the thumb which lifts the pen in the hand and allows the right degree of finger movement, and by holding the pen back from the point far enough to let the nails of the two little fingers carry the hand comfortably, which allows the right degree of arm movement.

3. *Slant.* Irregular slant is usually caused by not shifting the paper to the right often enough to keep the writing directly within the line of vision. Sometimes, however, with the paper held correctly, irregularity of slant is caused by a writing motion toward the right elbow instead of toward the center of the body. Too slanting a writing is usually caused by slanting the paper too much. Lack of slant in writing is usually caused by holding the paper so that the lines are horizontal. Correct slant can be secured by holding the paper so that the lines on the paper slant in the same direction as the fingers of the left hand when the hand is extended diagonally across the desk and by directing the writing motion toward the center of the body.

Experiments have shown an involuntary tendency toward this direction of motion, and also that this motion is most easy to control with regard to uniformity of performance. This is true as well for the left-handed person as for the right-handed person, and is the reason for the tendency to backhand slant in left-handed writing. This slant does not adapt itself easily to the modern alphabet, nor does it help in the matter of legibility.

4. *Handedness.* It is of most importance for the teacher to know all the reliable findings available concerning handedness. The old philosophy of method held that this is a right-handed world, that the left-handed person was socially misfit, and that for this reason he should be trained to use his right hand. This was largely a matter of opinion. Now we know from scientific research that two-thirds of such changes can be made successfully, but that one-third suffers many types of serious nervous reactions. The real danger lies in the fact that as yet we have no way of determining whether the outcome will be successful or not.

The teacher's problem with regard to handedness, especially with the very young children, becomes one of determining whether or not the child is left-handed. Some very definite helps in this matter have resulted from work carried on by Dr. Travis of the University of California. These include, particularly, an induction test, as well as simultaneous writing tests, mirror tracing tests, and tests for determining whether or not vision is "left-handed."

5. *Letter spacing.* Irregular letter spacing is usually the result of irregular slant. Crowded letter spacing is usually the result of too much slant. Scattered letter spacing is usually the result of a lack of slant. Correct letter spacing can be secured by making the upward curves of the letters in the standard slant. When this is done the curve will be that of a two space oval of correct slant.

6. *Beginning and ending strokes.* Irregular beginning and ending strokes occur when the letters are irregular in size. Long beginning and ending strokes are usually caused by writing the letters too large in size. Sometimes, however, they are caused by too much slant in the letters. Short beginning and ending strokes are usually caused by writing the letters too small in size. Sometimes, however, they are caused by a lack of slant in the letters. Correct beginning and ending strokes depend upon correct size of the letters. Correct beginning strokes can be secured by starting them on the line and curving them in correct slant for all the letters except a, o, d, g, q, and c. The beginning strokes for these letters should start at the top of the letter and curve down to the line. Correct ending strokes should be the same in height as the low letters.

7. Word spacing. Irregular word spacing is caused by irregular beginning and ending strokes. Crowded word spacing is usually caused by long beginning and ending strokes. Scattered word spacing is usually caused by short beginning and ending strokes. The beginning strokes of a word should start just under the tip of the ending stroke of the preceding word. When words begin with a, o, d, g, q, and c, space enough for a beginning stroke should be allowed.

8. *Alignment.* Irregular alignment is caused by not shifting the paper to the left often enough to keep the writing directly within the line of vision. Writing below the line is usually caused by slanting the paper too much. Writing above the line is usually caused by holding the paper so that the lines on the paper are horizontal. Correct alignment can be secured if the paper is held correctly and shifted to the left often enough to keep the writing directly within the line of vision.

9. *Form of letters.* Correct form of the letters depends upon a sensing of the units of rhythm which control the writing motion, as well as upon the elements of size, slant and spacing. Counting, which is descriptive enough to keep the writer keenly conscious of the vital or difficult strokes of letters, and which allows pauses for retracings, helps to control the rhythm of motion. Counting, both descriptive and numerical, however, has been much overdone. The count should be used only until a word is learned. Prolonging its use beyond this point hinders rather than helps.

Detailed and specific directions for diagnosing and treating these and other handwriting deficiencies are included in the manual for the Minneapolis Self-Corrective Handwriting Charts. They are adapted to the various stages of development of learning to write, and are too detailed for reproduction in this volume. There are several other well-known handwriting programs which include the use of diagnostic procedures and suitable remedial measures, for instance, those sponsored by Freeman and Zaner-Bloser (Columbus, Ohio).

Organizing the Upper Grades for Improvement

Systematic instruction in handwriting is completed by the end of grade 6. Beyond that level the program is essentially remedial. The purpose of instruction should be the attainment of desirable rate and quality of handwriting, the maintenance by pupils of satisfactory handwriting standards in all written work and the correction of deficiencies which have persisted.

A plan of self-help based on survey tests to measure quality of handwriting and suitable diagnostic and corrective exercises should be provided for all whose quality is below 60 in the Ayres Scale.

Secondary schools will vary their attack on the handwriting problem and adapt it to the needs of their situation. One Minneapolis school met its problem in this way:

1. Two home-room periods a week were devoted to handwriting.
2. Captains were selected for each home room to meet with a faculty advisor to survey needs and plan a program.
3. A school-wide test was given, papers were scored and turned over to captains for verification.
4. Medians were posted in home rooms.
5. Remedial classes were set up.
6. Retesting was scheduled at six week intervals.
7. Following the first test, the pupils wrote their test scores on all papers written for class assignment. Papers written with a quality less than their score were returned for rewriting.
8. At the end of the year's effort 98.2 per cent of the pupils rated Quality 60 or better on the Minneapolis Adult Handwriting Scale.

CORRECTING THE FAULTY WRITING OF NUMBERS

In the lower grades children frequently use the incorrect sequence or direction of strokes in writing the figures from 2 to 10, particularly the figures 5, 4, 8, and 9. Often they reverse the figures 2, 3, 4, 5, 6, 7, and 9. To overcome these faults, careful guidance by the teacher is necessary. Close observation of written work of pupils at their seats or at the blackboard will reveal these deficiencies. The correct strokes and format of the numbers should be demonstrated by the teacher. The movement then should be practiced by the children without pencil or pen so that they "get the feel." Finally the writing itself should be done under the close supervision of the teacher until she is satisfied the child has learned the correct format and strokes. At first, emphasis should be placed on form and movement. Gradually the rate of writing will increase as control improves.

In cases of unusually persistent reversal difficulties, children may be given the experience of tracing 3- or 4-inch figures made of fairly rough sandpaper or emery paper. Tracing strengthens the kinesthetic sensation and usually leads to rapid improvement.

SUGGESTED ACTIVITIES

1. Secure specimens of written work for a class and rate them on a standard handwriting scale.

2. Prepare a timed dictation test as described on pages 389-390 and administer it to a class. Rate the papers on a handwriting scale. Have the pupils construct an informal scale for judging the quality of handwriting.

3. How are legibility and quality related?

4. Prepare a test exercise for measuring rate of writing. The pupils should memorize a simple sentence containing as many letters of the alphabet as possible and write it as often as they can at their normal rate of writing for 2 minutes. Find the number of letters written. Compare rate and quality with the standards on page 388.

5. What use is made of diagnostic procedures in some of the better-known handwriting systems?

6. Try to make a diagnosis of deficiencies in letter alignment, letter spacing, and word spacing as described in this chapter for some pupil whose quality rates low.

7. Study the handwriting posture of several left-handed children in the primary grades; in the upper grades. Are changes needed? Describe them.

8. Observe a group of young children in the early stages of learning manuscript writing. What problems do they meet? Why is individual guidance necessary?

9. What was wrong with earlier systems of teaching handwriting in which "push-and-pull" exercises, speed standards, and quality norms were uniform for all members of a class? Compare with modern procedures.

10. How diagnose and correct faulty writing of figures?

11. Why are sandpaper tracing exercises often recommended as corrective measures?

SELECTED BIBLIOGRAPHY

BRUECKNER, L. J., and MELBY, E. O., *Diagnostic and Remedial Teaching* (Boston, Houghton, 1931), Ch. 11.

Child Development and the Curriculum, Thirty-eighth Yearbook, Part I, National Society for the Study of Education (Chicago, Univ. of Chicago Press, 1939), Ch. 12.

COLE, Luella, "Instruction in Penmanship for the Left-Handed Child," *Elementary School Journal,* Vol. 39 (February, 1939), pp. 436-448.

McKEE, Paul, *Language in the Elementary School* (Boston, Houghton, 1939), Ch. 10.

Pressey Chart for Diagnosis of Illegibilities in Handwriting (Bloomington, Ill., Public School Publishing Co.).

RICHARDSON, F. D., "Motivating Fluency in Penmanship," *School* (Secondary edition), Vol. 27 (1940), pp. 316-319.

Zaner-Bloser Progress Record and Scale (Columbus, Ohio, Zaner Bloser Co.); also *Functional Handwriting* by J. G. Kirk and F. N. Freeman, 1942 ed.

13 ORGANIZING THE SCHOOLS FOR DIAGNOSIS

THIS CHAPTER discusses the kinds of services and their organization that can be found in forward-looking school systems for dealing with handicapped children and for the diagnosis and treatment of the learning difficulties of normal children. The following topics are included:

1. Organizing special services for our schools.
2. Organizing the regular classroom for diagnosis.
3. Types of clinical services available.
4. Problems in maintaining clinical services.

ORGANIZING SPECIAL SERVICES IN SCHOOL SYSTEMS

The Provisions for Educational Clinics

Although classroom teachers should be able to handle correction of most learning difficulties, they need the special services offered by clinics to assist in the diagnosis and treatment of the more complex learning problems.

In the modern school system there are special services that deal with various aspects of the child's growth and development. The integration of related services into a single major department is a feature of modern school administration. For instance, in Seattle the Department of Guidance Services includes all divisions that deal with attendance, visiting teachers, psychological and testing services, counseling and guidance, remedial teachers, and group processes. This integrated approach enables the Department to bring to bear on any particular problem the attention of a group of specialists concerned with a wide variety of aspects of the child's growth and development. Under such circumstances, a well-rounded overview of the case is assured. Similar approaches to the integration of various special services are being made in a number of other school systems.

It is unfortunately true that such a forward-looking organization is not found in some of our larger cities at the present time. The various agencies often operate independently of each other, thus making an integrated approach to diagnosis practically impossible.

404

In a number of states—for instance, Minnesota—plans for establishing educational clinics in the various teachers colleges are being considered which could be maintained at state expense and whose services would be available to all schools of the area, primarily those that are too small to provide their own facilities. In other states, regional clinics have already been established.

In smaller school systems, special services of a less comprehensive variety are sometimes provided. An example is the Department of Educational Counsel in Winnetka, Illinois, which is in direct charge of all testing, psychological services, therapy, and diagnosis in academic areas, and works closely with all other special school services. An excellent example of the organization of these services in a larger area, including a whole county, is found in Orange County, California.

Special Provisions for Handicapped Children

In earlier times the care of handicapped children presented many problems for the classroom teachers. At the present time, legal provision is made in most states for the organization and maintenance of special instruction for exceptional children of various types, including the physically handicapped, the slow-learning child, the children with speech defects, and socially and emotionally maladjusted children. For children who are severely handicapped visually, auditorily, and orthopedically, or by delicate health, special facilities also are often provided, especially in the larger places. In some places instruction in the home is provided when necessary.

The problem of how to establish the needed services in smaller communities and rural areas is a serious one, since on the whole existing facilities are completely inadequate, even lacking in many of these localities, for dealing with handicapped children.

Many questions have been raised as to the desirability of complete segregation of handicapped children in separate classes and institutions. The value of association with normal children in regular classroom activities is generally recognized. The plan is frequently followed of enrolling children less severely handicapped in regular classrooms for the greater part of the day. They are taken out to special rooms for therapeutic treatment or for instruction modified to meet the nature of the handicap. When individuals require over a period of time treatment such as only a specialist can provide, they are returned to the regular classroom as soon as is feasible, where further adjustment is undertaken by the teacher under the guidance of the specialist. Part-time treatment is sometimes provided by transporting the individual to some conveniently accessible center during a portion of the day.

Children who are mentally retarded are often mistreated by their associates and this frequently leads to unfortunate consequences. The unfortunate mislabeling by their associates has sometimes caused emotional and social maladjustment. This problem must be dealt with so that these less fortunate children can have happier educative experiences, adapted to their various needs and ability.

ORGANIZING THE REGULAR CLASSROOM FOR DIAGNOSIS

The Grouping of Children

The classroom teacher faces the problem of guiding the learning experiences of all children assigned to a particular classroom. In small schools the group ordinarily includes all children of a given age or grade level. In larger schools, where the number of pupils in a particular grade or age group is large enough, the total group can be subdivided in various ways. Some schools prefer to group them according to levels of ability or readiness for the work to be done; other schools prefer to group children on an age basis or according to some other plan which eliminates any possibility of labeling classes by some general characteristic such as mental ability. Because of widespread interest in the education of gifted children, special classes for them have been organized in a number of schools, thus removing these children from regular classes where they can make valuable contributions to the learning activities of other, less able children.

Whatever plan of grouping is used by the school, the teacher still faces the problem of arranging educative experiences that are adapted to the needs and to the level and rate of development of each individual in the class. As has been indicated in preceding chapters, the range of individual differences will hardly be changed by any grouping plan, and the wide range in the level of development of the various traits of a single individual will still exist. Pupils also will differ in the rates at which they are learning and in the levels of achievement which they should be expected to reach because of differences in their potentialities.

For various reasons, minor learning difficulties often will arise in the course of regular instruction that the teacher can diagnose and remedy promptly. This may require the judicious grouping of learners according to common needs and the planning of learning experiences designed to alleviate particular conditions or factors that seem to underlie the difficulties. At the same time, the teacher must plan rich experience units and other kinds of learning activities in which all children in the class can participate regardless of their achievements or mental level, each contributing according to his ability and interests. This plan will give all children the opportunity to participate in learning experiences as members of a social group consisting of individuals who vary widely in ability, interest, social qualities, and other significant traits.

Studying the Needs of Individual Children

The school system faces the problem of assisting the classroom teacher to secure dependable information which will serve to determine the needs and ability of individual children. A well-planned city-wide testing program is essential. A city testing department should in addition make available suitable tests from which the teacher, under competent guidance, can select those that are most promising for the special study of some individual case. A modern cumulative record will also make available for the teacher valuable information about the individual's school history, his health, his achievements, social background, and the like.

Minor learning difficulties can be identified and remedied by informal instructional materials and practice exercises that are found in modern textbooks and workbooks. The instructional materials should be of various levels of difficulty so that a selection can be made to match the individual's progress and needs.

Special types of difficulties that must be dealt with on an individual basis, for instance, speech defects, are most suitably treated by special teachers who serve a number of schools. In other respects, the education of such children will be in the hands of the regular teacher.

TYPES OF CLINICAL SERVICES AVAILABLE

Varieties of Clinical Services

The clinical and advisory services that are available vary widely among the school systems of this country. Some communities have had clinical services of several kinds for many years, whereas in many others their development has hardly been begun.

The services rendered by clinics in some localities are sometimes comprehensive and many-sided, whereas in other places the point of view is exceedingly limited and narrow. Such titles as Department of Child Services, Department of Educational Counsel, Department of Guidance Services, Psycho-Educational Clinic, Child Study Center, and Child Guidance Clinic suggest the wide variety of contributions that a staff of specialists of various kinds can make to the diagnosis of learning problems. Other titles, such as psychological clinic, medical center, mental hygiene center, and reading clinic, suggest a narrower approach to the problem.

In recent years there has been a remarkable development of clinical services that are concerned with problems in mental health and emotional and social maladjustment. Unfortunately, in a number of instances the approach of clinics in this field has been limited to psychological problems believed to be closely related to mental health, and inadequate consideration has been given to the fact that learning difficulties often are closely related to poor mental health and often are contributory thereto. Usually this limited approach is due to the fact that mental hygienists have little, if any, training in the diagnosis of educational problems. However, the problem just pointed out is being more widely recognized, and the services of school psychologists and social workers are often utilized in case studies conducted in mental hygiene clinics.

The Referral of Cases

The general practice of clinics is to secure essential information from schools, social agencies, and parents when cases are referred for diagnosis and recommendations as to treatment. Blanks to be filled out by the schools quickly summarize available information about the individual's school progress, attendance, interests, behavior, previous test data, basic information about the nature and history of the difficulty involved, and the types of treatment that have been used but have proven to be ineffective. The home is asked to supply data about the previous health of the child, a record of the diseases he has had, and other kinds of information likely to assist the staff of the clinic to understand the case. One of the parents usually is requested to accompany the child on at least one of the days he is at the clinic, so that the staff of the clinic can interview the parent to secure additional data of value.

Specialists Available in Diagnosis

The function of specialists is not classroom teaching but the provision of services that will help the teacher to assist the individual learner to adjust through diagnostic study and therapeutic treatment. Teachers usually lack the specialized training necessary for diagnostic procedures of a technical nature. Nor do they have the time that is required. Often the necessary special equipment and apparatus are expensive and are available only in some clinical center.

Such specialists as those listed below supply services that are of undoubted value in planning an educational program that is adapted to the needs, ability, and interests of particular individuals:

1. Specialists in health, including school nurses, physicians, dentists, and psychiatrists.
2. Specialists concerned with the social aspects of the teaching-learning situation, including attendance officers, visiting teachers, social and welfare workers, and guidance and counseling personnel.
3. Technical clinical specialists, including psychometrists, school psychologists, educational diagnosticians, and psychiatric social workers.
4. Specialists in treatment and therapy, including speech correctionists, teachers of severely handicapped, mental hygienists, and remedial teachers.

In smaller places the various functions must be taken over by the members of a relatively limited staff. Many of them can be assigned to principals and to teachers with special training. Traveling clinics and regional centers are being established in a number of states.

Functions of Clinical Specialists

A recent survey of the activities of specialists in clinical services showed that their functions and contributions varied widely from system to system, depending on the leadership provided. The following descriptive analysis of functions is based on an examination of the services rendered by specialists in all parts of this country and is presented because of its possible suggestiveness for all clinical workers:

1. ADMINISTRATION OF TESTING PROGRAMS
   a. Intelligence and aptitude.
   b. Readiness testing.
   c. Achievement testing.
   d. Special testing for research and other purposes.
   e. Consultative service on selection and interpretation of tests.

2. DIAGNOSIS AND TREATMENT OF INDIVIDUAL CASES
   a. Mental health.
   b. Emotional stability.
   c. Social adjustment.
   d. Learning difficulties in all curriculum areas.
   e. Visual, auditory, and physical development.
   f. Vocational and educational aptitudes.

3. THERAPY
   a. Psychotherapy.
   b. Treatment of emotional and social problems.
   c. Remedial treatment of disabilities in basic learning skills.
   d. Correction of and adjustment to certain physical handicaps.

4. CONSULTATIVE AND ADVISORY SERVICES
   a. Methods of dealing with educational problems of school and community.
   b. Advising parents, teachers, individuals concerning educational problems.
   c. Consulting with courts, welfare agencies.
   d. Supplying information for placement and employment agencies.

5. EDUCATIONAL SERVICES
   a. In-service education of members of the staff.
   b. Parent education.
   c. Conducting workshops, courses, study groups.
   d. Assisting on problems in teacher selection.
   e. Conducting general types of educational research.
   f. Experimentation with educational programs.
   g. Assisting in the field of public information and relations.

Summary of Services of the Minneapolis Child Study Department

The following statement summarizes the kinds of services that are offered by a typical child study department which focuses on problems primarily related to personality, behavior, and emotional adjustment.

I. Assessment of scholastic abilities of children from kindergarten through high school. This service is asked for chiefly by:

A. Teachers and principals. The information is used for:
1. Correct grade placement of child.
2. Determination as to whether child is eligible for Special Class.
3. Decision as to whether child is achieving up to his true capacity for learning.
4. Broader and better understanding of the child.

B. Special Education Department. Information is used for:
1. Determination of eligibility to the following:
   a. Special classes for the retarded.
   b. Dowling School for physically handicapped.
   c. Sight Saving classes.
   d. Classes for the hard of hearing.

C. Department of Attendance and Census. This information is used chiefly for:
1. Recommended temporary School Excuse.
2. Recommended permanent School Exclusion.

II. Study of personality, behavior, and emotional patterns of children who present severe difficulties in the classroom. This service is asked for chiefly by teachers, principals, visiting teachers, counselors. Referral is made usually through the visiting teacher. The department attempts to determine the difficulties by the use of:

A. Special aptitude tests.
B. Diagnostic tests (such as in reading or arithmetic).
C. Personality measurements.
D. Observation of child in clinic or at school.
E. Interview with child.
F. Interview with one or both parents.

Counselors in Elementary Schools

The use of special counselors in elementary schools is a promising new development. Usually their function is to co-ordinate such activities as personnel work with all pupils, mental hygiene, measurement and evaluation, social work, clinical services, and adjustment problems. School psychologists often assume the responsibilities and functions of counselors. Bailard [1] has outlined the responsibilities of elementary school counselors in Long Beach, California:

---

[1] Virginia Bailard, in *Handbook for Counselors,* Long Beach, California Public Schools, 1952, pp. 70-71.

LEGITIMATE SERVICES OF AN ELEMENTARY SCHOOL COUNSELOR

The counselor is directly responsible to the principal in her building. Her services will be subject to his approval. The counselor's time should be used in promoting the services indicated below if a well-balanced guidance program is to be developed.

GENERAL SERVICES

An elementary school counselor should be responsible for:

1. A testing program.
   a. Make provision for ordering and administering tests—survey, intelligence, special building achievement, individual, and other.
   b. Interpret results.
   c. Make provision for the scoring of group tests. This may be done by junior clerk or classroom teacher, or by counselor when necessary.
2. Gathering, organizing and keeping significant pupil data (permanent record, pupil analysis blank, etc.).
3. Recording and filing of all pupil data.
4. Routine procedures for transferring pupils.
5. Aiding principal in registering pupils.
6. Assisting principal with the organization of pupils into socially satisfactory groups.
7. Aiding principal in the selection of pupils who need individual work.

SERVICES CONCERNING THE CHILD WITH A PROBLEM

1. Helping teachers to understand, accept, and deal more effectively with the individual child who presents special problems in behavior and learning, or who is emotionally and socially maladjusted.
2. Gathering data about the child through observation, testing, interviews, etc.
3. Utilizing and coordinating the services of school personnel workers who contribute to the welfare of the child.
4. Aiding principal in conferring with parents in an effort to arrive at a satisfactory plan of action which would be most beneficial to their child.
5. Cooperating with local agencies when they are concerned with an individual child with a problem.
6. Working with the child directly when that seems advisable.

SERVICES CONCERNED WITH TEACHERS

1. Helping teachers to accept and understand all children.
2. Helping teachers individually and in groups, through demonstrations and conferences, to develop acceptable techniques of collecting, interpreting, and using behavioral data.
3. Assisting principal in guiding teachers in making constructive and wise reports to parents.
4. Organizing pupil-study conferences and interesting teachers in participating in them.
5. Helping teachers use group work as an adjustive process for making pupils feel that they "belong."
6. Assisting principal in planning programs for faculty meetings which would make for greater understanding of the guidance point of view.
7. Being genuinely concerned about the mental health of the teacher, giving her as much help and support as possible.

Clinical Services in Colleges and Universities

Clinics operated by teacher training institutions often provide excellent facilities [2] and superior services that are available for small school systems which otherwise would completely lack them. An excellent example is the clinic at the St. Cloud Teachers College. Universities and teachers colleges generally use these clinical facilities to give teachers special training in the diagnosis and treatment of learning difficulties. In some universities, for example, the University of Minnesota, basic courses in the diagnosis and treatment of learning difficulties are a requirement for teacher certification of all elementary school teachers. Specialized courses for advanced study of diagnosis in such fields as reading, arithmetic, and spelling also are offered. Many other institutions offer courses for teachers in service in this field, including Columbia, Chicago, Temple, New York, City College of New York, Washington, Southern California, Florida, Northwestern, and many others. Enrollments in summer session courses have increased rapidly in recent years, indicating that there is a growing realization of the importance of competent educational diagnosis.

The following statement describes the services rendered by a typical psychoeducational clinic maintained by a major educational institution:

The Psycho-Educational Clinic is a department of the College of Education, University of Minnesota. It offers diagnostic and remedial services to children who have encountered special difficulties in school learning. In conjunction with this service, the clinic operates a training program for advanced student preparing to enter the field of specialized school services. By sustaining an active research program an attempt is made to broaden understandings essential to adequate training and service in the clinical aspects of Educational Psychology.

THE CLINIC STAFF

The staff of the clinic consists of the director, one instructor, three clinicians and a secretary. Graduate students with training in psychometrics, educational diagnosis and remedial teaching also participate directly in the activities of the clinic on a supervised basis. Members of the College of Education faculty, other than the clinic staff, often participate in the clinic's activities, particularly with respect to training functions and in a Summer Remedial Reading School sponsored by the Clinic. The training of all staff and students is in the area of Educational Psychology and closely allied disciplines. There is *no representation* of the fields of medicine, psychiatry, social work or speech pathology on the staff. There are service units in these fields in other departments of the University.

DIAGNOSTIC SERVICES

What kinds of referrals are accepted? The most common referral concerns reading difficulty. Referrals for reason of poor progress in other basic school

---

[2] Gertrude Boyd and O. C. Schwiering, "A Survey of Child Guidance and Remedial Reading Practices," *Journal of Educational Research,* Vol. 43 (March, 1950), pp. 494-506.

Gertrude Boyd and O. C. Schwiering, "Remedial Practice and Case Records: A Survey of Reading Clinical Practices." *Journal of Educational Research,* Vol. 44 (February, 1951), pp. 443-456.

subjects (arithmetic, spelling, handwriting, etc.) are less common, but welcomed. Other common bases for requesting clinic services include school readiness problems and special abilities and talents. The clinic also offers limited services in the case of mentally and physically handicapped children. Age limits are from five (school readiness) through eighteen (high school).

What kinds of referrals are not accepted? Generally, the clinic limits itself to the study of children in whose cases school personnel can be expected to carry the most active role in rehabilitation. The availability of other clinical facilities is also a consideration. Many of the children referred to the clinic present emotional or personality problems in some degree, but cases of primary personality or behavior problems are not accepted. Because of the difficulty in anticipating the nature of children's problems, the clinic often acts as a screening station; that is, brief studies are made as a basis for considering referral to other agencies.

What is the referral procedure? The first step in making a referral to the clinic is simply to call or write to the clinic asking for referral forms. Usually the parents or school officials make this first contact. The referral forms consist of two parts: (1) a part to be completed by parents or guardian of the child; (2) a part to be completed by school officials. When the referral forms have been completed and returned to the clinic they are studied. If it appears that the clinic is an appropriate diagnostic agency, the parents are contacted by phone or letter to arrange specific appointment dates. Referral procedure is modified in the case of referrals by physicians, social workers, welfare agencies, etc. In every case, however, it is required that the parents and a professional person (usually school officials) agree to and participate in the referral.

What is the nature of the Clinic's diagnostic services? Typically a diagnostic study will take about three half-day appointments. The clinic attempts to collect information about the child, his family, community and school in order to offer insights as to the nature of the problem and suggestions for rehabilitation. A typical study would include: (1) a parent interview; (2) individual mental testing; (3) screening tests for possible vision and hearing difficulties; (4) personality evaluation (including tests, observation and interviews); (5) survey testing in basic school subjects; (6) detailed diagnostic testing and evaluation in the areas of difficulty; (7) a final parent interview; (8) a full report of findings, interpretations and recommendations to the referring agency or person (usually a school official). No written reports on diagnoses are given to parents, but major results are summarized in the final interview.

When is the Clinic open? The Clinic operates five days per week through the entire year, except for the month of September and during school holiday periods (Christmas, New Year's Day, etc.).

What is the fee for the above diagnostic services? The fee for the "basic diagnosis" as described above is $30.00. In cases requiring less than three half-days, the charge is at the rate of $3.50 per hour. A limited scholarship aid, provided through the Greater University Fund, is available to those unable to pay the full fee.

REMEDIAL SERVICES

The clinic offers remedial services only after a diagnosis has been completed and then only in cases where its facilities seem definitely suited to the needs of the child. Remedial tutoring in reading is the most frequent service rendered.

All remedial services are on a highly individualized basis. During the school year a limited number of children can be served. Each child comes to the clinic for the period 9:30-11:30 A.M. each school day. During the summer a ten-week

Remedial Reading School is in operation. This program begins in mid-June and ends in late August. Children attend five days a week from 9:00-11:00 A.M. The clinic is not able to take responsibility for boarding or transportation involved in attending these remedial sessions, but can often suggest ways for making such arrangements.

Detailed daily records are maintained on all children enrolled for remedial work and periodic reports are sent to schools and parents. The clinic very frequently asks the privilege of consulting with parents and teachers in order to gain the advantage of their observations and in the interest of working out a more total and unified program for each child.

Fees for remedial tutoring during the academic year are as follows:

per day	$3.50	(if less than 10 days)
per 10 days	$30.00	(if 10 days or more)
per 35 days	$100.00	(if 35 days or more)

For the ten-week Summer School the fee per child is $140.00. Again there are limited Scholarship aids available, through the Greater University Fund, to those unable to pay the full fee.

Auxiliary Remedial Services

When there is a sufficient number of pupils who have similar learning difficulties, special centers for remedial treatment are sometimes established. Sometimes these serve the needs of single schools, such as the large schools of New York City and other metropolitan areas. In many junior high schools, pupils who are regarded as disability cases in such areas as reading, spelling, and arithmetic are scheduled for remedial work in special classes. Astonishingly successful results have been reported in many such cases.

Sometimes the children from several schools come by schedule to a center for treatment established in some readily accessible school. Sometimes they remain for several hours daily at the center and return then to their regular classrooms for the remainder of the day, while sometimes in cases of severe disability they may attend remedial classes on a full-time basis until enough improvement has taken place to warrant returning them to regular classes. Sometimes special remedial teachers who move from school to school provide remedial assistance for severe cases.

PROBLEMS IN MAINTENANCE AND SUPPORT OF CLINICAL SERVICES

Financial Resources

Funds for the maintenance and support of clinical services come from many sources. The main sources are local taxation and state aid. In many states, financial aid is provided to assist school systems to establish a wide variety of special classes for exceptional children. In a number of states, mental hygiene clinics are established with state support, sometimes in centers, sometimes as traveling clinics which schedule visits to small school systems in order to assist the local staff to deal with educational problems.

Most clinics charge a fee for diagnostic services rendered, whereas the services rendered by others are without cost to the schools or individuals concerned. Many private clinics are maintained by fees paid by those who utilize their services.

Funds advanced from other public and private sources also help to maintain clinical services. In some places the Community Chest provides the necessary funds; in several cities parent groups such as parent-teacher associations or parents of handicapped children have established special services which the local systems were not able to provide, for instance, for dealing with cerebral-palsied children and emotional or social maladjustment problems. In a number of clinics, private professional specialists contribute their services on a part-time voluntary basis without cost to aid in their maintenance.

It is perhaps literally true that "where there is a will there is a way" of securing the funds needed to maintain necessary clinical services. Their evolution in most localities shows that they began because of the activities of some interested individual or group of persons concerned about some problem and its solution. Often their efforts led to the development of simple, rudimentary services, the value of whose contributions in time were recognized and ultimately they were made an integral part of the community's educational program. A number of instances, for example, the State of Mississippi, can be cited where the funds needed to establish various kinds of clinics on an experimental basis were advanced by private foundations. After their value became recognized by the citizens, the costs were absorbed by funds raised by local taxation.

The extension of necessary clinical services so that they will become available for small school systems will involve the spending of considerable sums of money by the various states. These funds undoubtedly will become available as soon as the value of such services is more generally recognized.

Facilities Desirable for Clinics

The facilities that are available for clinics of various kinds in different parts of the country vary greatly in adequacy and suitability. In Fresno, California, there is an excellent new modern structure which houses many of the kinds of facilities that a modern child-guidance clinic requires, including reception rooms, rooms for interviews and individual testing, several rooms for therapeutic treatment, space for clerical staff, files, and records, and a professional library, all attractively and efficiently arranged. Unfortunately, the services rendered by this particular clinic are largely limited to the diagnosis and treatment of behavior problems that emerge in the home and at school, not including educational problems directly concerned with school learnings. The facilities of this clinic would have to be enlarged considerably before its program could be broadened to include the diagnosis of serious learning difficulties in the various curriculum areas.

The resourcefulness and ingenuity with which those concerned with diagnosis utilize the available facilities is clearly revealed when one considers the limitations of many of the structures in which current educational clinics operate. They range from old, previously abandoned school buildings, reconditioned homes, temporary portable structures, and dingy rooms in the basements of schools to splendidly equipped classrooms and clinical facilities in modern school buildings. In very few instances were the quarters actually designed by those concerned with diagnosis in its various ramifications, and with the need for special kinds of therapeutic treatment certain cases require. Clinics and necessary auxiliary services are often located in widely separated buildings, which greatly reduces the possibility of an integrated attack on problems. Interesting proposals as to the kinds of quarters that clinical services require are being advanced in a number of places. The essential point is that any clinic that is being established should have sufficient space to meet the needs of the various services which will assure a comprehensive many-sided view of each case.

In a number of places, clinical schools are established in connection with the clinical services. One of the most famous of these is the clinical school developed by Dr. Grace Fernald at the University of California at Los Angeles. Enrolled in this school are children of all age levels, including college students, who present serious educational and emotional problems that are too complex for the ordinary teacher to deal with in the classroom. Under the supervision of the clinic an educational program is organized that is adjusted to the needs of each individual. Those interested in the diagnostic procedures and remedial program used in this clinical school are referred to the book by Dr. Fernald, *Remedial Techniques in the Basic Skill Subjects,* published by McGraw-Hill Book Company.

At the University of Minnesota the Psycho-Educational Clinic is located in the building that houses the University Elementary School. Pupils who present serious problems are admitted to the clinic for diagnosis insofar as time and staff resources permit. During summer sessions, special use of the school and clinical facilities is made by providing at small cost clinical help for numerous problem cases from the Twin City area, especially in the field of reading. There is a one-way vision room in which up to forty persons can observe a demonstration diagnosis. Special training also is given to teachers in the use of diagnostic procedures and in the application of appropriate remedial treatment to cases assigned to them.

SUGGESTED ACTIVITIES

1. Investigate the special provisions for handicapped children that are provided in some state or in some school system. Could they be improved? How are they maintained?

2. Visit some educational or psychological clinic. Study the organization of

the clinic and staff, referral of cases, the services rendered, the facilities provided, financial support, and similar problems.

3. Discuss with some school psychologist or social case worker his functions and the services he renders.

4. Investigate the special provisions the community provides for remedial teaching, for instance, classes in remedial reading and mental therapy.

5. Determine the extent to which local teachers have had training in educational diagnosis. Suggest possible ways of improving this function.

SELECTED BIBLIOGRAPHY

BARHASH, A. Z., and others, *The Organization and Function of the Community Psychiatric Clinic* (New York, National Association for Mental Health, 1952).

BERNARD, Harold W., *Mental Hygiene for Classroom Teachers* (New York, McGraw, 1952).

BOYD, Gertrude, and SCHWIERING, O. L., "A Survey of Child Guidance and Remedial Reading Practices," *Journal of Educational Research,* Vol. 43 (March, 1950), pp. 494-506.

————, "Remedial Instruction and Case Records: A Survey of Clinical Reading Practices," *Journal of Educational Research,* Vol. 44 (February, 1951), pp. 443-456.

FENTON, Norman, *Mental Hygiene in School Practice* (Stanford, Calif., Stanford Univ. Press, 1943).

GLUECK, Sheldon, and GLUECK, Eleanor, *Unraveling Juvenile Delinquency* (New York, Commonwealth Fund, 1950).

Helping Teachers Understand Children (Washington, American Council on Education, 1945).

TRAXLER, Arthur, "Current Organization and Procedures in Remedial Teaching," *Journal of Experimental Education,* Vol. 20 (March, 1954), pp. 305-312.

WALLIN, J. E. W., *Personality Adjustment and Mental Hygiene* (New York, McGraw, 1949).

WILLEY, Roy D., *Guidance in Elementary Education* (New York, Harper, 1952).

The magazine *Exceptional Children* from time to time contains concrete descriptions of the organization of clinical facilities for dealing with exceptional children. It should be freely consulted by those concerned with this problem.

Index

Achievement tests: list of standard, 12; structure, 21; types, 12

Abney, F., 323

Adjustment, social and emotional, 12, 46-51

American Psychological Association, 14

Analysis of skills: arithmetic, 213, 216, 217, 218, 220, 274-278; language, 303, 315-317, 321; reading, 103-104, 136-138; handwriting, 395; spelling, 372-373

Analytical diagnosis: definition of, 64; in arithmetic, 213-219, 272-278; in handwriting, 390-393; in language, 313-331; in reading, 129-138; in spelling, 353

Analytical Scales of Attainment in Arithmetic, 233

Anderson, Irving H., 43

Anecdotal records, 9

Appraisal procedures: analysis of records, 9; criteria in evaluating, 13-14; informal testing, 9; interviews, 9; objective testing, 9; observation, 9; sociometric and projective, 9; typical testing programs, 11

Arithmetic operations: analytical diagnosis, 213-219, 272-278; basic teaching procedure, 197-199; case-study procedure, 219-233; complexity, 200-205, 216-219; construction of diagnostic tests, 217; deficiencies in operations, 225-233; diagnostic tests, 216, 218, 220-221; factors contributing to disabilities, 240-241; foundations of diagnosis, 199-208; fractional cutouts, 195, 258, 285-288; general diagnosis, 208-210; generalizations as aids to learning number facts, 261-269; intercorrelations of abilities and intelligence, 194; level of difficulty, 205-208; 219; manipulation aids, 244-251, 267-268, 280-281, 286-287; number boards, 266; number facts, 213, 255-269; number system, 199-200; objectives, 193-194; place-value pockets, 244, 249, 280-281;

principles of teaching, 295-299; principles of remedial teaching, 241-246, 282; readiness testing, 210-213; rate and accuracy, 214-215, 257; relationships among, 215, 297-298; screening tests, 274-278; steps in making case studies, 223; subskills in division, 202-203; teaching meaning of numbers, 246-254; teaching meaning of operations, 279-280; treatment of learning difficulties, 246-289; types of examples, 274-278; visualization of meanings, 198, 245, 248, 253, 260-262, 281

Arithmetic problem-solving: analytical diagnosis in, 234; case-study procedures, 235-237; deficiencies in, 293; factors contributing to deficiencies, 293; general diagnosis, 208-210, 233; manipulation aids in, 295-296; objectives, 193-194; principles of teaching, 292-293; reading in, 290-292; relationships in equations, 298; treatment of learning difficulties, 294-300; visualization, 295, 297; vocabulary development, 299

Arthur's Point Scale of Performance Tests, 12

Atkin, Samuel B., 355

Attitudes, faulty, 83

Audiometer, 44

Auditory deficiencies, 43-45

Auditory discrimination, test of, 378

Ayres Handwriting Scale, 387

Bailard, Virginia, 410

Basis of treatment, diagnosis, the, 77

Behavior records, 9

Bell Adjustment Inventory, 12

Betts, E. A., 42, 45

Bond, G. L., 25, 33, 43, 44, 48, 49, 51, 56, 96, 136, 142, 146, 148, 178

Bond-Clymer-Hoyt Development Reading Tests, 131, 144

Bond-Clymer-Hoyt Silent Reading Diagnostic Test, 70, 142, 145